D0233528

THE COMING OF THE SPANISH CIVIL WAR

The breakdown of democracy in Spain in the 1930s resulted in a torrent of political and military violence. In this thoroughly revised edition of his classic text, Paul Preston provides a deeply disturbing explanation of the democratic collapse, coherently and excitingly outlining the social and economic background.

Spain was a backward agricultural country divided by the most brutal economic inequalities. The coming of the Second Republic in April 1931 was greeted by the Left as an opportunity to reform Spain's antiquated social structure. Over the next two years, the Socialist members of a Republican–Socialist coalition pushed for reforms to alleviate the day-to-day misery of the great southern army of landless labourers. Paul Preston shows how the political activities of the Right, legal and conspiratorial, between 1931 and 1936, as well as the subsequent Nationalist war effort, were primarily a response to these reforming ambitions of the Left. His principal argument is that, although the Spanish Civil War encompassed many separate conflicts, the main cause of the breakdown of the Second Republic was the struggle between Socialists and the legalist Right to impose their respective views of social organisation on Spain by means of their control of the apparatus of state. The incompatible interests represented by these two mass parliamentary parties – those of the landless labourers and big landlords, of industrialists and workers – spilled over into social conflicts which could not be contained within the parliamentary arena.

Since the first edition of this book was completed more than fifteen years ago, archives have been opened up, the diaries, letters and memoirs of major protagonists have been published, and there have been innumerable studies of the politics of the Republic, of parties, unions, elections and social conflict, both national and provincial. This new edition updates the original text as exhaustively as possible to take account of the new material.

Paul Preston is Professor of International History at the London School of Economics. His many books on Spain include *Franco: A Biography* (1993), *The Politics of Revenge: Fascism and the Military in Twentieth-Century Spain* (1990) and *The Triumph of Democracy in Spain* (1986).

Q
46.081
PRE

THE COMING OF THE SPANISH CIVIL WAR

Reform, Reaction and Revolution in
The Second Republic

Second Edition

Paul Preston

WITHDRAWN
from
STIRLING UNIVERSITY LIBRARY

London and New York

POPLOAN

31239196

First published 1978 by
The Macmillan Press Ltd

First published in paperback 1983 by
Methuen & Co. Ltd

Second edition published 1994
by Routledge
11 New Fetter Lane, London EC4P 4EE

Simultaneously published in the USA and Canada
by Routledge
29 West 35th Street, New York, NY 10001

© 1978, 1994 Paul Preston

Phototypeset in Palatino by Intype, London

Printed and bound in Great Britain by
TJ Press (Padstow) Ltd, Padstow, Cornwall

All rights reserved. No part of this book may be reprinted or
reproduced or utilized in any form or by any electronic,
mechanical, or other means, now known or hereafter
invented, including photocopying and recording, or in any
information storage or retrieval system, without permission in
writing from the publishers.

British Library Cataloguing in Publication Data
A catalogue record for this book is available from the British Library

Library of Congress Cataloging in Publication Data
Preston, Paul
The Coming of the Spanish Civil War: Reform, Reaction and
Revolution in the Second Republic / Paul Preston. -- 2nd ed.
p.   cm.
Includes bibliographical references and index.
1. Spain--Politics and government--1931–1939. 2. Spain--Social
conditions--1886–1939. 3. Socialism--Spain--History--20th century.
4. Right and left (Political science) 5. Spain--History--Civil War,
1936–1939--Causes.
DP255.P73   1994
946.08--dc20   93–40967

ISBN 0–415–06354–X (hbk)
ISBN 0–415–06355–8 (pbk)

CONTENTS

ACKNOWLEDGEMENTS

During the preparation of the first edition of this book, I lived for more than three years in Spain as well as making many shorter visits. Not surprisingly, given the open-heartedness of Spaniards in general, I incurred a number of debts of gratitude for which I would again like to express my appreciation.

Many hours of conversation with two participants in the events described here helped me to comprehend the daily brutality of Spanish rural life in the 1930s. Miguel González Inestal was one of the libertarian movement's greatest experts on the land question. Ignacio Arenillas de Chaves, Marqués de Gracia Real, was a monarchist landowner from Salamanca who was active in Acción Popular and the Comunión Tradicionalista. After the Civil War, his experience as defending lawyer at the trial of Julián Besteiro together with Franco's failure to restore the monarchy inclined him to undertake a critical reassessment of the role of the Right during the 1930s. Both were more generous with time and information than a young unknown foreign historian could ever have expected.

Two Spanish scholars and friends helped me not to see Spain through English eyes. Jerónimo Gonzalo Rubio has been for many years unstinting with ideas, hospitality and friendship. Joaquín Romero Maura deepened my sense of the workings of Spanish history and taught me much about scholarship in general. Without wishing to implicate them as accomplices in the book's shortcomings, I reiterate my thanks to both for their contribution to it.

Norman Cooper, Frances Lannon and Martin Blinkhorn went to considerable trouble to read and comment on the text of the first edition. Christopher Seton-Watson supervised with unfailing patience the doctoral thesis on which the book is based. Hugh Thomas showed great kindness with books and advice in the early days of the research.

ACKNOWLEDGEMENTS

Herbert R. Southworth has for many years unstintingly made available to me the unrivalled resources of his library and his knowledge of the Spanish Right. I also benefited from the suggestions and criticisms of the following friends and colleagues: the late Edward A. Bayne, Juan José Castillo, Elías Díaz, Juan Pablo Fusi, Juan García Durán, Gabriel Jackson, Joe Harrison, Alistair Hennessy, James Joll, Victor Kiernan, Edward Malefakis, José Ramón Montero Gibert, Eduardo Sevilla Guzmán and Angel Viñas.

Subsequent to the publication of the first edition, I have derived enormous benefit from contact with many of the Spanish historians working on this period, particularly José Manuel Macarro Vera in Seville, Salvador Forner in Alicante, Francisco Moreno Gómez in Córdoba and Julio Aróstegui in Madrid. A great intellectual debt is also owed to Santos Juliá, who is responsible for some of the most important advances in the history of the Left in the Second Republic. I have derived the greatest pleasure and profit from ongoing collaboration with my friends Julián Casanova of Zaragoza, Enrique Moradiellos of Oviedo and Ismael Saz of Valencia, first during their periods as visiting scholars in London and thereafter in Spain. Among the growing band of British experts on Spain who have influenced my thinking through their work and given me encouragement to continue with my own, I would like to thank Helen Graham, Sheelagh Ellwood, Paul Heywood, Adrian Shubert and Nigel Townson.

Had it not been for the kindly prodding of Professor Robert F. Lesley when I was a recently appointed lecturer at Queen Mary College, this study might never have seen the light of day. However, he meant well and neither he nor anyone else mentioned above can be held responsible for any of the judgements or errors contained herein.

ABBREVIATIONS

ACNP: Asociación Católica Nacional de Propagandistas – an élite organisation of prominent Catholic rightists with influence in the press, the judiciary and the professions, linked to Acción Católica.

ASM: Agrupación Socialista Madrileña – the Madrid section of the PSOE, a stronghold of the Socialist Left.

BOC: Bloc Obrer i Camperol – the quasi-Trotskyist Worker and Peasant Bloc, led by Joaquín Maurín, which joined the POUM in 1935.

CEDA: Confederación Española de Derechas Autónomas – Spanish Confederation of Autonomous Right-Wing Groups, the largest political grouping of the legalist Right.

CMI: Círculo Monárquico Independiente – the monarchist organisation whose appearance in May 1931 triggered off church burnings across the country.

CNCA: Confederación Nacional Católico-Agraria – the political organisation of the Catholic smallholding peasantry in north and central Spain which provided the mass base of the CEDA.

CNT: Confederación Nacional del Trabajo – the anarcho-syndicalist National Confederation of Labour.

DRV: Derecha Regional Valenciana, led by Luis Lucia Lucia, the Valencian section of the CEDA.

FAI: Federación Anarquista Ibérica – the insurrectionary vanguard of the anarchist movement.

FJS: Federación de Juventudes Socialistas – PSOE youth movement which amalgamated with the Communist Youth in April 1936 to form the JSU.

FNTT: Federación Nacional de Trabajadores de la Tierra, the landworkers' union of the UGT.

JAP: Juventud de Acción Popular – the uniformed youth militias of the CEDA.

JSU: Juventudes Socialistas Unificadas – the joint Socialist–Communist Youth.

PCE: Partido Comunista de España – the Spanish Communist Party.

POUM: Partido Obrero de Unificación Marxista – the group of Left Communist dissidents from the BOC and the Izquierda Comunista who joined forces in late 1935 to create a revolutionary alternative to the PSOE and the PCE.

PSOE: Partido Socialista Obrero Español – the Spanish Socialist Workers' Party.

SOMA: Sindicato de los Obreros Mineros de Asturias – the Asturian Miners' Union, affiliated to the UGT.

UGT: Unión General de Trabajadores, the trade union organisation of the Socialist movement.

PROLOGUE

Spain in the 1930s was a backward agricultural country divided by the most brutal economic inequalities. The coming of the Second Republic in April 1931 was seen by many on the Left as an opportunity to reform Spain's antiquated social structure. In the course of the two years of the Republic's first legislature, between 1931 and 1933, the Socialist members of a Republican–Socialist coalition pushed for the introduction of a programme of reform aimed at alleviating the day-to-day misery of the great southern army of landless labourers (*braceros* and *jornaleros*). The prevailing economic system, however, depended on the fact that the day-labourers worked from dawn to dusk for a pittance at harvest time and were then unemployed for the rest of the year. The Socialists' reforms, improving working conditions and basic pay, necessarily implied a redistribution of wealth. Coming in the context of the Great Depression, these measures inadvertently constituted a challenge to the existing balance of social and economic power in Spain.

The activities of both the legalist and the so-called 'catastrophist' Right between 1931 and 1939 were primarily a response to these reforming ambitions of the Left. Unable to sustain improved labour conditions by higher profits, the landed and industrial oligarchies organised in order to block change. They were able to mobilise mass support because the laicising element of the Republic's project of modernisation permitted them to present the regime as anti-religious. They were able to secure the backing of the army because that same project included reform of the military promotion system and the concession of autonomy to the regions, which permitted the Right to present the Republic as unpatriotic and ready to divide Spain in the interests of foreign enemies. The right-wing victory in the Spanish Civil War paved the way for General Franco's re-establishment of the traditional social, economic and religious order.

1

This book is an examination of the part played by the Socialist Party in mounting the reformist challenge, of the determined resistance to reform put up by the political representatives of the landed and industrial oligarchies, and of the effects of the consequent conflict on the Socialist movement and on the democratic regime in Spain. The Socialists constituted the most important single group on the Spanish Left throughout the 1920s and 1930s. They were more decisive than their bourgeois Republican allies, in terms both of numerical strength and of their commitment to fundamental social reform. Moreover, as the largest parliamentary party of the Left, they had greater potential efficacy within the democratic system than their more revolutionary rivals. The desultory insurrectionism of the disorganised anarchist movement and the numerical insignificance of both the orthodox Stalinist and the dissident Trotskyist Communists deprived any of them of serious possibilities of conquering power. Nevertheless, the theoretical criticisms of the Socialists emanating from these groups and the attractions to the Socialist rank and file of their militancy constituted a crucial determinant of the Socialists' own drift from reformism to a self-destructive rhetorical revolutionism.

The Socialist role in the Second Republic is examined here in the light of the interaction of two main factors – party ideology and rank-and-file aspirations. Given that the Partido Socialista Obrero Español was a self-proclaimed Marxist party, the day-to-day tactics and strategies adopted by its leaders were often the consequence of their broader ideological interpretation of contemporary political and economic development in Spain. At the same time, Socialist policy was also a response, within these broad ideological parameters, to pressure emanating from the base of its working-class supporters. After all, the Republic was inaugurated at a time of acute economic crisis. The 1930s saw a massive influx into the Socialist movement of a rural proletariat deeply affected by that crisis, while its traditional membership already included mineworkers equally if not more savagely hit by its consequences.

These two poles of Socialist activity were naturally conditioned by the stout resistance to change organised by the parties of the Right. Accordingly, the book's second main theme is the legalist Right's attempts first to block reform and later to introduce a corporative state as a long-term solution to the leftist challenge. In fact, the principal argument of the book is that, although the Spanish Civil War encompassed many separate conflicts, the main cause of the breakdown of the Second Republic was the struggle between the PSOE and the legalist Right, particularly the Confederación Española de Derechas Autónomas, to impose their respective views of social organisation on Spain by means of their control of the apparatus of the state. The incompatible interests represented by these two mass parliamentary parties – the interests of landless labourers and big landlords, of industrialists and workers – spilled over into social conflicts which could not be contained within the parliamentary arena. Both the Socialists and the legalist Right felt at the time that theirs was the crucial battle. They were each confident that, once in power, their own loyal forces of order could deal with the activities of the extremists of the other side. What the PSOE feared more than the 'catastrophist' Right and the CEDA feared more than the anarchist Left was that the other would be able to use legal means to conquer power and give the Republic a legislative content which would damage the material interests of its followers.

In a predominantly agrarian society, both leftist and rightist considerations of social organisation centred on the land. Rural labourers constituted by far the largest single occupational group within the Socialist union, the Unión General de Trabajadores. The political formations of the legalist Right, the CEDA, the Agrarians and, to a lesser extent, the Radicals, received finance from and defended the interests of the landed upper classes. They also sought their mass support largely among smallholders. Inevitably, then, this study is concerned to a large degree with the class struggle in agricultural areas and its impact on national politics through the PSOE and the CEDA. Other socially conflictive sectors, especially mining, are also considered in some detail.

Since the first edition of this book was completed more than fifteen years ago, there has been a revolution in the historiography of the period. Archives have opened up, the diaries, letters and memoirs of major protagonists have been published, and there have been innumerable studies of the politics of the Republic, of parties, unions, elections and social conflict, particularly from the perspective of individual provinces. Many of these studies explicitly engage with this book, whether confirming or taking issue with points made in the first edition. Accordingly, while the book's basic theses seem still to stand scrutiny they have not survived unscathed. In general terms, then, this new edition has tried to update the original text as exhaustively as possible to take account of this new material. That has resulted in large numbers of relatively minor amendments throughout the text and the addition of fuller illustrative detail on the social conflicts of the time – particularly with regard to notorious flashpoints such as Castilblanco, Casas Viejas, Bujalance, Asturias and Yeste.

There are also substantial changes of three kinds. The opening of the

3

Socialist Party archives at the Fundación Pablo Iglesias has made it possible to study the internal conflicts of the PSOE in much more detail. The new text both reflects my own work in these archives and is a response to the work of a number of scholars, notably Santos Juliá and Helen Graham. There is, in consequence, both a change of emphasis and considerably more material than before on the radicalisation of the PSOE and its tragic consequences in 1934, 1935 and 1936. The other major changes are a response to my own reflections on what I have come to perceive as the weaknesses of the first edition. Its stress on the conflict between the PSOE and the CEDA somewhat simplified the complexity of the politics of the Republic. Now there is much more here on the allies of the principal protagonists, on the relationships between the Socialists and the Left Republicans, the Communists and the anarchists, and between the CEDA and the Radicals and the catastrophist Right. Similarly, the first edition did not satisfactorily explain the connections between right-wing popular militancy and the military uprising of 1936. Accordingly, I have added many pages which draw on my own subsequent work on the Spanish Army. They aim to relate specific military discontents to the broader political conflicts of the period and to illuminate the military readiness in 1932, 1934, 1935 and 1936 to intervene in domestic politics when the success of civilian rightists seemed in doubt.

Within the context of these changes, the overall structure remains broadly similar. The book begins with a chapter on the ideological and tactical developments of the Socialist movement between 1917 and 1931. Its purpose is to clarify the unspoken assumptions behind the behaviour of the three main Socialist factions when under pressure during the Second Republic. Chapters 2 and 3 deal with the period 1931–3 and examine separately the emergence and subsequent development of the legalist Right and the activities of the Republican–Socialist coalition in power. During that first so-called *bienio reformista* (two reformist years), the legalist Right and the Socialists were elaborating their respective stances towards the Republic and towards each other. The legalist Right moved from the disorganised defensive obstructionism of Acción Nacional to the development of a powerful mass party, the CEDA, determined to establish the corporative state. In response to the Right's success in blocking reform, the Socialists moved from an optimistic reformism, shared throughout the movement, to painful inner divisions manifested in a loud but empty rhetorical revolutionism.

Chapter 4 brings both groups together and deals with their constant interaction and growing hostility from the right-wing electoral victory of November 1933 to the late summer of 1934. In those ten months, the CEDA under Gil Robles dominated successive Radical cabinets, revealed its determination to protect the pre-1931 social order by introducing an authoritarian corporative state and enjoyed great success in tempting the Socialist unions into partial and destructive strikes. In reply, the Socialists tried to preserve the progressive character of the Republic by threats of revolution which they hoped never to have to carry out. Outmanoeuvred by the CEDA, the Socialists were obliged, unprepared and vulnerable, to make good their threats in October 1934. Chapter 5 examines the provocation of the rising, its course and its consequences.

The October 1934 rising and its defeat conditioned the tactics of both the Right and the Socialists until the end of 1935. Chapter 6 examines the attempts of the CEDA to proceed slowly towards the authoritarian state in a context of the proletarian resistance to such a state revealed by the events of October 1934. It shows how the CEDA in government in coalition with the Radicals contributed to the creation of reserves of social hatred which would spill out uncontrollably in 1936. The CEDA might have been able to act with impunity if the highly skilled strategy employed by the CEDA leader, Gil Robles, had been successful. However, his scheme to move crab-like to exclusive control of the government was undermined when a tactical miscalculation at the end of 1935 led to the calling of elections. Chapter 7 deals with the major internal dissensions and theoretical adjustments suffered by the Socialist leadership from the moment of defeat in October 1934 until the elections of February 1936. With their leaders in jail or in exile, the Socialists had been forced to withdraw from organised politics. An important part of the leadership wanted to bolshevise the party and reject the Republic. However, the severity of the right-wing repression persuaded a broad front of Republicans and Socialists to unite in the Popular Front electoral coalition.

The final chapter is concerned with the consequence of the Popular Front elections. A leftist victory ended the Right's chances of legally establishing the corporative state and the defence of the threatened social order passed to more violent groups. The Socialists, crippled by their own internal divisions, did not put their strength at the service of the government. Thus, when the bitterness of social conflict spilled over into a partly provoked breakdown of law and order, the Socialists were not in a position from which to take effective steps against the rightist resort to a military coup. A short epilogue considers the fate of leaders of both the Socialist Party and the CEDA after the military rising of 18 July 1936.

Day-to-day violence and the escalation of social hatred are central to the subject of this book. Frequent clashes between the forces of order and the retainers of the big landowners, on the one hand, and the rural and urban proletariat, on the other, were the long-drawn-out prelude to a savage civil war. Yet the origin of the conflict has to be sought not in extremist revolutionary efforts to overthrow established society but rather in limited reformist efforts to ameliorate the daily living conditions of the most wretched members of society. The implication is clear and underlines the similarities of the Spanish experience to those of Italy between 1917 and 1922, Germany from 1928 to 1933 and Chile from 1970 to 1973. The achievements of reformist socialism at a time of economic crisis are as likely as all-out revolutionism to provoke attempts to impose a fascist or corporative state.

1

THE ORIGINS OF THE SOCIALIST SCHISM: 1917–31

The Spanish army officers who took up arms in 1936 had a variety of grievances. They were outraged at attempts by the Republic to bring an end to the privileged position of the military within civilian society. This had taken the form of a series of military reforms which had threatened their promotions and their status. They were equally, if not more, infuriated by the Republic's programme of conceding regional autonomy to the historic nationalities of Spain, Catalonia, the Basque country and Galicia. In an army which had lost many battles, officers were obsessed with a determination to win the last battle, that for national integrity. They were also motivated by a belief, carefully cultivated by the rightist press, that the Second Republic had both been deeply anti-Catholic and done nothing to protect property against a rising tide of social disorder.

That many officers could hold such ideas and were prepared to risk their careers and their lives in a *coup d'état* pointed to a failure of conventional parliamentary politics. When the Second Republic was established on 14 April 1931, it faced social, economic and political problems which had bedevilled Spain for decades. The loss of imperial status and the consolidation of economic backwardness had coincided with the emergence of modern left-wing movements. In consequence, the century before 1931 had seen the profound division of Spain into two antagonistic social blocs. In simplistic terms, there were, on the one hand, the armies of urban and rural proletarians, bitterly split between socialism and anarchism, and the liberal intellectual petty bourgeoisie of enlightened lawyers and professors. And, on the other, stood the Church, the army, the great landowners, the industrial and mercantile bourgeoisie and the great mass of Catholic conservative smallholding farmers. The expectations of the Left exploded in April 1931 in an atmosphere of popular fiesta in the streets of many cities and in the workers' taverns of southern villages. Equally, there was much gnashing of teeth in the officers' messes of many garrisons, in the big houses of the great *fincas* (estates) and in churches all over Spain.

Nevertheless, on 14 April 1931, only the tiniest fractions of the most lunatic fringe of the extremes of Left and Right believed that the problems which lay deep in the social and economic structures of Spain would have to be resolved by war. Yet, five years and three months later, large numbers of the politically literate population had reached the sad conclusion that war was inevitable if not exactly desirable. When sections of the army rebelled on 18 July 1936, they did so with considerable civilian support. That would be starkly clear in the division of Spain over the next few days. The successes and failures of the rebels replicated the electoral geography of the 1930s. The rising, with a few exceptions, was defeated in areas of working-class strength and was successful in areas where the parties of the Right had won in the elections of the Second Republic.

The extent to which the politics of the Second Republic were reflected in the configuration of the war zones is not perhaps surprising. None the less, it stresses the fact that the reasons for the breakdown of parliamentary coexistence during the Republic are better sought in the failures of the mass parties of the period than in the activities of the extremists of Left and Right. The two great parliamentary parties of the time, the Socialist Party or PSOE (Partido Socialista Obrero Español) and the Catholic authoritarian CEDA (Confederación Española de Derechas Autónomas), represented the incompatible interests of landless labourers (*braceros*) and big landowners (*latifundistas*), of industrial workers and industrialists, particularly of miners and mine-owners. The PSOE, from 1931 to 1933, and the CEDA, throughout 1933 and 1934, attempted to use the power of the state to defend the interests of their supporters. In a context of world economic depression, the well-being of the Socialist rank and file could be defended only at the cost of major challenges to the economic power of the backers of the CEDA, and vice versa. Accordingly, the two parties brought to Madrid from the provinces, and especially from Andalucía, Extremadura and Asturias, the most embittered agrarian, mining and industrial struggles. Since it was impossible for such social conflicts to be contained within the parliamentary arena, they returned back to the fields and streets more embittered than before.

As the biggest party of the Left, the PSOE provided three ministers in the reforming governments of 1931–3 and the backbone of their parliamentary support. During the period of Centre-Right dominance from 1933 to 1935, the Socialists were the only major opposition force,

8

both in parliament and in the street, and even took part in a major insurrection in 1934. Without participating in them, the CEDA used its parliamentary power to dominate the Radical governments of 1934 and then, after October of that year, controlled a series of coalitions throughout 1935. From the so-called Popular Front elections of February 1936 until the outbreak of war in July of that year, the Socialists and the CEDA were both out of government. They were each bitterly divided, yet powerful sections of each advocated a move towards extreme solutions of violence.

The readiness to make way for the military had been apparent in the CEDA since the late summer of 1934. The appeal to violence was the most obvious symptom of a growing radicalisation of the PSOE which began in 1933 as a result of disillusion with the paucity of the Republic's reforming achievement; of fear that a less militant line would lead Spanish Socialists to share the fate of their German and Austrian comrades; and of a major reassessment of the ideology and tactics of the party.[1] The radicalisation or 'bolshevisation', as its advocates called it, was never complete and was advanced only at the cost of the most bitter polemic within the party. In fact, it was the continuing internal power struggle that virtually paralysed the more moderate groups of the Socialist Party and prevented them from contributing to the defence of the Republic when it was under threat in the spring of 1936. It is presumably to this fact that Salvador de Madariaga refers in declaring that 'what made the Spanish Civil War inevitable was the Civil War within the Socialist Party'.[2]

There has been considerable debate over the origins of the radicalisation of the Socialists. The present work interprets it in terms of acute social conflict in the great estates of the south and in the northern coalfields, probably the two areas of most endemic social violence during the Second Republic. In both areas, the hegemonic trade union was the Socialist Unión General de Trabajadores. Hundreds of thousands of landless labourers had flocked into the UGT's landworkers' union, the Federación Nacional de Trabajadores de la Tierra (FNTT), at the beginning of the Republic. They became one of the largest sections of the UGT and were in the front line of the social war fought in the area. The daily violence to which members of the FNTT were subjected was matched by the experience of another UGT union, the Asturian coal-miners' Sindicato de Obreros Mineros Asturianos.[3]

In the wake of defeat in the Civil War, many militants of the PSOE, and not only those who took the moderate side in the polemic, were harsh in their judgements of the attempts to 'bolshevise' the party.[4] In

9

the case of the moderates, this is not difficult to explain. Apart from an understandable resentment of the personal attacks to which they were subject, as long-standing militants they also opposed what they saw as an attack on the traditions of the party, which were anything but extreme. In the case of the repentant bolshevisers, it is also not difficult to explain their change of heart. One of the results of the 'bolshevisation' was that large sections of the PSOE fell under the influence of the Communist Party, whose behaviour during the Civil War left a legacy of great bitterness among its erstwhile Socialist and Republican allies. In the aftermath of defeat, they clearly regretted the part they had played in helping the Communists to prominence. In fact, neither of these critical stances substantiates the view of Madariaga, although both help to explain why such a view has been widely accepted as an explanation of the outbreak of hostilities in 1936. Criticisms of the attempted 'bolshevisation', however, should not blind us to the extent to which the radicalisation of the PSOE was a response, albeit a mis-judged one, both to a series of provocations by the Right at national as well as local level within Spain and to the context of the rise of fascism.

The radicalisation remains to be explained, not least because it made the Spanish Socialist Party unique in Europe at a time when most socialist movements were evolving towards ever more moderate posi-tions. The contrast was even greater in relation to the PSOE's own past history of deeply rooted reformism and its lack of a tradition of theoreti-cal Marxism.[5] The party never broke away from its origins among the working-class aristocracy of Madrid printers. Pablo Iglesias Posse, its founder, never gave his party much in the way of independent theory. *Pablismo*, as his ideas were later termed by Trotskyist critics, was always more preoccupied with cleaning up existing politics than with the class struggle, adopting an austere and monkish tone which made the party seem to at least one observer like a brotherhood of moralists. In fact, *pablismo* was a mixture of revolutionary ideology and reformist tactics, which, given the party's numerical weakness, was for Iglesias the only realistic alternative to either destruction or clandestinity. Julián Besteiro, his successor as party leader, also felt that austerity and aloofness were the only viable tactics in the corrupt politics of the restoration era.[6] Thus, after the tragic week of 1909, the PSOE joined the Republican forces in what was virtually a civil-rights campaign. In 1914, even though Spain was not involved in the hostilities, the PSOE leadership failed to take the opportunity to condemn the war and followed the French lead in breaking international solidarity, much to the chagrin of several groups within the party.

The aspirations of the reformist leadership were, until the 1930s, focused on the need to replace the discredited monarchy with a popular republic and hardly at all concerned with notions of social revolution and class struggle. Indeed, *El Socialista*, the party newspaper, at first ignored the Russian Revolution, then roundly declared it to be a sad deviation from Russia's real duty – the defeat of Germany.[7] A consequence of the poverty of the party's Marxism, the lack of revolutionary fervour was also partly the result of the fact that, from the PSOE's foundation in 1879 to the boom of the Great War, prices and wages remained relatively stable – albeit among the highest prices and lowest wages in Europe. Perhaps as a partial consequence of that stability, the Spanish working class remained largely demobilised.[8] In 1914 those circumstances began to change. Spain's position as a non-belligerent allowed her to assume the role of supplier of food, clothing and equipment to both sides. A vertiginous industrial boom was accompanied by fierce inflation, which reached its height in 1916. It was in response to the consequently deteriorating social conditions that the PSOE and its union organisation, the UGT, became involved in the nationwide reform movement of 1917. In complex circumstances, three anti-establishment movements shared a rhetoric of anti-monarchical reform while pursuing contradictory goals. The summer of 1917 saw a military protest about pay and promotion conditions, a bourgeois rebellion against a central government run in the interests of the landed oligarchy and a working-class determination to fight against rapidly crumbling living standards. Even when the UGT took part in a national general strike in mid-August 1917, the maximum aims of the Socialists were the establishment of a provisional republican government, the calling of elections to a constituent Cortes and vigorous action to deal with inflation.[9] Despite, or because of, its pacific character, the strike was defeated with relative ease by the government by dint of savage repression in Asturias and the Basque country, two of the Socialists' major strongholds – the other being Madrid. In Madrid, the strike committee consisting of the PSOE vice-president, Julián Besteiro, the UGT vice-president, Francisco Largo Caballero, the editor of *El Socialista* and leader of the printers' union, Andrés Saborit, and the secretary-general of the railway workers' union, Daniel Anguiano, was arrested and very nearly subjected to summary execution. They were finally sentenced to life imprisonment and spent several months in prison until they were freed on being elected to the Cortes in 1918.[10]

The repression of 1917 had a twofold effect on the Spanish Socialist movement. On the one hand, the leadership, and particularly the syndical bureaucracy, was traumatised, determined never again to risk their legislative gains and the movement's property in a direct confrontation with the state. On the other, those who had opposed the party line on the world war began to adopt more revolutionary positions. The consequent polarisation became increasingly apparent in the following years. Between 1918 and 1923 there was considerable revolutionary activity (mainly in the rural south and in industrial Barcelona), to which the Socialist leadership maintained an attitude of studied indifference.[11] Yet the continuing inflation and the rising unemployment of the post-war depression had created, in the wake of the Bolshevik Revolution, a climate of opinion within the Socialist movement, particularly in Asturias and the Basque country, in favour of a revolutionary orientation. This view was expressed in the journal *Nuestra Palabra*, which under the direction of Ramón Lamoneda and Mariano García Cortés adopted the view that events in Russia and the failure of the 1917 reform movement in Spain pointed to the irrelevance of the bourgeois democratic stage on the road to socialism. This brought them into conflict with the syndical bureaucracy and especially three key figures, the railway workers' leader, Trifón Gómez, the secretary-general of the Asturian miners' union, Manuel Llaneza, and one of the senior figures in the UGT, Francisco Largo Caballero, who were determined not to repeat what they saw as the senseless adventurism of 1917.[12]

There followed a lengthy, bitter and debilitating debate over what was to be the attitude of the PSOE and the UGT to the Russian Revolution and to the Third International. The pro-Bolshevik tendency was defeated in a series of three party congresses held in December 1919, June 1920 and April 1921. In a closely fought struggle, the leadership won the day by being able to rely on the votes of the strong union bureaucracy of paid permanent officials.[13] The defeated Left departed to form the Spanish Communist Party. Numerically, the Communist schism was not a serious blow, but it accentuated the Socialists' ideological weakness at a time of grave economic and social crisis. The party's fundamental moderation was strengthened and there was a plunge of morale which lasted for some years.[14] In the aftermath of the defeat of 1917, the 1921 split left the Socialists without a clear sense of direction and somehow remote from the burning issues of the day. The syndical battles which raged elsewhere attracted less Socialist attention than the parliamentary campaign against the Moroccan war and the King's alleged reponsibility for the great defeat of Annual.

The defensiveness and ideological conservatism of the Socialists became patently apparent with the coming of the military dictatorship of General Primo de Rivera on 13 September 1923. His seizure of power was largely a response to the social agitation of the previous six years. Yet the Socialists neither foresaw the coup nor showed great concern when it came, despite the fact that the new regime soon began to persecute other workers' organisations. A joint note of the PSOE and UGT executives announced that they had 'no tie of solidarity or political sympathy' with the political élite being overthrown by the army and questioned the right of the conspirators to take power but ordered workers to take no initiatives without instructions from the executive committees of the Socialist Party and the union. Rejecting CNT (Confederación Nacional del Trabajo) calls for a general strike, the Socialist leadership did nothing to impede the establishment of the regime, did little to analyse its nature and were soon to be found collaborating with it. Having failed to see any great significance in the rise of Mussolini, the Spanish Socialists were not tempted to make any comparisons between the Italian and Spanish dictatorships.[15] This reflected the extent to which the leadership had come out of the crisis of 1917 convinced of the need to stick to a legalist tactic, never again to risk the existence of the unions in direct clashes with the state, and to guard at all costs the achievements of existing social legislation.[16]

Years later, the collaboration with the Dictator was to become a moral burden to the Socialists. It is possible that some of the rhetorical extremism shown during the Republic was the symptom of a desire to expunge the egoistic reformism of the Dictadura period. Certainly several Socialist apologists went to some trouble to justify the failure of either the PSOE or the UGT to resist the coup. They claimed that it would have been absurd to risk the workers' movement to save the degenerate system of the Restoration monarchy.[17] This was a somewhat specious argument, since there was more at stake than Primo's overthrow of the old politicians, as was shown by the persecution suffered by other parties.[18] Moreover, critics on the Left felt that a general strike would have forestalled the coup and placed the Socialists in a dominant position within national politics.[19] More significantly, there were others within the PSOE itself who were shocked by the opportunism shown by the leadership. They accepted that strike action against the army would have been sentimental and infantile heroics, but could not admit that this justified close collaboration with it. They were disappointed that the party merely shrugged its shoulders instead of taking a strong stand on principle, which might have become a rallying point for later opposition to the Dictator.[20]

As it was, the Socialists took no significant part in the varied resistance movements to the Dictadura, at least until its later stages. This 'discretion' was to lead to division within the Socialist ranks, although left-wing Socialists were later to defend it as a refusal to play the game of the oligarchy.[21] As the Dictator's popularity fell, the Socialist movement in general began to dissociate itself from the regime, but in the early days only a small group was in favour of outright opposition. These were the followers of Indalecio Prieto, who had a certain amount of support in Bilbao and Asturias, and Fernando De los Ríos, whose supporters were to be found in Granada. Although the rest of the Socialist leadership was in favour of collaboration, it was not entirely for the same reasons. Indeed, the collaborationists were in practice equally reformist – as, for that matter, were Prieto and De los Ríos. In theory, however, two distinct factions could be discerned: the practical trade unionists led by Francisco Largo Caballero, and those trade unionists who followed the Marxist revisionist Julián Besteiro. Their differences became apparent only very gradually, and even then they were far from clear to the rank and file. Nevertheless, they were to lead to the bitter polemics of the 1930s and to split the movement, owing to the wide personal following which each of the front-rank leaders commanded.

After Pablo Iglesias, the founder of Spanish socialism, Julián Besteiro was the PSOE's most significant figure and one of its very few theoreticians. When Iglesias died in December 1925, Besteiro became president of both the party and the UGT. His theoretical position was analogous to that of Kautsky, of whom he was an open admirer.[22] With Kautsky, he shared an orthodox Marxist analysis of the inevitable progress of society through a bourgeois democratic revolution towards socialism, and he derived from this a pacific and gradualist praxis. Like Kautsky, he rejected the notion of the dictatorship of the proletariat, regarding much of the Bolshevik experience as irrelevant to Spanish conditions.[23] Besteiro, like Iglesias, looked far more towards the British Labour Party and the Fabians for example. In 1924, he spent seven months in England consolidating his admiration for the British model of gradualist socialism. It was hardly surprising then that he was in favour of the Spanish Socialists taking advantage of the opportunities offered by Primo de Rivera in order to defend their material interests.[24]

Those trade unionists within the movement who were not followers of Besteiro tended to be supporters of Largo Caballero, although Prieto also had his adherents, particularly in the north. Largo's attitude to the Dictatorship was similar to Besteiro's although he lacked the latter's theoretical foundation for it. Largo was essentially a pragmatic trade unionist, who always claimed that he owed his prominence in the movement to his assiduous performance of syndical duties and his close attention to the everyday round of organisational chores. Largo had once written that the workers' movement was the product of their unchanging need to improve their moral and material conditions within the capitalist system.[25] Not unnaturally, he was hostile to any enterprise which might endanger that movement, particularly after the disaster of 1917. When the Dictatorship came, he and his followers reasoned that, although the political struggle was suspended, the syndical struggle had to go on. An economic recovery was being staged after the post-war crisis and they felt that the first task of the UGT was to use any means possible to protect the material interests of their members in the factories and workshops.[26] In practice, this meant going beyond simple pragmatism to a narrow opportunism based on a desire to steal an advantage over the anarcho-syndicalists.[27] This sectarian egoism was to meet considerable rank-and-file opposition, particularly in Asturias, but also among the agrarian sectors of the UGT.

The formal initiative for the collaboration came from the Dictator himself, who could be confident of a sympathetic response in view of the Socialist passivity during his coup – the joint communiqué of the PSOE and UGT had ordered the Socialist movement not to follow the example of the Bilbao workers who had declared a general strike. The approach came in a manifesto to the workers on 29 September 1923 in which Primo thanked the working class for its attitude during his seizure of power. The manifesto was clearly directed at the Socialists. On the one hand favouring social legislation, so dear to the reformists of the UGT, it then called upon the workers to leave the organisations which led them 'along paths of ruin'. This reference to the revolutionary CNT and PCE (the Spanish Communist Party) was a scarcely veiled offer to the UGT that it could become the exclusive working-class organisation and, in return for collaborating with the regime, eliminate its anarchist and Communist rivals.[28] It struck the chord of the long-standing Socialist hostility to the CNT. Soon after, Pablo Iglesias was gleefully, and in similar terms, predicting the downfall of the CNT, implying that the workers in its ranks had found themselves there either by mistake or because they were forced. Two days after his manifesto, Primo made a direct offer to Manuel Llaneza, secretary-general of the Asturian Miners' Union (SOMA: Sindicato de los Obreros Mineros de Asturias), to join a committee to examine the problems of the mining industry. Getting the erroneous impression that the SOMA would thereby be able to defend its achievements in the way of wages and hours, on the following day Llaneza enthusiastically addressed an already favourably predisposed

posed meeting of the joint national executives of the PSOE and UGT.[29] The meeting decided to support the collaboration begun by Llaneza, although there were three votes against this resolution, including those of Prieto and De los Ríos.[30]

The moderate Llaneza had been leader of the SOMA during the strike of 1917 and, having witnessed its brutal repression, was one of the Socialists most shaken by the events of that year. He wrote of the 'odio africano' (African hatred) that had been unleashed against the mining villages, in an orgy of rape, looting, beatings and torture. Llaneza claimed that only one officer, a Colonel Borbón behaved in a civilised manner as a result of which he was relieved of his post.[31] It was fear of the consequences of another clash with the army which was the basis of his collaborationism. However, his views were opposed even at that early stage by Teodomiro Menéndez, another of the 1917 leaders, and a staunch follower of Prieto.[32] This was symptomatic of nascent division between the UGT rank and file and the reformist leadership. The SOMA, besides constituting one of the UGT's most substantial sections, was also one of its most militant, and even after the 1921 schism had cordial relations with local Communists.[33] For the moment, however, the opposition to the executive's tactic was expressed only by De los Ríos and Prieto, who wrote to Besteiro at the end of 1923 protesting against it. Meeting on 9 January 1924, the National Committee of the PSOE ratified the collaborationist line adopted so far, but it made a small but significant concession to Prieto. This was a declaration that no government positions would be accepted without their recipients' being designated by the Socialist organisation concerned.[34]

Nevertheless, the integration of the national leadership into the new regime was considerable and the UGT had representation on several state committees.[35] The Socialist 'Casas del Pueblo' remained open and most UGT sections were allowed to continue functioning, while anarchists and Communists suffered a total clamp-down on their activities. The first indication of the Military Directory's price for the privileged position accorded the Socialists came in March 1924, when workers' demonstrations were prohibited, prior to the planned May Day celebrations.[36] In return for the workers' docility, the UGT was offered its greatest prize yet, a seat on the Council of State. On 2 June 1924 the Instituto de Reformas Sociales was replaced by a Labour Council, the UGT delegation passing in its entirety from one body to the other. Then, on 13 September, a royal decree allowed for one workers' and one employers' representative from the new council to join the Council of State. The UGT representatives chose Largo Caballero. Within the

UGT itself this had no unfavourable repercussions – Besteiro was vice-president and Largo himself secretary-general. However, there were protests within the PSOE.

Prieto and De los Ríos both wrote letters to the PSOE executive denouncing the opportunism of Largo's acceptance of the position and warning that it would be exploited by the Dictator for its propaganda value. In fact, Primo did cite Largo's presence on the Council of State as a reason for not re-establishing democracy.[37] The executive met on 17 October to consider the complaints and decided that the PSOE should not interfere with something concerning the UGT. This was not entirely honest, since the same individuals made up the executive committees of both bodies and it was normal practice to hold joint deliberations on important national issues. As a result of this Prieto resigned.[38] The issue was placed before a plenum of the PSOE National Committee on 10 December and Largo's acceptance was ratified by fourteen votes to five. De los Ríos called for a referendum among the rank and file, but his proposal was defeated.[39] This division within the party was to have repercussions right up to the Civil War, if only for the personal enmities created. In fact, faced by rumours of schism within the party, Prieto declared publicly that the tactical discrepancies had in no way affected the cordiality and unity among the party's leaders. Nevertheless, it is clear that, both at the time and later, Largo Caballero harboured tremendous personal rancour against Prieto.[40]

The collaboration was to continue and increase despite evidence from Asturias that such a tactic was doing little to protect the workers' interests. The mine-owners provoked a strike in November 1924 by demanding a reduction in wages. While Llaneza hurried to Madrid to see Primo, the owners struck a pre-emptive blow by sacking 350 workers. When the strike came, it was no more than defensive and barely managed to maintain wages at their previous level. This gave rise to criticism, by elements to the left of the Socialists, that collaboration meant handing over the miners bound and gagged to the owners.[41] In no way dismayed, the UGT maintained its pacific attitude, refusing to join movements of resistance to the Dictatorship. Citing the Asturian industrial action as a triumph resulting from collaboration with the regime, Pablo Iglesias claimed that, despite censorship and limits on meetings and strikes, both the UGT and the PSOE were growing under the Dictatorship. In fact, 1926 was to see the most substantial co-operation yet by the UGT. Largo Caballero, speaking at the Madrid Casa del Pueblo, roundly condemned industrial sabotage, go-slows and strikes as likely to provoke lock-outs. He declared that opposition to

17

the regime could prove disastrous for working-class organisation. Besteiro would not authorise a move against the regime unless this involved no risk for the Socialists. Later PSOE apologists were to point out with some justification that most of the resistance movements aimed at restoring the monarchy and therefore offered little benefit to the workers' movement.[42]

In November 1926, Primo's Minister of Labour, Eduardo Aunós, set up the National Corporative Organisation. Largely the result of a study-tour that he had made in Italy, and incorporating much existing social legislation, its long-term aim was to eliminate the class struggle.[43] Its most practical manifestation was the creation of arbitration committees, *comités paritarios*. The UGT decided to accept the regime's invitation, on the grounds that there were immediate material benefits to be obtained. They reasoned that, if the best conditions for the workers were to be negotiated through the committees, and workers' representation were exclusively in the hands of the UGT, then non-Socialist workers would flock to their ranks. The main activities of the committees consisted of negotiating wages and working conditions (*bases de trabajo*) and arranging compensation for unfair dismissals. It was the belief of the trade union bureaucracy that the committees prevented many strikes and unnecessary sacrifices for the working class.[44] Years after, when the UGT was criticised for its opportunism in accepting them, it was claimed that UGT orators used them as a front for propaganda against the Dictatorship.[45] There is little evidence for this, and, if it happened, it was probably after the tide of popular opinion had turned against the Dictator and the UGT was trying to dissociate itself from the regime.

In any case, it is difficult to calculate how many strikes were avoided by the work of the *comités paritarios*. Certainly by 1927 the economic boom which had so favoured the Dictatorship at first was beginning to come to an end and there was growing evidence of syndical unrest and significant increases in unemployment. In 1927 there were 107 recorded strikes, involving 70,616 workers and with 1,311,891 working days lost. In 1928, with approximately the same number of strikes and strikers, only 771,293 days were lost. In 1929, the numbers dropped even further: 96 strikes, 55,576 strikers and 313,065 days lost.[46] This seems to reflect the success of the *comités paritarios* in anaesthetising working-class dissent. In Barcelona, for instance, unemployment almost doubled between early 1927 and late 1929.[47] Moreover, after rising slowly until 1925, wages began to fall steadily thereafter, albeit with great regional and trade variations. Staple working-class foods such as potatoes, bread and olive oil also rose in price.[48] Besides affecting the stability of the

regime, the intensification of labour unrest was to have major repercussions within the Socialist movement, since it suggested the existence
of a rift between the militancy of the rank and file and the timid
conservatism of the UGT leadership. Nowhere was this more apparent
than in Asturias. In the autumn of 1927 the mine-owners tried to
increase working hours and decrease piece-work rates. Llaneza was
against strike action because he feared that the army would be sent
against the miners. The SOMA overruled him and went ahead with the
strike, which was successful. The effect of this in national terms was
that the Asturian leaders began to favour abandonment of the UGT's
collaborationist line. They had little choice since members were drifting
away from the SOMA at an alarming rate, membership dropping from
its peak of 20,000 in 1921 to 5,998 in 1928.[49]

Opposition to the leadership was not confined to the Asturian miners,
but also affected the UGT's rural sections. Agricultural workers were
the most numerous occupational group within the UGT and alarm
at the drop in their numbers indicated that their importance was being
recognised within the Socialist movement.[50] They constituted, moreover,
the section which had derived least benefit from UGT co-operation
with the Dictadura. Rural comités paritarios were never established and
Aunós's half-hearted attempts to help rural labourers were instrumental
in uniting the landowners of the south against Primo.[51] Sixty-five rural
sections of the UGT, with 15,000 members, were closed down by 1928.
By December 1929 the UGT had only 30,000 rural members; in August
1922 there had been 65,405.[52] A significant reflection of feeling within
the agrarian section of the movement came from Gabriel Morón, a
veteran leader from Córdoba and an important voice within the party.
In a devastating critique of the leadership's failure to make a stand
against the Dictadura, he claimed that the UGT's egoistic attitude was
dividing the workers' movement, and complained that nothing was
being done to prepare the masses for the end of the regime. He
demanded that official posts be relinquished, on the grounds that their
retention signified exchanging the party's historical prestige for short-
term official patronage.[53]

The discontent now emerging seemed to vindicate the stand taken
four years previously by Prieto and De los Ríos. Moreoever, it seemed
as though their position was gaining adherents, particularly within the
PSOE. In September 1927 Primo offered six Socialists seats in his new
National Assembly, which was to deliberate on a possible constitutional
reform. All six – Largo Caballero, Núñez Tomás, Llaneza, De los Ríos,
Santiago Pérez Infante and Lucio Martínez Gil – rejected the offer.

Extraordinary congresses of the UGT and the PSOE were called for 7 and 8 October respectively. The rejection was ratified – a clear victory for the anti-collaborationists. Indeed, the PSOE issued a statement demanding the re-establishment of liberty and democracy. Nevertheless the followers of Besteiro clung to the collaborationist tactic. Besteiro himself was ill, but two of his most loyal supporters, Trifón Gómez of the railway workers' union and Andrés Saborit of the printers' federation, proposed that Primo's offer be accepted if the Socialists could choose their own representatives. The polemic provoked by this proposal was so bitter that it was decided to shelve the issue.[54]

The debate over the National Assembly showed that the intensification of social conflict was having a gradual but significant effect on the configuration of forces within the Socialist movement. Of the three tendencies within the movement – the social democrats following Prieto, the 'Kautskyism' of Besteiro and the pragmatic trade unionism of Largo Caballero – it was the last that was most noticeably affected by the changing mood of the Socialist working masses. In 1924 Largo had opted for co-operation with the Dictatorship for no more theoretical reason than that he could see substantial material benefits for the UGT in doing so. By the same token, now in 1927, he began to change his mind in the face of growing evidence that such a tactic was having a deleterious effect on the UGT's membership rolls. Collaboration had already earned the Socialists the opprobrium of others on the Left.[55] The loss of prestige could be justified only if it were compensated by an increase in numbers. Yet there was little indication that the UGT's virtual monopoly within the state industrial arbitration machinery had a significant positive effect on recruitment. Indeed, two of the UGT's strongest sections, the Asturian miners and the rural labourers, had suffered appreciable losses during the Dictatorship.

It is difficult to establish trade union membership gains during the period. The UGT admitted the loss of 15,000 rural labourers, but claimed in compensation a gain of 17,000 industrial workers by the time of the Sixteenth Congress in September 1928.[56] Even in the mining sector, despite the spectacular losses in Asturias, there were some gains. Llaneza managed to secure better wages and conditions for the copper-miners of the British-owned Tharsis mines near Huelva. This success led miners in the area to join the Federación Minera of the UGT.[57] Overall gains within the UGT were not substantial. Membership rose as follows: 1923, 210,617; 1924, 210,742; 1925, 217,386; 1926, 219,396; 1927, 223,349; 1928, 210,567; 1929, 238,501.[58] This represented a poor return considering the UGT's privileged position; hardly a greater increase than might have been expected in normal years and certainly not in any sense the hoped-for absorption of CNT rank and file. Equally the figures represent only fully paid-up members and times were hard. At the Sixteenth Congress of the UGT, held between 10 and 15 September 1928, the 591 delegates represented only 141,269 affiliates but that low figure probably represents the fact that some sections just could not afford to send a delegate.[59] The PSOE fared slightly better, increasing from 5395 members in 1923 to 12,815 in 1929. It has been claimed that the increase merely represented existing UGT members who had also joined the PSOE. In major industrial centres PSOE membership was extremely low. In Asturias it dropped from 528 in 1923 to 391 in 1929; in the Basque country from 670 to 631.[60] The material welfare of the Socialist movement in general and of the UGT in particular was always to mean more to Largo Caballero than any theory and he was therefore always responsive to shifts in rank-and-file feeling. This goes some way towards explaining some of his otherwise inexplicable changes of tactics during the Republic, when again it was the Asturians and the landworkers who were in the forefront of militancy.

The extent to which opposition to the Dictatorship was growing within the Socialist movement was shown clearly at the Twelfth Congress of the PSOE, which was held from 9 June to 4 July 1928. De los Ríos was in South America, but Prieto and Teodomiro Menéndez defended a line of outright resistance. And it was soon apparent that they were no longer alone. A special committee was created to examine the party's tactics. The tactic of collaboration was rejected by this committee by six votes to four. The majority included Morón from Córdoba and Teodomiro Menéndez from Asturias, who also, in the main Congress, made a resounding speech against collaboration.[61] For censorship reasons, the discussions of the committee on tactics were given no publicity. However, involving as they did the defeat of supporters of Largo Caballero, they seem to have had an effect on his views regarding the Socialist role in the Dictadura. But for the moment, despite the increasingly vocal opposition in favour of a stand for liberty and democracy, the majority view remained pro-collaborationist. This was reflected in the elections for party offices at the PSOE's Twelfth Congress, and for posts in the UGT at the union's Sixteenth Congress. Besteiro was elected president of both the PSOE and the UGT. All senior offices went to followers either of Besteiro or of Largo Caballero. In the PSOE, the division of posts was as follows: president, Besteiro; vice-president, Largo Caballero; treasurer, Saborit; secretary, Lucio Martínez Gil; minutes secretary,

Wenceslao Carrillo; and in the UGT: president, Besteiro; vice-president, Saborit; secretary-general, Largo Caballero; treasurer, W. Carrillo.[62]

Nevertheless, conflict between the workers' movement and the regime was increasing. After a strike in Seville had been crushed by the forces of order, Socialists of the south retained little faith in the efficacy of co-operation.[63] This was the beginning of what by 1930 would become a massive wave of strikes throughout the south.[64] In Asturias, the inability of the *comités paritarios* to resolve the problems of the mines was ever more apparent. The mines were inefficient and their coal not of high quality. In 1928 the coal industry began to suffer badly from the dumping of cheap British coal. Four thousand miners were laid off. Negotiation was impossible and reformist solutions irrelevant. The miners called for nationalisation of the mines; the owners for wage-cuts and redundancies. Primo clearly could never accept any policy which implied an attack on the structure of property. When Llaneza complained to him that many miners could get work for only two weeks in any month, the Dictator replied, 'You people panic too easily; it's better to work two weeks than not at all.' As increasing numbers were being laid off, mines being closed and shorter working becoming the norm, the SOMA began to divide on the issue of a general strike. The internal polarisation of the union showed that the miners were already being pushed towards the radicalisation which was to become a major issue during the Republic.[65]

It was becoming increasingly difficult for the Socialist leadership to maintain that collaboration with the Dictatorship was working for the benefit of the working class, yet in January 1929 Largo Caballero was still arguing against direct action and in favour of government legislation.[66] Nevertheless, he was pulling away from close commitment to the regime. He had little choice since it was obviously foundering. In the latter stages of the Dictadura, following strikes (particularly in Santander and Vigo), 150 UGT sections were dissolved, ninety-three workers' centres were closed down and hundreds of Socialists were arrested.[67] The universities were in an uproar. Intellectuals, republicans and even monarchist politicians protested against the abuse of the law and went so far as to prepare resistance movements in collaboration with progressive elements in the army. Support from the army derived from the bitter resentment in the more professional artillery and engineering corps, which had seen their commitment to promotion by strict seniority flouted by Primo, who high-handedly imposed promotions by merit. The bourgeoisie was alarmed to see the peseta falling, and, as 1929 advanced, the first effect of the world depression began to impinge on the Spanish economy. The Socialists were gradually being isolated as the Dictator's only supporters outside his own Unión Patriótica.

Fear of being left behind by the changing circumstances and of losing rank-and-file support finally began to have its effect on the collaborationist majority within the Socialist leadership. On 26 July 1929, Primo offered the UGT the chance to choose five representatives for his National Assembly. His original offer of September 1927 had been rejected only because the Socialists had not been allowed to choose their own delegates. On 11 August, the National Committees of the PSOE and the UGT held a joint meeting to discuss the offer. Two main proposals were presented. The first, from Largo Caballero, called for rejection of the offer on the grounds that acceptance would be a contravention of the agreement made at the UGT's extraordinary congress of 7 October 1927. This, apart from bending the truth somewhat, represented a significant change of position by Largo. He had clearly decided that the Dictatorship was discredited and that further association with it would be counter-productive for the Socialist movement. The other proposal, by Besteiro, was in favour of accepting Primo's offer.

The debates in the meeting showed the extent to which the trade union leaders had realised the danger of losing their hold over the Socialist masses. Only Enrique Santiago and Wenceslao Carrillo supported Besteiro's proposal. Yet the change of direction was executed only with the greatest reluctance and because of the pressure of the rank and file. Andrés Saborit, Besteiro's most loyal follower, commented, 'Our vote was based on the examination of the political circumstances. Really it was a case of rectifying a correct policy out of pure opportunism.'[68] Besteiro had called for an extraordinary congress of the UGT to settle the issue. The objections raised to this proposal showed the extent to which the changing mood of the Socialist masses had begun to influence their leaders. Largo Caballero stated that he was entirely in agreement with Besteiro's reasons for being in favour of collaboration with the regime, but not with the proposal for a congress. It was clear that he did not want to confront a revolt from the rank and file in an open congress. Trifón Gómez, leader of the railway workers' union and a Besteirist, said in defence of voting against the president:

I have no objection whatsoever to supporting what Besteiro says in his declaration, but I am taking into account the sentiments of the organised working class. I believe it useless and damaging to call a congress, because the delegates will come to vote in a majority against participating in the National Assembly.

23

In the final vote, only Santiago voted with Besteiro, since Wenceslao Carrillo was also convinced that the delegates to any congress would vote against the executive.[69]

Even Besteiro was affected by the circumstances, albeit with greater theoretical consistency. If he was driven now to criticise the Dictadura, it was for reasons of an intellectual reformism and not in response to the practical considerations which swayed the trade union bureaucracy. The National Assembly to which the UGT had been invited was to discuss a project of constitutional reform which effectively would have blocked any return to 'democratic' normality. Besteiro had been in favour of accepting the invitation in order to contest the project in the Assembly. In fact, the rest of the Socialist leadership was in basic agreement with him, except for the Prieto group, but preferred to make a major gesture to rank-and-file sentiment. With the Dictator's invitation rejected, Besteiro drew up a manifesto containing his thoughts on the projected constitutional reform. Signed by Besteiro and Saborit for the PSOE and by Besteiro and Largo Caballero for the UGT, this manifesto was issued on 13 August 1929. Its publication was prohibited by the censorship apparatus and it was printed clandestinely and distributed by hand.[70]

The text of the manifesto represented an ample demonstration of Besteiro's thought concerning the political crisis and the role of the Socialist movement therein. It represented no inconsistency with his position regarding collaboration with the regime. On the long road to the establishment of socialism, Besteiro felt that it was legitimate to use all legal means to maintain or improve the situation of the Socialist movement. Seeing the Dictatorship as a transitional stage in the decomposition of the monarchical regime, it seemed logical to him to accept the privileges offered by the Dictator. This was because, according to his rigidly orthodox Marxist analysis, the monarchy had to be overthrown by a bourgeois revolution and therefore the job of the Socialists was to keep their organisation intact until their day should come. In 1929, Primo's project for constitutional reform seemed an attempt to legitimise, and make permanent, the transitional nature of the Dictatorship. Besteiro saw the road to socialism as a legal one and now Primo's scheme was trying to close the legal possibilities. His first reaction was to contest the project legally within the Assembly. When the movement decided against this, he drew up the manifesto. His criticisms of the project were of two sorts. The more immediate and short-term criticisms were based on the fact that the project made only the vaguest promises of social reform and declared an intention to restrict the right to strike.

More important were his criticisms of the long-term effects of the project if it were ever put into practice. The powers to be given to the King would make it impossible for the parliament ever to introduce reforms which undermined the interests of the oligarchy. Accordingly, Besteiro reached the conclusion that the precondition for the democratic road to socialism was 'a republican state of liberty and democracy within which we might reach the political power which corresponds to our growing social power'. If Primo destroyed the possibility of establishing the necessary political conditions for the development of socialism, then neither the UGT nor the PSOE could be responsible for the actions to which this might drive them.[71]

This forthright statement did not, however, signify the union of all three tendencies within the Socialist movement. It might have been thought, for instance, that Besteiro's rejection of the Dictatorship would bring him nearer the position of Prieto and De los Ríos, but the co-incidence was only accidental. Not being committed Marxists in any specific way, they were always more concerned with liberty and democratic rights as ends in themselves. Besteiro was also a committed democrat, but he accepted the Marxist view that the establishment of basic liberties was the role of the bourgeoisie. Hence, while Prieto and De los Ríos were in favour of Socialist co-operation with middle-class republicans against the monarchy, Besteiro was afraid that the working class would be exploited to achieve bourgeois goals and, in the process, suffer attrition and lose sight of its own long-term objectives. Largo Caballero's position was different again. Ever pragmatic and opportunist, he was concerned always with two things: the material interests of the Socialist movement as against any other group and the maintenance of the Socialist bureaucracy's control over the rank and file. This pragmatism made Largo's position more subject to sudden and inconsistent shifts than were either of the other two tendencies.

Largo was already moving towards the Prieto position of collaboration with the republicans, although still within a context of profound reformism. Nevertheless, it was a shift and it soon became apparent that it was an adjustment to the wishes of the militants of the base. On 16 September 1929, he made a speech to the Santander branch of the printworkers' union (Federacíon Gráfica Española). He declared that the Socialists could no longer confine their attention to exclusively union matters, 'because, *against our wishes*, circumstances are forcing us to play a part in all kinds of national problems'. He made it clear that he was looking ahead to the end of the Dictadura and was altering tactics accordingly:

I, who have been accused of rightist tendencies, am one of those who believe that, as long as the working class can act within a legal context which allows it to develop its organisation, it would be madness to leave that context. However, I also believe that if eyes are closed to the desires of the country and if possibilities are closed whereby the country might have developed towards progress, then the working class will know how to do its duty.[72]

This new militancy on Largo's part was perhaps not unconnected with the fact that Santander had seen major clashes between local Socialists and the Dictatorship. Hundreds of UGT members had been imprisoned in Santander after a strike by the local metalworkers' union, the Sindicato Metalúrgico Montañés.[73] Largo was moving away from Besteiro's position towards that of Prieto. On 12 January 1930 he declared that on the road to socialism it would be necessary to pass through a longer period of transition, in which Socialists could collaborate in republican bourgeois governments and even become the 'administrators of capitalism'.[74] When, in 1933, that position too proved damaging to the workers' movement, Largo just as easily abandoned it in favour of greater radicalism.

Even though it is possible to distinguish three main tendencies within the PSOE, they were partly masked by some coincidences of political analysis. As befitted a party which had rejected bolshevism, all three tendencies shared an essentially reformist approach. This was made abundantly clear after the decision not to join the Third International. It was further underlined in early 1924, when all sections of the party were to be found rejoicing over the establishment, in January, of the first Labour cabinet in Britain. Pablo Iglesias commented in fulsome terms that it was an event which would repair the damage done to world socialism by the tactics of the Russian Communists. Largo Caballero called it 'the most important event in the entire history of international socialism'.[75] Luis Araquistain, later to be one of Largo's radical advisers, emphasised the importance of following the British road to socialism.[76] Besteiro, of course, was already something of a Fabian and a close follower and admirer of British socialism. In 1924 Besteiro spent a long period in England, studying the Workers' Educational Association. It was the culmination of a growing interest in the achievements of the Labour Party and in the English guild movement. At the height of the polemic surrounding the so-called bolshevisation of Spanish socialism in 1934, Besteiro published an introduction to a series of essays by English socialists, including Stafford Cripps.[77] De los Ríos was

26

also delighted with the Labour victory and saw it as proof that the class struggle could be avoided.[78] In fact, for many reasons, a gradualist road to socialism in Spain was to prove impossible in the 1930s. The realisation that this was the case, an insight unavoidable by 1933, would affect each of the three tendencies of the PSOE in different ways. It was these differing responses that exaggerated the divisions apparent in the 1920s and that formed the basis of the savage polemics which split the Spanish Socialists in the 1930s.

For the moment, however, this was far from apparent. The Dictator resigned on 28 January 1930, and in the subsequent euphoria the Socialists seemed less divided than at any time since 1923. Moreover, they were in a better position than at any time in their history. The old Liberal and Conservative parties, separated for so long from the old mechanisms of electoral falsification and demoralised by the King's espousal of a dictatorship, were in complete disarray. New republican parties were still in their most embryonic form. Accordingly, at the beginning of 1930 the PSOE was the only properly organised political party in Spain. The situation of the UGT was even more favourable, given the difficulties under which the anarchists and Communists had been forced to operate. Inevitably, the growing opposition to the monarchy looked to the Socialists for support. Republicans were sure of a favourable response from Prieto and his social-democratic followers. And, as the crisis sharpened and the rank and file grew increasingly militant, Largo Caballero moved ever more quickly towards Prieto's position. Only Besteiro was hostile, believing that it was up to the bourgeois republicans to make their own revolution and determined that the Socialist masses should not be exploited as cannon-fodder. Yet even he adopted something of a passive attitude.

At first, Besteiro threw himself into his academic life as Professor of Logic at Madrid University.[79] He drew up the joint UGT–PSOE manifesto which greeted the government of Primo's successor, General Dámaso Berenguer. Expressing doubts about Berenguer's pledge to re-establish the basic liberties, the manifesto condemned his regime as illegitimate and without a popular mandate. Yet, critical as it was, Besteiro's text contained no hint of active opposition to Berenguer or of any interest in trying to force a change of regime. Indeed, it stated that, if political liberties were re-established, the Socialist movement would resume its participation in normal political life.[80] Not surprisingly, Berenguer was confident that he need expect no trouble from the Socialists. On 29 January 1930, the day he assumed power, he received a report drawn up by the Director-General of Security, General Bazán, on the political and social situation of the country. The report praised the Socialist leaders for keeping the rank and file out of political agitation. Its conclusion was that the Socialists, far from constituting a danger to the established order, could be seen as a guarantee of it.[81] Bazán's successor, General Emilio Mola, was also confident that the trade union bureaucracy could be relied on to try to keep the rank and file out of militant action, although he was worried about their ability to do so.[82]

It was not long before the Socialists were subjected to mounting pressure by republican forces to add their weight to the movement against the monarchy. Besteiro was firmly against any such Socialist collaboration and spoke out several times, insisting that the republicans show themselves to be united and make clear their programme before requesting Socialist support.[83] Prieto remained as strongly tied to the cause of republicanism as he had been during the Dictatorship, and was playing an ever more important role. One by one, the most significant politicians in the country were declaring themselves against the King. On 20 February 1930, Miguel Maura, son of the great Conservative Prime Minister Antonio Maura, announced his newly adopted republicanism. On 27 February, another great Conservative, José Sanchez Guerra, declared his lack of faith in Alfonso XIII. They were followed by other significant monarchists, Angel Ossorio y Gallardo and Niceto Alcalá Zamora. But the speech which had the greatest popular effect came from Prieto on 25 April in the Madrid Ateneo. To the chagrin of both Besteiro's group and Largo Caballero, Prieto advocated a revolutionary movement against the monarchy with the participation of the Socialist masses. Largo demanded that the PSOE executive censure Prieto for appearing at a banquet with Sánchez Guerra.[84]

Before the summer of 1930 was out, however, Largo Caballero was showing as much enthusiasm as Prieto for Socialist collaboration in the republican movement. There was no theoretical consistency in his attitude. He was acting, as he had done throughout the 1920s, out of an opportunism based on what he instinctively felt to be in the immediate material interests of the UGT. Two things in particular impelled Largo to his change of tactics. They were the increasingly evident economic crisis and its effect on the day-to-day militancy of the Socialist rank and file, and, above all, the rapid gains being made by the anarchist CNT and, on a smaller scale, by the Communist Party.

As in the late 1920s, the contraction of the economy was particularly apparent in the mining and agricultural sectors. The militant tendencies of the Asturian miners had been held in check by Llaneza at the cost of falling numbers, but he died in January 1930. Thereafter, the influence of Prieto became ever more powerful. In March, under the leadership of a Prietista, Ramón González Peña, the SOMA successfully fought for a 7 per cent wage increase. And, despite orders from the executive committee of the PSOE not to make pacts with republican groups, the Asturian Socialist Federation was soon following a Prietista policy of making alliances in the battle against the monarchy.[85]

On a national level, labour militancy was increasing at a vertiginous rate. 1930 saw, in comparison with 1929, four times as many strikes, involving five times as many strikers, with the loss of ten times as many working days.[86] The UGT leadership seemed unaware of the scope of the economic crisis and was far from prominent in the labour troubles of the spring. Indeed, General Mola even considered proposing an agreement between the UGT and the government-sponsored 'yellow' unions, the Sindicatos Libres, in an effort to combat anarchist and Communist agitation.[87] The CNT had been legalised in April and recovered its old strength with astonishing speed. By June, strikes were breaking out in Catalonia, the Levante, Aragón and Andalucía. The Communists did not attain the same influence, but they had substantial and militant support in the Basque country and in Seville, where the conclusion of Primo's extravagant works programme left a mass of unemployed construction workers.[88]

The wave of strikes made it clear that the UGT rank and file were considerably more militant than their leaders. Mola was convinced that what he called the CNT's 'revolutionary gymnastics' was gradually forcing the UGT leadership to follow suit for fear of losing members. A jealous vigilance towards other organisations had always been a characteristic of the Socialist trade union bureaucracy and it seems to have had a crucial influence upon the syndical leaders in mid-1930. To go along with the rank and file clearly clashed with the economic interests of the leadership. Mola trusted their reformism because of the stipends the Socialist bureaucracy received for running the *comités paritarios*. They had a vested interest in making the wage-arbitration machinery work.[89] It is all the more significant, then, to note the opinion of a member of the UGT bureaucracy renowned for his multiple posts in the state machinery, Manuel Cordero.[90] Explaining how the UGT came to join the movement against the monarchy in 1930, he says, 'Our revolutionary optimism had hardly been excited at all. It was just obvious that we were faced with an imminent revolution, which would take place with us or without us or even against us.'[91]

Police information led the Director-General of Security to believe that CNT prominence in strikes was damaging the UGT's membership figures, particularly among the young. The main consequence of this, above all in the south, was that the UGT passed gradually, in the summer of 1930, from a secondary role in anarchist-led strikes to a more independent and dynamic one. With the exception of the Basque country, where Prieto had considerable support, the initiative for Socialist participation in the republican movement came from the masses, with the Besteiro- and Largo-Caballero-dominated leadership trailing behind. During the summer, the greatest labour agitation took place in the south, with general strikes in Seville, Granada and Málaga. By September, this had spread to the industrial north. Galicia, Asturias and the Basque country were also becoming active. Moreover, if at first the strikes tended to have limited economic aims, it was not long before they manifested a clearly political orientation, beginning with protests against the repressive measures of the government and finally developing into demands for a change of regime. In October, for instance, a one-day strike called by the UGT in Bilbao on the 4th was met by the Civil Guard. The strike was then extended in protest for another four days. Then on 23 October, the Basque PSOE and UGT decided in favour of joining the republican movement. In mid-November, a construction accident in Madrid killed four workers; the UGT, seconded by the CNT, called a general strike, and this too saw clashes between workers and the forces of order. It was becoming increasingly clear that the spontaneous tendency of the Socialist masses was towards the line of action advocated by Prieto and away from that of the syndical bureaucracy. Indeed, one of the Besteirista executive committee of the UGT, Manuel Muiño, told Mola that the leadership could not oppose the general trend within the UGT.[92]

It is not without significance that the UGT participation in strikes increased after the foundation in April 1930 of the Socialist Landworkers' Federation (FNTT: Federación Nacional de Trabajadores de la Tierra). Founded with 157 sections, embracing 27,340 members, within two months the FNTT was able to boast 275 sections and 36,639 members. This was the beginning of a rapid expansion which was to take the UGT to over 1 million members by 1932. The importance of the FNTT within the UGT was soon apparent, since the UGT as a whole registered relatively smaller increases than the FNTT on its own. In December 1929 the UGT had 1511 sections, with 228,507 members. One year later it had grown to 1734 sections, with 277,011 members.[93] Such figures are, of course, not definitive, since they are based on subscription payments. Many workers, particularly in the rural south, might obey UGT instructions regarding a strike without being able to afford the membership dues. Nevertheless, the disproportionate growth of the FNTT clearly reflects its growing influence within the Socialist movement. Moreover, the figures suggest that Mola was right when he said that the CNT was making inroads into UGT membership, since virtually all the 1930 increases represent rural workers. In industrial areas, UGT membership can hardly have been better than static.

A large proportion of the wave of strikes which broke out in the second half of 1930 took place in the south. If this was partly a result of frenetic anarchist and Communist agitation, it was above all a response to the intense crisis which was affecting Andalusian agriculture. Storms in the spring had ruined the olive crop. Not only did this deprive the landless labourers of the greater part of their yearly income, normally earned during the mid-November to mid-January olive harvest, but in addition it limited the amount of work available in the intervening period. Jaén, two thirds of whose agricultural production consisted of olives, was the worst-hit province, followed by Córdoba and Seville. The spring storms were then followed by a summer drought so severe that in November the Sierra Nevada was without snow. This seriously damaged the cereal crop. The resulting unemployment ranged from 12 per cent in Cádiz, 13 per cent in Huelva and Córdoba and 16 per cent in Granada to 50 per cent in Jaén and Seville.[94] The consequent economic hardship of the *braceros* was clearly reflected in the increase of strikes in the south.

The FNTT was led by a Besteirista, Lucio Martínez Gil – that is to say, a member of the group which opposed any form of collaboration with the republicans. Nevertheless, there was a growing feeling among the working class in general and the landless southern labourers in particular that only a republic could solve Spain's economic and social problems. The growth of the popular notion of the republic as a panacea centred on the prospects of a fundamental agrarian reform.[95] It seems that this attitude and evidence of rising militancy had some influence on Largo Caballero. Certainly, the alacrity with which, when in April 1931 he became Minister of Labour, he introduced decrees favouring the southern labourers demonstrated considerable sensitivity to these workers' problems. And, in general terms, it is clear that the increase of labour agitation was accompanied by a parallel increase in his interest in Prieto's links with the republican movement.

Prieto and De los Ríos attended a meeting of republican leaders in San Sebastián on 17 August. From this meeting emerged the so-called Pact of San Sebastián, the republican revolutionary committee and the future republican provisional government. Immediately afterwards, De los Ríos went to Madrid to inform the PSOE executive committee. Besteiro did not take the republican requests for Socialist collaboration very seriously. Nevertheless, after a meeting between Besteiro, Saborit and Cordero, and Prieto, De los Ríos and the republican Alvaro de Albornoz, it was decided to call a full meeting of the National Committee of the PSOE. This was held on 16 September and saw a direct clash between the Besteiristas and De los Ríos. Neither group had changed since the Dictatorship. While Prieto and De los Ríos, in supporting the coming of a republic, did so for reasons of social-democratic ethics, Saborit, for the Besteiro group, adhered to the rigid Marxist line that it was for the bourgeoisie to make the necessary bourgeois revolution. Significantly, Largo Caballero was not present. The outcome of the meeting was a non-committal declaration that no agreement with the republicans had been reached.[96]

Largo had been in Brussels for an international congress, but he was back in Spain in time to hear, in the second week of October, of the revolutionary committee's offer to the PSOE of two ministries in a future republican government. The National Committees of the UGT and the PSOE met on 16 and 18 October (respectively) to discuss this offer and the price asked: the support of the Socialists in a *coup d'état* by means of a general strike. The positions of the Besteiristas and the Prietistas remained as before. The balance was swung by Largo Caballero. So long in agreement with the Besteirista union bureaucracy, he suddenly began to support the Prieto line, declaring that the PSOE should be one more party in the republican movement. This shift was the result of that same opportunism which had inspired his early collaboration with, and later opposition to, the Dictatorship. He said himself at the time, 'This was not a question of principles but of tactics.' It was decided that the UGT would support the military insurrection in return for assurances that the republic when established would take action to redistribute property, introduce workers' control in industry and establish the mixed-jury system of arbitration machinery. The republican committee then extended its original offer to three ministries. When the executive committee of the PSOE met to examine the offer, it was accepted by eight votes to six, with Prieto, De los Ríos and Largo Caballero being designated as the three Socialist ministers in the provisional government.[97]

As before, there was no theoretical reason for Largo's brusque change of direction. Given his well-known sensitivity to the mood of the UGT rank and file, it is not difficult to see in his action a response both to the rise in labour troubles and to the increasingly political character thereof. Moreoever, since Largo was throughout his career obsessed by a sense of rivalry with the CNT, he must have been influenced by the anarchist successes of 1930. Here, then, is discernible a characteristic of Largo's behaviour already visible during the Dictatorship and that would become increasingly obvious during the Republic – a tendency to lead from behind. He cannot have been unaware of a growing dis-satisfaction at a local level with the line adopted by the Besteirista leadership in Madrid.[98] Largo never permitted himself to be out of step with the rank and file.

There was also a personal element in Largo's sudden switch. His bitterness with regard to Prieto is patently evident in his memoirs, and it was evident to Miguel Maura in the meetings of the revolutionary committee.[99] Saborit felt that Largo was irritated by seeing Prieto in the limelight and enjoying immense popularity among the workers.[100] It is interesting to note that, soon after his conversion to republicanism, Largo was outdoing Prieto in enthusiasm.[101] However, the crucial element in his change of mind may be seen in the offer of ministries in the provisional government. Concerned as he was with the material welfare of the UGT, he cannot have been unaware of the advantages to be derived from tenure of the Ministry of Labour. Control of arbitration machinery could be used to the advantage of the UGT as against the CNT. Members of the UGT bureaucracy could be placed in lucrative posts within the ministry. And, above all, wide-ranging social legislation could be introduced. All these things were done when the Republic was established. They demonstrate the primacy of the material interests of the UGT in Largo Caballero's mind.

Tending, as he did, to see things in personal terms, Largo soon developed a strong resentment towards the Besteirista faction of the Socialist Party.[102] This became immediately apparent during the arrange-ments for the UGT's participation in the revolutionary movement agreed upon in October and finally, after various delays, scheduled for mid-December. It was arranged that the UGT would support a military coup with a strike. Things were complicated somewhat by the precipitancy of Captains Galán and García Hernández who rose in Jaca (Huesca) on 12 December, three days before the agreed date – an action perhaps motivated by a suspicion that the other conspirators could not be relied upon. Nevertheless, there was no change of plan, despite the scarcely veiled opposition of the Besteirista leadership in Madrid. Partly at least because of this opposition, the movement planned for 15 December was a total failure. After the execution of Galán and García Hernández on the 14th, the artillery withdrew from the plot. And, although forces under General Queipo de Llano and aviators from the air base at Cuatro Vientos went ahead, they realised that they were in a hopeless situation when the expected general strike did not take place in Madrid.[103]

Given that within four months a Republic was established after municipal elections, the failure of the December movement was not a definitive set-back. Moreover, if the Republic had been brought in by a military coup, this would have considerably altered its character and perhaps its ability to contemplate sweeping reforms. Nevertheless, the failure of the Madrid strike was the object of bitter discussion within the Socialist movement. It was debated at the Thirteenth Congress of the PSOE, in October 1932, and led to the defeat of the Besteiristas in the leadership. It is difficult to find the truth among so many personal accusations, but the evidence does suggest that the failure derived from the Besteiristas dragging their feet, if not actually sabotaging the strike, as supporters of Largo Caballero were later to claim.[104]

On 10 December, for instance, Julio Alvarez del Vayo, one of the Socialists involved in the conspiracy, tried to have the revolutionary manifesto for the day of the proposed strike printed at the Gráfica Socialista, the printing works at which the PSOE newspaper, *El Socialista* was produced. Saborit, the editor, refused point-blank.[105] Moreover, it is significant that Madrid was the only important city where there was no strike, since Madrid was the stronghold of the Besteiro faction of the UGT bureaucracy. General Mola, who was in touch with Manuel Muiño, the president of the Socialist Casa del Pueblo, was confident on the night of the 14th that the UGT would not join in the strike on the following day. He based his certainty on police reports and other 'assurances'.[106] Such assurances are unlikely to have come from sources other than the syndical bureaucracy, since Largo Caballero was actively working for the strike and his dismay when it did not take place seems to have been genuine. Largo's job was to pass on the final instructions for the strike on the night before. This he did, with Muiño as his contact.[107] Yet the defence later put forward by the Besteiro group was that Largo Caballero failed to pass on the necessary information. In any case, Besteiro told the Thirteenth Congress of the PSOE that, having seen planes dropping revolutionary propaganda over Madrid and being pressed by members of the Socialist Youth Federation (FJS: Federación de Juventudes Socialistas) to take action, he called the strike at mid-day on the 15th. Yet, after he told Muiño to go ahead, nothing was done except that a message threatening a strike if any more executions took place was sent from the Casa del Pueblo to the government. None of the powerful unions controlled by the Besteirista syndical bureaucracy stopped work. This was later attributed to the apathy of the rank and file. It is odd that this apathy was not apparent in the preceding months and that in the provinces there was substantial strike action. The UGT was prominent in stoppages throughout Asturias and the Basque country and even in Barcelona.[108]

The debate within the Socialist movement over responsibility for the failure was of considerable importance. It indicated that, although Besteiro was a theoretical Marxist, he represented a strong current of practical reformism, which was centred on the Madrid-based union bureaucracy and was prepared to act against the wishes of sections of the rank and file. The debate also indicated the extent to which Largo Caballero, impelled always by a pragmatic assessment of the mood of the grass-roots militants and a keen sense of the practical advantages to be derived by the UGT, had travelled away from the positions he had maintained in the 1920s. The debate also created a reservoir of bitterness which later was to exacerbate internal divisions within the Socialist movement. It was perhaps because of this that Besteiro later admitted that the responsibility for the December 1930 failure was entirely his.[109]

The immediate result of that failure was the defeat of the Besteiristas and the acceptance by the Socialist Party and the UGT of a policy of complete co-operation with the republican movement. A joint meeting of the National Committees of the PSOE and UGT took place on 22 February 1931. Besteiro called for the Socialists to leave the revolutionary committee, a proposal which was defeated by thirty-five votes to twelve. Besteiro resigned from the executive, along with Saborit, Trifón Gómez and Lucio Martínez Gil; the remaining members proposed a new set of candidates, all in favour of collaboration, and these were elected by a considerable majority. It was clear that the desire of the rank and file for a change of regime, encouraged by the stance adopted by Prieto and Largo Caballero, had finally influenced the entire movement. Only the Agrupación Socialista Madrileña remained as a staunch bulwark of Besteiro.[110]

In fact, the two positions, of collaboration and abstention, had a shared assumption – that the Republic about to be established would be a bourgeois democratic republic which would carry out a bourgeois revolution as the first essential step on Spain's road to progress and socialism. Of course, the conclusions that the two sides drew from that assumption were different. Besteiro felt that the Socialists should leave the bourgeoisie to make their own revolution, for there was a possibility that the Socialists would find themselves in the contradictory position of carrying out bourgeois policies. Prieto felt that the Socialists should collaborate – first because the establishment of democratic rights was a worthy end in itself, and secondly because he was convinced that the bourgeoisie was too weak to carry out its own revolution unassisted. Largo Caballero was also in favour of collaboration, but rather more because of the immediate material benefits which would accrue to the Socialist movement and because of the opportunity to prepare for the future implantation of socialism. The fact that the assumption on which these conclusions were based was erroneous was to lead to even wider divisions in the Socialist movement as each sector reacted in its different way to the realisation that the hopes placed in the Republic were not being fulfilled.

The Socialist belief that the old Spain was about to undergo transformation into a modern bourgeois society was based on two mistaken notions. The first mistake was simply to regard the republican politicians of the revolutionary committee and the provisional government as the 'bourgeoisie' about to undertake the historical role of the English bourgeoisie in the seventeeth century and the French in the eighteenth. In fact, the republican politicians were merely members of the urban petty-bourgeois intelligentsia. The economically powerful oligarchy was not, as the Left supposed, a feudal structure, but had already integrated sections of the bourgeoisie.[111]

This was the second error of analysis. The moment when the Spanish 'bourgeoisie' might have tried to sweep away the outmoded structure of the *ancien régime* had long since passed. The progressive impulse of the bourgeoisie had been sufficiently weak to preclude any major change in the structure of political and economic power. In the first two major periods of pressure, 1833–43 and 1854–6, the bourgeoisie had been virtually bought off by the disentailment of Church lands and release of common lands onto the open market. This process saw much urban mercantile capital invested on the land and the consolidation of the system of large latifundia estates. The class that the Socialists expected to be progressive was already tied to the old oligarchy. Henceforth the *latifundios* were part of the capitalist system and not, as the Socialists thought, feudal vestiges. Part of the process of integration of the urban bourgeoisie with the landholding oligarchy was a certain penetration of the financial oligarchy by aristocratic and ecclesiastical capital.[112] The second two major periods of bourgeois impulse, 1868–74 and 1916–17, emphasised more than ever the weakness of the bourgeoisie as a revolutionary force. On both occasions, the conjunction of worker and peasant agitation was enough to induce the urban oligarchy to accentuate its ties with the rural.[113] Once the Catalan industrialists had withdrawn from the alliance of progressive forces in 1917 and accepted participation in the 1918 coalition government, the possibility of a bourgeois revolution as the PSOE leaders conceived it was no longer viable.[114]

To a large extent, the development of the Socialist movement during the 1930s was influenced by the importance of an essentially incorrect historical analysis of what was happening in Spain. The calculations of all three sectors of the PSOE were based on the certainty that a bourgeois-directed progressive revolution was about to take place. When it became apparent, by 1933, that this was not happening, each sector reacted according to the norms of behaviour it had established during the pre-Republican period. Besteiro made a quietist withdrawal into his theory; Prieto tried in every way he could to reinforce the Republic and to help it fulfil its historical tasks; and Largo Caballero began opportunistically to channel the discontent of the most vocal sections of the embittered rank and file.

2

BUILDING BARRICADES AGAINST REFORM
The legalist Right, 1931–3

The victory of Republican and Socialist candidates in the big towns in the municipal elections of 12 April 1931 generated considerable apprehension among many members of the middle and upper classes. The subsequent decision of Alfonso XIII to leave Spain, and the coming of the Republic on 14 April, signified for them rather more than a simple change of regime. The monarchy symbolised in their minds a hierarchical concept of society, with education controlled by the Church and the social order jealously guarded against change. Hitherto, growing popular resentment of harsh industrial conditions and a manifestly unjust distribution of land had been kept in check by the Civil Guard and, in moments of greater tension, the army. Until 1923, albeit with increasing difficulty, the monarchy's parliamentary system was so managed by means of electoral falsification that universal suffrage never seriously challenged the monopoly of power enjoyed by the great oligarchical parties, the Liberals and the Conservatives. However, in that year, the parties had been supplanted by the Dictatorship. Those of the old politicians who did not throw in their lot with the Dictator never forgave the King for his unceremonious destruction of the constitutional system. Now the Dictator had gone and the King too in his wake. In the changed situation, the upper classes were caught momentarily without the necessary political formations to defend themselves from the threat implicit in the implantation of a popular Republic. Even if the great bourgeois revolution anticipated by the Socialists was not to be, a Republic supported by the Socialist movement clearly implied some kind of reform, however mild, and some adjustment of political and social privilege.

The privileged classes were not entirely helpless. The peaceful way in which the Republic had been established had left their social and economic power intact. Moreover, there existed organisations of the Right which had been endeavouring to combat the rising power of the urban and rural working class for the previous twenty years. Prominent among them were the ACNP (Asociación Católica Nacional de Propagandistas), an élite Jesuit-influenced organisation of about five hundred prominent and talented Catholic rightists with some standing in the press, the judiciary and the professions, and the CNCA (Confederación Nacional Católico-Agraria), a mass political organisation of the Catholic smallholding peasantry particularly strong in north and central Spain. Both the ACNP and the CNCA were in a position to mobilise mass support against any progressive tendencies in the Republic.[1] So successful did they prove that they shattered completely the hopes that the Socialists had placed in the Republic.

Before the ACNP and CNCA achieved their success, however, it was somewhat more combative groups which tried to take up the cudgels on behalf of the old order. In Burgos, one eccentric monarchist unsuccessfully tried to recruit an army of 'legionaries' to combat the revolution. In Madrid, others, headed by the ACNP member Eugenio Vegas Latapié, tried to found a counter-revolutionary journal and were soon plotting the violent destruction of the Republic. Before the elections, the ex-ministers of Primo de Rivera had founded the UMN (Unión Monárquica Nacional), to strengthen the monarchy with the authoritarian ideas of the Dictator. The UMN had undertaken a large provincial propaganda campaign to fight against republicanism in the elections. The tone of the campaign showed the party's awareness of the issues at stake in a possible change of regime. In a meeting at Santander, a talented and energetic young Catholic lawyer, José María Gil Robles, also a member of the ACNP, told his audience that, 'by defending the monarchy, you defend the basic principles of society'. The point was underlined elsewhere by Antonio Goicoechea, a well-known Madrid dandy and one-time minister of the King: 'The monarchist candidacy does not only mean the permanency of fundamental institutions, it also means order, religion, family, property, work.'[2]

Electoral defeat, and the King's recognition of the futility of defending his throne by force, had caught conservatives by surprise. While the Left had prepared for success, the Right had barely conceived of such resounding failure. However, for all its apparent disarray, the Right was quick to produce a response to the new regime. This took two forms. The first, that of the Carlists and the more ultraist supporters of Alfonso XIII, was a determination to overthrow the Republic by violence.[3] The other, that of the ACNP, was less dramatic and more immediately realistic: an acceptance of the democratic game in an attempt to take over the Republic and draw its teeth. This response grew out of an awareness of the political weakness of the Right and of the tactical insight that its interests could best be defended within the law. This legalistic tactic, known as 'accidentalism', was, in terms of the development of the Republic, far more important than violence. Admittedly, the 'catastrophists' were behind the military rising of 1936 which eventually destroyed the regime. Nevertheless, until that moment most of their activities were external to the mainstream of Republic politics. The accidentalists, on the other hand, built up a mass right-wing party, using it to block the reformist path of the Republic, and thereby completely altered the Socialists' perception of the possibilities of bourgeois democracy. This accelerated the polarisation of Republican politics and created the context which gave a spurious relevance to the activities of the catastrophist conspirators.

The theory behind accidentalism was that forms of government were accidental, of secondary importance, and that the essential issue was the 'content' or socio-economic orientation of a regime. It was propounded by the leader of the ACNP, Angel Herrera, editor of the militantly Catholic and, hitherto, monarchist daily *El Debate*. A shrewd political strategist, Herrera would be the brains behind political Catholicism in the early years of the Second Republic, although by 1935 his religious vocation would lead him to withdraw altogether from politics, going to Switzerland in May 1936, taking holy orders in July 1940 and eventually becoming Bishop of Malaga in April 1947 and a cardinal in February 1965. His advocacy of accidentalism, which derived from the encyclicals of Leo XIII and the writings of the traditionalist thinker Balmes, implied no surrender of fundamental objectives, but, rather, a prudent tactical adjustment to unfavourable circumstances, unhindered by any need to defend lost causes. It was more convenient to fight for one's objectives within the established system, especially when its overthrow was patently beyond one's means. The accidentalism of *El Debate* was clearly this, a politic accommodation to an unpleasant situation. On the morning of 14 April, *El Debate*'s editorial had said, 'The Spanish monarchy, after fifteen centuries of life, cannot end like this.' On election day it had proclaimed the need for a grand monarchist affirmation, to protect 'the basic principles of society' against 'negative barbarism' as represented by the Republic. Even as the election results came in, the editorial board was meeting to find a formula to get the King to stay. Yet on 15 April *El Debate* proclaimed the need to respect the new, *de facto* regime. Republicans of all shades had reason to believe that this sudden abandonment of yesterday's ardent monarchism was not entirely sincere. It was seen rather as an example of that 'sacristy cleverness' which enabled *El Debate* to be always on the winning side.[4] The other editorial printed on 15 April was entitled 'Our Homage to King Alfonso XIII'. Indeed the accidentalists' handbook gave a retrospective indication of their attitude to the advent of the Republic: 'The rabble, always irresponsible, took over the resorts of government . . . the sewers opened their sluice gates and the dregs of society inundated the streets and squares.'[5] In fact, it was only after Alfonso's decision to leave became final that it was decided to 'continue the struggle in the only terrain possible: within Republican legality'.[6]

Angel Herrera maintained this combative tone when he addressed members of the ACNP on only the second day of the Republic's existence. He urged them to throw themselves into the defensive battle against 'the avalanche which was overwhelming the bases of the Church'. Their objectives were to be the reorganisation of dispersed forces, the provision of a common ideology to the Spanish Right and, within legality, 'the reconquest of everything that has been lost'.[7] As Gil Robles, the deputy editor of *El Debate* who had taken part in the monarchist election campaign and who was to become leader of the accidentalists, put it, 'with the conservative parties liquidated, the reaction of the dispersed monarchist elements rendered impossible, there was an urgent necessity to establish a strong nucleus of resistance'. The 'resistance' was to be directed against any threat of change in the religious, social or economic order. The propagandists went all over Spain and began a zealous campaign to 'group together the *non-Republican* forces, destroyed and badly damaged'.[8]

The unrolling of the campaign revealed something of the political interests for which the 'struggle' was to be undertaken. On 21 April *El Debate* addressed itself to 'all the elements of order not tied before or now to the triumphant revolution', and called upon them to join in a single organisation. Since the 'triumphant revolution' had done nothing to change any aspect of Spanish life except the form of government, the appeal could be seen to be to those who nurtured a prior hostility to the Republic, and whose objective the Left could not but suspect was, if not the rapid return of the King, at least the limitation of the nascent regime to a form indistinguishable from the monarchy. The slogan under which the 'anti-revolutionary' forces were to unite was 'Religion, Fatherland, Order, Family and Property'. The reflective Republican could hardly have failed to see the resemblance to the slogans used by the Unión Monárquica Nacional less than a fortnight before. The connection was in any case underlined by the same *El Debate* appeal, which said, 'Perhaps someone misses from our slogan an element – a word affirming the monarchy. We omit it deliberately despite our well-known and sincere monarchist sentiments.'

As clear as the tie with the monarchy was the connection with the Vatican. The ACNP and *El Debate* had a tradition of submission to the wishes of the Church hierarchy, and, throughout the years of the Republic, Angel Herrera scrupulously followed instructions from Rome, which he received through the Papal Nuncio, Monsignor Tedeschini.[9] Not surprisingly, *El Debate*'s editorial line and the tactics adopted by the ACNP closely followed the instructions telegrammed by Cardinal Pacelli, the Secretary of State to the Papacy, to Cardinal Vidal i Barraquer. Pacelli recommended that Spanish Catholics follow the Bavarian example of 1918 and unite against the Communist menace.[10] Vidal responded immediately with a pastoral letter, framed in similar terms, that virtually enjoined adherence to the organisation that Angel Herrera was founding. Catholics were instructed to vote, in the forthcoming elections for the Constituent Cortes, for those candidates who would protect the rights of the social order.[11] In mid-May, the Pope issued the anti-socialist and anti-liberal encyclical *Quadragesimo Anno*.

Close ties with the Church hierarchy merely underlined the extent to which the new group's omission of overt monarchism from its slogan was manifest opportunism. Alfonso XIII had always been identified with militant clericalism.[12] Moreover, taking sides in religion involved a clear social alignment, since it was the middle and upper classes whose piety was to be outraged by the Republic's laicism. A close bond with the Church had increasingly become limited to the aristocracy, the large landowners of the south and the conservative smallholders of Castile, Levante and the Basque–Navarrese provinces. Consequently, the nascent accidentalist organisation was to be characterised by a blend of religion and reaction: 'We must all defend Spain and ourselves and our material and spiritual goods, our convictions . . . , the conservation of property, hierarchy in society and in work.'[13] This hardly suggested open-mindedness on questions of social reform and it was the corollary of active clericalism. The Church was still the living symbol of the old Spain which the Republicans hoped to modernise, and was, on a par with the monarchy, a central pivot of the conservative world. Besides, religion was an issue which could be used to mobilise mass peasant support behind the interests of the oligarchy. Having lost the political hegemony in April 1931, the ruling classes clung all the more to the Church as one of the key redoubts of their social and economic dominance. Equally, the Church hierarchy, as a major landowner, had a somewhat similar view of the value of an alliance with the new political formation being created to defend oligarchical agrarian interests.[14] Not surprisingly, throughout the Republic, the clergy used both pulpit and confessional to defend the existing socio-economic order and to make electoral propaganda for the successive political organisations of the Right. This crucial backing from thousands of priests was directed above all to the organisations of the accidentalists – Acción Nacional, Acción Popular and the CEDA.

The growth of accidentalism received a considerable boost on 10 May. Followers of Alfonso XIII had tried publicly to regroup as the Círculo Monárquico Independiente (CMI). The provocatively timed stance of these extreme rightists created a fervent popular reaction which formed the background to the notorious church burnings which took place in Madrid, Malaga, Seville, Cadiz and Alicante from 10 to 12 May. The origins of the incendiarism remain obscure, although Miguel Maura, the Minister of the Interior, was convinced that the fires were the work of provocateurs drawn from the scab unions, the Sindicatos Libres, aiming to discredit the new regime. Some eyewitness reports tend to support Maura's view. Others believed that the attacks were carried out by hotheads from the anarchist movement, in the belief that the Church was the spider at the heart of the web of reactionary politics in Spain. In support of this view are allegations that the first fires were started with aviation spirit secured from Cuatro Vientos aerodrome by Ramón Franco, the aviator brother of the future dictator, who declared: 'I contemplated with joy those magnificent flames as the expression of a people which wanted to free itself from clerical obscurantism.'[15]

The provocation of the Círculo Monárquico led to its being closed down on 12 May. For many on the Right, indifferent to the identity of the true culprits, the church burnings sealed their hostility to the Republic. Summing up the views of many right-wing army officers like himself, Francisco Franco later described the church burnings as the event which defined the Republic.[16] Such a view, prevalent at the time, reflected the extent to which priests and conservative officers were flung into each other's arms as the self-perceived victims of Republican persecution. Whether the burnings be attributed to left-wing extremists or to right-wing *agents provocateurs*, one thing is clear: the response of the crowds showed how strongly the Church was identified with monarchism.[17] And the intensity of the popular reaction to an open demonstration of monarchist sentiment highlighted the great advantage of accidentalism. Angel Herrera and Gil Robles had already decided on 26 April to form a group, to be known as Acción Nacional, to unite the 'elements of order' for the forthcoming elections. It started from a strong base in the form of a powerful press network at the heart of which stood *El Debate*, a general staff of well-educated professionals from the ACNP and the tacit support of the Catholic Church. *El Debate* alone, with its five daily editions, sold more than 150,000 copies per day – an astonishingly high figure in the Spain of the early 1930s. While ACNP *'propagandistas'* began the work of preliminary organisation in the provinces, Herrera held a meeting with other right-wing leaders to arrange the formation of a circumstantial coalition for electoral campaigning. Bereft of other political mechanisms after the collapse of the monarchy, the conservative newspaper *ABC* encouraged monarchists to join the new organisation. Conservatives of all kinds, including the most extreme monarchists who were chastened by the swift closure of the Círculo Monárquico, flocked into the organisation.[18]

Prospective members were not asked for any profession of Republican faith. Indeed, in León, Acción Nacional was founded in the offices of the monarchist youth.[19] Even the rabidly anti-Republican Carlists were anxious to join.[20] In Madrid, a giant task of issuing circulars and making file indexes of voters was undertaken by volunteers. One of them wrote later:

> into Acción Nacional came the first offers of help, the first import-
> ant sums of money and almost all the hopes of those who could
> never come to terms with, let alone recognise, the new order . . .
> All those who came were monarchists. I didn't meet a single
> Republican in the considerable time I was there writing cards and
> checking electoral lists.[21]

It followed then that the interim president of the organisation should be the monarchist leader, Antonio Goicoechea – until the formal election of Angel Herrera on 18 May. Other prominent Alfonsists, who were simultaneously plotting the armed overthrow of the Republic, also held important positions in Acción Nacional – as did the leader of the Carlist Comunión Tradicionalista, the Conde de Rodezno.

The conservative, not to say reactionary, nature of the new group was even more marked in the provinces. In Cáceres, 'all the people of sub-stance of the province, the great landowners, the politically significant and persons of social influence' met under a monarchist president to found the local section. In Córdoba, the local eleven-man committee included four landowners, two factory directors and four engineers. In Jerez, the dominance of bigwigs was even more marked.[22] Less spectacu-larly rightist but equally conservative, and much more plentiful, was the kind of support found in Old Castile and Salamanca. There Acción

Nacional inherited the influence of the CNCA. Founded by the Palencian landowner Antonio Monedero-Martin, and largely financed by donations from big landlords and subscriptions organised by *El Debate*, the CNCA claimed to have 500,000 members by 1919. It is certain that the organisation had built up a large following among the conservative smallholders of northern and central Spain by providing a series of services. Rural savings banks, agrarian credit entities, co-operatives for selling crops and bulk-buying, insurance facilities and the hiring out of machinery all contributed to the mitigation of social conditions in the Castilian plain. The various facilities were available only to peasants who made clear their conservative and religious sentiments. Its main inspiration was traditionalism; its main enemies the 'pagan principle of liberalism' and socialism. The CNCA affirmed 'the principles of religion, family and property as the bases of the social order against the negations of socialism'. The CNCA had a marked counter-revolutionary orientation and occasionally organised strike-breaking. Before his abdication, Alfonso XIII was president of one of its most important branches.[23]

The immediate heir to this body of ultra-conservative peasants was Acción Castellana, based in Salamanca, one of the principal component organisations of Acción Nacional. The development of Acción Castellana showed the extent to which the Catholic organisations were prepared to throw the weight of their peasant masses behind the local territorial oligarchy. Some of the more reactionary local landlords, such as the Carlist José María Lamamié de Clairac and Candido Casanueva y Gorjón, were prominent in the leadership. The branch organisations of Acción Nacional in this area consistently defended the interests of the agrarian élite throughout the Republic. This commitment was always skilfully generalised in their propaganda, largely for the consumption of the poorly educated middle-size farmers who made up the basis of their support, into a patriotic concern for 'agrarian interests'. Often poverty-stricken and scraping a bare living from their holdings by working also as day-labourers on the big estates, these peasants still considered themselves to be 'landowners'. Since they occasionally employed casual labour themselves at harvest time, the right-wing press had little difficulty in persuading them that the rural labour legislation and Socialist trade unions hit them in the same way as they did the bigger owners. This apparent identification of interest was skilfully achieved by the use of words like *labrador* and *agricultor* to describe all landowners, large and small alike. *Labrador* (ploughman) and *agricultor* (husbandman) implied at once someone who worked the land and was a respectable man of substance. Thus, the conservative and Catholic smallholder of Castile, already imbued by his parish priest with a deep distrust for democracy, readily felt an identification of interest with the local oligarchy, sharing with it a commitment to the monarchy and the Church as the twin pillars of the social order.

On joining Acción Nacional, a statement was issued by Acción Castellana to the effect that it would have preferred to give battle to 'the enemies of the social order' while still in the shadow of the monarchy, but that, since this no longer existed, the fight would go on without it. An inflexible attitude to social reform was revealed in the declaration that any alteration in the landholding structure would be communism and make the landowner a slave. Salamanca was to provide some of the most belligerent support for Acción Nacional during the Republic, but it was not atypical. The orange-growers who formed the basis of its branch in Valencia, the Derecha Regional Valenciana, had more progressive, social Catholic leaders, particularly Luis Lucia Lucia and Luis García Guijarro, but it also had a powerful Carlist tradition. That, together with the overwhelming influence within the organisation of the wealthy orange-growing élite, ensured that they were also the first accidentalists to take up arms in 1936.[24] Unión Castellana Agraria of Palencia was probably nearer the norm in its simple aim of defending the interests of 'conservative social forces'.[25]

Acción Castellana's unwilling tactical acceptance of the Republic was typical of the national body. As early as 21 April *El Debate* showed why it was adopting accidentalism: 'Without certainty of success, and in fact with certainty of failure, we have no right to destroy Spain with civil and fratricidal strife.' So the 'moderate' Right was eschewing violence not out of conviction but out of a recognition of weakness. Herrera felt that it would be easier to render the Republic innocuous by working within it than by attacking it.

The strictly limited nature of even this kind of acceptance of the Republic was shown by the bellicosity of Acción Nacional's campaign for the June 1931 elections. Its candidates included several ex-leaders of the UMN, and its manifesto set the tone of ill-masked hostility to the Republic. The keynote was the battle against Soviet communism, with which the Republic was taken to be consubstantial – a demagogic exaggeration, to say the least. The manifesto described the Republic as:

> the rabble that denies God, and, therefore, the principles of Christian morality; which proclaims instead of the sanctity of the family the inconstancy of free love; which substitutes for individual prop-

erty, the basis of individual well-being and collective wealth, a universal proletariat at the orders of the state.

Given the fact that this sort of propaganda was launched at semi-illiterate, politically immature rural audiences, at a time when the government could be characterised by its timidity in social questions, it can be seen only as deliberately or irresponsibly provocative. In fact, the manifesto was openly couched in terms of a declaration of social war 'to decide the triumph or extermination of imperishable principles. This was not to be resolved in a single combat; it is a war, and a long one, which is being unleashed in Spain.'[26]

The first electoral meeting confirmed the impression given by the manifesto. Held at Avila, it was opened by Antonio Bermejo de la Rica with a call for intransigence: 'Only the lack of masculinity of the aristocracy and bourgeoisie has allowed the rise of the lowest and vilest rabble.' Another speaker, José María Pérez Laborda, later to become leader of the Acción Nacional's youth movement, equated the Republic with bolshevism and appealed to his audience of local farmers either to stand back and see the Republic murder 2 million people or to defend the principles of Acción Nacional. Other speakers, including Angel Herrera, openly revealed their monarchist convictions and admitted that they silenced them only out of expediency. Herrera said that it had been decided not to raise the standard of the monarchy, despite the monarchism of the majority of the movement's members. The example to be followed was that of Hindenburg. This all derived from the insight that nothing could more effectively consolidate the Republic than frontal attacks – the lesson of 10 May.[27]

Characteristic of the campaign was the constant linking of religion with social conservativism. It was stated at the Avila meeting that the social order had been based on two principles, the monarchy and the Church, and that with one gone, defence of the other had to be the more resolute. Gil Robles said at a meeting in Tamames (Salamanca), 'Religion is a brake which stops society driving into anarchy ... we defend property, not its abuses ... we make no impossible promises of land division or of socialisation, projects which led to disaster in Russia.' Posters were distributed which stated simply, 'Landowners! Acción Nacional will be the great safeguard of property in the Constituent Cortes!'[28]

The election results were, nevertheless, disappointing. The campaign produced twenty-four deputies from the two Castiles and León; they became known in the Cortes as the Agrarian Minority. Only five were members of Acción Nacional, although the majority owed their election to its campaign. They were all of monarchist origins. Angel Herrera, who had stood as a candidate for Madrid, did not gain a seat and therefore remained as the strategist of the movement from his powerful position as editor of *El Debate*, president of the ACNP and also president of Acción Nacional. He and Gil Robles had founded Acción Nacional initially to organise propaganda for the elections. Now, precisely because the 'revolutionary threat' had been confirmed by the left-wing victory, it was decided to maintain the organisation as a permanent means of defending rightist interests within the legal political arena. This was the prelude to a massive effort to build up the provincial bases of Acción Nacional.[29]

Acción Nacional appealed to the widest spectrum of the Right as the organisation most likely to succeed in defending the interests of the Church and property owners within the new order. Many of its members, however, while prepared to go along with Herrera's accidentalism, considered the army as the appeal of last resort if right-wing interests were seriously endangered. Throughout the Republican period, the relationship between the accidentalists and the military would be publicly and privately close. The army had been severely divided by the experience of the Primo de Rivera Dictatorship to the extent that it had been unable or unwilling to defend the monarchy. Nevertheless, although there existed a substantial number of officers of genuine Republican convictions, the majority of the officer corps regarded the new regime with considerable suspicion. That suspicion was fed by a right-wing press which daily described the regime as the enemy of the Church, property and traditional values. Throughout the summer of 1931, the army's exiguous loyalty to the new regime was to be stretched to the limit.

The new Minister of War, the brilliant intellectual Manuel Azaña, was determined to eradicate the problem of militarism from Spanish politics, a problem which he equated with the army's technical deficiencies. He believed that Spain had an army completely disproportionate to her economic possibilities and, in consequence, overmanned and underequipped. He believed that these problems pulled the army away from its proper task of defending Spain and inclined it instead to intervene in domestic politics. An austere intellectual, Azaña set about his task with some urgency to the distress of the officer corps. Moreover, Azaña and the Republican–Socialist government were determined to eliminate where possible the irregularities of the Dictatorship of Primo de Rivera. Some of the most prominent and influential officers, including Francisco

Franco and Manuel Goded, had admired the Dictatorship and had been promoted by it. They bitterly resented any attack on its achievements, the more so because Azaña was believed to be influenced by, and to reward the efforts of, those officers who were most loyal to the Republic and, indeed, had worked to overthrow the monarchy.[30]

The military reforms which Azaña introduced in the spring and summer of 1931 were skilfully manipulated by the rightist press in order to propagate the notion that the military, along with landowners and the Church, was being singled out for persecution by the new regime. That was a distortion of Azaña's intentions. By a decree of 22 April 1931, army officers had to take an oath of loyalty (*promesa de fidelidad*) to the Republic just as previously they had to the monarchy. According to the decree, to stay in the ranks, an officer simply had to make the promise 'to serve the Republic well and faithfully, obey its laws and defend it by arms'. An officer's refusal to give the promise would be taken as an application to resign his commission. A number of prominent officers, like Alfredo Kindelán, the founder of the Spanish air force, felt obliged by their monarchist convictions to leave the service, but most officers had no difficulty about making the promise. For many, it was probably a routine formula without special significance and the oath was made by many whose real convictions were anti-Republican.[31] After all, few had felt bound by their oath of loyalty to the monarchy to spring to its defence on 14 April. On the other hand, although a reasonable demand on the part of the new minister and the new regime, the oath could easily be perceived by the more partisan officers as an outrageous imposition. Adept at manipulating the military mentality, the right-wing press generated the impression that those whose convictions prevented them swearing the oath were being hounded penniless out of the army.[32] In fact, those who opted not to swear were considered members of the reserve and were to receive their pay accordingly.

Significantly more infuriating to right-wingers in the officer corps was the decree announced on 25 April, which came to be known as the Ley Azaña. It offered voluntary retirement on full pay to all members of the officer corps, a generous and expensive way of trying to reduce its size. However, the decree stated that after thirty days, any officer who was surplus to requirements but had not opted for the scheme would lose his commission without compensation. This caused massive resentment and further encouragement of the belief, again fomented by the rightist press, that the army was being persecuted by the Republic.[33] Since the threat was never carried out, its announcement was a gratuitously damaging error on the part of Azaña or his ministerial advisers.

Many officers were equally outraged by what was known as the 'responsibilities' issue. General Berenguer had been arrested on 17 April, for alleged offences committed in Africa, as Prime Minister and later as Minister of War during the summary trial and execution of Galán and García Hernández.[34] General Mola was arrested on 21 April for his work as Director-General of Security under Berenguer.[35] These arrests were part of a symbolic purge of significant figures of the monarchy which did the nascent Republic far more harm than good. The issue of 'responsibilities' harked back to the Annual disaster and the role played in it by royal interference, military incompetence and the deference of politicians towards the army. It was popularly believed that the military coup of 1923 had been carried out in order to protect the King from the findings of the 'Responsibilities Commission' set up in 1921. Accordingly, the issue was still festering. To the 'responsibilities' contracted by army officers and monarchist politicians before 1923 the Republican movement had added the acts of political and fiscal abuse and corruption carried out during the Dictatorship and after. The greatest of these was considered to be the execution of Galán and García Hernández. With the Dictator dead and the King in exile, it was inevitable that Berenguer would be an early target of Republican wrath. Others, such as civilian collaborators of the Dictatorship, of whom José Calvo Sotelo was the most prominent, went into exile.

The campaign for 'responsibilities' helped keep popular Republican fervour at boiling point in the early months of the regime but at a high price in the long term. In fact, relatively few individuals were imprisoned or fled into exile but the 'responsibilities' issue created a myth of a vindictive and implacable Republic, and increased the fears and resentments of powerful figures of the old regime, inducing them to see the threat posed by the Republic as greater than it really was.[36] The 'responsibilities' trials were to provide the Africanistas with a further excuse for their instinctive hostility to the Republic. The issue of 'responsibilities' was deeply divisive, with moderate members of the government, including Azaña, keen to play it down. After a venomous debate, on 26 August, the Cortes empowered the 'Responsibilities Commission' to investigate political and administrative offences in Morocco, the repression in Catalonia between 1919 and 1923, Primo de Rivera's 1923 coup, the Dictatorships of Primo and Berenguer and the Jaca court martial.[37] To the fury of Azaña, who rightly believed that the commission was dangerously damaging to the Republic, a number of aged generals who had participated in Primo's Military Directory were arrested at the beginning of September.[38]

No issue inflamed military sensibilities, however, as much as Azaña's decree of 3 June 1931 for the so-called *revisión de ascensos* (review of promotions) whereby some of the promotions on merit given during the Moroccan wars were to be re-examined. It reflected the government's determination to wipe away the legacy of the Dictatorship – in this case to reverse some of the arbitrary promotions made by Primo de Rivera. The announcement raised the spectre that, if all of those promoted during the Dictadura were to be affected, many distinguished right-wing generals including Manuel Goded, Luis Orgaz and Francisco Franco would go back to being colonels, and many other senior African-istas would be demoted. Since the commission carrying out the revision would not report for more than eighteen months, it was to be at best an irritation, at worst a gnawing anxiety for those affected. Nearly one thousand officers expected to be involved, although in the event only half that number had their cases examined.[39]

The right-wing press and specialist military newspapers mounted a ferocious campaign alleging that Azaña's declared intention was to *'triturar el ejército'* (crush the army).[40] Azaña never made any such remark, although it has become a commonplace that he did. He made a speech in Valencia on 7 June in which he praised the army warmly and declared his determination to *triturar* the power of the corrupt bosses who dominated local politics, the *caciques*, in the same way as he had dismantled 'other lesser threats to the Republic'. This was twisted into the notorious phrase.[41] To the fury of the Africanistas, it was rumoured that Azaña was being advised by a group of Republican officers known among his rightist opponents as the 'black cabinet'. One of Azaña's informal military advisers, Major Juan Hernández Saravia, complained to a comrade that Azaña was too proud to listen to advice from anyone. Moreover, far from setting out to persecute monarchist officers, Azaña seems rather to have cultivated many of them, such as General José Sanjurjo or the monarchist General Enrique Ruiz Fornells whom he kept on as his under-secretary. Indeed, there were even some leftist officers who took retirement out of frustration at what they saw as Azaña's complaisance with the old guard, and the offensive and threatening language which Azaña was accused of using against the army is difficult to find. Azaña, although firm in his dealings with officers, spoke of the army in public in controlled and respectful terms.[42] However, the conservative newspapers read by most army officers, *ABC*, *La Época*, *La Correspondencia Militar*, presented the Republic as respons-ible for Spain's economic problems, mob violence, disrespect for the army and anti-clericalism.

However, more than for anything else that had happened since 14 April, Franco was to bear Azaña the deepest grudge of all for his order of 30 June 1931 closing the Academia General Militar de Zaragoza of which he was director. He had loved his work there and he would never forgive Azaña and the so-called 'black cabinet' for snatching it from him. He and other Africanistas believed that the academy had been condemned to death merely because it was one of Primo de Rivera's successes. Franco's outrage could not be masked by the formal tone of his farewell speech to the cadets at the academy on 14 July 1931. He commented on discipline, saying that it 'acquires its full value when thought counsels the contrary of what is being ordered, when the heart struggles to rise in inward rebellion against the orders received, when one knows that higher authority is in error and acting out of hand'. He made a rambling but bitter allusion to those who had been rewarded by the Republic for their disloyalty to the monarchy. He made an oblique reference to the Republican officers who held the key posts in Azaña's Ministry of War as 'a pernicious example within the army of immorality and injustice'.[43] Azaña issued a formal reprimand (*reprensión*) in Franco's service record for the speech to the cadets.[44]

That Franco was not the only prominent officer infuriated by the activities of the Minister of War can be deduced from an important incident of military indiscipline which took place in late June. It involved General Goded, at the time head of the General Staff, an officer whose career paralleled that of Franco in many respects and whose rival he was considered to be.[45] Within the army, they were both regarded as outstanding officers of talent and bravery. They were both ambitious and, in addition to having their rapid promotions called into question by the *revisión de ascensos*, both found their career prospects curtailed by Azaña's military reforms. Both despised the officers who made a show of their Republicanism.[46]

Manoeuvres involving the cadets of the military academies were being held at Carabanchel, on the outskirts of Madrid. Various regiments of the Madrid garrison visited the camp, and after a breakfast together, the second-in-command in Madrid, General Federico Caballero García, commander of the First Brigade, made a speech about the army's distress regarding the political situation and particularly its dismay at the autonomy statute for Catalonia. It was followed by another in similar vein from Major General Rafael Villegas Montesino, commander of the Madrid military region. This in turn was followed by another by General Goded, who should not have spoken since he was there as a private guest and not in an official capacity. Goded ended his speech with the shout '*Un viva único: ¡Viva España! y nada más*', which was an unmistakable rejection of the more usual '*¡Viva la República!*'. As Azaña later told the Cortes, the speeches did not constitute a breach of discipline but they were 'inopportune, indiscreet, out of place'. An enraged Republican, the infantry Lieutenant Colonel Julio Mangada, refused to shout '*¡Viva España!*', insulted Goded and was arrested by Villegas. While upholding the punishment of Mangada for indiscipline, Azaña also had the three generals immediately removed from their posts.

The impulsive Goded was replaced as Chief of the General Staff by General Carlos Masquelet y Lacaci, a quiet hard-working liberal engineer who specialised in fortifications. Before deciding on Goded's fate, Azaña had two long conversations with him, during which he talked about his prestige, his merits and the curtailment of his career as a result of the military reforms. Goded spat out a stream of rancour, frustrated ambition and spite, leaving Azaña with the impression of someone 'who carries a scorpion within'. Goded was upset by the truncation of further promotion and the diminution of the legal powers and social prestige of senior army officers implied in the abolition of the rank of Lieutenant General and the post of Captain General. He was disturbed by the presence of Socialists in the government and by the moves towards Catalan autonomy. He was also afraid that the rank-and-file soldiers were being influenced by leftist ideologies. The things that Goded said were an accurate barometer of opinion within the army and across the Right as a whole.[47]

The determination of the Right to halt the reforming progress of the Republic could be perceived in the activities in the Cortes of the newly elected group of right-wing deputies who took the title Minoría Agraria (Agrarian Minority). Its most immediate and urgent task was to make its mark on the fashioning of the new Constitution. The sort of mandate they held was indicated by a series of meetings against agrarian reform held by landowners' federations all over the country, but especially in the south. *El Debate* reported the meetings sympathetically and took up the complaints in its editorials.[48] Inevitably, the clauses in the Constitution which most interested the deputies of the Agrarian Minority were those which had implications regarding the position of organised religion in society and the possibility of agrarian reform. Effectively this meant that their opposition to the Constitution crystallised around two main points, articles 26 and 44. The first of these concerned the cutting off of state financial support for the clergy and religious orders; the dissolution of orders, such as the Jesuits, that swore foreign oaths of allegiance; and the limitation of the Church's right to wealth. The

Republican attitude to the Church was based on the belief that, if a new Spain were to be built, the stranglehold of the Church on many aspects of society must be broken. Religion was not attacked as such, but the Constitution was to put an end to the government's endorsement of the Church's privileged position. This was presented by the Agrarian Minority in parliament, and by the newspaper network of which *El Debate* was the centre, as virulent anti-clericalism, thereby allowing the opponents of any kind of reform to hitch their reactionism to the cause of religion. Article 44 stated that 'Property of all kinds can be the object of expropriation with adequate compensation for reasons of social utility unless a law to the contrary receives an absolute majority in the Cortes.'

In alliance with the ultra-Catholic Basque–Navarrese minority, the Agrarians put up stout resistance to every progressive clause which implied a change in the prevailing social order. When accused of being monarchist, anti-democratic cavemen, the Agrarians responded with feeble protestations of accidentalism, democratic conviction and a love for the poor. However, when it came to debating the articles concerning regional autonomy, private property and a more flexible and humane approach to labour relations, they piled amendment upon amendment in an attempt to block the passing of the Constitution.[49] It was difficult to avoid the impression that the existing structure of society as it had been under the monarchy was being defended with the banner of persecuted Catholicism. Yet the cordial relations of prominent Republicans such as Manuel Azaña, Luis de Zulueta, Jaume Carner and Luis Nicolau d'Olwer with liberal churchmen such as Cardinal Vidal belied the accidentalist cries that the Church was being mercilessly persecuted.[50]

Despite the efforts of the Agrarians, both articles 26 and 44 were included in the final approved draft of the Constitution. This clinched the opposition of the Right to the new regime. The accidentalist handbook described the passing of article 26 in terms which revealed the extent of the group's flexibility: 'Reason fell, smashed by the hoof of the beast, with all the horrors of the Apocalypse and all its majority mocked and trampled underfoot.'[51] The Agrarian Minority immediately withdrew from the Cortes and announced the launching of a campaign for the reform of the Constitution. The call for revision now became the rallying cry against the Republic. A huge effort of propaganda, through the press and a nationwide series of meetings, attempted to build up a store of conservative resentment against the Republic. Gil Robles, who during the campaign emerged as the major figure in Acción Nacional, wrote later that the aim was to give the Right a mass following which would be prepared to fight the Left 'for the possession of the street'.[52] The tone of the campaign was belligerent and incendiary and had some considerable success in changing the way in which the Catholic population, particularly in rural areas, perceived the Republic. It opened with an appeal in *El Debate* to all Catholics to 'defend yourselves, and at the same time defend, by all methods and with all resources, the threatened existence of Spain'. Miguel Maura, who, in an attempt to maintain his own credibility on the Right, had himself resigned from the government in protest at its markedly laic tone, had already commented that Gil Robles's language regarding the Constitution was a call for religious warfare and would irreparably harm the Republic. Maura's own attempt to create a democratic Right was doomed to failure because the rightist press would never tolerate his refusal to tie Catholicism to a given social and economic order.[53]

The Catholic press diffused an intepretation of the Constitution which presented it as a blueprint for the persecution of religion and of the respectable citizen. Hundreds of orators were sent all over Spain to present a deliberately distorted view of the political situation. The Republic's reforming aspirations were portrayed as violent revolutionism; its laicism as a Satanic assault on religion. At the first meeting of the campaign, held at Ledesma (Salamanca), Gil Robles said, 'While anarchic forces, gun in hand, spread panic in government circles, the government tramples on defenceless beings like poor nuns.' Acción Nacional of Toledo issued a manifesto which claimed that 'When religion is not respected in a state greater consideration cannot be expected for property or the family.'[54] An English Catholic in Spain at the time commented:

> I welcomed the Republic as a step towards better social conditions and much as I disliked the mob violence and the burning of churches I felt that the people in Spain who professed most loudly their Catholic faith were the most to blame for the existence of illiterate masses and a threadbare national economy.[55]

Certainly, the terms of such Acción Nacional propaganda were entirely out of proportion with the halting steps to reform taken so far by the Republic. These were phrased to make the unsophisticated and conservative rural smallholders or the urban owners of small businesses, whose interests were not threatened by the Republic, feel that they had everything to fear from the new regime. The wealthy backers of Acción Nacional's expensive press and propaganda drives thereby gained mass support against prospective reforms which threatened *their* interests. By the end of 1931, Acción Nacional had twenty-six affiliated organisations in the provinces and by late 1932 this figure had risen to thirty-six.

In Madrid, in a meeting held under the auspices of Acción Nacional, Goicoechea told a cheering audience that there was to be a battle to the death between socialism and the nation, and that it was thus necessary to defend property and strengthen the forces of order. Gil Robles told the rich businessmen of the Circle of the Mercantile Union that all right-wingers, monarchist or Republican, should join together. The boisterousness of all this propaganda did not go unnoticed on the Left, and the Socialist Minister of Labour, Largo Caballero, protested about the bitterness of attacks on his party. The campaign was reaching the momentum which was to force the government to ban it. On 8 November there was a great revisionist meeting in Palencia which was addressed by all members of the Agrarian Minority and some Traditionalists. Joaquín Beunza, a far from extreme Carlist, thundered to an audience of 22,000 people:

Are we men or not? Whoever is not prepared to give his all in these moments of shameless persecution does not deserve the name Catholic. It is necessary to be ready to defend oneself by all means, and I don't say legal means, because all means are good for self-defence.

After declaring the Cortes a zoo he said, 'We are governed by a gang of freemasons. And I say that against them all methods are legitimate, legal and illegal ones.' This was followed within a week by a lecture attacking parliament and the Socialist Party delivered by the vituperatively clever Alfonsist professor, Pedro Sáinz Rodríguez, deputy for Santander. At that point, the government stopped the campaign as anti-Republican.[56]

In December, Acción Nacional held a deliberative assembly which did nothing to dispel the impression created by outbursts such as Beunza's. While it confirmed that Gil Robles was to take over the presidency from Herrera, the assembly nevertheless adopted a programme drawn up by the latter. Minimal and circumstantial, it recognised the freedom of the individual member to defend his own views on forms of government. Drafted in such a way as to allow the extreme Alfonsists to remain within the organisation, the programme made it inevitable that Acción Nacional would be tarred with the brush of its own extremists. The Carlists, however, increasingly open about their violent opposition to the Republican regime, did begin to establish their distance from Acción Nacional from December 1931.[57] For the moment, the Alfonsists stayed, although ten days later the publication began of their journal *Acción Española* which consistently criticised the defeatist collaborationism implicit in Acción Nacional's accidentalism.[58] The basic premise of the programme agreed at the assembly was that the nation was threatened by international socialism and extremist separatism. The principle of private property was reaffirmed and a fundamental hostility to agrarian reform expressed. Such reform was dismissed as an attempt to sacrifice individual rights and public wealth to the 'unhealthy convenience' of pandering to the working masses with 'pompous schemes'. Above all, the Constitution was to be revised.[59] The Left could only regard this as a declaration of war on the essence of the Republic.

Meanwhile *El Debate* was speaking of founding a political party. A disturbing glimpse of the intransigence it could bring into Spanish politics was afforded by the manifesto issued on the foundation of the Juventud de Acción Nacional. Closely tied to the parent organisation, this youth movement declared:

> We are men of the Right . . . we will respect the legitimate orders of authority, but we will not tolerate the impositions of the irresponsible rabble. We will always have the courage to make ourselves respected. We declare war on communism and free-masonry.[60]

Since these latter concepts were represented in the eyes of the Right by the Socialist Party and the Left Republicans, such outbursts did little for the credibility of Acción Nacional's much-vaunted notion of constructive opposition within Republican legality.

This belligerence seems to have been an accurate reflection of the tone which Gil Robles wished to give his group. Opening a massive recruitment drive, he said at Molina de Segura (Murcia) on 1 January:

> In 1932 we must impose our will with the force of our rightness, and with other forces if this is insufficient. The cowardice of the Right has allowed those who come from the cesspools of iniquity to take control of the destinies of the fatherland.

There was no doubt on whose behalf this militancy was being drummed up:

> I speak to the powerful, to those who have plenty to lose, and I say to them – if you had sacrificed a small sum at the right moment, you would lose less than you might now, because what you give for the press, the rightist press, which defends the funda-

mental principles of every society – religion, the family, order, work – is a real insurance policy for your personal fortune.

In similar vein, a journalist in the Acción Nacional orbit wrote that 'the danger which threatens our altars also threatens our pockets'.[61]

To defend these interests, then, a political party was being created. Parliament was accepted as the most conventional battleground. This emerged clearly in meeting after meeting as Gil Robles worked to produce a great mass party of the Right. In Málaga he said, 'The ideal of the Spanish Right . . . is to form a united front to put an end to socialism. We must struggle for the conquest of parliament.'[62] Gil Robles made a superhuman effort of organisation and propaganda, travelling ceaselessly around Spain, trying to gain for Acción Nacional the mass support necessary for the legal 'conquest' of power. At one point, he made speeches in fifteen villages in less than two days. And on his own admission he was always pushing his audiences towards escalatory conflicts with the authorities. Yet at this time the Republic had taken only the most faltering steps towards a limited agrarian reform. In 1937 and in his memoirs, Gil Robles claimed proudly that the fund of mass rightist belligerence which he had built up during the Republic made possible the victory of the Right in the Civil War.[63]

The movement grew rapidly, particularly in conservative areas likely to be affected by agrarian reform. In New Castile and Extremadura, organisations such as Acción Popular Agraria de Badajoz, Derecha Regional Agraria de Cáceres, Acción Agraria Manchega and Acción Ciudadana y Agraria de Cuenca affiliated to the parent organisation. Growing numbers highlighted the ambiguity of the movement's programme. The many monarchists within Acción Nacional found outright opposition to the Republic much more congenial than accidentalism. Virulent statements to this effect were made under the aegis of the supposedly legalist organisation. Of course, while recruitment was still a major priority, propaganda tended towards demagogy. In April the movement survived a change of name to Acción Popular, and it continued to grow.[64]

A profitable zone of operations for the agrarian oligarchy and its political representatives was the question of wheat prices and supplies. It was an issue which could advantageously be exploited to foment hostility against the Republic and to do so in such a way as to mobilise the support of the many smallholders who produced wheat. This was possible because wheat was grown mainly in Castile, Aragón and parts of Andalucía; that is to say, in both smallholding and *latifundio* areas.

In problems relating to stocks and prices at a national level, it was always relatively easy to create an apparent identification of the interests of all wheat-growers, large and small.

Such was the case with a campaign in the autumn and winter of 1931 to secure an increase in the minimum price for wheat, the *tasa*, which stood at 46 pesetas per metric quintal. Organised by the bigger producers, the campaign enjoyed the support of small farmers, leaseholders and sharecroppers, for obvious reasons. In reality, however, only the big owners stood to benefit. Their production costs were lower, because of economies of scale, and often because their land enjoyed superior yield. Many substantial producers, even in the Castilian smallholding areas, had sufficient capital and the necessary storage facilities to enable them to keep their wheat off the market until the most favourable moment for selling. Clearly this meant that a price increase would widen their already comfortable profit margins and certainly not harm the interests of the smallholders. Nevertheless, the small growers did not stand to enjoy any improvement in their precarious position. At all times short of ready cash, be it for seed, fertiliser or food for his family, the smallholder was usually at the mercy of the local *acaparador*, when it came to disposing of his grain. The *acaparador*, sometimes a merchant, sometimes a money-lender or even a landowner, bought up the crops of the smaller growers, who had neither warehousing nor transport facilities of their own. Irrespective of the official minimum price, the smallholder normally had to sell at the price dictated by the *acaparador*, because either immediate necessity or the need to repay a loan to the *acaparador* himself forced him to sell at times of surplus.

Nevertheless, a campaign to raise prices could rely on the support of all wheat-growers. The owners wanted to increase the price from 46 to 53 pesetas. Their campaign was headed by two deputies from Valladolid, Antonio Royo Villanova and Pedro Martín y Martín, whom the Socialists accused of being an *acaparador* himself.[65] Speaking in the Cortes, Royo claimed that the increases in agricultural wages permitted by Largo Caballero had pushed up the cost of producing wheat by 30 per cent, to 54 to 55 pesetas per metric quintal. Pedro Martín, by stating that an increase in bread prices could be easily absorbed in the towns, skilfully implied that it was urban workers who kept the smallholder poor. The campaign continued with the support of the Acción Popular press network. When a new Minister of Agriculture, Marcelino Domingo, took over in December, he immediately investigated the need to revise the *tasa*. Local information showed that production costs varied from 33.25 pesetas per metric quintal in Salamanca to 41.77 pesetas in Badajoz. In the light of this, because he was not prepared to raise bread prices at a time of high unemployment and wage cuts and because he realised that the *acaparadores* would prevent the smallholders from deriving any benefit, he opted against any increase of the *tasa*.[66]

The minister was subjected to a virulent press campaign which made his action seem responsible for all the ills of the countryside. Those owners who held stocks and had hoped to benefit from 1931's rather poor harvest now began to hold back supplies. Reports reached Domingo in January 1932 that there was a scarcity and he replied with a somewhat ineffectual decree prohibiting clandestine hoarding. Some stocks were forced out onto the market, but not enough to allay fears of bread price rises and consequent public order problems. The press began to talk of the need for lifting restrictions on the import of foreign wheat – a politically sensitive decision given the weakness of the peseta and the fact that high-cost Spanish wheat survived against Argentinian and American competition only by means of rigid protection. On 12 April, Domingo authorised just 50,000 tonnes to be imported for the neediest provinces and then called for stockists to reveal existing supplies and for growers to estimate the forthcoming harvest. The reports received suggested that a drastic shortage was on the horizon. Domingo authorised more imports: 100,000 tonnes on 27 April, 100,000 on 26 May and 25,000 on 15 June.[67]

The prices continued to rise, reaching their highest figure ever in July, at which point about 250,000 tonnes miraculously appeared on the market, coinciding with the delivery of foreign shipments. There followed a lengthy period of fine weather and stable labour relations which produced a bumper harvest. Throughout the autumn, wheat prices fell steadily until they reached their lowest figure since 1924. Approximately 2 million wheat-producers were hit by the fall, which had been caused largely by the speculation of the big owners. Nevertheless, the rightist press immediately went to work to ensure that Domingo's imports were firmly planted in the minds of smallholders as the cause of the disaster. He was accused by the Agrarians of deliberately setting out to destroy Spanish agriculture. The campaign against Domingo had considerable success and was one of the central issues in clinching the electoral support of the smallholders of Castile for the parties of the Right in the elections of November 1933.

In the spring of 1932 the question of how best to oppose the proposed agrarian reform and the Catalan statute, discussion of which began in May, raised the question of how far respect for the Republic should go. The ultra-monarchists of the Acción Española group were actively conspiring against the Republic without seeing any incompatibility between this and their membership of Acción Popular. The 'catastrophists' also enjoyed the co-operation of some ostensibly 'moderate' members of Acción Popular. Even the so-called social Catholic from Toledo, Dimas de Madariaga – in reality, a hard-liner of Traditionalist views – was involved in anti-Republican activities with the monarchist plotter, Juan Antonio Ansaldo. Madariaga also led a riot at the Madrid première of the play *AMDG*, by the Republican writer Ramón Pérez de Ayala.[68] Gil Robles, on the other hand, believed that there was no immediate possibility of successful solutions by force and that the same objectives could best be achieved by the Right infiltrating the Republic to make it its own.[69] It was purely a tactical point. According to Gil Robles himself, the 'immense majority' of Acción Popular members were monarchists and felt an 'insuperable repugnance' to the idea of accepting the Republic. The same applied to himself: 'In a theoretical sense, I was and am a monarchist . . . The same motives which prevented 90 per cent of the members of Acción Popular from declaring themselves Republican held me back, not least for reasons of good taste.'[70]

The efficacy of the legalist tactic was demonstrated during the spring and early summer. *El Debate* ran hostile commentaries on both the agrarian and Catalan projects, while the Agrarian Minority began an intense campaign of obstruction in the Cortes. Their success was remarkable. Between May and September 1932, one-third of the debating time in the Cortes was taken up by discussion of the agrarian reform. Debate was held up while the rightist deputies asked complex technical questions. Each member of the Agrarian Minority had an amendment to each clause of the bill. By August, only four out of twenty-four clauses had been passed.[71]

However, this success was nullified by the first manifestation of the other, 'catastrophist', tactic. This was the abortive rising of 10 August, which came to be known as the Sanjurjada – a play on the name of its leader, General Sanjuro, and the word *carcajada*, a burst of laughter. Gil Robles was fully aware that it was being prepared, and was likely to fail, having discussed it with General Franco at a dinner in the home of their mutual friend, the Marqués de la Vega de Anzó. The fiasco of the rising highlighted the relative success of the parliamentary tactic in stalling reform. According to Gil Robles, 'The tenacious obstruction of various projects and the constant criticism of the government's labour not only prevented the passing of many laws, but also produced enormous wear and tear in the governments of the Left.'[72] Now the decisive response of the government to the defeated coup showed that the 'catastrophist' tactic was counter-productive to the material interests of the Right. The wave of Republican fervour produced allowed both statutes to be passed without difficulties in September. Moreover, there was a general crack-down on the activities of the Right. The point was proved once more that frontal attacks could only strengthen the Republic. For all that the Right applauded the motives of 10 August, and it did so fulsomely, in practical terms it was a considerable set-back.

Gil Robles was determined that it should not happen again. The ambiguity of the Acción Popular programme, once an advantage, was now a liability. An assembly of Acción Popular was called for October to create a political party and, at the same time, to clear the air after the rising. *El Debate* had said in its first number after the rising, 'We have been and always will be the paladins of the legal struggle and of respect for the constituted power ... We were not in the secret of the conspiracy.' This was not entirely true. A series of meetings of right-wing leaders, including one in Biarritz on 7 August, had put Gil Robles in the picture. Of course, the Alfonsist members were clearly implicated, while he had kept his hands publicly clean. Understandably, he was anxious for his movement not to suffer unnecessarily. The Alfonsists were disillusioned by a manoeuvre aimed at disowning them, convinced as they were that, had the rising not been a failure, his attitude would have been very different.[73]

The assembly opened in Madrid on 22 October. Apart from delegates representing the many provincial sections of Acción Popular, there was also representation of another dozen affiliated organisations such as the Bloque Agrario de Salamanca, Acción Regional Independiente de Santander, the Derecha Regional de Cáceres and the Derecha Regional Valenciana. The debate illustrated the divergency of views within Acción Popular. Angel Fernández Ruano, delegate of the Juventud de Acción Popular from Málaga, asked, 'What can we do?' and answered, 'A declaration of Republican faith? Never!' to rapturous applause. José María Fernández Ladreda, head of Acción Popular's powerful Asturian section, declared that within Acción Popular there were those who regarded a Republic in Spain not as a regime but as a revolutionary doctrine. They were opposed by José Cimas Leal, editor of *La Gaceta Regional* of Salamanca, who pushed the boundaries of accidentalism to breaking point when he claimed that 'to obey is to accept'. He was greeted with cries of 'No! No! No!'

Underlying the heated debate, there was intense awareness that the object of the congress had been announced as being to settle the questions of tactics raised by the events of August. And there was a broad sweep of agreement that violent rebellion against the Republic was counter-productive. A call for a round of applause for Goicoechea – currently in prison for his part in the Sanjurjada – was rejected by the chair. Even Dimas de Madariaga stated roundly that the Toledo section of Acción Popular would 'respect the constituted regime whatever happened'. Julio Moreno Dávila from Granada put the final and successful argument for accidentalism when he said, with an eye on the rapid passage of Republican legislation in September, 'What has been lost is because of 10 August; our tactics have lost what had been gained. Let us return to yesterday's tactic.' Despite a fierce Alfonsist rearguard action led by Sainz Rodríguez, the assembly voted for the legalist tactic.[74]

This victory was not pushed to its logical conclusion of a declaration of full acceptance of the Republic, for fear of alienating strong monarchist groups (for instance, the Asturian section, with nearly 30,000 members) within Acción Popular. However, preparations went forward for the creation of a federal Catholic party at another assembly to be held in the new year. The emphasis was on accidentalism, but, if this excluded the active conspirators of Acción Española, it implied no definite split with monarchism. Indeed, the majority of Acción Popular's members 'conserved their anti-Republican spirit intact'.[75] Obviously, Gil Robles did not break with the Alfonsists because he found their monarchism offensive. If that had been the case, he could have declared himself Republican. It was rather that their publicly anti-Republican 'catastrophist' tactic was undermining the effectiveness of his 'Trojan horse' policy. This was made abundantly clear when Goicoechea resigned from the Acción Popular executive. Gil Robles's letter of reply declared that any incompatibility between the group and Goicoechea 'is not for reasons of ideology or political position regarding forms of government, but for reasons of tactics'.[76] And the members of both groups continued to mix socially, to attend each other's meetings, to read each other's press and even to belong to more than one organisation. Goicoechea remained a member of Acción Popular.

The Left in general and the Socialists in particular were understandably not impressed by the accidentalists' Republican credentials. The sort of political ideals that Acción Popular seemed to value were regularly indicated in *El Debate* during late 1932. A growing interest in Italian Fascism was emphasised by the eulogistic editorial of 28 October. Entitled 'Ten Years of Fascism', it was couched in terms which suggested a strong identification with fascism's fundamental objectives. The great triumph of Mussolini was seen as the replacement of 'daily rioting' with 'authority, discipline, hierarchy, order', which was significant since *El*

Debate, in common with other rightist papers, was placing increasing stress on disorder in Spain. This was an attempt to arouse the fears of conservative farmers. In fact, for all the talk of endemic social break-down, the harvest was one of the biggest of the century.[77] Praise for fascism was unstinted: 'The Fascist state may be justly proud of having liberated Italy from parliamentarism and having thus been able to stimu-late its activities, direct the economy, resist the economic crisis and strengthen the moral resources of the nation.' The key to this achieve-ment was the destruction of socialism. The Spanish Socialists were not slow to draw the conclusion that a similar fate awaited them, if ever the Right came to power: 'This isn't the first time that we've pointed out fascistic tendencies in *El Debate*. But never before have we heard such spine-chilling language from the Spanish Right.'[78] The tone of *El Debate* editorials hardly admitted of any other interpretation. The paper was manifesting a growing sympathy towards the adoption of fascist political and economic institutions as the solution to Spain's problems and a regular theme was the need for right-wing unity to annihilate socialism.[79] The constant reiteration of such hostility naturally made the Socialists apprehensive.

Meanwhile, Gil Robles was preparing the ground for the formation of his political party. A significant step forward took place in late Nov-ember at the Third Assembly of the Derecha Regional Valenciana, which was attended by Gil Robles and other Acción Popular luminaries. The DRV, under the leadership of Luis Lucia Lucia, was already a function-ing model of the kind of party Gil Robles wanted to create on a national basis – inter-classist and social Catholic. Since the defeat of the Sanjur-jada, Lucia had campaigned against the idea of armed opposition to the Republic and, at the Third Assembly, he threw his weight behind Gil Robles's project, calling for a broad confederation of autonomous right-wing groups which the DRV could join.[80] On 23 December, Gil Robles announced that the congress to create the great national confederation of autonomous right-wing groups would take place in early February. He also outlined how the various organisations of Acción Popular would federate with similar groups like the DRV.[81] However, fearful of restricting the appeal of the new group, he announced in a speech in Salamanca on 25 December that, in the future party, 'there is room for monarchists and Republicans'.[82] He repeated the point in an open letter to the editor of *El Nervión* of Bilbao published on 5 January 1933, which made it clear that the demands to be made on the consciences of the members of the proposed confederation of right-wing groups would not be excessive. Its legalist programme would leave them free to maintain their convictions and defend them outside the organisation. It was the natural outcome of the October assembly: only those who insisted on attacking the Republic openly would be excluded. The point was reiterated by Gil Robles at local assemblies of Acción Popular in Ciudad Real, Pontevedra, Málaga, Salamanca and elsewhere. The consequence was that, while prominent Alfonsists followed the Carlists out of Acción Popular, Gil Robles had blurred the distinctions sufficiently to permit large numbers of rank-and-file monarchists to stay in the new organisation. None the less, some local organisations split on the issue of acceptance of the Republic. Lamamié de Clairac and part of the Bloque Agrario de Salamanca and several other groups did not intend to join the new confederation and remained simply as *agrarios*.[83]

The projected congress of the various provincial groups affiliated to Acción Popular finally took place in Madrid at the end of February 1933. Five hundred delegates representing 735,058 members of forty-two rightist groups attended. The most powerful delegations came from Acción Popular and the DRV. The delegates agreed on the creation of the Confederación Española de Derechas Autónomas (Spanish Confederation of Autonomous Right-wing Groups). The new party's general aims were 'the defence of the principles of Christian civilisation' and the revision of the Constitution, especially in those clauses which referred to religion, education and property. In his closing speech, Gil Robles clarified the ostensibly moderate terminology of the programme:

> When the social order is threatened, Catholics should unite to defend it and safeguard the principles of Christian civilisation . . . We will go united into struggle, no matter what it costs . . . We are faced with a social revolution. In the political panorama of Europe I can see only the formation of Marxist and anti-Marxist groups. This is what is happening in Germany and in Spain also. This is the great battle which we must fight this year.

Having thus aligned himself with the mainstream of the European Right, it was fitting that, later on the same day, in a meeting at the Teatro Fuencarral (Madrid) held to celebrate the creation of the CEDA, he said that he could see nothing wrong with thinking of fascism to cure the evils of Spain.[84]

The inaugural congress of the CEDA produced much talk of an advanced social programme. In view of the social forces which the CEDA represented, the Left was not impressed. *El Socialista* saw the new party as a mixture of all the regressive tendencies in Spain, the unification of everything that was old, crumbling and rotten.[85] Besides,

Hitler's rise to power and the Reichstag fire were fresh in the minds of the Socialists. And they were determined that agrarian and Catholic elements should not do to the Second Republic what they had done to Weimar. The CEDA's determination to revise the Constitution was seen as the beginning of the end, as the first provocation: 'how can we trust the spiritual and material allies of Italian fascism, of Hitler, or Horthy?' Intensely aware of what was happening already to Jews, communists, socialists and liberals in Germany, the Spanish Left was highly sensitive to the behaviour of the Right. The persistent harping on disorder by the rightist press was seen as the preparation for a move towards fascism.[86] Above all, the Spanish Socialists were determined not to make the same mistakes as their comrades abroad.[87] Their anxiety was understandable when *El Debate* said of the German situation that Nazism had ideals worthy of praise, especially in its reinforcement of 'many concepts indispensable for society'. Gil Robles's attitude to fascism was ambiguous. He was attracted by its modes of social organisation and its ruthless elimination of the class struggle, but he found its reliance on violence distasteful. To the Socialists, this was not a meaningful reservation. Moreover, on the one occasion when Gil Robles spoke against fascism in a public meeting, in Barcelona on 21 March 1933, his followers greeted his words with boos and hisses. He did not repeat the exercise.[88]

Throughout 1933 the CEDA spread discontent with the Republic in agricultural circles. It was hardly surprising that the Left chose to regard declarations of legality as a mere fiction, a tactical device whereby the CEDA could work for anti-Republican aims but with all the convenience of doing so legally. *El Debate* proclaimed openly that accidentalism as a tactic made it difficult for the authorities to restrict the group's activities.[89] The concerns of the CEDA were those of its wealthy backers rather than of its poorer voters. In May, *El Debate* gave a cocktail party for a deputation of landowners and employers from Seville, who had come to complain to the government about growing disorder and rising wages. They saw the problem not in terms of a need for reform, but as the lack of government repression before 'a monstrous, anarchic, anti-social offensive against commerce, industry and agriculture'.[90] At the same time, the CEDA was making its own demands of the National Cereal Growers' Association for an increase in minimum wheat prices and action against existing labour legislation. This referred to the two main reforms introduced by Largo Caballero as Minister of Labour: *jurados mixtos*, or arbitration committees, and the Law of Municipal Boundaries. The latter prevented labourers from outside an area from being hired while there were still local unemployed. It had effectively prevented the import of cheap labour to back wage cuts, and the use of blackleg labour in time of strikes. The Castilian cereal-growers wanted the *jurados mixtos* 'reformed' so that they would not favour worker interests, and they wanted the Law of Municipal Boundaries abolished. It was an attack on much that the Socialists regarded as progressive in the Republic, as well as being a blow at the urban worker, who relied heavily on cheap bread.[91]

El Socialista commented bitterly that the claims of the Seville deputation were equivalent to a demand for a return of the profits made 'in the days when there was no social legislation, when pathetic wages were the norm and all conflicts were settled by calling in the Civil Guard'. Three months later, *El Socialista* pointed out that 50 per cent of the population in the province of Seville went to bed hungry every night. It claimed that the salvation for which the upper class had looked to the military conspirator General Sanjurjo on 10 August 1932 was salvation from wage-claims and from laws which attacked feudal privilege.[92] The Socialists claimed persuasively that the disorder which was always cited in condemnation of the Republic was provoked by an upper class enraged by the limitation by law of their exploitation of the working classes.[93] Just how far disorder went at this time it is difficult to say. The American Ambassador went on regular safaris in search of it without finding any: 'We had travelled from one end of Spain to the other in search of the disorders "bordering on anarchy" of which we had heard so much in the drawing rooms of Madrid and found nothing of the sort.' Certainly the Left had nothing to gain from disorder, while the Right could always use it to support demands for more authoritarian government.[94]

During this time the CEDA regularly made a show of social-Catholic ideas, both in the press and in the party's frequent meetings. A typical example was a speech made in Seville in May by Federico Salmón, one of the more liberal of the CEDA leaders. He spoke in the vaguest terms about 'class harmony', the need for Christian charity and the need to work for the elimination of inequalities. It seemed a pious embroidery barely related to the real interests served by the CEDA. Moreover, any given listener who applauded the announcement of a determination to do away with the abuses of property naturally never imagined the orator's strictures to be directed at himself.[95] The only practical remedy for the agrarian situation which was ever suggested with any regularity was that of an increase in the forces of order and an adoption of the methods used in Italy against anarchy.[96]

Most CEDA declarations were double-meaning, but the social-

Catholic aspect was the one that seemed least to correspond to the party's actions. In August, there could be seen in the Cortes the familiar sight of the Agrarian Minority – with Gil Robles in the vanguard – obstructing reform. This time it was the draft law on rural leases, a crucial element in the projected agrarian reform. It could have improved the lot of the tenant farmers of northern and central Spain, who had in fact voted for the deputies of the Minority. Two hundred and fifty amendments were tabled as part of a planned technical obstruction. Gil Robles disingenuously explained the amendments as the fruit of his group's concern for the leaseholders. Once given security of tenure, they might lose the land to money-lenders and thereby contribute to the creation of *latifundios*, or else divide it among their heirs and create *minifundios*. The level of boredom created by this evident cant so discouraged attendance at the Cortes that, when the time came to vote, a quorum could never be obtained.[97] The Agrarian opposition in parliament to the leases bill, and the Acción Popular campaign against the Republic's religious legislation, inevitably conditioned the Left's response to the CEDA. This was to be emphasised during the build-up to the November 1933 elections, when the CEDA campaign hinged on opposition to everything which the Left might regard as progressive in the Republic.

The continuing identification of the CEDA and its leader with anti-Republicanism had been underlined during the summer. Always aware that the majority of his followers were monarchists, Gil Robles dreaded that Alfonso XIII would declare membership of the CEDA incompatible with monarchist ideals. Accordingly, in June he went to see the exiled King at Fontainebleau, where, it seems, he had little difficulty in persuading Alfonso that the CEDA was a useful method of building up right-wing sentiment without in any way consolidating the Republic.[98]

Gil Robles was closely tied to the old Spain for family reasons. His father was the famous Carlist theoretician Enrique Gil Robles. The Carlist in José María spoke when he referred later to 'the almost physical repulsion which was caused me by having to work within a system whose defects were so patently obvious to me. My doctrinal training, my family background, my sensibility rebelled daily.' In December 1932 he had declared publicly that only its lack of overt monarchism divided his movement from Traditionalism.[99] It was inevitable that the Left would assume that he was using the legalist tactic as the best means available to defend the socio-economic structure and the cultural-religious values of traditional Spain.

Suspicion of Gil Robles's essential hostility towards democracy was strengthened by the knowledge that he had held an official post under the Dictatorship and had been an editor of *El Debate* when it was one of the most lyrical apologists for Primo's regime. But there were more topical reasons for the Left's growing tendency to see Gil Robles and the CEDA as proto-fascist. In the first place, the similarity between the CEDA and the Catholic Party of Dollfuss in Austria was becoming more marked. Both groups were authoritarian, corporativist and fiercely anti-Marxist. The coincidences were many: both manifested an implacable hostility towards socialism, both found their mass support among backward rural smallholders who resented the socialist dominance of the capital city, and both had a semi-fascist youth movement.

During the summer of 1933, the Spanish Left was becoming highly sensitive to the danger of fascism. Weimar was persistently cited as a warning.[100] Parallels with the Spanish situation were not difficult to find. The Catholic press applauded the Nazi destruction of the German Socialist and Communist movements. Nazism was much admired on the Spanish Right because of its emphasis on authority, the fatherland and hierarchy – all three of which were central preoccupations of CEDA propaganda. Once Von Papen had signed a concordat with the Vatican, *El Debate*'s enthusiasm, previously restrained by unease at Nazi anti-Catholicism, knew no bounds. The Nazis were aware of this and grateful. When Angel Herrera visited Germany in May 1934, officials of the Wilhelmstrasse tried to arrange an interview with Hitler, because of the importance attributed to what was seen as the Herrera-inspired pro-Nazi line. In the event, however, the German Foreign Minister, Constantin von Neurath, said that an interview was impossible.[101]

In justification of the legalistic tactic in Spain, *El Debate* pointed out that Hitler had attained power legally. In reply, *El Socialista* was scathing about the Church's readiness to overlook persecution in authoritarian regimes.[102] The parallel between Nazism and Fascism and the CEDA was starkly underlined in the most eulogistic editorial of all, on 4 August 1933, when the leader-writer, having praised Hitler and Mussolini for their stand against 'communist levelling', rejoiced that the Spanish middle class now had its own organisation to fulfil that task. At the same time, regular calls were made for the adoption of a corporative economic organisation to bring Spain into line with Italy, Austria, Germany and Portugal. While the Catholic press urged its readers to follow the example of Italy and Germany and organise against the dragon of revolution, the CEDA could hardly wonder why the Left regarded it with trepidation.[103] A brilliant and influential book by a Socialist on the rise of Hitler, published in 1933, neatly pointed the parallel with accidentalism, by showing how 'the enemies of democracy take it up to reach power, and once there bury it with every dishonour'. And, when *El Debate* praised Hitler for renewing Germany's moral and spiritual values, *El Socialista* asked itself if the CEDA, which often proclaimed Spain's need of a similar renovation, intended to use the same methods.[104] The rise of Hitler increased apprehension, especially among the left wing of the Socialist Party, one of whose most distinguished theoreticians, Luis Araquistain, had been Ambassador in Berlin. Nor could it have escaped the notice of this group that *El Debate*'s Berlin correspondent, Antonio Bermúdez Cañete, later to be a CEDA deputy, was an ardent sympathiser with early Nazism. He had even translated parts of *Mein Kampf* and was involved in the Conquista del Estado group, one of the earliest attempts to introduce fascism into Spain.[105]

There was thus considerable suspicion surrounding the intentions of the CEDA when the campaigns for the November elections began.[106] The extreme bellicosity of Gil Robles's tone was not reassuring. He had just returned from the Nuremberg rally and appeared to be strongly influenced by what he had seen. He recorded his impressions in the CEDA party bulletin, favourably describing his official visit to the Brown House, to Nazi propaganda offices and to concentration camps, and how he saw Nazi militia drilling. While expressing vague reservations about the pantheistic elements in fascism, he pinpointed those elements most worthy of emulation in Spain: its anti-Marxism and its hatred of liberal and parliamentary democracy. The same issue carried a reprint of a piece called 'Towards a New Concept of the State', which he had written in September. This was a eulogistic account of how totalitarianism dealt with 'corrosive liberalism', and in it Gil Robles expressed his readiness to follow the new trends in world politics.[107]

The CEDA's election campaign showed just how well Gil Robles had learned his lessons. The German tour had been made 'to study details of organisation and propaganda' and he had been on a similar visit to Italy in January.[108] The keynote of the campaign was to be anti-socialism. *El Debate*'s announcement of the imminence of elections was combative in the extreme. Appealing to all those of right-wing views to co-operate, the paper stated that 'The miserly now know that for each coin they didn't want to give, they lost ten times its value.'[109] It was made clear that the CEDA was determined to win at any cost. The election committee decided for a single anti-Marxist counter-revolutionary front. In other words, the CEDA had no qualms about going to the elections in coalition with groups such as Renovación Española and the Carlists, who were conspiring to destroy the Republic by force of arms. It was an acknowledgement that the Right's material interests could best be defended within parliament, irrespective of how a majority was obtained. The manifesto of the CEDA youth movement, JAP (Juventud de Acción Popular), stated that it expected nothing from the obsolete parliamentary system but that it accepted the Cortes merely as the battleground for the moment.[110]

The climax of Gil Robles's campaign came in a speech given on 15 October in the Monumental Cinema of Madrid. His tone could only make the Left wonder what a CEDA victory would mean for them:

> We must reconquer Spain ... We must give Spain a true unity, a new spirit, a totalitarian polity ... For me there is only one tactic today: to form an anti-Marxist front and the wider the better. It is necessary now to defeat socialism inexorably.

At this point, Goicoechea, who was present, was made to stand and he received a tumultuous ovation. Gil Robles continued with language indistinguishable from that of the extreme conspiratorial Right:

> We must found a new state, purge the fatherland of judaising freemasons ... We must proceed to a new state and this imposes duties and sacrifices. What does it matter if we have to shed blood! ... We need full power and that is what we demand ... To realise this ideal we are not going to waste time with archaic forms. *Democracy is not an end but a means to the conquest of the new state. When the time comes, either parliament submits or we will eliminate it.*[111]

This speech, described by *El Socialista* as an 'authentic fascist harangue', was regarded by the Left as the most crystalline expression of CEDA orthodoxy. Certainly every sentence was greeted by ecstatic applause. Fernando De los Ríos, a moderate Socialist and a distinguished professor of law, pointed out with horror that Gil Robles's call for a purge of Jews and freemasons was a denial of the juridical and political postulates of the regime.[112] There was something ominous about the way Gil Robles ended a plea for financial assistance by threatening 'a black list of bad patriots' who did not contribute. The tenor of the speech was carried over to election posters, which emphasised the need to save Spain from 'Marxists, Freemasons, Separatists and Jews'. José Antonio Primo de Rivera, leader of the Falange, whose public launch was imminent, commented:

These are fascist principles; he may reject the name but the name is not the thing. By speaking thus, Gil Robles does not express himself as the leader of a Christian Democratic Party... This speech has been warm, direct, 'fascist'. I applaud him for it and am in agreement with him. But what mysterious reason makes him say that he is in disagreement with us?[113]

A vast amount of cash was spent on a campaign technically reminiscent of Nazi procedure. Millions of leaflets were printed and scattered on villages from the air. Two hundred thousand coloured posters were printed. Lorries drove around the streets of the bigger towns carrying screens on which were projected films of Gil Robles's speech. Twenty times a day there were radio spots exhorting listeners to 'Vote for the Right!' or to 'Vote against Marxism!'[114] The election fund was gigantic and based on generous donations from the well-to-do, particularly Juan March, the millionaire enemy of the Republic, and the Conde de Romanones, the ex-confidant of Alfonso XIII. Apart from radio, full use was made of modern transport and neon signs to carry CEDA propaganda to every part of Spain. Throughout November, it was made clear that if the CEDA won an outright victory then it would proceed to the establishment of an authoritarian regime of semi-fascist character along Austrian lines.[115]

The basic minimum programme which held the CEDA in coalition with its monarchist running mates could hardly have been more extreme. Its three points were (1) the revision of the laic and socialising legislation of the Republic, (2) a defence of the economic interests of the country, especially agriculture and (3) an amnesty. This was an open challenge to the Republicans. Religious legislation was widely regarded on the Left as the only blow so far against the *ancien régime*. Social legislation, in the form of the *jurados mixtos* and the boundaries law, was the only practical reform in favour of the landless peasantry. 'Defence of economic interests' meant, in the jargon of the Right, protection of land and industry against the demands of the workers. An amnesty would apply to the collaborators of General Primo de Rivera and those who had been implicated in the 10 August rising. For these latter it was a virtual invitation to continue their plotting, as indeed they did. Alliance with monarchist groups known to be violently hostile to the Republic irrevocably associated the CEDA with them in the eyes of the Left. Statements that the coalition was merely circumstantial could not dispel an impression of coincidence of purpose and method. There was little difference in tone between the speeches of Gil Robles and the pieces sent from abroad by José Calvo Sotelo, the extremist leader-in-exile of the monarchist Renovación Española. At a meeting in Valladolid at the beginning of November, Gil Robles made a menacing reference to 'a strong movement against democracy, parliamentarism and liberalism taking place in Italy, Germany and other countries. The Cortes about to be elected can be the decisive trial for democracy in Spain.'[116]

In addition to the national right-wing coalition, the CEDA made a number of alliances at local level before the first round of the elections. These local alliances took place in areas where the anti-Marxist coalition was relatively weak and there existed some other substantial conservative force in the area. Thus, in Asturias, a deal was made with the Reformist Party of Melquíades Alvarez; in Alicante, with Joaquín Chapaprieta, a monarchist turned conservative Republican; in the Balearic Islands, with Juan March; in Guadalajara, with the Conde de Romanones. In Badajoz, Cáceres, Ceuta, Granada, Jaén and Zamora, an arrangement was made with the local Radicals. The elections were held on 19 November. Despite the various alliances and the fact that, in rural areas especially, the Right disposed of quite considerable pressure over the unemployed, the results were disappointing. Out of 378 deputies elected in the first round, there were sixty-seven Cedistas (members of the CEDA) and seventy-eight Radicals. It was an appreciable gain, but far from remarkable in view of the previous year's vast investment in propaganda. So Gil Robles, anxious to take advantage of the fact that the electoral law favoured coalitions, decided to widen his alliances even further. He now clinched local deals with Radicals in the south, the great masters of electoral falsification. This involved going back on previous commitments and created considerable bitterness on the Right. In Córdoba, for instance, the monarchist José Tomás Valverde had only with difficulty been persuaded to run in the first round. Now he was unceremoniously dropped to make way for a local Radical, to the annoyance of the local monarchists. Nevertheless, the tactic paid off. After the second round, the Cedistas numbered 115 and the Radicals 104.[117] The fact that the local alliances had been made at the expense of rightist allies proved nothing to the Left if not that Gil Robles was prepared to do anything and compromise any principles to get a parliamentary majority and deform the Republic from within.[118]

3

SOCIAL DEMOCRACY AND SOCIAL CONFLICT

The PSOE in power, 1931–3

Unaware of just how successfully the Right would be able to organise its opposition to reform, the Socialist leadership saw the coming of the Republic with great optimism. Two weeks before the municipal elections which were to convince the King that he no longer enjoyed 'the love of my people', Largo Caballero spoke at an electoral meeting in Madrid and expressed the hopes which he and many others placed in a change of regime. Declaring that because he was a Socialist he was also necessarily a Republican, he claimed that only the overthrow of the monarchy could remedy the hunger in Andalucía and change a situation in which the social order had to be defended by the Civil Guard. At a similar function in Granada, Fernando De los Ríos said that the Socialists were about to help the middle classes make their democratic revolution.[1] In so far as they analysed the situation at all, the majority of the Socialist leadership were convinced that a classic bourgeois revolution was imminent. If they differed over the tactics to be followed – Besteiro counselling that the bourgeoisie be left to get on with its own task, Prieto convinced that without Socialist help the bourgeoisie would be too weak to do so, and Largo keen to participate in government in the hope of benefit for the party and the UGT – they were all united in the conviction that progress was inevitable.

In fact, the 'bourgeoisie' was not about to make an assault on feudalism. The commercial middle class had long since been integrated into the old landed oligarchy, and the one-time feudal ruling class had adopted capitalist modes of exploiting the land and had varied interests in industry and commerce. The adoption of democratic forms, far from being a stage in the advance of capitalism in Spain, was accepted by the economically dominant classes with great reluctance and only because of the demonstration of the monarchy's bankruptcy. That they grudgingly accepted the change in political form did not signify that they would

74

countenance any change in the social and economic structure of the country. Socialist optimism was based on a seriously flawed application of simplistic Marxism to the Spanish situation. Broadly speaking, the bulk of the bourgeoisie had hitherto been represented politically by the monarchist forces which had been defeated on 12 April. Moreover, even within the anti-monarchical coalition forged at San Sebastián in 1930, the political representatives of the most liberal sections of the bourgeoisie, the Radical Party under Alejandro Lerroux, had a significantly more conservative view of what the Republic should be than either the left-wing Republicans or the Socialists.

The Socialists seemed to have taken the great surges of popular rejoicing which greeted the proclamation of the Republic as a kind of plebiscitory approval for their vision of the Republic. That part of the Socialist leadership which embraced governmental collaboration did not fully take on board that several strands within the popular reception of the Republic were potentially inimical to their ambitions for social and economic reform. The Radicals, who, as the 1933 elections would show, enjoyed a substantial proportion of the electoral support for the Republic, had no commitment to sweeping social reform. Indeed, Lerroux had opened the doors of his party to erstwhile supporters of the monarchy.[2] To make matters worse, the Socialists' closest allies within the coalition, the left Republicans, were more concerned with institutional than agrarian reform. The anarchist masses, who formed a large part both of the joyous crowds on 14 April and of the electorate which voted for the coalition on 28 June, regarded the Republic with considerable suspicion and barely restrained impatience. Had the Socialists realised all this, and been prepared to adjust their policies accordingly, their bitterness on eventually realising the strength of the opposition to their timid attempts at reform would perhaps have been less.

Accordingly, the King's departure on 14 April and the establishment of a parliamentary regime constituted far less of a change than was thought either by the joyful crowds in the streets or by many Socialist leaders. Believing that a period of classic bourgeois democracy must now be lived through before socialism could be established, the PSOE hierarchy assumed that the new Republic would allow the improvement of social conditions within the existing economic order. Given their own origins in the trade union movement, the Socialist leaders knew well enough that the brutal conditions of the southern day-labourers (*jornaleros*) or the Asturian miners could hardly be improved by half-measures. What they failed to realise was that the great mine-owners and landlords, unaccustomed to making concessions, would regard any

75

attempts at reform as an aggressive challenge to the existing balance of social and economic power. In fact, in the context of the primitive Spanish economy, the owners were right. Thus, the Socialists' hopeful vision of a social-reforming Republic was to leave them trapped between an impatient popular clamour for more and faster reform and the determined resistance to change of the possessing classes. Differing responses to the realisation that the attempt to make the Republic socially meaningful involved the party in harmful contradictions were to lead to a stark and painful intensification of the divisions which had already become apparent during the 1920s.

For the moment, however, the PSOE was to be publicly committed to the defence and protection of the Republic. As the crowds began to celebrate in the streets, the executive committees of the PSOE and the UGT issued a joint declaration, which ended with the undertaking that, 'If at any time it became necessary to use our strength to safeguard the nascent regime, the Socialist Party and the UGT would carry out their duty without any kind of vacillation.'[3] Elsewhere in Madrid, the Socialist youth prevented the burning of General Mola's house and also linked arms to form a human barrier around the Royal Palace to hold back the crowds and to avoid any unpleasant incidents.[4] This symbolised the role that the Socialists were to find themselves adopting in the early years of the Republic, that of restraining the enthusiasm of their followers in order to give the regime an image acceptable to the middle classes. The conservative Republican and Prime Minister, Niceto Alcalá Zamora, gratefully emphasised the point in an article written six weeks after the establishment of the Republic. He saw the Socialist movement as 'a wall of defence against assault and a reassuring strength within the new regime'.[5]

That the Socialists should make sacrifices for a regime that was not their own seemed natural in the euphoric atmosphere of the spring and summer of 1931. But the optimism with which the politically unsophisticated masses, particularly in the rural south, associated the coming of the Republic with proletarian emancipation was soon to be a cause of regret for some Socialists, particularly followers of Besteiro. The moderate trade unionist Manuel Cordero regarded the enthusiasm and illusions of the masses as an impediment to the Socialists' need to take advantage of the Republic slowly. Assuming that, on the day after the Republic was proclaimed, all the problems facing the country would be solved, class privileges would disappear and a regime of equality and social justice would be established, the rank and file were soon to be disappointed by the slowness of progress towards reform.[6] Largo

Caballero did not share this view. In fact, he was sufficiently enthusiastic about the situation to assume that the party's internal divisions of the previous year would now automatically heal. He offered Besteiro's lieutenant, Andrés Saborit, a senior post in the Ministry of Labour, an offer which was immediately turned down. The cabinet, in which Largo, Prieto and De los Ríos now sat, also offered Besteiro himself first an attractive job as state delegate to the national petrol monopoly, CAMPSA, and then the post of Ambassador to France. He refused both.[7]

It was not just the traditional abstentionist right wing of the party which had its doubts about the wisdom of becoming too involved with the Republic. There soon emerged other discordant voices, only this time more radical ones. Although for the moment in a minority, significantly they belonged to party members whose opinions were of some weight with key militant sectors of the Socialist movement. Javier Bueno, who published a book on the possibilities of state power for the Socialists in June 1931, was later to be editor of the Asturian miners' daily *Avance*. Under his editorship, and impelled by the worsening conditions in the mining valleys, *Avance* became increasingly radical after its foundation in November 1931. Bueno's book urged his fellow Socialists to seize the opportunity presented by the birth of the new era. Declaring that capitalist society was finished, he rejected the party's evolutionary reformism: 'If the future lies in a social order which liberates mankind, there can be no reason for delaying the moment of breaking the chains.'[8]

In the optimistic atmosphere of the early summer of 1931, Bueno's views had little impact. Yet before long he was to be a vocal member of a section of the PSOE which came to feel that it was precisely the party's commitment to the Republic which was delaying the breaking of the chains. Perhaps of greater significance were the misgivings of Gabriel Morón, the militant rural leader from Córdoba who had spearheaded the inner-party protest against collaboration with Primo de Rivera. Morón and a group of his friends were concerned that the reformist hopes of a progressive Republic were illusions. Arguing that contemporary events suggested that socialism was now the object of a worldwide offensive by the bourgeoisie, they believed that bourgeois democracy and bourgeois liberties had become meaningless concepts. Accordingly, the PSOE tactics of reformism and revisionism were now obsolete. Instead, claimed Morón, the Socialists must learn that a fundamental struggle was coming between the old capitalist order and the new political aspirations of the workers.[9]

What gave added significance to the views of Morón was that it was in the agrarian south that the front line of the battle for a progressive

Republic was to be found. Moreover, it was there too that a massive influx of recruits into the UGT was taking place. The vertiginous growth of the landworkers' federation, the FNTT, was greatly out of proportion with the overall growth of the UGT. The total union membership grew from 277,011 in December 1930 to 958,451 in December 1931 and to 1,041,539 in June 1932. The FNTT's membership rose from 36,639 in June 1930 to 392,953 in June 1932.[10] The shift in orientation of the UGT as a whole was immense. In mid-1930, as the agrarian crisis had first got under way, rural labour had made up 13 per cent of UGT membership. Two years later, with class bitterness in the southern villages intensifying by the day, the proportion of landworkers in the UGT had risen to 37 per cent. Largo Caballero was delighted just to see his beloved union growing faster than the anarchist CNT: 'Our rapid growth cannot frighten us,' he declared, 'nay, must not frighten us.'[11] More cautious members of the trade union bureaucracy were concerned that the illiterate day-labourers now flooding into the movement, brutalised by conditions on the southern estates, would push the UGT into violent conflict with the landowners. They were anxious that the union organisation should face up to the task of moderating the untutored exaltation of the *jornaleros*.[12] If their fears were born of bureaucratic paternalism, they were none the less justified. The change in orientation of the UGT, from a predominantly élite union of the working-class aristocracy to a mass union of unsophisticated unskilled workers and rural labourers, at a time of economic depression and rising unemployment, was to place it at the centre of the major conflict of the Republic, the one between the large landowners and the landless labourers. Each side in that conflict was represented in the national political arena by a mass parliamentary party: the landowners by the Acción Popular–Agrario coalition, the labourers by the PSOE. Thus, the survival of the parliamentary regime depended to a large degree on the successful resolution of the conflict.

In the first days of the Republic, few Socialists were aware of the sombre implications of the recruiting boom in the UGT. Moreover, the three Socialists in the provisional government were involved as early as 15 April 1931 in a solemn undertaking to improve the living conditions of the Spanish peasantry. This took the form of clause 5 of the Juridical Statute of the Republic, a formal declaration in which the provisional government laid out its objectives and circumscribed its powers until such time as a parliament could be elected.[13] Clause 5 declared that private property was guaranteed by law and could be expropriated only for reasons of public utility and with compensation.

It went on to recognise the neglect that previous governments had shown of the great mass of peasants and of agriculture in general, and undertook to alter agrarian legislation in such a way as to make it correspond to the social function of the land. At a cabinet meeting on 21 April, the specific application of this commitment was discussed. The three Socialist ministers were prevailed upon to shelve their party's desire for a sweeping redistribution of the land, at least until such time as parliamentary assent were possible. In return for this forbearance, they were to be allowed to issue a series of decrees to deal with some of the immediate causes of hardship in the countryside.[14]

A Ministry of Labour report commissioned in November 1930 and published in early 1931 gave a sombre picture of the misery caused in the south by the drought during the winter.[15] Such was the hunger of the landless labourers that immediate palliatives were urgently needed. The usual solution of increased public works was inadequate. The Republican government had come to power with the biggest budgetary deficit in the history of Spain, the legacy of the grandiose projects of General Primo de Rivera. Public works contractors were owed 300 million pesetas and, in a context of international financial uncertainty, long-term loans were not to be had. Deficit financing was impossible. Thus, an improvement in the conditions of the rural poor could be sought only in some readjustment of the prevailing economic inequalities. That effectively meant legislation to introduce higher wages and better working conditions and to guarantee protection against arbitrary dismissal, the rural lock-out and the artificial maintenance of low wages by the unfettered importation of cheap labour. These were all reforms which were issues of life and death for hundreds of thousands of *jornaleros* but they could be introduced only at the cost of the rural rich. The *latifundio* system of landholding depended to a large extent for its economic viability on the existence of a large reserve of landless labourers paid the minimum wages for the shortest period possible. Increased wages and protection against dismissal for those labourers therefore challenged the basis of the entire system. What may have seemed to the Socialists to be merely limited reformist palliatives were thus to have far-reaching and deeply conflictive implications.

At a time of economic boom, wage increases might perhaps have been absorbed by higher profits. As it was, the period in which the Socialists were attempting to ameliorate conditions coincided with the years of the Great Depression. The consequent situation of exacerbated class struggle could not but impel the landless labourers to push for more reforms and the landowners to oppose any reform at all. The depression affected the Spanish countryside in two main ways – by closing the safety valve of emigration and by forcing down agricultural prices. After forty years of high net emigration, averaging at 32,000 per year, 1931 saw a net return of emigrants of 39,582. By the end of 1933, barriers to immigrants in France and Latin America had caused over 100,000 Spaniards to return to Spain, joining a similar number who would normally have emigrated but could not do so. The industrial depression ensured that there would be little relief in terms of internal migration to the towns and that the returning emigrants would be forced to go to the countryside. During the boom of the 1920s there had been a considerable rural exodus, not least provoked by Primo's great building schemes. Since the collapse of his artificial boom, unskilled building labourers were returning to their villages in droves. Given that the world downturn was soon to take its toll of Spanish agricultural exports of wine, fruit and olive oil, the great landowners had no reason to want to find employment for the rural masses. Since 45.5 per cent of the active population, 3.9 million landed or landless peasants, worked the land and 2 million of them were landless day-labourers, the resolution of the conflict of interest between the landowners and the labourers was the central issue facing the provisional government.[16]

This then was the context in which the Minister of Labour, Largo Caballero, and the Minister of Justice, Fernando de los Ríos, began at the end of April 1931 to issue decrees concerning the rural question. Between 28 April and the opening of parliament on 14 July, they passed a series of edicts of crucial importance. Those emanating from the Ministry of Justice concerned rural leases; those from the Ministry of Labour dealt with the working conditions of the *braceros* (landless labourers). A decree of 29 April froze all leases, automatically renewed any which fell due, and prevented eviction other than for failure to pay rent or lack of cultivation. Its object was to prevent hitherto absentee landlords from taking possession of their land to avoid the consequences of the proposed agrarian reform. As of 11 July, tenants were allowed to petition local courts for reduction of rents. The decrees introduced by Largo Caballero had a more dramatic impact. The most important of them was the decree of municipal boundaries (*términos municipales*), issued on 28 April. It prevented the introduction of outside labour into a municipality while there remained local workers unemployed. On 7 May, agrarian mixed juries (*jurados mixtos*) were introduced, to arbitrate in rural labour disputes. Significantly, General Primo de Rivera had never dared extend his arbitration committees (*comités paritarios*), on which the mixed juries were based, to rural areas, for fear of the owners' reaction. A decree of 1 July established, in theory at least, the eight-hour day in the countryside. Given that labourers had traditionally been expected to earn their day-wage by working from sunrise to sunset (*de sol a sol*) and that sixteen-hour days were not uncommon, this decree implied a substantial additional income for the *braceros*, either in the form of overtime pay or in terms of more work for more men. To prevent the owners' sabotaging these various measures by simply ceasing to cultivate their land, a supplementary edict of obligatory cultivation (*laboreo forzoso*) was passed by the Ministry of National Economy, on 7 May.[17]

The cumulative effect of these decrees was, on paper, to strike at the heart of the repressive economic relations prevailing in rural Spain, particularly in the areas of the great estates. Yet it seems that, in promulgating them, Fernando de los Ríos and Francisco Largo Caballero were not aiming at revolutionary objectives. They meant their edicts rather as a palliative to the conditions of acute misery in which Andalucía found itself in the spring of 1931. Apart from the Ministry of Labour report on the agrarian crisis, the cabinet also had at its disposal a number of alarming warnings. General Sanjurjo, head of the Civil Guard, reported to the Minister of War, Manuel Azaña, that agitation was on the increase. On 21 July all the mayors of the towns and villages of the province of Jaén, one of the worst hit, came to beg the government for help. They claimed that, just to prevent widespread starvation and an insurrection, subsidies of 2 million pesetas per day would be necessary for at least three months.[18] Projects for public works were drawn up with the limited funds available but the initial grant for the entire south was only 10 million pesetas.[19] In such circumstances, it was not surprising that the government began to think that the employers should contribute towards alleviating the crisis.

However limited the intentions of the ministers involved, the implicit threat to the hitherto dominant position of the owners remained. The law of municipal boundaries effectively curtailed the introduction of blackleg labour to break strikes and keep wages down. The mixed juries recognised that the labourers also had legal rights and were not simply subject to the economic necessities of the owners. The eight-hour day would increase costs in a depressed market. The decree of obligatory cultivation introduced a notion of social utility which limited the owners' right to dispose of their land as they willed, and did so in such a way as to neutralise one of their principal weapons of social domination. The big landowners began to mobilise to meet the threat. Various employers' federations – the Agrupación de Propietarios de Fincas

Rústicas, the Confederación Española Patronal Agrícola, stock-breeders' associations, olive-growers' associations, and so on – were either founded or revitalised.[20] Much of the success of the Acción Nacional recruiting campaign of the summer of 1931 can be attributed to the resentment generated by these first decrees and to fear of more thoroughgoing measures to come. The press and propaganda network of the ACNP (Asociación Católica Nacional de Propagandistas) was soon at work attacking the decrees. It had considerable success on this issue, as on others, in creating the appearance that the interests of smallholders were the same as those of large landowners. This was relatively easy to do, since many of the decrees' consequences affected any employer of labour, large or small. Indeed, many poor small farmers who employed only one or two men during harvest times were particularly vulnerable to any increase in wages for the simple reason that they were often little better off than those they employed. The same big owners who ostentatiously lamented this situation did so only when the perceived enemy as the Republic. Their loud solidarity for the smallholders did not inhibit them, in other contexts, from foreclosing mortgages, calling in loans and evicting tenants at will.

In fact, several of the rightist criticisms were, from the owners' point of view, justified, but others were part of a campaign of denigration which skilfully distorted the real details and functions of the recently introduced measures. The decree of municipal boundaries, for instance, deprived migrant workers of labour and also hit the inhabitants of smaller, 'satellite' villages near to, but outside, the legal boundaries of a bigger village. However, that such was the case was not so much a criticism of the decree as proof of the need for fundamental changes in Spain's agrarian structure. Complaints on the workers' behalf came from those who wanted to be able to pay them less than the going rate. It is also likely that local workers used their new-found job security to drag jobs out longer and so guarantee their exiguous wages for a few days longer. That, however, was not sufficient to justify Gil Robles's charge, on a visit to the Ministry of Labour at the end of November, that the decree benefited none but 'professional layabouts' (*vagos profesionales*). There is evidence to suggest that the Socialist municipal councillors in charge of applying the decrees showed little restraint in taking advantage of the shift in the legal balance of power. In some cases, for instance, they used the decree of obligatory cultivation to plough pasture. Again, the loudest complaints often came from those who defined as pasture land which was wastefully used to graze fighting bulls. The readiness of the landless labourers and their union representatives to derive benefit from the new legal context is hardly surprising given the scale of deprivation and despair in which many of them lived. The owners had equally not hesitated in the preceding decades to squeeze all the economic benefit possible from the prevailing situation.

The Socialist *alcaldes* (mayors) and councillors did not have it all their own way, however. The machinery to enforce the decrees was almost non-existent. Yet the problem was immense. While thousands of *braceros* were on the point of starvation, vast areas of land lay uncultivated. In Andalusia and Extremadura, between 40 and 60 per cent of all useful land was uncultivated.[21] Nevertheless, fines for infringements of the decree of *laboreo forzoso* did not exceed 500 pesetas and were usually much less. In fact, Largo Caballero complained bitterly of the way in which senior officials, such as the civil governors of several provinces, sabotaged the application of the various decrees by rulings which were contrary to their spirit. Moreover, in remote villages particularly, the power of the Civil Guard remained untouched. Even General Sanjurjo commented to Azaña that the Civil Guard's social commitment was to the rural upper classes and against the Socialist and anarchist *alcaldes* and councillors, whom not so long ago they had been putting in jail. Above all, the power consequent upon being the exclusive providers of work remained to the owners.[22]

The propaganda campaign carried out by the Catholic press merely inflamed the determination of the southern landowners not to abide by the provisions of the decrees. The belief was created that one of the consequences of the law of municipal boundaries was that unemployed barbers, cobblers, school-teachers and other unsuitable workers, unskilled in agricultural jobs, were being used for highly specialised tasks to the detriment of the nation's agriculture. Yet, by a supplementary ruling of 6 August, the importation of necessary specialised labour was permitted. By another, of 30 September, it was laid down that the list of workers from a given municipality who had to be employed before the introduction of outsiders could be permitted was to be composed only of agricultural labourers. The rightist press also complained that valuable crops were lost because the law's rigidity prevented the hiring of essential extra labour. In fact, once all the labourers in a village had been hired, there was nothing to prevent the introduction of outsiders. Moreover, the law was suspended altogether on 15 October for the duration of the orange harvest, and on 29 October for the duration of the olive harvest, in the provinces concerned. The various original decrees required some adaptation when put into practice.

Nevertheless, it was the theoretical rigidity and not the practical flexibility which attracted the attention of the rightist press.[23]

Less directly offensive to the big landowners, but no less irritating to them, were the decrees passed by Fernando de los Ríos to improve the situation of the hard-pressed leaseholders. Besides the traditional smallholding areas of the north and centre of Spain, there was an increasing amount of land cultivated in small leaseholdings in the predominantly *latifundio* areas. Given the acute land-hunger and consequent competition for plots, leases were accepted by tenants on economically ruinous terms and for periods as short as one year. De los Ríos's decrees mitigated some of the worst results of the disastrous 1930–1 harvest by making eviction almost impossible and preventing rent rises at a time of falling prices. This was seen as an intolerable infringement on property rights by many large landowners. However, the real battle over this issue did not come until 1935, when, to the outrage of his own party, the liberal CEDA Minister of Agriculture Manuel Giménez Fernández would rashly take up the defence of the smallholder. It is reasonable to suppose that the reason for the delay was that the political formations which protected the big owners' interests were too anxious to gain the support of the small farmers to risk taking up the issue on behalf of their real masters.

Indeed, by the end of 1931, it was obvious that the owners' initial resentment of the decrees concerning the working conditions of the *jornaleros* was maturing into a determination to destroy them by means of a virtual rural lock-out. However, in the early summer this future conflict was not foreseen by most of the PSOE leaders. Besteiro's abstentionist faction remained doubtful, but others tended to see the raised expectations of the rural workers and their consequent influx into the UGT as an indication of the possibilities offered to the Socialist movement by a reformist bourgeois democracy. In the elections of 28 June for the Constituent Cortes, the PSOE had gained 116 seats. In the flush of victory, little thought seems to have been given by the Socialist leadership to the significance of the fact that Lerroux's Radicals, with a campaign that was unashamedly conservative, not to say right-wing, had gained 94 seats and become the second largest party in the Constituent Cortes. Lerroux campaigned for reconciliation rather than divisive reform, denounced the 'Utopia' of sweeping agrarian reform and raised the flag of law and order against anarchy. He made it clear that for him the Republic was the end of a political process not the beginning of a period of social change.[24] For the Socialists, in contrast, the establishment of the new regime was merely the first step on a long road of social and economic reform.

The long-term implications of the potential conflict with the Radicals, who constituted a large and powerful section of the Republican–Socialist coalition, were not directly confronted within the PSOE, although *El Debate* was already delightedly discussing the prospects that such divisions opened up for the Right.[25] To an extent dazzled by their electoral triumph, many Socialists were none the less determined not to stand aside to the benefit of Lerroux. An extraordinary congress of the party was called for 10 July, four days before the Cortes was due to open, to discuss the policy to be followed by the PSOE deputies. Its proceedings concentrated narrowly on the continuing role to be played by the PSOE within the government of the Republic. It was to be a debate in which both the meaning of Lerroux's rightwards move and the substantial electoral support that it seemed to enjoy were not discussed explicitly. An indication of rank-and-file enthusiasm for collaboration came in the voting for delegates to the congress. In the hitherto strongly pro-Besteiro Agrupación Socialista de Madrid, the abstentionist Andrés Saborit was surprisingly not elected.[26]

The specific question at the congress was whether or not the three Socialist ministers in the provisional government should continue to participate. The sub-committee delegated to examine the question was dominated by Besteiro but included a Prietista, Teodomiro Menéndez, Prieto's under-secretary at the Ministry of Public Works, and Largo's close theoretical adviser, Luis Araquistain. The central recommendation of its report was that the three ministers should remain in the government during the elaboration of the Constitution. Prieto then proposed an amendment of its text. This amendment stated that:

1 In this historic moment, the fundamental obligation of the PSOE is to defend the Republic and contribute by all means to its definitive consolidation.

2 Since the task entrusted to the provisional government is unfinished, the party will continue to be represented in the government until the Constitution is approved and the supreme organ of power is elected.

3 The parliamentary group, although directly responsible for its activities to the congresses of the party, in cases of exceptional importance in which its attitude could have a decisive effect on

the direction of Spanish politics, will appeal to the Executive Committee of the party for a decision.

4 After the Constitution is approved and the supreme organ of power is elected, if the party is requested to continue in the government and the request comes at a time when an extraordinary congress cannot be called, the parliamentary group and the Executive Committee will decide together. If they do not agree, the National Committee will decide.

5 As a general norm, the party declares in principle against participation in power. However, faithful to article 1 of this declaration, and in defence of the Republic, the party would accept such participation if it felt that not to do so would lead to rightist policies contrary to the profoundly radical aspirations revealed by the country on 12 April and confirmed on 28 June and contrary also to the vehement desire for a rigid administrative austerity and a break with the traditional political vices. The party would also accept power if it felt that lack of cohesion between the Republican groups deprived the government of indispensable solidarity.

Prieto's text implied that participation was a necessary sacrifice on the part of the PSOE but encapsulated an awareness of the threat from Lerroux. It opened the way to full collaboration and clearly implicated the PSOE in the success or failure of the Republic. Besteiro opposed it on the grounds that the party would be doing the bourgeoisie's job and consequently would lose contact with its own followers, but Prieto's text was accepted by the congress by 10,607 votes to 8362. For the rest, the congress was concerned with elaborating Socialist objectives in the Constituent Cortes. These were basically reformist, but were none the less ambitious, including as they did the establishment of civil rights, the nationalisation of railways, banks, mines and forests, the solution of the agrarian problem, the introduction of divorce, the construction of a laic educational system and the declaration of the religious independence of the state.[27]

The full implications of the Socialist commitment to the defence of the bourgeois Republic were soon apparent and tended to justify Besteiro's worst fears. Despite the Socialists' readiness to postpone their more ambitious reforms, the upper classes were not satisfied. The peseta began to fall as large sums of capital were spirited out of the country – to such an extent, indeed, that the old adviser of the King, the Conde de Romanones, declared that if he were in power he would shoot the pessimists.[28] At the same time as the upper classes thus expressed their hostility to the Republic, the working class began to reveal its own impatient expectations by a number of strikes throughout 1931. It was an awkward situation for a working-class party in a bourgeois government. To prevent industrial and agrarian unrest from discrediting the Republic, the Socialist ministers acquiesced in the often-violent suppression of strikes involving anarchists and Communists, while the UGT trade union bureaucracy worked hard to curtail the militancy of its own members. Given the traditional rivalry with the CNT, few tears were shed for the repression of the anarchists. However, the rank and file did not always share the egoistic vision of the paid bureaucrats and felt a more basic class solidarity. This was particularly the case in rural areas. Although the Socialist press referred to anarchist unrest,[29] there was little to choose between anarchists and FNTT members. In many villages, the local organisation of *braceros* was, in a naïve spirit of class solidarity, affiliated to all three of the principal worker organisations, the UGT, the CNT *and* the Communist Party. Elsewhere, the fact that illiterate day-labourers joined the FNTT did not make them sophisticated Marxists overnight and there was little difference in political maturity or aspirations between them and members of the CNT. In the mines too, the essential harshness of conditions created a solidarity which rose above the rivalries of the political factions. Not surprisingly then, the acute anarchist and Communist criticisms of class collaboration and reformism made against the Socialist leadership could not fail to have an effect on the UGT rank-and-file militants. Significantly, it was precisely those Socialist leaders who were nearest to the problems of the workers – Largo Caballero, Luis Araquistain, his second-in-command at the Ministry of Labour, and Carlos de Baraibar, his Director-General of Labour – who were eventually to reject reformism as worse than useless.[30]

The basic cause of the Socialists' discomfort was the fact that the anarchists regarded the bourgeois Republic as little different from the monarchy and were not disposed to listen to PSOE pleas for patience. At the end of May there was a strike of port workers in Pasajes (San Sebastián). The Minister of the Interior, Miguel Maura, sent in the Civil Guard, and eight workers were killed and many more wounded. The Pasajes incident had an immediate repercussion in Asturias. There, the UGT-affiliated SOMA (Sindicato de los Obreros Mineros de Asturias – the Asturian Miners' Union) was coming under increasing pressure from the far more militant Sindicato Unico, jointly controlled by anarchists and Communists. Since the death of the great reformist Manuel

Llaneza, the SOMA had been led by Prietistas such as Teodomiro Menéndez and Ramón González Peña, strong believers in the party line which was to prevail at the extraordinary congress. They condemned the proposed solidarity strike as reactionary irresponsibility designed to discredit the Republic. Nevertheless, rank-and-file sympathy with anarchist claims that the SOMA leadership was acting as the ally of the hated mine-owners eventually forced SOMA participation in the general strike which began on 1 June. The Socialists then used all their influence to bring the strike to a rapid and peaceful end.[31]

Elsewhere, the story was similar. In Andalusia and Extremadura, hungry *braceros* and *yunteros* (ploughmen for hire with their own yokes of oxen) were attacking the great estates and again the Civil Guard was sent in. The Besteirista leadership of the rapidly swelling FNTT had to use all its powers of persuasion to keep the militancy of its new members within Republican legality. The major conflicts of the summer took place in Madrid, Barcelona and Seville. The first of these, the great telephone strike which broke out on 6 July, starkly highlighted the dilemma of the Socialists in the government. The telephone monopoly in Spain had been established during the Dictadura by the American ITT Corporation, in the midst of a great scandal. Throughout the late 1920s and up to the coming of the Republic, the Socialists had condemned its irregularities and promised support for the wage-claims of the telephone workers. However, when the strike broke out, the cabinet was frantically trying to create confidence in the regime and was also under considerable pressure from the American Ambassador. Accordingly, Miguel Maura, with the agreement of his Socialist cabinet colleagues, mobilised a considerable police apparatus against the strikers, instructions being issued to shoot any worker caught trying to sabotage company property. The Socialist press denounced the strike as a reactionary provocation and the UGT recommended militants not to cooperate with the strikers. However, it was a popular strike against a multinational corporation and many UGT sections sent messages of solidarity and money to the strikers. The strike failed and left a considerable legacy of bitterness between the Republic and the CNT.[32]

Even more dramatic was the outcome of a period of anarchist agitation in Seville. As the culmination of a series of strikes, the CNT called a general stoppage on 18 July. This was the signal for a number of disorders and gun-battles between the anarchists and the Civil Guard. At the cabinet meeting of 21 July, Largo Caballero demanded that Miguel Maura take action to put an end to the disorders which were damaging the Republic's image. When the Prime Minister, Niceto Alcalá

Zamora, asked if everyone was agreed that energetic measures against the CNT were called for, the cabinet assented unanimously and Largo actually produced a draft decree for declaring strikes illegal under certain circumstances. The following day, the irascible and impulsive Maura authorised the artillery shelling of an anarchist meeting-place, the Casa Cornelio, in Seville.[33] This ended the strike, but it also provoked a wave of criticism of the Socialists, both in the press and in the Cortes. The point of view of the CNT was put in the Cortes by Catalan deputies who had been elected with anarchist votes. In reply to their accusations that the UGT was exploiting the Socialist presence in the government to damage the CNT, Largo Caballero and Manuel Cordero replied that the CNT was prepared to bring down the Republic in order to hurt the UGT and that governmental participation involved nothing but sacrifice for the Socialists.[34]

It was extremely wearing on the Socialists to have to bear the brunt of the defence of the Republic against both Right and Left. Yet in the summer of 1931 it still seemed a worthwhile task. This was emphasised by Luis Araquistain in a series of articles which he published at the time of the Seville strikes and with the telephone strike still under way. In 'The Syndicalist Antichrist', he tried to show how the CNT's behaviour was playing into the hands of the Right by allowing a picture of chaos and disorder to be created of the Republic. In the second article of the series, 'Why Are There So Many Strikes?', he suggested that the anarchists were motivated by a desire for revenge against the Socialist collaboration with the Dictadura. In contrast to this egoistic irresponsibility, he praised the 'civic heroism' of the UGT's members, who were hit by the economic depression every bit as much as the anarchists, yet put the health of the Republic before their own interests. In the third and final article, 'Against the Abuse of the Strike', he claimed that the existing conciliation and arbitration machinery could meet any just complaints without recourse to strikes.[35] This was not true, but the Socialists were intensely anxious to reduce social tension and unrest.

As the summer wore on, the attacks from both sides of the political spectrum began to take their toll of the Socialists. Prieto, who always tended to pessimism, was becoming thoroughly disillusioned about his inability to alter the financial structures of the country, and talked of resignation. He also expressed the opinion that, by having a Socialist as Minister of Labour, the PSOE was drawing on itself the popular discontent consequent on the impossibility of solving all social problems at once. Largo remained convinced that, by being in the ministry, he was helping to improve conditions, but he too expressed concern at the hostility it was provoking among the anarchists and, on 7 August, also talked of resigning. Two days earlier he had stated in the Cortes that the *labradores* of Cádiz, Málaga and Seville were refusing to plant seeds, in an attempt to break the *jurados mixtos*. Both Prieto and Largo were persuaded by their cabinet colleagues to stay on, although the intensity of upper-class resistance to reform would probably have been sufficient to remind them that social conditions would deteriorate dramatically if the PSOE left the government. Largo's attitude was revealed in his preamble to a draft law on work contracts, in which he described himself as a 'Socialist who for thirty years has collaborated with the capitalist classes in order to take from them, gradually and by legitimate means, their impossible privileges'. Provided reformist policies were making some advances for the working class and particularly the UGT, he would continue to collaborate in the government of the Republic. However, the precedent of his reaction to the frustration of his hopes under the Primo de Rivera Dictatorship suggested that a rapid change of tack could be expected in the case of a similar disappointment now. Already there were those to the left of the PSOE who were thoroughly disillusioned with the collaboration. Significantly enough, when in 1929 Largo rejected co-operation with the Dictator, his decision was preceded by an acute critique of collaborationism by Gabriel Morón. Now, in a book written in late 1931, Morón denounced participation in the government as pointless, and predicted that, if the Socialists did not withdraw from power and prepare for battle with the bourgeoisie, they would be destroyed when eventually their reforming efforts provoked a reaction from the ruling classes. It was only a matter of time before Largo would arrive at similar conclusions.[36]

However, as a result of the failure of the various strikes, there came a lull in the wave of anarchist agitation. Indeed, besides exhausting the anarchist workers, the strikes were provoking a division within the CNT. This came to a head in August when thirty moderates issued a manifesto (*el manifiesto de los Treinta*) against the sporadic violence of the pure anarchists of the Federación Anarquista Ibérica.[37] Unrest was to break out again soon, but this respite allowed the Socialists to concentrate during the autumn on the parliamentary debates concerning the elaboration of the Constitution.

After an earlier draft by the conservative politician Angel Ossorio y Gallardo had been rejected, a new constitutional committee, under the Socialist law professor Luis Jiménez de Asúa, met on 28 July. It had barely three weeks to draw up its draft. In consequence, some of its unsubtle wording was to give rise to three months of acrimonious debate. Presenting the project on 27 August, Jiménez de Asúa described it as a democratic, liberal document with great social content. Fernando de los Ríos, speaking in its favour on 3 September, declared his commitment to liberal democracy and the planned economy. Luis Araquistain chalked up the first Socialist victory when he prevailed on the chamber to vote in favour of a text for article 1 which read, 'Spain is a Republic of workers of all classes.' However, he also reminded his listeners that a paper constitution did not of itself alter the existing relation of economic forces within the country. Nevertheless, the draft constituted enough of a challenge to provoke bitter opposition from the Agrarians and other rightist deputies. This was particularly so with the clause which probably meant most to the Socialists, number 42 in the draft, 44 in the final text. It stated that all the wealth of the country must be subordinate to the economic interests of the nation and that all property could be expropriated, with compensation, for reasons of social utility. It required a magisterial speech by Besteiro on 6 October before it was approved. Besteiro's speech, like that of De los Ríos a month earlier, expressed a more or less Fabian commitment to a mixed economy. Yet, for the Alfonsist monarchist Pedro Sáinz Rodríguez, the very notion of social utility was 'a sword of Damocles hanging over property'. In the main, however, the Constitution was satisfactory to the Socialists and fulfilled the objectives that they had set themselves in the extraordinary congress. Perhaps only on one major issue did they fail. That was when they were persuaded by a brilliant speech by Azaña not to push for the complete dissolution of the religious orders. That aside, the Constitution finally approved on 9 December 1931 was as democratic, laic and reforming as the Socialists might have wished.[38]

After the approval of the Constitution, there arose the question of whether the Socialists could continue in the government, or, indeed, whether the government should not dissolve the Cortes and call new elections. In fact, throughout the period of debate over the Constitution, there had been some controversy on the subject, both in the press and within the cabinet.[39] De los Ríos and Largo Caballero were enthusiastic about staying on; Prieto, as ever, was ready to resign. At one point, Largo even talked of an entirely Socialist government. With UGT recruiting at an all-time high and with many union bureaucrats enjoying well-paid government posts, Largo was satisfied that the existing arrangement was beneficial to the UGT.[40] Moreover, despite the southern landowners' growing aggressiveness against his reforms, he must have reflected that, with the Socialists out of the government, conditions would have been worse. Nor can he have been unaware that, with the massive political mobilisation being undertaken by Acción Nacional, if the Cortes were dissolved, the Socialists would probably lose a number of seats in the consequent elections. So great was Largo's commitment to the Republic that he had been prominent in elaborating the rather authoritarian Law for the Defence of the Republic and also, in a vain attempt to clinch conservative confidence in the regime, had supported the candidacy of Alcalá Zamora for the post of President of the Republic. Despite Alcalá Zamora's hostility to the Constitution, which had led him to resign as Prime Minister on 14 October, Largo and Prieto, in the meeting held by the parliamentary minority of the PSOE to discuss the candidacies, managed to prevail over Besteiro by fifty-three votes to thirty-eight.[41]

The extent to which the Socialist ministers were prepared to make sacrifices in order to defend the Republic was made particularly clear throughout November, when they helped to avert a major railway strike. The railwaymen's leader, Trifón Gómez, a Besteirista, was hostile to the idea of a strike but was unable to restrain the militancy of the rank and file. At one point, when his men had refused an offer by the government, Trifón Gómez made an extraordinarily significant remark to Azaña:

> If there were not three Socialist ministers in the government, the concessions would have been received by the workers with applause and gratitude. However, since there are Socialist ministers, they think the railways should be handed over to them lock, stock, and barrel.

Apart from what this revealed about the paternalistic attitudes of the syndical bureaucracy, it emphasised the dilemma faced by the ministers, and in particular Largo Caballero. Azaña underlined the anomaly of their situation when he asked himself in his diary, 'If the presence of three Socialist ministers in the government cannot prevent a strike, what use is it?' Eventually, by dint of frantic persuasion, Trifón Gómez managed to prevail at the congress of railwaymen called to debate the proposed strike.[42]

The railway dispute typified the way in which the Socialists were prepared to sacrifice their popularity by restraining the militancy of their followers. Nowhere was this more true than in Asturias, where the UGT found itself in the crossfire between the employers and the militants of the anarchist Sindicato Unico. On 6 December the SOMA managed to end a miners' strike in Mieres, declaring that 'Surprise stoppages, without a premeditated study of their possible consequences, inevitably fail.' When the anarchists started a general strike in Gijón, during which at least four workers were killed by the Civil Guard, the Asturian UGT condemned it as leading only to hunger and misery for the workers. The union of gas and electricity workers, the SOMA and the provincial Federation of Building Workers issued specific instructions that their members were not to go on strike.[43] This constituted a considerable risk, since, at a time of acute economic crisis, particularly in the mining sector, there was a growing rank-and-file sympathy for militant action. Moreover, while accusations of class betrayal from anarchists and Communists abounded, the UGT's moderation did nothing to abate the hostility of the Right. Under such circumstances, continued sacrifices on behalf of the Republic would be made in large part because of an intensifying awareness that only the Republican—Socialist coalition stood as a bulwark against ever more ferocious reaction.

The recognition of this became increasingly apparent in the Socialist movement towards the end of 1931. Disinterested enthusiasm for the Republic was giving way to a harder line. The PSOE press recalled that the Socialists were in the government to secure social reforms. If the spirit of the Constitution were not carried over into the auxiliary laws which were to put it into practice, this would be a challenge to the Socialists to resort to revolutionary tactics. As *El Socialista* warned, it was time that 'the bourgeois elements realised that the people had not surrendered their revolutionary weapons but simply held them in readiness'. The PSOE executive committee met on 12 November to decide whether to continue to collaborate in a new government headed by Manuel Azaña. Aware that abstentionism could open the way to elections which might be manipulated to the benefit of Lerroux, the executive decided to offer their collaboration.[44] Alongside the growing sense of beleaguerment in the highest reaches of the party, there was a feeling within the wider Socialist movement that, to justify ongoing sacrifices, Azaña's government, having seen the Constitution through the Cortes, must now, with Socialist collaboration, fill its framework with a socially progressive content.[45]

The test for social progress had inevitably to be the most backward sector of Spanish society, the rural south. There, despite promises of agrarian reform and the improvements introduced by the early decrees of Largo Caballero, where they could be enforced, conditions remained brutal. All over the south, many owners had declared war on the Republican–Socialist coalition by refusing to plant crops. The Socialist deputies from Badajoz, Jaén, Málaga and Huelva denounced such cases in the Cortes. In Jaén, for instance, where landowners had systematically ignored the social legislation of the Republic, the provincial Sociedad de Labradores openly called on its members to cease cultivating their lands, in order to combat the various decrees which defended the *braceros*.[46] With the exception of the olive harvest, during which the law of municipal boundaries was suspended, there was, thereafter, massive agrarian unemployment in the province. In Badajoz the story was the same. The governor of the province and the colonel in charge of the province's Civil Guard connived with the local *caciques* against the existing labour legislation. Eventually, on 21 December 1931, the local section of the FNTT resolved to call a general strike in order to get both of them transferred. In the most dramatic way imaginable, this strike was to force the Socialists to face the question of whether social reform was possible without revolutionary change.

The Badajoz strike took place on 30 and 31 December. It was in the main a peaceful strike, in accordance with the instruction of its organisers. In an isolated village called Castilblanco, however, there was bloodshed. Castilblanco is in that most arid and inhospitable part of Extremadura known as 'Siberia *extremeña*'. Its inhabitants lived in the most crushing poverty and misery. The village's common lands had been taken from it in the nineteenth century by legal subterfuge. It was now controlled by the local *latifundista*, and the *alcalde* was his nominee. Castilblanco was not untypical of hundreds of villages in southern Spain. When the strike was called, the workers of Castilblanco had already spent the winter without work. They were all members of the FNTT. On 30 December they held a peaceful and disciplined demonstration, which they intended to repeat on the following day. They did so and were dispersing to their homes when the *alcalde*, frightened that their display of discipline heralded a change in the village's power structure, instructed the Civil Guard to break up the crowd. Some women were pushed, protests were heard and one guard opened fire, killing one man and wounding two others. At that moment, the villagers, in a frenzy of fear, anger and panic, fell upon the four guards and beat and hacked them to death with stones and knives.[47]

The consequent uproar starkly revealed the gulf which existed between those who defended and those who hoped to change the prevailing social order. The Right accused the Socialists of inciting the *braceros* against the *Benemérita*, the eulogistic term used for the Civil Guard by its devotees. The Socialists believed the real criminal of Castilblanco to have been the repressive land system and reflected ruefully that workers were regularly killed by the Civil Guard without a flicker of interest by the rightist press. General Sanjurjo, the Director-

General of the Civil Guard, visited Castilblanco. Speaking to the press, he inadvertently revealed the contempt for the working class felt by many army officers when he compared the killings to atrocities committed against Spanish soldiers by Moorish tribesmen in Morocco. He blamed the outrage on the extreme leftist Socialist deputy for Badajoz, Margarita Nelken. He also demanded justice for the Civil Guard.[48] Castilblanco was a great blow to the new Republican–Socialist coalition government, which had been formed by Manuel Azaña in mid-December, not without some difficulty. Prieto had not wanted to continue in the cabinet and only a sharp reminder of party discipline by Largo Caballero had brought him around. In fact, although the Socialist executive and the parliamentary group were in favour of continued governmental participation, after Castilblanco, collaboration was subjected to increasingly hostile scrutiny among the rank and file.[49] Castilblanco thus came as an unwelcome warning of the obstacles still to be faced on the road to reform. Even before the cabinet had had time to come to terms with it, there occurred an equally disturbing tragedy, in which the Civil Guard's hostility to the working class yet again played a leading part.

Arnedo is a village in the northern Castilian province of Logroño. One of its main sources of employment was a shoe factory, whose owner, Faustino Moro, was a man of extreme right-wing convictions. Towards the end of 1931, he sacked several of his workers for belonging to the UGT. The case was put before the local *jurado mixto*, which declared in favour of the workers, but still Moro refused to give them back their jobs. A public protest meeting was held in front of the *ayuntamiento* (town hall) on 5 January 1932. Without apparent motive, the Civil Guard opened fire, killing four women, a child and a worker, besides wounding at least thirty more. The incident had all the appearance of an act of revenge for Castilblanco, particularly in the light of the remarks made by General Sanjurjo after the killings there. As more of the wounded died, the Socialist press expressed its indignation. The Civil Guard's action seemed to justify the accusation that it was a repressive force at the service of the ruling classes. Luis Araquistain declared that it had been created by a despotic regime in order to keep the people down with terror, and that, although the monarchist regime was no more, those who had benefited from it still used the Civil Guard as a weapon against the reforming spirit of the Republic. Two weeks later, at a Traditionalist meeting in Bilbao, two Socialists and two Republicans were killed by rightist gunmen. The Civil Guard was nowhere to be seen.[50] That such a situation existed made it all the more difficult for the UGT to justify appeals for union discipline by claims that the Republic was putting an end to the injustices of the old regime.

Nevertheless, there was a strong body of feeling in the UGT that hundreds of years of oppression could not be rectified overnight. Long committed to gradualism, the union officials were determined that the democratic regime should be allowed to consolidate itself. Accordingly, when the CNT called a national general strike in the fourth week of January 1932, the condemnation from UGT leaders was unanimous. On a national level, the UGT's official note declared against any actions of solidarity. In Asturias the SOMA denounced the terrible waste of workers' energies. Even the FNTT, under its Besteirista leader, Lucio Martínez Gil, called for discipline. Not surprisingly, the UGT's reformist hierarchy was not prepared to leave the Republic 'at the mercy of extremists'. The general feeling was that anarchist activities played into the hands of reactionaries and 'erected barriers to the serene march of the proletariat towards emancipation'.[51] After all, some visible progress was being made, despite the hostility of the Right and the economic depression. This was particularly true in the field of labour legislation, but in education too great strides were being made. Between 1908 and 1930, the monarchy had built 11,128 schools, an average of 505 per year. In its first year alone, the Republic had built 7000.[52]

Yet, despite this evidence that the Republic was worth defending, there was still a perceptible slackening of Socialist enthusiasm for continued participation in the government. This was revealed at a meeting of the UGT National Committee on 1 February 1932, only a week after the anarchist strike had been put down, with considerable severity, especially in the Alto Llobregat in Catalonia. The UGT leadership had little sympathy for CNT adventurism. Nevertheless, it was impossible to ignore the invidious position of a government containing Socialists apparently reserving its greatest energies for the repression of strikes. The rank and file did not always take the long-term view. Antonio Muñoz, one of the leaders of the Federation of Printing Workers, expressed concern that the presence of Socialists in the government was damaging relations between the PSOE and the UGT masses. This was understandable, since the government was responsible, in theory at least, for whatever the Civil Guard did. Muñoz also said that, because the hopes raised by the coming of the Republic had been so great, disappointment at the slowness of reform was all the more acute. Alleging that much of this disappointment stemmed from the fact that the Socialist ministers were helping to defend the bourgeois economy, he appealed for them to withdraw from the cabinet. When the issue was debated, however, persuasive speeches by Largo Caballero and De los Ríos caused the meeting to pass a resolution of solidarity with the ministers.[53]

For the moment, the union bureaucracy was committed to the continuation of its policy of restraining militancy. Other advantages of the Republic aside, there was one positive consequence of Largo's tenure at the Ministry of Labour which could not but influence union officials – the UGT recruiting boom. In the first months of 1932, new members were flocking in at the rate of 4000–5000 per week. However, 2000–3000 of these were joining the FNTT.[54] If discipline were to be maintained, progress would have to be made on the agrarian problem. Yet in all sectors of the economy the depression was beginning to bite, and the rank-and-file workers were being impelled to militancy by the actions of the employers. The devaluation of the pound sterling lowered the return on Spanish agricultural exports and made British coal more competitive. This provided the excuse for an offensive against the unions by both landlords and mine-owners. Perhaps the most remarkable feature of the spring of 1932 was the restraint shown by both the FNTT and the SOMA in the face of intense hostility.

The theme of the UGT's May Day manifesto for 1932 could hardly have been more reformist: 'For democracy and the forty-hour week!' It typified the mood of the entire movement. The FNTT, for instance, was under intense pressure, yet did not waver in its counsels of moderation. At the beginning of the year, with the olive harvest over, there was massive unemployment in Andalusia. In addition, landowners were systematically ignoring the law concerning obligatory cultivation and were not undertaking essential agricultural tasks. In places where the authorities sent workers into estates to do the crucial jobs (a procedure known as *alojamiento*), the owners refused to pay them.[55] Throughout La Mancha, members of the FNTT were being refused work simply because they were trade unionists. The landworkers union stood firm in its policy of moderation and ordered its members not to be provoked. In the second week of February, 200 delegates, representing 80,000 members of the union from Andalusia and Extremadura, met at Montilla in Córdoba for a congress. They resolved to avoid all extremism and to meet attacks with the tactics advised by the UGT nationally. Moreover, at a time when its members were becoming impatient at the government's failure to produce an agrarian reform, the FNTT's newspaper reiterated that reform would take years and warned members not to expect too much.[56]

Considering the provocation to which the *jornaleros* were subject, it was remarkable that the summer did not see even more rural conflict than did in fact break out. On 1 April, in Miguel Esteban (Toledo), the local landowners organised a demonstration of their fixed employees (*pegados*), and during this a worker was shot and the Casa del Pueblo stormed. Boulders were dropped down a well in which it was believed that the local UGT president was working.[57] This and similar incidents led to a demand in the Cortes for the disarming of the caciques. The howl of protest from the rightist press was revealing of the attitudes of the large landowners. If their guns were taken away, it was claimed, they would be forced to use less dignified weapons, such as clubs and knives, and with greater frequency.[58] In this context, the FNTT continued to advocate moderation, despite pressure for action from the local rank-and-file organisations. Violence and extremism were condemned, especially in the case of a Communist-inspired rising at Villa Don Fadrique (Toledo) on 8 July, in which three workers were killed.[59] However, the owners' campaign against the Republic's social legislation was making the rural masses, already impatient for agrarian reform, even more desperate. Yet the nearest that the FNTT leadership got to militant action was in protesting to the government about the owners' refusal to abide by the labour laws, and about the slow passage of the agrarian statute. In fact, 83 per cent of all the infractions of labour edicts in 1932 were committed by employers, according to Ministry of Labour statistics.[60] While the rightist press inveighed against the agrarian reform and praised the existing land system, the Agrarian deputies in the Cortes organised systematic obstruction of the bill's passage. Given the conservative tone of the bill, the FNTT press could not but reflect on the intransigence of the possessing classes.[61] The rank and file increasingly took matters into their own hands, joining anarchist workers in machine-breaking and strike action throughout the summer.

A similarly conflictive situation was developing in Asturias. The Republic had opened up to the miners the possibility of essential reforms in the application of safety regulations, accident legislation, working conditions and pensions. However, the mine-owners were unwilling to accept the increase in costs which these reforms involved. Profits were falling as the industrial depression hit demand. Imported British coal was 12 pesetas cheaper per tonne than the inferior Asturian variety. Thus, reforms like the introduction of the seven-hour day became challenges to the existing system. The owners were determined to reduce wages, increase hours and lay workers off. The SOMA's initial response to this crisis was to condemn strikes, since the leadership feared that a stoppage would result in temporary coal imports, allowing the owners to build up stocks, and, when the strike was over, begin sackings. In its May Day manifesto, the SOMA declared that its first priority had always been to obtain social concessions from the coal-owners without violent conflicts or unnecessary cost to the workers. Yet moderation was becoming increasingly difficult. After the *jurado mixto* for the mines introduced improved working conditions, the miners began to experience delay in receiving their wages. Despite the miners' declared readiness to accept work-sharing schemes, the owners began to close down some pits. The SOMA claimed that the mines could be made profitable if properly run, and called for nationalisation. Union officials were convinced that the owners' actions were designed simply to break the new work agreements. With great reluctance, they called a total stoppage for 15 May, appealing to the government to prevent the monarchist coal-owners from sabotaging the Republic. For the moment at least, the strike was successful in holding back most of the threatened closures.[62]

The difficulty of the Socialist position can be easily imagined. In order to justify appeals for rank-and-file patience and to counter Communist accusations of 'social fascism', some visible reforms were essential. Yet the economic situation and the hostility of the employers made it almost impossible to translate paper reform into practice. Nevertheless, the Socialist movement still stuck to its self-appointed task of watch-dog of the Republic, albeit with growing inner doubts. On 24 June the UGT issued a manifesto underlining the absurdity of strikes at a time of high unemployment:

> Even if they are carried out peacefully, the final balance of strikes originating in the unemployment crisis can be no other than the loss of wages for those fortunate enough to have work. Our comrades should see that all the strikes called in protest against unemployment have failed ... and, in many cases, the number of unemployed has increased rather than diminished.

Instead of striking, the manifesto urged, the workers should devote their energies to forcing employers to fulfil work contracts and to apply the existing legislation. How this was to be done without recourse to strike action was not specified. Indeed, strikes were condemned yet again as playing into the hands of the extremists of Right and Left.[63]

If anything, opposition to the reforming intentions of the government tended to confirm to the Socialist ministers that their participation was essential. There remained less now of that conviction that, by collaborating with the Republic, they would be helping the bourgeoisie to carry out its historic role of destroying feudalism. The rise of fascism abroad and the determined resistance to reform of both the urban and rural bourgeoisie at home indicated the erroneous nature of the party's analysis of Spain's development. However, the conclusion drawn from this was that, if progress to reform was less and slower than had been hoped, without the Socialists in the government it would have been virtually non-existent. This was illustrated in July by the Socialist reaction to a speech by Lerroux in Zaragoza, in which he advocated their departure from the government. The animosity between Lerroux and the Socialists was growing ever more intense. Not without reason, they regarded him as corrupt and power-hungry.[64] They were particularly disturbed by the fact that, in his quest for power, he had moved considerably to the Right, accepting into his party many monarchist landowners from the south.[65] Lerroux, in his turn, saw the Socialists as an obstacle to the power which he, as the senior Republican, felt was his by right.

Lerroux was in touch with Sanjurjo and other generals who were plotting a rising. In his speech, therefore, he said that the country was under the threat of a military dictatorship because of injuries done by the Republic to the Church and the army. If the Socialists left the government, all would be well. At best, it was a clumsy attempt at intimidation. Largo Caballero was furious and inspired a joint PSOE–UGT manifesto on 16 July. Not only did the manifesto state the Socialist movement's determination to meet any threat of a coup with resolute action, but it also rejected in unmistakable terms Lerroux's attempted blackmail. On 20 July, Prieto rose in the Cortes to clarify the manifesto in rather more measured and statesmanlike language. Reiterating the Socialist determination to stay in the government until the passing of the auxiliary laws to the Constitution, he exposed the fatuity of Lerroux's arguments. He pointed out that the measures which had provoked the enmity of the generals were not the work of the Socialists. If the Socialist presence in the government was being attacked by the Republic's enemies, then, according to Prieto, that proved how it strengthened the regime. It was not without significance that *El Debate* had printed an editorial praising Lerroux's speech as evidence of the success of the great rightist propaganda campaign against the Constitution. Lerroux was forced to back down.[66]

General Sanjurjo's rising took place as planned on 10 August. It was a fiasco. Confident that the government could deal with it, the UGT ordered its militants not to leave their work. In a sense, this attack on the Republic by one of the heroes of the old regime, a monarchist general, benefited the government, by generating a wave of pro-Republican fervour. It was this which made possible, on 9 September, the passing of the agrarian reform bill, which had been delayed for so long in parliament. Mild and contradictory as the reform was, the anarchists denounced it as a farce. Although the FNTT had already warned its members not to expect too much, the disappointment felt in its ranks could not be hidden. The second congress of the Federation was held almost immediately after the passing of the agrarian reform bill. Besteiro, addressing the congress, condemned the excessively legalistic language in which the bill was couched. On 1 October the FNTT issued a manifesto expressing its disappointment at the unwieldy and bureaucratic structure of the Instituto de Reforma Agraria. The fact that the workers' representation in the institute was far outnumbered by agronomists, technicians and others (including even a mortgage-bank representative) was seen as confirmation that the reform would not be far-reaching.[67]

Although the reform was limited, it provoked the landowners into a declaration of all-out war on the Republic. A determination to break the reforming legislation passed by the Republican–Socialist coalition had long been apparent, but never before had the Right expressed itself so openly. The Bloque Agrario of Salamanca spearheaded a campaign to get owners not to cultivate their lands. Claiming that the wages decreed by the provincial *jurado mixto* were ruinously high, the Bloque circularised the landowners, large and small, of the province, asking them to sign a pledge not to cultivate their lands. The provincial governor had the governing body of the Bloque arrested.[68] Immediately, the political representatives of the Bloque, Gil Robles, Cándido Casanueva and Lamamié de Clairac, went into action to carry the dispute beyond the narrow confines of the province. According to Gil Robles, the absurdly high wages being paid to day-labourers did not make it economically viable to sow crops. Although he claimed to be thereby representing the interests of the smallholders, who were indeed badly hit by the increase in wages, he did not acknowledge that the Bloque's tactic could be carried out only by those large landlords who could turn their land over to pasture. In a vehement Cortes speech, in which he defended the call for rural lock-out, he produced a number of contentious figures, purporting to show that day-labourers were earning fifteen pesetas per day. In reality, the day-wage decreed in the mixed jury's *bases de trabajo* (work conditions) was five pesetas.[69]

These figures become more meaningful when examined in context. To begin with, Gil Robles's figure can be discarded, since it is inconceivable that some of the most anti-Republican landowners in Spain would pay three times more than the officially decreed wage. It must also be remembered that these were harvest wages, from which the *braceros* had to save for the six to eight months of unemployment which faced them. Moreover, not all the *braceros* could find work even at harvest-time.[70] Yet Gil Robles had stated in the Cortes that 'Previously there existed a regime of oppression in the countryside, but things have now gone radically to the other extreme.' What did five pesetas per day mean in 1932? Taking no account of the need to save for the months without work or to repay credit advanced by the village shopkeeper, an average three-child family needed more than thirty-five pesetas per week in order to attain the most meagre subsistence diet. Such a diet never contained more than secondary sources of protein, since meat, fish and eggs were beyond the means of the day-labourer.[71] It is not without significance that at this time there were growing numbers of thefts of acorns and other livestock fodder from large estates. The Right did not hesitate to brand the FNTT's members as common thieves, without pausing to reflect that hunger rather than perversity drives men to steal acorns. If, as Gil Robles claimed, the *labradores* could not plant crops unless wages were drastically reduced, then he was admitting that the existing economic system depended for its survival on the rural labourers' accepting starvation wages.[72]

The improvements in working conditions introduced by the Republic constituted an economic challenge to all landowners. The hardest-hit were naturally the smallholders. However, while securing the votes of farmers for Acción Popular, the rightist campaign against (allegedly) inflated rural wages ignored the extent to which much of the hardship suffered by leaseholders and sharecroppers was a consequence of the unfavourable leasing arrangements imposed upon them by their landlords. The limits of Acción Popular's concern for the smallholders were to be revealed unequivocally by the group's unremitting opposition to any attempts to introduce leasehold reform. There is little doubt that, in the 1932 protest over rural wages, the propaganda value among the small farmers was considerable, but their interests were really marginal. The call for the abandonment of cultivation had more directly political ends than a determination to improve the cash-flow of the smallholders. The central issue of the autumn 1932 rural lock-out was the existence of the agrarian legislation introduced by the Republic.

Even taking into account the profit squeeze caused by the decrees of Largo Caballero, many *latifundios* were far from the economic ruin depicted by Gil Robles. In wheat-growing areas, for instance, profits made by the larger farmers were quite substantial.[73] In other areas growing export crops, that was, of course, not the case. Nevertheless, the owners' refusal to plant crops was not motivated entirely by the economic problems of the day. The FNTT response to the lock-out showed that there was more at stake than just economic self-defence. If it is not worth the owners' effort to cultivate their land, declared *El Obrero de la Tierra* on 8 October, let the land be turned over to the FNTT's members, who will cultivate it collectively and scrape from it a far better living than under the present system. However, armed guards prevented the labourers from entering the estates and there were increasing numbers of clashes throughout the following year.

The determination of the big owners to put an end to the Republican legislation seemed to be justified by the fact that there were many owners who fell in between the categories of *latifundista* and subsistence smallholder. Their sympathies were not unnaturally with the big landlords. They were Catholics, read the local rightist press and were *labradores*, like their more powerful neighbours. And, above all, the Republican–Socialist attempt to end starvation wages for the *jornaleros* was costing them money. In a period of prosperity, the almost irreconcilable conflict of interest on the land would certainly have been softened by a reduction of surplus labour, drawn off to the industrial towns, and by an increase in productivity, stimulated by irrigation and fertilisers. However, the economic depression merely exaggerated the fundamental dichotomy highlighted unconsciously by Gil Robles: either there existed starving labourers or there had to be a transfer of wealth away from the large owners, with many of the middle and small farmers suffering in the process. A collective solution incorporating the smallholders would perhaps have been a viable answer. But the purpose of the lock-out proposed by the Bloque Agrario was not to hasten a future agrarian solution which benefited the greatest number but to force a return to the pre-1931 situation.

It was thus becoming increasingly difficult for the Besteirista leadership of the FNTT to contain the militancy of its followers. The visible improvements which had hitherto been the best justification for discipline were now being eroded by the employers' offensive. Another sector of the UGT which was being pushed towards militancy and yet managed to retain its faith in the government was the SOMA. More mines were closing down and the miners were being asked to accept short-time working, reduced wages and even payment in kind. In the context of this crisis, it infuriated miners and pit-owners alike that the total production of Spanish mines was still 2 million tonnes less than the nation's coal consumption. The SOMA called an extraordinary congress to debate strike action. Held on 11 September, the congress called on the government to solve the coal crisis and resolved on a general strike to start on 19 September if nothing were done. In fact, the government was frantically trying to find a solution. The Minister for the Navy was examining the possibility of Asturian coal being used in warships. Railway chiefs were being pressured to use Spanish coal too. Undertakings were made that the existing legislation on coal imports would be tightened up. In the light of this, the SOMA called off the strike. 'Never has a government taken so much interest in our problems,' said its declaration. To go ahead with the strike was felt to be simply counter-productive intransigence.[74]

The whole question of whether or not the Republic represented a positive benefit for the workers was thus foremost in the minds of delegates to the PSOE and UGT congresses held in Madrid in October 1932. The Thirteenth Congress of the PSOE opened on 6 October. Since the previous year's extraordinary congress, the Besteirista faction, as hostile as ever to Socialist participation in the government, had regained control of the Agrupación Socialista Madrileña. Besteiro himself, however, had considerably modified his position. Prieto put forward a motion in favour of continued ministerial participation. Speaking effectively in its favour, Besteiro said, 'If the Socialist ministers leave the government, the political equilibrium of the Republic will be broken, the life of the Cortes will be considerably shortened and premature elections could be too dangerous an adventure.' Prieto's proposal was passed by 23,718 votes to 6356. The main issue debated in the congress was the failed strike of December 1930. Largo considered that the party had been betrayed by the machinations of the Besteiristas Andrés Saborit and Manuel Muiño. Apart from this desire to settle an old score, however, the issue, concerning as it did the party's role in establishing the Republic, had some relevance for the question of continued collaboration in the government. After a vitriolic struggle between Largo and Saborit, the debate had to be cut short lest it lead to a schism in the party. The activities of those who had been in favour of a strike – that is to say, Largo, Prieto, De los Ríos and many of the rank and file – were approved. Largo Caballero was also voted president of the PSOE by 15,817 votes to Besteiro's 14,261. Besteiro had not stood for the post. However, it is difficult to say whether the high number of votes that he received reflected anything more than veneration for a respected and senior member of the party. His apparent approval of ministerial participation may also have had some effect on the voting.[75] Whatever the case, the Thirteenth PSOE Congress represented the last major Socialist vote of confidence in the efficacy of governmental collaboration.

The PSOE congress ended on 13 October. On the following day, the Seventeenth Congress of the UGT began. The contrast in mood between the two assemblies was remarkable. The UGT congress was a major triumph for Besteiro. This was not entirely surprising, given the way in which UGT congresses were organised. Each national section of the UGT – railwaymen, printers, bakers, building workers, miners, land-workers, and so on – was represented by its own union officials and enjoyed a voting strength corresponding to its overall membership. This meant that the block votes cast for a given federation at the congress represented the views of that federation's syndical bureaucracy, and not necessarily of its rank and file.[76] This put Largo Caballero at a consider-able disadvantage since, although he enjoyed immense popularity among the workers in general, he did not control the votes of a specific union. The Besteiristas, on the other hand, did enjoy such control – through Saborit (printers), Trifón Gómez (railwaymen) and Lucio Martínez Gil (FNTT).

An illness, which was probably no more than diplomatic, kept Largo away from the congress. Yet again the strike of December 1930 was discussed, and this time the behaviour of the executive committee of the UGT, which had been hostile to the strike, was approved. A new executive was elected, with Besteiro as president, and all his senior followers in key positions. Largo was in fact elected as secretary of the UGT. However, he immediately sent a letter of resignation, claiming that the congress's vindication of the 1930 executive constituted a dis-avowal of his own activities in December of that year. The other Caba-lleristas elected, Rafael Henche and Pascual Tomás, also resigned, leaving the UGT executive entirely in Besteirista hands. Largo com-plained that the block votes of Lucio Martínez Gil's FNTT and Trifón Gómez's Sindicato Nacional Ferroviario went against the spirit of the congress.[77] That was possible but difficult to prove, then or now.

In fact, rightist opposition to reform and the growth of fascism abroad were soon to be undermining Largo Caballero's faith in the efficacy of governmental collaboration with the left Republicans. Nevertheless, this change, when it came, would not bridge the gulf between him and the Besteiristas. They might all have been reformists but they were reform-ists of radically different kinds. The union officials who followed Besteiro felt it their duty to stand back and let the bourgeoisie get on with its historic task. In the meanwhile, they would get on with defend-ing the working class within the existing economic system as they had done under the monarchy. Largo Caballero's views were more prag-matic. He was aware that his participation in the government had led to great advances in the living conditions of the Spanish working class and to a massive increase in UGT recruiting. Since both of these achievements had been his lifelong ambitions, he would do everything in his power to prevent a return to pre-1931 conditions. Now in late 1932, the Right was mounting a challenge to his reforms and to the UGT masses' expectation of continued reform. If to the Besteiristas this was proof that collaboration was dangerous to the working class, to Largo Caballero it could only be a stimulus to defend his work so far.

Thus, 1932 saw the beginnings of the radicalisation of Largo Caballero. Above all, this was a response to the mood of the rank and file, rendered impatient by the slowness of reform and by the success of right-wing obstruction of its application. However, it was also strongly influenced by a growing awareness of the spread of fascism. Largo's closest advisers, Carlos de Baraibar, Luis Araquistain and Antonio Ramos Oliveira, kept him informed of the failure of social democratic reformism around Europe.[78] The belief was emerging within the PSOE that a fascist role might be played in Spain by Gil Robles. Accordingly, the rightist resistance to reform was taken by Largo as proof that, far from retreating along Besteirista lines into classical reformism, the Socialists should perhaps advance to some more radical form of social organisation. However, this conviction was a long time in gestation, and it was not until he was being forced out of the government in the summer of 1933 that he began the process of public radicalisation. Even then, given his fundamental moderation in practice, it never went beyond rhetoric.

Two factors during the winter of 1932–3 made Largo begin to reflect on the inadequacies of reformism as a means of changing economic structures in a time of depression. The first was the employers' offensive, which put great strain on the discipline of UGT militants. The second was the obstruction of all government legislation by the Radical Party. In both cases, the section of the UGT most directly hit was the FNTT. At a national level, with Besteiristas controlling the executive, the FNTT remained committed to moderation and gradual reformism. The reports which it had sent to both the PSOE and UGT congresses had laid special stress on the need for stricter enforcement of existing legislation.[79] At a local level, however, rank and file militancy was becoming impatient with the ineffectiveness of that legislation. In Salamanca, for instance, the success of the employers in evading the rulings of the mixed jury was creating intense bitterness among the local federation of landworkers. Thousands of workers had not been paid their harvest wages and yet not one landowner had been fined. The local leaders, headed by teacher-turned-lawyer José Andrés y Manso, felt that, by obeying UGT discipline and submitting to the mixed jury, the workers were worse off. Largo Caballero was held 'morally and materially responsible'.[80] It was no longer possible to restrain the militancy of the local workers, who had exhausted every legal means of protecting their rights. There was talk of seceding from the UGT. This almost certainly had a considerable effect on Largo Caballero. He had, after all, been intensely anxious about 'what the workers would say' if he wore tails at the President's inauguration.[81] His sudden change of tactic at the end of the Dictadura was the result of his realisation that the workers were leaving the UGT in protest at the policy of collaboration. He was unlikely to react differently now.

In protest at the landowners' failure to pay the wages that they owed and at the inadequate functioning of rural social legislation, the Salamanca Federation of Socialist Workers called a general strike on 10 December 1932. The strike was almost total and paralysed the province for ten days. A certain amount of violence broke out, but it was quickly repressed by the forces of order. From Madrid, the UGT executive called for a rapid end to a senseless strike. Not only was the call ignored, but it was regarded as evidence of the betrayal of the rank and file by the national union bureaucracy. Given the determined intransigence of the Salamanca owners, it is difficult to see what the strike could have gained. Equally, with the unemployed driven to desperation by the lockout, appeals for patience and discipline were bound to fall on deaf ears and, indeed, provoke local bitterness against the Socialists in the government. The strike finally ended in stalemate, with prisoners being freed, the Casas del Pueblo reopened, and promises made, but not kept, to solve the problem of unemployment.[82]

Growing rank-and-file militancy was creating divisions between the central UGT hierarchy, the government and the local union leadership. So as not to lose their members to more extreme groups, local leaders were increasingly being forced to acquiesce in strike action. In Asturias, for instance, after simmering since September, a general strike was called for mid-November. The SOMA leaders, Amador Fernández, Ramón González Peña and Teodomiro Menéndez, had little choice. On the one hand, the owners were closing pits, laying off miners and ignoring safety regulations. On the other, the jointly anarchist and Communist Sindicato Unico de Obreros Mineros was increasing in both numbers and militancy. If the leaders did not go along with the miners' demands for action, the SOMA would risk losing members as it had done during the 1920s. Their demands were not extreme: simply that the government take action to remedy the crisis in the industry. Such action would involve limiting the importation of cheap scrap-iron, which was cutting demand for smelting-coal, obliging government entities to use Spanish coal and persuading consumers to reduce the immediate surplus by building up their stocks. The anarchists in the region called wide solidarity strikes, particularly in Gijón, where they had complete union hegemony. The SOMA repudiated these strikes as irresponsible. Nevertheless, they represented a growing solidarity at rank-and-file level which would gradually force the moderate UGT leadership to vie with the anarchists and Communists in militancy. The strikes ended with the defeat of the CNT in Gijón, and with government assurances to the SOMA that action would be taken to help the mines.[83]

Further evidence of the rift between the union bureaucracy and its rank-and-file militants was provided in the second half of December when the railway strike which had been narrowly averted in late 1931 threatened finally to break out. Dissidents from the Sindicato Nacional Ferroviario, in opposition to Trifón Gómez's reformist leadership, had created a rival union, the Federación de la Industria Ferroviaria, and were pushing for a revival of the claims left in abeyance the previous year. On 10 December 1932, the UGT issued a note, signed by Besteiro and Trifón Gómez, calling upon affiliated federations not to call strikes without first consulting the executive. This increased the risk of losing members, but was typical of the responsible moderation being shown by the reformist leaders. It was particularly galling for the Socialists when the Radicals, always keen to make things difficult for the government, claimed somewhat demagogically that the railwaymen's claim should be met. Prieto exposed the Radical manoeuvre in the Cortes. He adopted a patriotic line and declared that, if the strike did break out, he would not hesitate to sacrifice the interests of his party in order to defend the Republic. This was unmistakably a threat to subject the railwaymen to the same harsh treatment which had, in the main, hitherto been confined to anarchists and Communists. The strike did not take place, but several thousand members of the Sindicato Nacional Ferroviario drifted away from it.[84]

The greatest blow to Largo, and, indeed, to the entire cabinet, came in mid-January. The anarchists had organised a rising for 8 January. It was repressed without great difficulty in Catalonia, Zaragoza, Seville and Madrid. However, in the village of Casas Viejas (Cádiz), the most violent events of the rising and its repression took place. Casas Viejas (today known as Benalup de Sidonia) formed part of an area of endemic hunger and unemployment, exacerbated by the employers' boycott of the Republic. It was, if anything, even poorer than Castilblanco. The dwellings of the *braceros* consisted of a cavity in the ground, mud walls built up for about three feet, and a covering of branches. The fact that some of the best land around the village was given over to the breeding of fighting bulls only added to a situation in which, according to one observer, 'the poor were maddened with hunger and the rich were maddened with fear'. When the FAI (Federación Anarquista Ibérica) declaration of libertarian communism reached the local Centro Obrero, the villagers hesitantly followed instructions from Barcelona. Assuming that their strike would be linked to others in Jerez and Cádiz, they did not expect bloodshed. They decided, rather naïvely, to wipe the slate clean and offer the local landowners and the Civil Guard the opportunity to join the new collective enterprise. To their surprise, the Civil Guard replied to the offer with gunfire. Many fled to the fields and some took refuge in the hut of the septuagenarian Curro Cruz, known as Seisdedos. Reinforcements were brought in and, after a night-long siege, the Civil Guard and the Assault Guard (Guardia de Asalto, the highly trained urban armed police) set fire to Seisdedos's house. Inside were Seisdedos, his son-in-law, his two sons, his cousin, his daughter, his daughter-in-law and his two grandchildren. Those who tried to escape were shot down. Another twelve people were also shot in cold blood.[85]

The immediate reaction of the rightist press was relatively favourable, since it had long been calling for harsh measures of law and order in the countryside.[86] However, when the enemies of the government realised what political capital could be made out of the incident, a great cry of indignation went up. The anarchists were naturally incensed, but rightist groups which normally applauded such actions by the Civil Guard also added their voices to the campaign. Before the full details were known, all three Socialist ministers, especially Prieto, expressed to Azaña their satisfaction at the repression of the anarchist rising. Fernando de los Ríos said that what had happened at Casas Viejas was necessary, given the anarchist antecedents of the province of Cádiz. Largo Caballero advised vigorous measures as long as the unrest continued.[87] However, despite their hostility to the anarchists, the Socialists could not approve of the gratuitous brutality displayed by the forces of order. They were angered, moreover, by the attempts of the Right and, especially, the Radicals to prove that the savage reprisals taken at Casas Viejas were the result of specific government orders.[88] That seems most unlikely in the light of the efforts made by the government to investigate the affair. Nevertheless, the smear campaign took its toll of the government's time and morale. Efforts to clear the government absorbed

109

virtually its entire efforts for the first three months of 1933. Since the campaign was linked to systematic obstruction of attempts to pass legislation through the Cortes, it demoralised the cabinet considerably.[89]

Casas Viejas and its repercussions graphically brought home to the Socialists the cost of collaboration in the government. It emphasised more than ever that, in order to defend a bourgeois Republic, they were sacrificing their credibility with the Socialist masses. That sacrifice may have seemed worthwhile in 1931, when the new regime's reforms were visibly benefiting the working class. In 1933, however, with legislation paralysed in the Cortes by the Radicals and the Agrarios and in the rural areas by the employers' boycott, only the conviction that things would be even worse if they left persuaded the Socialists to stay on in the government. The cabinet was convinced that government by Lerroux would be disastrous for reform, as well as being corrupt and inefficient.[90] Paradoxically, it was the Radical opposition which convinced the reluctant PSOE Cortes deputies to continue supporting Socialist participation in the cabinet although it took an energetic speech by Prieto to talk the PSOE executive out of abandoning the cabinet.[91]

In the spring and summer of 1933, the Socialist presence in the government increasingly assumed a defensive stance, designed largely to exclude the Radicals. Not only did this mean that little was done in the field of new legislation, but also that the component groups of the Republican–Socialist coalition were under increasing strain as the opposition widened. The Radicals, anxious for power, were drawing nearer to the rightist groups; while the Radical–Socialists were dividing into three factions, one of which opposed the government from a rightist position, another from the left. The two motives used to justify opposition were Casas Viejas and the municipal elections of April 1933.

Approximately 20 per cent of Spain's voters were going to choose new municipal councillors to replace those who had been returned unopposed in April 1931. The municipal elections of 12 April 1931 had, of course, been held under the then prevailing monarchist electoral law of 1907. According to its article 29, in any district where there were not more candidates than seats, unopposed candidates were declared elected without the need for any votes to be cast. Article 29 had traditionally been most invoked in areas dominated by *caciques*. On 12 April 1931, 29,804 candidates had been declared 'elected' in this way – 37 per cent of the total number of municipal council seats, leaving 20.3 per cent of the electorate without a vote. They were concentrated in the conservative provinces of the two Castiles, León, Aragón and Navarre. Catalonia, the large urban conglomerations and much of the south were not taking part in the elections. Of the 16,000 councillors elected on 23 April 1933, approximately 10,000 were Republicans of one kind or another. Of these, 1826 were Socialists, 3222 were left Republicans supporting groups represented in the government, 2479 were Radicals and the remainder other Republicans; 4954 were declared rightists. Since the areas in which voting occurred were traditionally rightist and, indeed, as the previous (April 1931) elections had shown, were dominated by the local *caciques*, this was a good showing by the government parties, particularly in the aftermath of Casas Viejas. Yet it did not meet the expectations of either the Socialists or the left Republicans and was hailed by the Right and the Radicals as a national plebiscite against the government and the Socialists.[92]

The parliamentary obstruction which followed the elections was seen by Besteiro as a good pretext for Socialist withdrawal from the government.[93] Largo did not agree, largely because the growing social conflict which was visible in the rural areas convinced him that his presence was essential to protect the interests of the working class. Considerable bitterness was created by the slowness with which the Instituto de Reforma Agraria was functioning, not least because much of the delay was the consequence of the hearings of the grandees' claims for exemption from the September 1932 confiscation of aristocratic lands.[94] An extended decree on *laboreo forzoso* introduced by the Radical-Socialist Minister of Agriculture, Marcelino Domingo, infuriated the landowners but did little to mitigate the growing crisis of unemployment in rural areas. If the decree was not respected, an inspector could be called in. He then had a week in which to report to the Central Technical Committee of the province, which in its turn had eight days in which to pass sentence. If the sentence went against the employer and he still did not undertake the tasks prescribed in the decree, then the local union was empowered to start the work after twelve days had passed. Even then, there was no mechanism to make the owners pay for the work done.[95] Accordingly, in village after village in the south, every day the unemployed thronged the market places. Violence was accumulating. Some estates were invaded. Hungry *braceros* stole acorns and olives. Bloodshed was not uncommon, as the owners opened fire on workers who were trespassing and stealing their crops, or workers attacked owners who denied them work.[96] The latent violence at a local level was transmitted to national politics, where the mutual hostility of the PSOE and the CEDA was growing rapidly.

This hostility was accentuated by the Socialist conviction that the CEDA was likely to fulfil a fascist role in Spain, a charge only casually denied by the Catholic party, if at all.[97] From this belief two very different conclusions were drawn. Largo was soon to be proclaiming that, if bourgeois democracy was incapable of preventing the rise of fascism, it was up to the working class to seek different political forms with which to defend itself. Besteiro, on the other hand, drew a far more defensive conclusion. Throughout the spring and summer of 1933 he made speeches condemning the collaborationist line and advocating that the Socialist movement withdraw entirely into the syndical sphere. Besteiro was celebrated as the PSOE's most accomplished Marxist. Yet, although his speeches had a veneer of Marxist rhetoric, they totally failed to come to terms with the phenomenon of fascism. The line taken by Largo, although hardly the last word in theoretical sophistication, was to be rather nearer to some of the more advanced Marxist thought on the subject. The differences between the two were greatly to accentuate the existing divisions within the PSOE.

Since Besteiro held the rigidly orthodox Marxist view that Spain must pass through a classic bourgeois revolution and concluded that the working class should not get involved in the bourgeoisie's historic task, he considered his stance to be more revolutionary than that of Largo Caballero. Thus, on 26 March, at the Agrupación Socialista Madrileña's commemoration of the fiftieth anniversary of Marx's death, he condemned the reformism of the collaborationists. Denouncing the insufficiency of reformism at a time of economic crisis, he also pronounced against radicalism. In other words, he was counselling inaction. His apparent revolutionary purity was no more than extremely puritanical reformism. This was confirmed on 2 July when he spoke at the Casa del Pueblo of Mieres in a tribute to Manuel Llaneza, the great Asturian union leader. He reaffirmed his view that the bourgeoisie should be left to carry out its own task and advanced the remarkable view that the Italian and German socialists were suffering fascism as a consequence of having participated in bourgeois governments. The implication of this view was that, if the socialists had not tried to defend the working class with the backing of the state, they would not have provoked the bourgeoisie into turning to fascism. The notion was extended on 26 July in the closing speech to the congress of the Sindicato Nacional Ferroviario. Echoing some of the ideas put forward by Turati during the period in which the Italian socialists were being subjected to the attacks of the fascist *squadristi*, Besteiro claimed that the Spanish Socialists must not risk provoking the vengeance of their enemies. Yet, he also declared at a meeting of the National Committee of the UGT that fascism was 'the noise of mice in an old house which frightens the cowardly'.[98]

Largo's position was very different. Believing that the Republic was seriously threatened by fascism, and fully aware of the German and Italian socialists' failure to oppose fascism in time, he advocated not retreat but a seizing of the initiative. Throughout the first half of 1933 the Socialist press had fully registered both its interest in events in Germany and its belief that Gil Robles and his followers intended to follow in the footsteps of Hitler and Mussolini. Largo Caballero received frequent letters from his friend, Luis Araquistain, now the Spanish Ambassador in Berlin, which commented on the growing power of the Nazis. Now, in the summer, Largo and his advisers became conscious of a united assault by both industrial and agricultural employers on the Republic's social legislation.[99] It was obvious that the days of Socialist presence in the government were numbered, since Alcalá Zamora had already tried to persuade Azaña to form a cabinet without PSOE participation. Thus Largo Caballero set about trying to regain his close contact with the rank and file, which had faded somewhat during his tenure of a ministry.

Largo's public revelation of his newly acquired radical views began with a speech, in the Cine Pardiñas in Madrid on 23 July, to the most militant sector of the Socialist Party, its youth movement (the Federación de Juventudes Socialistas). One of his main reasons for breaking his silence, he said, was the growing hostility against the Socialist movement. His speech was essentially moderate and was primarily concerned with defending ministerial collaboration against the criticisms of Besteiro. However, a hardening of attitude was apparent. He took issue with Besteiro's claims that governmental participation had brought fascism upon the heads of the German and Italian socialists and pointed out that fascism was the bourgeoisie's last resort at a time of capitalist crisis. From this he went on to emphasise that the PSOE and the UGT had a duty to prevent the establishment of fascism in Spain. If this meant seizing power, then the Socialists, albeit with the greatest reluctance, should be prepared to do so. It is conceivable that the principal motive behind the speech was a desire to warn the President and the Radicals of the consequences of forcing the PSOE out of the government. However, the enthusiastic cheers which greeted the more extremist portions of his speech could not but confirm Largo in the validity of his new line.[100]

Clearly the PSOE was dividing as the employers' offensive provoked varying responses in the Socialist movement. This was starkly revealed at the summer school held by the FJS at Torrelodones near Madrid in the first half of August. Besteiro was the first of the faction-leaders to address the young Socialists. His speech was mainly concerned to refute the new line adopted by Largo in the Cine Pardiñas. For him, the aggression of the capitalists was not a reason for going onto the attack, but rather a test of discipline: 'If a general staff sends its army into battle in unfavourable circumstances, then it is fully responsible for the consequent defeat and demoralisation.' Without actually naming him, Besteiro accused Largo of adopting a radical line to gain cheap popularity with the masses and, in doing so, of risking a proletarian defeat. He condemned any talk of Socialist dictatorship to defeat fascism as 'an absurdity and a vain illusion'. 'It is often more revolutionary', he said, 'to resist the collective madness than to allow oneself to be carried along by it.' His speech revealed him to be either unaware of contemporary post-Hitlerian currents of Marxist thinking on fascism or else unsympathetic to them. It was received with some hostility and *El Socialista* refused to publish it.[101]

On the following day, 6 August, Prieto spoke. His language was far more moderate than Besteiro's had been, although he also warned against the dangers of a too facile radicalism. He defended, as Largo had done, the achievements of the Republic so far. Only someone who had expected the Republic to change Spain's economic structure overnight, he declared, could be dissatisfied, particularly in view of the disastrous economic depression. He did acknowledge that the savagery of the ruling class's attacks on the Republic's legislation and on the Socialists was infuriating. In fact, in the most radical, and inevitably the most applauded, part of his speech, he reflected that it might have been better to have taken some reprisals in 1931 for the years of oppression that had gone before. Nevertheless, he called upon his audience to consider that the strength of the rightist assault threw doubts on the Socialists' capacity to challenge the immense economic power which still remained in the hands of the upper classes. Realism, said Prieto, showed that 'our kingdom is not of this moment'. The advocates of radicalism had compared Spain in 1933 to Russia in 1917 to justify, as the bolsheviks had done, a leap across the bourgeois democratic stage in the revolution. Prieto pointed out that it was not a valid comparison, since the weakness of the ruling classes and their state and military institutions in Russia in 1917 could hardly be said to be reflected in the Spain of 1933. He also warned that, even if a Socialist seizure of power were possible, capitalists in other parts of Europe were unlikely to stand idly by. It was a skilful speech, accepting the moral justification of radicalism, but rejecting the notion that there should be a dramatic change of party policy. Realistic as it was, the speech was not what

114

Prieto's youthful audience wanted to hear. It was received coolly, if not quite so icily as Besteiro's had been, and was not published by *El Socialista*.[102]

Largo Caballero was not at first scheduled to speak at the summer school. However, leaders of the FJS informed him of the disappointment created by the speeches of Besteiro and Prieto. Largo, always proud of his rapport with the masses, was not a man to ignore the feelings of the rank and file. During the Dictadura, he had shown ample evidence of what Trotsky called 'tailism', or leading from behind. The enthusiasm of the rank-and-file militants had turned him into a Republican then; now it was apparently turning him into a revolutionary. His speech was on the impossibility of truly socialist legislation within the confines of bourgeois democracy. It was a rather bitter speech, reflecting his dismay at the virulence of rightist attacks. He claimed to have been radicalised by the intransigence of the bourgeoisie: 'We thought before that capitalism was a little more noble, that it would be more accommodating, more open to compromise. No, capitalism in Spain is obdurate [*cerril*], no one can convince it.' Nevertheless, Largo affirmed a continuing commitment to legality, despite talking of a future transition to socialism. Just as it alarmed the Right, the speech delighted the young Socialists because of its implication that the party would soon be adopting a full-scale revolutionary policy.[103]

To a certain extent, Largo Caballero's revolutionary rhetoric was not entirely what it seemed to the youthful radicals. It was not just the result of seeing the Marxist light. An element of personal rivalry with Besteiro, and even perhaps with Prieto, cannot be discounted. It is also possible that, with his new stance, Largo was hoping to warn the President against trying to replace the Republican–Socialist coalition with the Radicals. However, Largo's new revolutionism responded above all to a sense of outrage at the mounting aggression of employers against social legislation and the effect that this was having on the UGT. Throughout the summer, evidence had been growing that the mixed juries and the various social laws were simply being ignored. Official labour exchanges were being by-passed and work was only offered to those who would renounce membership of the UGT and join patronal unions. Land was being withdrawn from cultivation. There were increasing instances of landowners firing on groups of workers. A lengthy meeting of the National Committee of the UGT, held on 16, 17 and 18 June, discussed the extent to which the Socialists' attempt to maintain worker discipline in the face of provocation was simply losing members for the union.[104] Largo was thus determined to maintain the loyalty of the rank and file.

In a sense, it was a terrible dilemma. Since the workers were being forced into increasing militancy by the employers' refusal to compromise with social legislation, Largo was effectively committing himself to ever-escalating verbal radicalism. Not to do so would be to see workers drifting away to the CNT and the Communists and into counter-productive strike action. To do so could only exacerbate the polarisation of Republican politics, as well as providing a justification for rightist extremism.[105] Moreover, even if Largo opted for the harder line called for by a growing number of militants, it was unlikely to solve the problem of employer intransigence without a corresponding advance towards active revolutionary praxis. Prieto had recognised this in his speech, but there clearly were limits to the extent to which a policy of moderation could be imposed on the rank and file, who were, after all, in the front line of an increasingly bitter class struggle. It was a dilemma which was greatly to strain Socialist unity and eventually to lead Largo to half-hearted participation in the insurrection of October 1934.

While the Socialists remained in the government, it was possible to call on the unions for discipline and patience while social reform was carried out. However, that situation was unlikely to pertain for much longer. In June, Alcalá Zamora had used Azaña's need to replace the sick Finance Minister, Jaume Carner, as an excuse to withdraw his confidence from the government. Since no one else could get a majority in the Cortes, the President was obliged to let the cabinet continue through the summer. Conscious of growing opposition to the govern-ment, and always on the look-out for a more pliant Prime Minister than Azaña, Alcalá Zamora was anxious for a change, even if it meant elections. The difficulties of remaining in power under such circum-stances were underlined in August, when the rightist deputies, with Radical complicity, managed to emasculate Marcelino Domingo's bill on rural leases, thereby belying their much vaunted concern for the smallholder.[106] In early September, despite a parliamentary vote of con-fidence for Azaña, the President decided that a conservative victory in the elections for the Tribunal of Constitutional Guarantees justified his asking Lerroux to form a government. He did so on 11 September, but could not face the Cortes without certain defeat. He governed with the Cortes closed. To the delight of the landowners, Largo Caballero's social legislation was virtually abandoned. The law of municipal boundaries was lifted in entire provinces and infractions of the law were not punished.[107]

There had long been a feeling of rage and frustration within the Socialist movement that the mild social reform achieved so far should have given rise to such fierce opposition. Now the speed with which a Republican government without the Socialists permitted the evasion of social legislation began seriously to undermine Socialist faith in bourgeois democracy. Interviewed by the FJS newspaper, *Renovación*, on 23 September, Largo Caballero declared that the new government had created grave doubts about the possibility of the workers' attaining even their minimum aspirations within the Republic. For many leftists, the rightist assault on the achievement of reformist socialism was the thin end of the wedge of fascism. It had not been a difficult association of ideas. The landowners had launched the most violent attacks on the Republic's social reforms. Hitler and Mussolini had been quick to dismantle social legislation once they were in power. The press and political representatives of the Spanish landowners never tired of praising Nazi and Fascist achievement. In August, *El Debate* had commented on Spain's need for an organisation like those ruling in Germany and Italy and hinted coyly that Acción Popular was that 'necessary organisation'.[108] Gil Robles may not have been a fascist, but the Spanish Left certainly perceived him to be one.

The working class soon felt the effects of Largo Caballero's absence from the Ministry of Labour. UGT officials complained to the National Committee that they would lose members if the executive did not make a stand against the government's abandonment of social legislation.[109] That Largo had already realised this was made clear by a speech to the tramworkers on 1 October. He declared that the first task of the Socialist movement was to protect its gains to date. For Largo, most Socialists and many Republicans, the Republic was consubstantial with its reforms; otherwise, it did not differ from the monarchy. Thus, reasoned Largo, since an assault was being made on its reforms, the Republic was in danger. The events of the previous month showed Lerroux to be a saboteur of the regime. He had already collaborated with the monarchists and the Agrarians in blocking reform. Largo went on to reflect that the vehemence of opposition to legislation that merely helped the workers to defend themselves did not bode well for the Socialists' long-term ambitions. Thus, while affirming his commitment to legality, Largo recalled the PSOE's revolutionary commitment to a complete transformation of the economic structure of society. If, he concluded, the government fell into the hands of those who would use legality and the Constitution against the working class and its aspirations, then the Socialists would have to consider leaving legality behind.[110]

117

It is likely that at this stage Largo was adopting radical positions in part as a warning to the President. However, that was soon to change. Speaking in the Cortes on the following day, Prieto declared that all Socialist commitments to the Republicans were at an end. On the day after that, the government fell.[111] Alcalá Zamora asked Diego Martínez Barrio, the deputy leader of the Radicals, to form a government which would hold elections. Marcelino Domingo persuaded Martínez Barrio that such a government should include all Republican forces, including the Socialists. Largo Caballero, after consulting the rest of the PSOE parliamentary minority, agreed, which rather confirms the premonitory element of his radicalism. However, just as it was becoming clear that Socialist participation was precluded by a constitutional technicality, there arrived news of opposition within the party proper to such a move. The PSOE executive committee had circularised the local *agrupaciones* for their opinions about collaboration with the Republicans in the next elections. The majority had opposed any such collaboration.[112] Martínez Barrio formed an exclusively Republican government on 8 October and elections were announced for 19 November.

Largo Caballero, the Federación de Juventudes Socialistas and many of the UGT rank and file went into the electoral campaign with enthusiasm and optimism. Other party leaders did not share Largo's euphoria and were uneasy about the rashness of going to the polls alone in an electoral system which favoured wide coalitions. De los Ríos confided his doubts to the American Ambassador.[113] Prieto, by including Azaña and Domingo in the Socialist list, ensured that in Bilbao there would be no division of the left-wing vote.[114] The Socialists could not match the massive propaganda campaign mounted by the Right and only began their campaign two weeks after their opponents. Largo Caballero dominated the campaign, just as Gil Robles did for the 'anti-Marxist front'. He made a tour of the country in the first half of November and his language grew more revolutionary as he travelled. That was a response first to the virulence of the rightist campaign whose leitmotiv was the need to smash socialism and secondly to the unrestrained enthusiasm of the crowds, who cheered his speeches long after they were over.[115]

On 15 October, Gil Robles had expressed his determination to establish the corporative state. Largo's speeches announced the Socialist determination to stop him doing so. On 5 November, in the Jaén bullring, the PSOE president told 12,000 workers that they should prepare to defend the Republic's achievements so far and to take them further along the road to socialism. In Albacete on 12 November, Largo was more explicit.

He claimed that the opposition to his mild reforms showed that legal reformist tactics were futile. If social progress were made impossible, as it surely would be in a rightist corporative regime, the Socialists would have to abandon bourgeois democracy and proceed to the revolutionary seizure of power. On 14 November, speaking in Murcia, Largo declared that there could never be real democracy in Spain while glaring economic oppression was still rife. He acknowledged that only the dictatorship of the proletariat could carry out the necessary economic disarmament of the bourgeoisie.[116] Such remarks, of course, much as they delighted his audiences, could not but antagonise the Right and justify its already aggressive stance. Given the strength of the Spanish Right, both economically and politically the line adopted by Prieto at Torrelodones appeared far more realistic than the objectives, understandable but unrealisable, put forward by Largo Caballero.

The election results brought bitter disappointment for the Socialists, who gained only fifty-eight seats. A variety of factors contributed to the defeat. The efficacy of the rightist propaganda campaign cannot be underestimated. The Left also claimed that there was considerable rightist pressure, in the form of bribery and intimidation, on potential leftist voters. There appears to have been considerable harassment of peasant voters in the south by Civil Guards and thugs in the pay of local landowners.[117] Many observers believe that the introduction of the female vote worked against the Left. Working-class women voted with their husbands, it is argued, while middle-class wives whose husbands voted Republican followed the advice of their confessors.[118] However, the two most potent reasons for the Left's poor showing were its electoral fragmentation and the opposition of the anarchists. Because of the Socialist refusal to ally with the left-wing Republicans, it took twice as many Socialist votes to elect a deputy as it did rightist ones. Leftist orators were greeted with cries of 'Assassin!' and chants of 'Casas Viejas' from anarchists in their audiences. In 1931, despite the CNT's apoliticism, most anarchists had voted for Republican candidates. Now they either voted Radical or else abstained. The national average of abstentions was 32 per cent; in areas of anarchist influence it was much higher. In Barcelona, Zaragoza, Huesca and Tarragona it was around 40 per cent, and in Seville, Cádiz and Málaga it was over 45 per cent. The rightist victory was, in fact, not nearly so overwhelming as it appeared. Even with the widest coalitions, including Radicals, they did not get more than 40 per cent of the vote anywhere.[119] All these factors could only serve to increase the Socialists' disillusionment with bourgeois democracy and ease the way to greater radicalisation.

4

THE POLITICS OF REPRISAL
The CEDA, the PSOE and the polarisation of 1934

Between 1931 and 1933 the Republican–Socialist coalition had endeavoured to create a socially progressive Republic. In a context of world depression, it is inconceivable that their programme of tentative reform could have resolved the highly conflictive social and economic problems inherited from the monarchy. Nevertheless, Left Republicans and Socialists believed that they had done enough to distinguish the new regime from the old and to set Spain off on its first faltering steps to modernity. They agreed that any step backward from the minimum achieved so far would be disastrous for the majority of the population. The Socialists, however, had been disturbed by the vehemence of opposition to what they regarded as basic humanitarian legislation. In the light of this, a growing sector of the trade union movement and the FJS, encouraged by rather reckless rhetorical support from Largo Caballero, were losing faith in the possibility that bourgeois democracy would allow the establishment of even a minimal social justice, let alone full-blown socialism.

A variety of reasons had led many of the Socialist rank and file to this conclusion. The immense rightist propaganda campaign against the Republic and its reforming projects had had sufficient success to convince them that the democratic process could be easily manipulated. Considerable disillusionment was created by the inability of a large parliamentary majority to overcome determined minority obstruction of reform. The ease with which employers evaded the provisions of the legislation that had been passed further undermined faith in the equitable nature of the bourgeois regime. Of even more importance was an awareness of the fate of similar regimes abroad. The Spanish Right had not hidden its sympathy for the achievements of Hitler and Mussolini. The CEDA had many of the trappings of a fascist organisation, with its rallies, its uniformed youth movement and its blanket propaganda techniques. During the campaign for the November elections, Gil Robles had confirmed the worst fears of the Socialists when he had declared his determination to establish a corporative state in Spain. He had announced his preference for doing so legally, just as Hitler and Mussolini had done, although he also proclaimed his readiness to do so by other means if necessary. There was a growing conviction among European socialists that the only way to deal with the fascist threat was to destroy the very capitalist system which, in its moment of crisis, had spawned it. It is not surprising then that a significant sector of the Spanish Socialist movement should start to think along similar lines.[1]

Socialist disappointment with the Republic was a direct consequence of the success of Gil Robles's legalist tactic in frustrating the reforming zeal of the new regime. In fact, the politics of the Republic were increasingly a battle between the PSOE and the CEDA to decide which of the two was to impose its stamp on the regime. Certainly, that was how both groups perceived the situation. For all that violent extremists of Right and Left played a considerable role in the polarisation of Republican politics, they were never the principal targets for the denunciations of the Socialist or the Catholic press. Socialist propaganda singled out the Catholic party rather than the Carlists or the Alfonsist monarchists as the most dangerous enemy on the Right. Equally, the ACNP propaganda machine, despite the revolutionary insurrectionism of the anarchists, consistently pinpointed socialism as the enemy to be destroyed. This is not surprising. Both the PSOE and the CEDA were confident that the repressive apparatus of the state could deal adequately with monarchist conspiracy or anarchist subversion. What each really feared was that the other would come to power legally and give the regime a consitutional and legislative content which would damage the material interests of their supporters. In a democratic regime, the numerical advantage might normally have been expected to lie with a working-class party. Accordingly, in 1931 the Socialists took part in the government with optimism. However, by the end of 1933 Acción Popular had demonstrated that ample financial resources and skilful propaganda could also conjure up substantial popular support.

What particularly disturbed many Socialists and Republicans in the winter of 1933 was the probability that the rightist victory in the elections would be used to rescind the reforms achieved so far. The re-establishment of the repressive social relations obtaining under the monarchy would be regarded by them as an assault on everything for which the Republic stood. Nevertheless, CEDA hostility to the Republican–Socialist legislative programme had been so marked as to make clear the party's determination to annul it at the first opportunity. Now, victory in the elections made it possible for the CEDA to give legal sanction to the resentment that its financial backers felt against the reforming challenge of the first two years of the regime.

This reversal was about to come at the moment when the unemployment crisis reached its peak. In December 1933 there were 619,000 out of work, 12 per cent of the total work-force. This was considerably lower than in Germany and Italy, whose economies were so admired by *El Debate*, but given Spain's lack of social welfare schemes, it still represented widespread and immense physical hardship. Without Largo Caballero at the Ministry of Labour to help cushion the blow, the impact on the labour force was even greater. Worsening conditions were the basis of rank-and-file pressure on union officials for militant action. The worst-hit sectors were agriculture, the metal industries and construction, all of which were represented by substantial groups within the UGT. In the agrarian south, the number of unemployed was much higher than elsewhere. The worst-hit provinces were Jaén, Badajoz and Córdoba, where the percentage of unemployed was 50 per cent above the national average. Once landowners began to ignore social legislation entirely and take reprisals for the discomforts of the previous two years, unemployment rose even further. By April 1934 it had reached 703,000.[2] The consequent growth of militancy within the FNTT was soon to lead to the replacement of its Besteirista president, Lucio Martínez Gil, by a radical follower of Largo Caballero, Ricardo Zabalza. The other two unions badly hit by the crisis were already led by faithful Caballeristas. The leader of the metalworkers was Pascual Tomás, and the building labourers were led by Anastasio de Gracia. These three unions represented over half the UGT's total strength of 1,041,539 members – the FNTT accounting for 445,414, the metalworkers 33,287, and the building labourers 83,861. Of the next three most powerful unions – the railway workers with 49,117 members, the miners with 40,635 and the urban transport workers with 34,435 – two were increasingly adopting a militant line. The railway workers remained under the leadership of the Besteirista Trifón Gómez, but the urban transport workers were led by Largo's most extremist young supporter, Carlos Hernández Zancajo, and the miners, albeit without a change of leadership, were developing a harder line.[3]

Rank-and-file militancy was thus a crucial element in Largo Caballero's adoption of revolutionary rhetoric. There were, however, other factors. The most compelling was, paradoxically, a desire to make good the mistake, made before the elections, of rejecting the alliance with the Left Republican forces. The Socialists had only themselves to blame for failing to take advantage of the electoral system, but that fact did little to mitigate their bitterness at the results. They were anxious to persuade Alcalá Zamora to call new elections because, in their opinion, the recent ones had no real validity as a popular vote. The Socialists had gained 1,627,472 votes, almost certainly more than any other party running alone could have got. With these votes, they had returned fifty-eight deputies as against their 116 in 1931, while the Radicals, with only 806,340 votes, had obtained 104 seats. The Left Republicans – that is to say, Azaña's Acción Republicana, Marcelino Domingo's Radical-Socialist Party, the Esquerra Catalana and Santiago Casares Quiroga's Organización Regional Gallega Autónoma – fell from their 1931 collective total of 139 to a mere forty seats. According to calculations made by the PSOE secretariat, the united Right had gained a total of 3,345,504 votes, as opposed to the disunited Left's 3,375,432, winning 212 seats to the Left's ninety-nine.[4] The results were open to various interpretations. Even if the PSOE's somewhat sophistical calculations were correct, it would not alter the fact that the main factor in determining the results was the party's own tactical error in failing to take advantage of a system which favoured coalitions.

However, the Socialists had other reasons for rejecting the validity of the elections. They firmly believed that in the south they had been swindled out of parliamentary seats by electoral malpractice. In villages where one or two men were the sole source of employment, it was relatively easy to get votes by the promise of a job or the threat of dismissal. For many workers on the verge of starvation, the offer of food or a blanket was worth a vote. In Almendralejo (Badajoz), the Marqués de la Encomienda distributed bread, olive oil and *chorizo* (sausage). In Granada, Fernando de los Ríos was prevented from speaking by armed thugs and, in Extremadura, there were two attempts on the life of Juan Simeón Vidarte.[5] Glass voting urns and the presence of the caciques' strong-arm men made a mockery of the secret ballot. The authorities turned a blind eye to malpractice carried on in favour of the Radicals, who were in coalition with the CEDA in much of the south. In some provinces (particularly Badajoz, Málaga and Córdoba), the margin of rightist victory was sufficiently small for electoral malpractice to have affected the results. After the elections, the Minister of Justice, Juan Botella Asensi, resigned, in protest at the level of electoral falsification. The Socialists were also convinced that the cynical way in which the rightists and centrist Republicans formed electoral coalitions made a mockery of the democratic system. Nowhere was this better illustrated than in Asturias. There it looked as if there was going to be a three-way fight between the Socialists, Acción Popular and the Liberal Democrats of Melquíades Alvarez. The campaign started with the liberal press reserving its most ferocious attacks for the *'trogloditas'* (cavemen) of Acción Popular. Then, in late October, the Liberal Democrats, the one-time monarchist Reformists, made a pact with Acción Popular and turned their efforts against the Socialists. A contest which the Socialists might reasonably have expected to win resulted in a victory for the Centre-Right coalition, which gained thirteen seats to the PSOE's four. Had the local anarchists not abstained, the Socialists would almost certainly have won the majority. There were numerous other places where a united front of Socialists and Left Republicans would almost certainly have ensured left-wing victory – Alicante, Badajoz, Ciudad Real, Córdoba, Granada, Jaén and Murcia, to name only the most clear-cut cases. Moreover, a united front would have ensured such a triumph after the first round of the elections, thereby depriving the Radical Party of the temptation and the opportunity to ally with the parties of the Right in the second round, something they did with great success in many southern provinces.[6]

At the end of 1933, then, the Socialist leaders were faced with a rising tide of mass militancy, which was a consequence both of the employers' offensive and of a feeling of bitterness at unfairly losing the elections. Largo Caballero was not a man to fly in the face of the rank-and-file militants. Accordingly, his pronouncements in late 1933 and thereafter resumed that revolutionary tone which he had first adopted earlier in the summer in his speeches at the Cine Pardiñas and the Torrelodones summer school. His rhetoric was not, however, matched by serious revolutionary intentions. No concrete plans for a rising were made, and in December 1933 the Socialists ostentatiously stood aside from an attempted insurrection mounted by the CNT. Moreover, the Socialists broadcast their revolutionary aspirations in a manner which was totally inimical to subversive efficacy. It is far more likely that the PSOE's verbal revolutionism was intended merely to satisfy rank-and-file aspirations and, at the same time, to impress upon Alcalá Zamora the need to call new elections. It was a dangerous game, since, if the President did not succumb to such pressure, the Socialists would be left with the choice of stepping up their threats or losing credibility with their own militants. The resulting situation could be of benefit only to the CEDA.

Gil Robles was also faced by the need to play a subtle game. The election results had vindicated his tactics but they were far from constituting the overall victory which would have enabled him to install his 'new state' and a corporative system. Moreover, he realised that his victory was much more precarious than it appeared. Even if asked by the President to form a government, he could not have done so. To try to govern with a right-wing coalition was out of the question, since all the rightist elements in the chamber did not make up an absolute majority. Besides, a government containing the declared enemies of the Republic could only arouse the Republican fervour of the Left, including a substantial section of the Radical Party. Gil Robles knew that, with leftist divisions healed, any such rightist government would be defeated. There would then be either a coalition government of left-wing and centrist Republicans or, if that were not possible, new elections. It was inconceivable that the Socialists would make the same tactical error twice. Anxious, therefore, not to have to risk his fragile victory in further elections, Gil Robles sought another solution. Lacking the force to seize power by violence, he thus turned to the notion of a centrist government backed by CEDA votes. His party would not participate in the cabinet but it would remote-control it.

On 19 December, Gil Robles rose in the Cortes to express the CEDA's position and to spell out the sort of politics for which the new Radical government might expect his support. Although the speech was moderate in tone, it could not fail to cause great concern on the Left. If he did not demand power immediately, said Gil Robles piously, it was because tempers were still too high on the Right after the tensions and frictions of the first two years of the Republic. This altruism merely reflected his awareness of the basic weakness of his position. He claimed that the right-wing victory in the elections showed a national revulsion against the policies of the first *bienio*, and demanded that the new government carry out a policy in accordance with what he saw as the wishes of the electorate. The actual details of the desired policies revealed the narrow interests defended by the CEDA. Gil Robles called for amnesty for those sentenced to imprisonment for the military rising of August 1932. He also demanded a revision of the religious legislation of the Constituent Cortes. However, it was with regard to social reforms that his demands were most sweeping. All the decrees which had been most welcomed by the landless peasantry – the law of municipal boundaries, that of obligatory cultivation and the introduction of mixed juries – were the subject of swingeing attack. Then Gil Robles called for a reduction of the area of land subject to expropriation under the agrarian reform bill, justifying his demand with a condemnation of the socialising concept of settling peasants on the land. Having thus succinctly dismantled the entire social legislation of the Republic as it applied in rural areas, the CEDA leader went on, somewhat cynically, to affirm his party's commitment to social justice. CEDA votes, he claimed, would never 'serve to perpetuate social injustices'. He also called for action against unemployment, suggesting public works projects and pledging CEDA support for the fiscal reform necessary to finance such schemes.[7] In fact, over the next six months, CEDA votes would carry through the abrogation of social legislation, but, when the party supported a mild fiscal reform in 1935, there would be an internal revolt.

In reply to Gil Robles, Prieto claimed that Lerroux's collaboration with the CEDA in the dismantling of the work of the Constituent Cortes was a betrayal of the Pact of San Sebastián. He went on to threaten that the Socialist would defend the Republic against the dictatorial ambitions of the Right by unleashing the revolution. For the Socialists, that legislation which Gil Robles was determined to overthrow was what made the Republic worth defending.[8] Convinced that the CEDA, with the complicity of Lerroux, was about to destroy the progressive content of the Republic, the Socialists were playing the only card left to them. The threat of revolution was intended to make Lerroux and Gil Robles think twice before proceeding with their plans and to impress upon Alcalá Zamora the need for new elections.

In the context of this kind of opposition to CEDA plans, the tactic of supporting the Radical government from outside was the best available to Gil Robles. Such a government could be controlled without moral compromise and without the risk of provoking the formation of a left-wing coalition. Showing no qualms of conscience, Gil Robles abandoned his monarchist electoral allies. Their chagrin can be imagined. On 27 September he had sworn not to accept pacts or deals with anyone until article 26 of the Constitution was revoked. In his great 15 October speech he claimed, 'We will not govern with anybody else.' His erstwhile allies, more perhaps even than his leftist enemies, regarded this as gross cynicism.[9] Apologists for Gil Robles have seen his decision to co-operate with the Radicals as a supreme gesture of self-sacrifice which kept the Republic in existence and was therefore the greatest proof possible of his loyalty to the Republic. Indeed, it has been stated that CEDA and Agrarian benevolence made government possible and perhaps saved the country from immediate civil war.[10] It is difficult, however, not to see more self-interest than idealism in a decision which derived from the double knowledge that the CEDA could only lose its gains in another election and that the Right was not yet ready for a violent showdown with the Left. In other words, it was the obvious and unavoidable tactic.

In any case, a partnership with the Radicals was useless as a gesture of Republican faith. The Radicals' lack of a consistent political stance had already done the Republic considerable damage. By supporting the group most likely to win, Lerroux had dangerously exaggerated the pendulum effect built into the electoral system and thereby encouraged the politics of reprisal. The Left regarded the Radicals' brusque move to the right in search of votes as the prime cause of the CEDA's success. It was felt that, despite its reputation as the 'historic' Republican party, the Radical Party had been infiltrated by monarchist elements. In August 1931, Lerroux had declared that the Radical Party was basically con- servative and opened its arms to ex-monarchists. In many parts of the south, to the horror of the rightist press, many monarchists decided that they could best defend their interests from within a Republican party and joined the Radical Party.[11] This merely confirmed the leftist convic- tion that Lerroux was unprincipled and would always sell his services to the highest bidder. *El Socialista* regularly highlighted Radical corrup- tion, of which there was a long history. Largo Caballero believed that the Radical Party included elements who, 'if they have not been in jail, deserve to have been'. He claimed that, in early 1931, when the majority of the Republican revolutionary committee had been in jail, Lerroux had started a public subscription for them, the proceeds from which mysteriously disappeared.[12] A CEDA deputy commented that 'This Rad- ical minority reminds me of the voyage of a ship: people of all ages and conditions, of the most diverse ideologies, brought together merely to travel.'[13] The Left was also aware of the Radicals' ominous connection with Juan March, the millionaire smuggler and declared enemy of the Republic, who had partly financed the Right's election campaign.[14]

The Radical Party was thus a party without ideas or ideals, united only by a certain loyalty to Lerroux, a nostalgic recollection of the struggle against the monarchy especially in its Valencian sections and, above all, the prospect of enjoying power. Lerroux himself admitted to Santiago Alba that he understood none of Spain's problems in depth.[15] The Radicals were interested in power as an end in itself, as access to a spoils system. Once in the government, they set up an office to organise the distribution and sale of ministerial prizes in the form of monopolies, commissions, concessions, government orders, licences and letters of introduction.[16] The Socialists feared, understandably, that this was not the party to defend the basic precepts of the Republic against the attacks of the Right. In fact, in return for keeping the Radicals in power with its votes, CEDA support depended upon the implementation of satisfactory policies by the Radicals. Gil Robles had

127

declared unequivocally in his policy statement to the Cortes on 19 December:

> Today I will facilitate the formation of centre governments; tomorrow when the time comes, I will demand power and I will carry out a reform of the Constitution. If we do not receive power, if events show that a right-wing evolution of politics is not possible, the Republic will pay the consequences. This is not a threat but a warning.[17]

It was in reply to remarks of that nature that Prieto had referred to Gil Robles's ill-concealed dictatorial ambitions. The Socialists appear to have been extremely anxious about the use to which the Right would put its new power. They were convinced that not only the Republic's legislation but also their own persons were in considerable danger from a possible fascist coup. On 22 November, De los Ríos placed information before the PSOE executive committee which suggested that plans were afoot for a rightist seizure of power and the detention of the Socialist leaders.[18] It was probably no more than a rumour, but the Socialists were genuinely afraid. Ever since the Republican–Socialist coalition had left power in September, there had been constant reports of rightists in rural areas adopting increasingly violent and provocative attitudes with the acquiescence of the Civil Guard.[19] With a Radical government dependent on CEDA votes, the situation could only deteriorate. Throughout November and December, the Socialist press broadcast its certainty that Lerroux was serving as a bridge to power for the fascism of Gil Robles. Documents were reprinted which showed that Acción Popular was trying to create a citizen militia to face any revolutionary activity on the part of the working class. Other documents showed that Acción Popular was, with the connivance of the police, trying to build up a massive file on all of Spain's politically active workers. The activities of the uniformed militias of the Juventud de Acción Popular were taken as confirmation that an attempt would soon be made to establish fascism in Spain.[20]

Acción Popular was not in a position to seize power; nor, with a pliant Radical Party in the government, did it need to. Socialist fears were exaggerated, but, in the light of contemporary events in Germany, understandable. There was a deep conviction in the Socialist Youth particularly that the only effective answer to fascism was social revolution. This had been strengthened during the election campaign by an extraordinarily influential speech by Luis Araquistain on 29 October. The speech was reprinted as a pamphlet and distributed by the Federación de Juventudes Socialistas.[21] Araquistain had been Spanish Ambassador in Berlin during the first month of Hitler's rule and had been active in trying to organise the escape of Jews and leftists from the Nazi terror.[22] In his view, it had been the passivity of the German Social Democratic Party which had facilitated the victory of Nazism. If they needed any encouragement, the Socialist Youth were quick to seize on Araquistain's belief that only revolution could meet the fascist threat.

The combination of a newly confident employer class taking advantage of the changing political situation and the fears of fascism had a rapid effect on the Socialist rank and file. According to Largo Caballero, delegations of workers' representatives from the provinces came to Madrid to beg the PSOE executive committee to organise a counter-offensive. Accordingly, the Caballerista party executive proposed sending a delegation consisting of De los Ríos, Wenceslao Carrillo and Enrique de Francisco to meet the Besteirista executive of the UGT and to reach an agreement 'to carry out the action deemed necessary against any attempt to establish fascism, restore the monarchy or create a dictatorship'. Besteiro and Trifón Gómez proposed instead a joint meeting of both the PSOE and UGT executives at party headquarters on 25 November.

De los Ríos, who had just come back from a trip around the province of Granada, addressed the meeting. He painted a sombre picture of the sufferings of the rural proletariat at the hands of the newly confident and vengeful *caciques*. The PSOE executive, convinced that this was only the beginning of a nationwide rightist offensive, was keen to take positive action. The UGT executive was hostile to any kind of adventurism. Besteiro, Saborit and Trifón Gómez all argued that the most prudent thing to do would be to wait on events and keep the organisation together until circumstances improved. Largo was infuriated by their immobilism, which he found incomprehensible. Revealing his own sense of priorities, Largo opposed the UGT executive on the grounds that 'the workers themselves were calling for rapid and energetic action'. As usual, he was frightened of a rank-and-file drift away to more determinedly revolutionary organisations. Prieto finally agreed with Largo on the need for 'a defensive action'. The meeting issued a declaration urging workers to be ready to rise up and oppose 'reactionary elements in the event that they went beyond the bounds of the Constitution in their public determination to annul the work of the Republic'. On 26 November the PSOE executive submitted its view of the situation to the party's National Committee. The executive's line was approved and a statement issued warning that, with working-class rights threatened by fascism, all party organisations should be ready to oppose the 'sinister fulfilment of the Right's ambitions'. This was a reference to Gil Robles's declared intention of implanting the corporative state in Spain. However, what it meant in practical terms was not specified and a joint committee of the PSOE and the UGT was set up to elaborate this 'defensive action'. The UGT was represented by Besteiro's closest lieutenants, Trifón Gómez, Lucio Martínez Gil and Andrés Saborit, the PSOE by the Caballeristas Juan-Simeón Vidarte, Enrique de Francisco and Pascual Tomás.[23]

The CEDA may not have been a fascist organisation in the terms of post-1945 academic definition. In 1933 the full extent of Nazi horrors was as yet unknown.[24] In the light of what was known of Nazi and Fascist persecution of leftists, the CEDA's broadcast intention to smash socialism, Gil Robles's corporativist ambitions and CEDA-encouraged employers' attacks on unionised labour were, to most Spanish leftists, indistinguishable from contemporary fascism. With a degree of nervous exaggeration, the Socialists in particular were obsessed with the need to avoid the tactical errors made by their German and Italian comrades. However, behind the consequent revolutionary posturing stood a long tradition of reformism. There can be little doubt that even the most verbally radical of the Socialist leaders viewed with considerable trepidation the prospect of actually organising a revolution. Rather, they hoped that their threats of revolution would serve the same purpose as the real thing, satisfying the demands of the rank and file and giving the Right pause. It was a tactic subject to the law of diminishing returns, but desperate Socialist politicians trapped between their own militant masses and an aggressive Right understandably grasped at it.

The limits of the Socialists' rhetorical revolutionism were shown two weeks after the creation of the joint PSOE–UGT committee. The anarchists, as a corollary to their electoral abstentionist campaign, had organised an uprising for 8 December. The aim of abstentionism had been to ensure the return of an undiluted bourgeois government, in order, thought the anarchists, to let the working class see without confusion that the Republic was as oppressive as the monarchy had been and to help rid the Socialists of their reformist illusions. Now they denounced the Socialists as being objectively fascist and proceeded to unleash an unco-ordinated and ill-prepared rising. Like electoral abstentionism, random insurrectionism was an irresponsibly naïve strategy.

Only a scattering of the traditionally anarchist areas responded to the call for a rising. The anarchists of Asturias and most of Andalusia were hostile to the rising. Nevertheless, there was a wave of violent strikes, trains were blown up and Civil Guard posts were assaulted. In the Rioja, the rising was briefly successful, with libertarian communism being proclaimed in many villages, before being put down with surprising ease. Despite the lack of bloodshed, several hundred prisoners were taken. In Zaragoza, despite arms seizures by the police, the general strike was accompanied by gun-fighting in the streets. Twelve people were killed on 9 December. By 14 December, the strike was defeated and more than four hundred CNTistas were in jail. In Galicia, Catalonia and Alicante, the insurrectionists were easily repressed. In parts of Andalusia, there were sporadic clashes. Cars were burnt in the streets of Seville. In Bujalance in Córdoba, there was nearly a re-run of Casas Viejas – armed peasants took over parts of the town and tried to capture the *ayuntamiento*. In thirty-six hours of fighting, five civilians, including a child and an old man, and one Civil Guard were killed. Two hundred prisoners were taken and two alleged ring-leaders were shot by the Civil Guard 'while trying to escape'.[25]

The entire insurrection left the CNT decimated and played into the hands of the Right. Nowhere had Socialist organisations taken part although some individual militants had done so believing it to be precisely the 'defensive action' advocated on 26 November. At the suggestion of the joint committee, the PSOE and UGT executives met in Madrid on 11 December to thrash out their attitude to the anarchist action and to establish what was meant by the proposed joint PSOE–UGT action to prevent the Right fulfilling its ambitions. Besteiro argued forcefully against making empty threats of a Socialist seizure of power and Saborit criticised the revolutionary rhetoric of the editorial line of *El Socialista*. (Years later, Largo Caballero was to claim that its bolshevising tone was a reflection of the chagrin of its editor, Julián Zugazagoitia, at not being elected to the Cortes for Bilbao.) In response to Besteiro, Largo Caballero continued to advocate 'an anti-fascist movement' but, when Trifón Gómez proposed issuing concrete instructions to local workers' organisations, he merely talked in the vaguest terms about 'being prepared'.

After acrimonious wranglings which went on until late in the evening, agreement was finally reached on the text of a communiqué or manifesto to be published on the following day. This note announced roundly that the Socialist movement had 'had no participation whatsoever in the rising' but blamed the rising on the government, 'which, by its contempt for workers' rights, has diverted the Republic from those paths on which the will of the people set it'. In the Cortes, Prieto condemned 'this damaging movement' (*movimiento perturbador*). Yet, when Goicoechea and Gil Robles offered their enthusiastic support to the government to help crush subversion, Prieto reacted angrily. It disturbed him that the 'enemies of the Republic' only ever supported the regime for enterprises which involved the repression of the working class. By its determination to silence the workers' organisations, declared Prieto perceptively, the Right was 'closing all exits to us and inviting us to a bloody conflict'. The Socialists' revolutionary stance was intended to inhibit the Right from going too far. In the previous day's note the joint executives had emphasised this by reaffirming their 'firm decision, when the time comes, to fulfil the duties which our ideals impose upon us'.[26] In other words, the revolutionary threats would be applied if an attempt were made to establish fascism. However, the text of the note could not conceal the growing rift between the moderate Besteirista executive of the UGT and the increasing verbal extremism of Largo Caballero and the party leadership.

The premonitory nature of the revolutionary declarations of leaders like Prieto and Largo Caballero cannot be underestimated. Nevertheless, among the younger union members there was a great surge of irresponsible enthusiasm for revolutionism. This was taken by Largo Caballero as justifying his position and, at the same time, it was making the position of the UGT executive committee untenable. On 13 December 1933, at a tense session of the UGT's National Committee, the political situation and the policies being proposed by the PSOE executive were discussed. While Saborit and Trifón Gómez spoke in terms of calming the spirits of the rank and file, Amaro del Rosal, the hot-headed young Caballerista president of the Federación de Trabajadores de Banca y Bolsa (Federation of Bank and Stock Exchange Workers), proposed that the UGT join the PSOE in organising a revolutionary movement to seize power and establish socialism. There was a lengthy debate, in which sympathy for Rosal's position was expressed, in rather more reasoned terms, by Pascual Tomás, the Caballerista leader of the metalworkers' federation, and by Carlos Hernández Zancajo, leader of the transport workers and president of the FJS. Anastasio de Gracia of the building workers' federation wavered while the printers' and railway workers' delegates supported the Besteirista executive. Besteiro himself declared that he regarded Rosal's proposal as 'an impossible absurdity'. When the proposal was put to the vote, it was roundly defeated. However, it was decided, after further acrimonious debate, to call an extraordinary congress of the UGT to resolve the bitter divisions between moderate Besteiristas and revolutionary Caballeristas.[27]

The proposal was overtaken by events. On 16 December, Lerroux formed a government with the support of CEDA votes. The PSOE executive had hoped to persuade the President of the Republic to dissolve the Cortes and call new elections. As might have been predicted, he did not choose to take such unconstitutional action. Faced now with the reality of Lerroux in power following the instructions of Gil Robles, the PSOE executive sought a meeting with its UGT counterpart, which took place at party headquarters on 18 December. Largo Caballero, fearing that Lerroux planned to appoint the right-wing General Manuel Goded as Under-Secretary of War as a prelude to the establishment of a more authoritarian government, proposed that the two executives agree to launch a revolutionary movement if the appointment was made. Besteiro and the rest of the UGT executive refused on the grounds that to do so was irresponsible and precipitate. Largo Caballero declared that henceforth there would be no more consultation with the UGT. The Besteiristas therefore called a further meeting of the National Committee of the UGT on 31 December to resolve the dispute with the PSOE leadership. At that meeting, one after another, the leaders of the major federations of the UGT rose to declare that they supported the line of the PSOE executive and not that of the UGT. This view was expressed with varying degrees of vehemence by Ramón González Peña for the mineworkers, Salvador Vidal Rosell for the textile workers, José Díaz Alor for the bakery workers, Mariano Muñoz for the hotel workers, Pacual Tomás for the metalworkers, Amaro del Rosal for the bank workers and Carlos Hernández Zancajo for the transport workers. They were opposed by the representatives of the Besteirista strongholds, the printers, the FNTT and the railwaymen.

Amaro del Rosal again put forward a motion for 'the immediate and urgent organisation, in agreement with the Socialist Party, of a national revolutionary movement, to take political power exclusively for the working class'. The voting revealed the disarray of the Socialist trade union. Impotent rage at the election results and the subsequent erosion of the Republic's social legislation led many senior union leaders to follow their rank and file in adopting revolutionary rhetoric. However, they drew back when faced with Amaro del Rosal and Carlos Hernández Zancajo talking of establishing the dictatorship of the proletariat. The proposal was defeated by twenty-eight votes to seventeen. Apart from the expected votes against the motion from the executive – excepting Besteiro himself, who had been taken ill and left the meeting – and the FNTT and Saborit's printers, 'conservative' votes came from Anastasio de Gracia, the construction workers' leader, and Ramón González Peña of the Sindicato de Obreros Mineros Asturianos. This confirms that it was the younger element which was pushing for revolutionary tactics. The voting was reversed for the other motion of the day, presented by the executive committee, which simply reiterated the UGT's total identification with the joint executives' declaration of 25 November, which had threatened revolutionary action only if the Right went beyond the limits of the Constitution.[28]

The strident revolutionary rhetoric of the Federación de Juventudes Socialistas increased the pressure on the PSOE leadership to adopt an insurrectionary line. The dilemma this created for them was revealed by De los Ríos, who visited Azaña on 2 January 1934 to seek his advice. Azaña's account of the meeting is extremely revealing:

> He recounted to me the incredible and cruel persecutions that the political and union organisations of the workers were suffering at the hands of the authorities and the employers. The Civil Guard was daring to do things it had never dared do before. It was impossible to restrain the exasperation of the masses. The Socialist leaders were being overwhelmed. Where would it all end? In a great misfortune, probably. I was not unaware of the barbaric policy followed by the government nor of the conduct of the landowners with the rural labourers, reducing them to hunger. Nor of the retaliations and reprisals which were taking place against other workers. I know the slogan 'Let the Republic feed you' [*Comed República*]. But all of this and much more that De los Ríos told me, and the government's measures, and the policy of the Cortes majority, which apparently had no other aim but to undo the work of the Constituent Cortes, did not make it advisable, nor justify, that the Socialist Party and the UGT should throw themselves into a movement of force.

Azaña told De los Ríos in no uncertain terms that it was the duty of leaders to make the masses see sense, even at the risk of their own popularity. Shortly afterwards, De los Ríos reported this conversation to the PSOE executive committee. Yet, for all that their language was intemperate, it is difficult to see how, given the intransigence of the employers, the Socialist leadership could tell their followers to be patient.[29]

From all over Andalusia and Extremadura came reports of considerable provocation from owners and Civil Guards alike. The law was flouted at every turn. In Real de la Jara (Seville) some workers who had stolen acorns were savagely beaten by the Civil Guard. In Venta de Baúl (Granada) the armed guards of the *cacique*, a member of the CEDA, beat up local union leaders. In Fuente del Maestre (Badajoz) it was the Civil

Guard which did the beating. Members of the FNTT were systematically being refused work, and wages had dropped by 60 per cent. The FNTT executive had sent several appeals to the Minister of Labour, Ricardo Samper, for the full implementation of existing social legislation. A delegation went to visit Samper on 8 January. It was to no avail.[30]

This was hardly surprising given the composition of the government and the nature of its parliamentary support. On forming his government, Lerroux had looked for collaboration to the Agrarian Party of José Martínez de Velasco, parliamentary deputy for Burgos, one of the founders of Acción Nacional and, in the Constituent Cortes, head of the Minoría Agraria, to which Gil Robles and the other Acción Nacional deputies had belonged. Martínez de Velasco's party represented the wheat oligarchy of Valladolid and Burgos and was so strong in the latter province that the CEDA had acquiesced in its hegemonic role there. When José María Cid Ruiz Zorrilla, the aggressively conservative Agrarian deputy for Zamora, became Minister of Communications, his party announced that he did so in a personal capacity. Since the Agrarians and the CEDA remained virtually indistinguishable in the eyes of many Republicans, such an announcement was regarded as no more than a self-serving deception.[31]

The inclusion of Cid in the cabinet caused a crisis of conscience for Diego Martínez Barrio, the most genuinely liberal Republican among the Radicals. The loyalty of the Agrarians to the Republic was little more confidence-inspiring than that of the CEDA. Indeed, when Martínez de Velasco announced his group's decision to adhere to the Republic in January 1934, going further in his accidentalism than Gil Robles was ever to do, eight of his thirty-one deputies passed to the CEDA in protest. The Left was convinced that CEDA and Agrarian votes in the Cortes gave the Radicals a licence for corruption in return for the protection of the agrarian oligarchy's material interests. In late December, a draft law had already been presented to the Cortes for the expulsion of those peasants who had occupied land in Extremadura the previous year. In the third week of January the law of municipal boundaries was provisionally repealed. The CEDA also presented projects for the emasculation of the 1932 agrarian reform, by reducing the amount of land subject to expropriation, and for the return of land confiscated after the 10 August 1932 military rising.[32]

The increase in the 'preventive brutality' of the Civil Guard was a consequence of the government's appointment of conservative provincial governors. In fact, the maintenance of authority became one of the CEDA's greatest preoccupations in the Cortes. On 26 January, Gil Robles and a CEDA deputation visited Lerroux to complain about disorder. Although they admitted its origin in unemployment, they demanded sterner measures from the forces of order. *El Debate* devoted a favourable editorial to Hitler's law for the regimentation of labour. There was talk that the Ministry of Justice might set up concentration camps for unemployed vagabonds. The Socialists were disturbed by further evidence that the CEDA was building up files on workers in every village, with full details of their 'subversiveness', which was equated with their membership of a union. As clashes between the Civil Guard and the *braceros* increased daily, *El Socialista* commented that 'never, not even in the worst days of the monarchy, did the peasants feel more enslaved and wretched than now'. The President of the Supreme Court called for the application of the principles of social justice in the workings of the mixed juries, now under rightist control. Gil Robles, however, aligned himself openly with the owners when the CEDA tabled a proposition for increased credits for the Civil Guard.[33]

In this context, it was difficult for the Socialist leadership to hold back its followers. Largo Caballero tended to give way to the revolutionary impatience of the masses, although his rhetoric, which they cheered, was unspecific and consisted largely of Marxist platitudes. To make the revolution, he said, it was necessary to control the apparatus of the state. If the working class were to gain power, the people would have to be armed. To gain power, the bourgeoisie would have to be defeated. No concrete relation to the contemporary political scene was ever made in Largo's speeches of early 1934 and no timetable for the future revolution was ever given. He did, however, dwell on one thing. That was the lesson of defeated European socialism as expressed by Otto Bauer: that only the destruction of capitalism could remove for ever the threat of fascism. Yet it is likely that Largo hoped to avert that menace with his own revolutionary threat. In one speech he asked rhetorically if the Republicans in the government did not see that by their policies they were giving the working class the idea that the legal struggle was useless. They could only do such a thing, he said, if they did not realise that it was provoking a revolutionary movement.[34]

Since the threats and appeals of Largo Caballero's speeches did little to mitigate the aggression of the rural employers and the Civil Guard, rank-and-file pressure for the radicalisation of the Socialist movement continued throughout January and February. The PSOE named a special commission, presided over by Largo and with Enrique de Francisco as secretary, to examine the practical side of organising a revolutionary movement. A further tumultuous meeting of the UGT National Committee on 9 January agreed on UGT participation in this revolutionary committee but brought the two factions no nearer to agreement. The Besteiristas were losing ground. Largo then insisted that the PSOE's policies be submitted to the UGT's National Committee. This was to meet on 27 January.[35]

In the meanwhile, Besteiro and Prieto agreed, at a joint meeting of the two executives on 11 January, that a revolutionary programme should be prepared. Largo Caballero believed that this was just a delaying tactic. Prieto and Besteiro spent many hours trying to hammer out such a programme, but could never reach agreement. Eventually they each elaborated separate programmes. Prieto produced a ten-point project which proposed (1) the nationalisation of land; (2) the dedication of the biggest proportion possible of the nation's savings to irrigation projects; (3) radical reform of the education system; (4) the dissolution of the religious orders, the seizure of their wealth and the expulsion of those considered dangerous; (5) the dissolution of the army and the immediate organisation of a democratic military body; (6) the dissolution of the Civil Guard and the creation of a popular militia; (7) the reform of the bureaucracy and the removal of anti-Republican elements; (8) an improvement in the working conditions of the industrial working class, but not, for the moment, the socialisation of industry; (9) the reform of the tax system and the introduction of an inheritance tax; and (10) that the previous nine measures be carried out in the form of decrees to be ratified by a freely elected legislative body and that the present President of the Republic be replaced. This programme, which curiously contained no proposals to nationalise the banks, the railways or principal industries, was approved by the PSOE executive on 13 January. At the executive meeting which approved the programme, a five-point programme of immediate action was added, drawn up by Largo Caballero himself. This called for (1) the organisation of a frankly revolutionary movement; (2) the declaration of such a movement at the right moment, preferably before the enemy could take definitive precautions; (3) contacts to be made between the PSOE and the UGT and any other groups ready to co-operate in the movement; and, in the event of triumph, (4) the PSOE and the UGT with other participants in the revolution to take over political power; and (5) the ten-point programme drawn up by Prieto to be applied. Besteiro's project proposed that a great corporative assembly be called to advise on a massive programme of national economic regeneration and nationalisation over a period of years. It was rejected by the PSOE executive on 17 January.[36]

The National Committee of the UGT met on 27 January to discuss the various projects. The executive opposed the PSOE's revolutionary line. Besteiro used some strange arguments against Prieto's project, claiming that it would involve the Socialists in war on the CNT. He also asserted that the violent seizure of power was contrary to the spirit of Marxism, the weapons of which were science and economic technique. When it was submitted to the vote, the PSOE's revolutionary project was approved by thirty-three members of the committee. Only the Sindicato Ferroviario Nacional and the FNTT voted for the executive, which immediately resigned en masse.

Two days later, a new executive was elected, with Anastasio de Gracia as president and Largo Caballero as secretary-general and a membership which included the most radical leaders of the Socialist Youth, Ricardo Zabalza, Carlos Hernández Zancajo and Amaro del Rosal. On 30 January, the National Committee of the FNTT had also met to debate the revolutionary proposals. An identical situation had arisen. The entire executive, all Besteiristas, resigned, and a new committee of young Caballeristas was elected under the presidency of Ricardo Zabalza. The organisations of the Socialist movement were falling in quick succession to the extremist youth. A meeting of the Agrupación Socialista Madrileña was packed by young Socialists, who passed a motion of censure against its president, Trifón Gómez, obliging him to resign. He was replaced as president by Rafael Henche with Julio Alvarez del Vayo as vice-president supported by a group of the most fervent Caballerista 'bolshevisers' including Hernández Zancajo and Santiago Carrillo.

With Largo Caballero now controlling both the UGT and PSOE executives and the FJS in the hands of his most fervent supporters, a joint committee was immediately established to make preparations for a revolutionary movement. It consisted of Juan Simeón Vidarte, Pascual Tomás and Enrique de Francisco for the Socialist Party, Felipe Pretel, José Díaz Alor and Carlos Hernández Zancajo for the UGT and Santiago Carrillo for the FJS. Operating from the UGT headquarters in Calle Fernández de la Hoz, the committee established links with PSOE, UGT and FJS organisations in each province and issued seventy-three instructions for the creation of militias, the acquisition of arms, the establishment of links with sympathetic local units of the army and the Civil Guard and the organisation of squads of technicians able to take over the running of basic services. The response from the provinces was deeply discouraging and there is little evidence that, apart from the flurry of communications generated by the committee, any practical action was taken.[37]

The resort to revolutionary verbalism was a reflection of the bitterness and frustration felt in all sections of the Socialist movement at the election results and the rapid overturning of the social advances of the first *bienio*. However, the apparent unity created across the PSOE, the UGT and the FJS as the Caballeristas gained a monopoly of executive posts was illusory. It was not only that large numbers of union functionaries and militants still shared the cautious moderation of Besteiro despite the change in leadership positions. There was also a hidden gulf between Prieto, Largo Caballero and the older trade union leaders like Pascual Tomás and Anastasio de Gracia, on the one hand, and the young radicals like Amaro del Rosal and Carlos Hernández Zancajo, on the other. For the older generation, revolutionary threats were little more than threats, which they had neither the inclination nor the expertise to implement. The young bolshevisers, in contrast, felt a real revolutionary exhilaration – although they too had little idea of how to implement their rhetoric – which was to be translated, at the Fifth Congress of the FJS held in mid-April 1934, into a vague commitment to an armed insurrection. Thus, the young and old radicalisers were united only in irresponsibility and incompetence. The real differences between the older trade unionists, who were cautiously pulling back from revolutionary action, and the the young bolshevisers, who were loudly advocating it, damagingly weakened the Socialist movement during the severe trials to which it was to be subjected in the course of 1934.

The exiguous response of the provincial sections to the hopeful missives of the revolutionary committee, together with Largo Caballero's cautious trade union instincts, ensured that – Asturias aside – the activities of the committee never went much beyond rhetoric. However, that rhetoric glimmered through the editorials of *El Socialista* which were sufficiently virulent in their denunciation of the 'betrayal' of the Republic to provoke considerable trepidation on the Right. The loud revolutionism of the younger elements of the movement was used to justify the government's uncompromising repression throughout the spring and summer of 1934 of strikes that were anything but revolutionary in intent. The revolutionary movement was to be launched in the event of 'the constitution of a government with the participation of the CEDA'. In theory, this was a secret instruction but, as might have been expected given the premonitory nature of the entire operation, the President of the Republic was warned of it and Gil Robles and other leaders of the Right were fully aware of its existence. The virtual lack of secrecy and the implicit separation of the chosen 'revolutionary moment' from any real working-class struggles effectively gave all the cards to the government. On 3 February, the new UGT executive had met to decide whether to try to stop all strike action in order for the movement to harness its energies for the projected revolution. Revealingly, it was decided, at the urging of Largo Caballero, that the UGT should not ask its members to abstain from strike action in defence of their economic interests.[38]

Accordingly, the joint revolutionary committee would have no control over the UGT rank and file as its strength was dissipated in a series of economically motivated and ultimately destructive strikes. While it vainly laboured at its task of preventing the CEDA from taking over the government, Gil Robles was gradually achieving his aim of coming to power legally. Lerroux's need for CEDA votes in the Cortes ensured that the Radicals carried out a policy acceptable to the Right. Gil Robles backed up his demands on the Radicals with scarcely veiled threats. Addressing the Radical deputies in the Cortes, he announced that, if the Right were unable to achieve its programme in full within the parliament, it would be forced to transfer its field of action elsewhere. He made these remarks in a debate which had largely centred on the Socialist adoption of a revolutionary line. Prieto had stated that the PSOE's stance was a direct consequence of the daily violence being carried out against the working class by Gil Robles's supporters. Gil Robles denied that such was the case, on the rather specious grounds that the CEDA was fulfilling its ambitions legally. That was true, but it was precisely the protection of the law which made possible the violence to which Prieto referred. The debate had started because a number of rightist deputies had demanded that the Minister of the Interior, the liberal Radical Martínez Barrio, take firm action against the 'acts of indiscipline' being committed in rural areas. Such 'acts' included the robbery of acorns and olives by hungry day-labourers. Gil Robles, who regarded Martínez Barrio as too liberal, demanded assurances that the government would take action against such 'criminality' and would also oppose the revolutionary aspirations of the Socialists. To Gil Robles's annoyance, Martínez Barrio replied that it was his job to deal with violence, whether committed by the Right, the Left or the Centre. It was in reply to this that Gil Robles made his threat to go beyond parliament if he did not get his way within it.[39]

What his threats could mean was illustrated by contemporaneous events abroad. At the end of the second week in February, the Austrian government began its repression of the Socialist movement in Austria. Reporting the fighting in Linz and Vienna, *El Socialista* drew the obvious analogy when it referred to the 'offensive of clerical fascism against the proletariat'. The reaction of the ACNP press to Dollfuss's bombardment of the Karl Marx Hof was enthusiastic. It was 'a lesson for us all'.

The Spanish government was exhorted to follow the examples of Italy, Germany and now Austria in dealing with 'disorder'. The extravagant praise for Dollfuss brought forth a ready response from the Socialists:

> as always the Spanish clericals extend a certificate of good states-manship to the Austrian chancellor after a ferocious and inhuman repression which easily emulates the cruelty of Italian fascism or the horrors of Hitlerism ... For us, the best governor is not one who, like Dollfuss, shoots women and children.

The Socialists heeded the warnings of Otto Bauer and Julius Deutsch, which began to fill their publications. They were determined not to share the fate of their Austrian comrades. Reading the CEDA press, they were confirmed in their conviction that to avoid such annihilation they would have to fight. The fate of German and Austrian Social-ists figured largely in Largo Caballero's daily conversation.[40]

Gil Robles's attitude did little to calm the young Socialists. For them, any attack on the Republic as created by the Constituent Cortes was fascism and a prelude to an attack on the Socialist movement. The Caballeristas, and indeed many other Socialists and Republicans, regarded the new Cortes as essentially monarchist. Significantly, the CEDA leader showed a consistent aversion to declaring his loyalty to the Republic. On 4 January in the Cortes, he sidestepped a direct chal-lenge to shout '¡Viva la República!' His normal device in such cases was to use expressions like 'readiness to work within', 'respect for', 'defer-ence to' the Republic, and then only as sparingly as possible, when under direct pressure, and presumably with mental reservations. Miguel Maura, who was shocked by El Debate's fulsome approval of events in Austria, remarked that, despite Gil Robles's acceptance of the Republic's existence, he was still manifestly in contact with Alfonso XIII.[41] The CEDA leader, however, was not concerned for the moment with the restoration of the monarchy. He was interested in state power, Republic-an if necessary, to carry out concrete objectives. Speaking in Pamplona on 18 February, he admitted as much: 'Are we to govern with the present regime? Why not? A political party has a programme and this can only be carried out from a position of power.' The objectives to be pursued once the apparatus of the state was secured were, as the behaviour of his party from its foundation had made clear, inimical to the work of the Constituent Cortes. This was emphasised three days later when El Debate called for a united front of the employer class to mobilise against socialism.[42]

The CEDA's commitment to the promotion of these class interests was illustrated throughout March. The most disturbing event from the Republican point of view was the calculated elimination of the more moderate members of the cabinet at the beginning of the month. In speeches on 19 and 26 February, Gil Robles had threatened to bring down the government unless critics of the CEDA were not silenced or removed. Martínez Barrio had long expressed his discomfort at the government's being forced to carry out the CEDA's policies. Although the Minister of the Interior had acquiesced in the toughening of Civil Guard attitudes and had appointed right-wing provincial governors, it was not enough for Gil Robles. The landowners were unhappy at the idea of having a liberal in such a key position of social control. Martínez Barrio's attempts at fairness were denounced as laxity. After he had publicly expressed his opposition to the eventual inclusion of the CEDA in a coalition government, Gil Robles withdrew his support from the government, proclaiming it 'thoroughly exhausted', and demanded a cabinet which more closely corresponded to the forces in the Cortes. Martínez Barrio and two other moderate Radical ministers, Antonio de Lara y Zarate (Finance) and José Pareja Yébenes (Education), were forced to resign. The reactionary and volatile Rafael Salazar Alonso became Minister of the Interior. This was to lead in April to the schism of the Radical left wing, which then became the Partido Radical Demócrata under the leadership of Martínez Barrio on 17 May. That group would eventually join the right wing of the Partido Radical-Socialista, led by Félix Gordón Ordás, to become Unión Republicana, whose founding congress was to take place between 28 and 30 September 1934. With the departure of Martínez Barrio and eighteen other Radical deputies who followed him, the remainder of the Radical Party was left even more a prisoner of the CEDA. It was Gil Robles's first major move in a skilful process of gradually eliminating the Radicals from the CEDA's path to power.[43]

The CEDA's success in subverting the progressive nature of the Republic had been analysed in a monumental speech by Azaña given at the Teatro Pardiñas on 11 February. Gil Robles, said the Republican leader, was exploiting Lerroux's desire for power to impose a narrow class policy. The counter-revolutionary reversal of the Republican–Socialist coalition's modest attempt to improve the living standards of the lower classes was now provoking social war. It was tragic that because of the government's contempt for social justice the Socialists were being forced to adopt a revolutionary stance. Azaña considered that it suited the Right for the Socialists to be provoked into a rising. After the Radicals had used the state's repressive apparatus to smash the proletariat, Gil Robles would demand that he be allowed to govern in order to establish his corporative state.[44] This is largely what was to happen between October 1934 and November 1935, although, in the event, Gil Robles was to miscalculate his final bid for power. In a very real sense, the Socialists were just playing into his hands. Many of them, of course, hoped that it would never be necessary to launch the threatened rising. Speaking in the Pardiñas a week before Azaña, Prieto had made it clear that, for him at any rate, the aim of the revolution would be to defend the work of the Constituent Cortes. Its programme, the same one he had drawn up and presented to the UGT, was not incompatible with the Constitution.[45] The trend of politics in general and the appointment of Salazar Alonzo in particular, however, showed that Prieto's hopes that the government would modify its aggressively right-wing policies were unlikely to be fulfilled.

Moreover, Prieto, for all his reluctant acceptance of a revolutionary line, was still far from being the most extreme of the Socialists. The Socialist Youth, who had gained control of union after union, including even the printers, a Besteirista stronghold, were set on revolution not, as Prieto was, to revive the bourgeois Republic but to establish socialism. At the Fifth Congress of the FJS in April, the most energetic revolution-ists had clinched their hold over the youth movement: Carlos Hernández Zancajo became president and Santiago Carrillo became secretary and editor of the FJS newspaper *Renovación*.[46] In practice, however, the revolutionism of the youthful extremists, like that of their elderly hero Largo Caballero, did not go beyond verbal infantile leftism. Their radical propaganda, not backed by any serious revolutionary preparations, was used to justify an increasingly authoritarian stance by the government. In early March, in union after union where control was in the hands of Caballeristas, the new leadership, fearful of losing the initiative to the even more militant CNT, took the bait offered by the employers' intransi-gence and launched a series of strikes. It is a telling comment on the extent to which the preparations for a revolutionary movement were not being taken seriously. If they had been, then energies would not have been dissipated in local, economically motivated strikes. Those in the metal and construction industries dragged on into the early summer and ended in stalemate, but that of the printers ended in a major defeat for the hard-liners.

In fact, it was the printing dispute which revealed to what extent the recent cabinet shuffle marked an abrupt surge to the right. On 7 March, Salazar Alonso declared a state of emergency (*un estado de alarma*), closing down the headquarters of the FJS, the Communists and the

CNT. A printers' strike had been declared at the monarchist daily *ABC* in protest against the violation of a long-standing 'closed shop' agreement and the introduction of non-union labour. The owner of *ABC*, Juan Ignacio Luca de Tena, advised by the lawyer Cándido Casanueva, the CEDA deputy for Salamanca and a close crony of Gil Robles, got Salazar Alonso's assurance that the government would support his attempt to break the strike. Thus, when the workers expressed a willingness to return to work, Luca de Tena locked out the strikers and produced the paper with the labour of right-wing volunteers. The Asociación del Arte de Imprimir, the Socialist printers' union, declared a general strike in the newspaper industry to the considerable alarm and discomfit of the bulk of its members who did not regard themselves as affected by the local dispute at *ABC*. Salazar Alonso made no attempt to conciliate the two sides. He was determined to defeat a strike which, he claimed in a provocative exaggeration, would have brought 'the triumph of the red tyranny'. Most other newspapers of the Right took advantage of the minister's support and the unemployment crisis to sack union labour and to create pliant work-forces. The general strike which started on 12 March ended in defeat for the Socialist printers after only five days. It was an unnecessary and irresponsible defeat. It is indicative of the essential caution of Largo Caballero and the other senior leaders of the Socialist Party that, at the initiative of Indalecio Prieto, the PSOE executive agreed to issue a statement that the strikes in the metal, building and newspaper industries had social and economic origins and were not meant to be revolutionary strikes against the threat of fascism. The leaders of the Madrid Casa del Pueblo visited the Ministry of Labour to assure the minister that the strikes had no revolutionary intention.[47]

The Right was delighted with Salazar Alonzo. On the day after his declaration of the state of emergency, his energy was applauded by Gil Robles, who declared that, as long as the Minister of the Interior thus defended the social order and strengthened the principle of authority, the government was assured of CEDA support. What Gil Robles had in mind was clarified by a series of articles in *El Debate* demanding severe measures against what was called the 'subversion' of workers who protested at wage cuts. The CEDA press demanded the abolition of the right to strike. The government responded with an announcement that strikes would be ruthlessly suppressed if they had any political implications. For the right-wing press and, indeed, for Salazar Alonso, all strikes seemed to fall into this category. On 22 March *El Debate* referred to stoppages by waiters in Seville and by transport workers in Valencia

THE POLITICS OF REPRISAL

as 'strikes against Spain', and recommended the adoption of anti-strike legislation like that current in Italy, Germany, Portugal and Austria. The government attempted to extend its repressive armoury by increasing the numbers of the Civil Guard and the Assault Guard and by re-establishing the death penalty.[48]

Simultaneously, the religious legislation of 1931–3 was being reversed. It was thus part of an overall trend when the CEDA called on the government to introduce the amnesty for attacks on the Republic which had been one of the Right's election pledges. Its text was drafted by the leaders of the four largest right-wing parties, Gil Robles, the Alfonsist Antonio Goicoechea, the Agrario José Martínez de Velasco and Carlist Conde de Rodezno. Since the main beneficiaries were to be those associated with the Dictatorship and the 10 August rising, the Socialists and Left Republicans tried, unsuccessfully, to block the measure. For them it was confirmation if any were needed that the Republic was being taken over by its enemies. Even after the Cortes had passed the amnesty, the President of the Republic withheld his consent for fear of the return to the Army of officers who had clearly manifested their determination to overthrow the regime. He hesitated over the weekend of 20–3 April before finally signing. He also issued a note making public his reservations.[49]

While the President dithered, the CEDA made a sinister gesture in the form of a large rally of its youth movement, the JAP (Juventud de Acción Popular). It had been planned swiftly but thoroughly. Hundreds of meetings were held to drum up support and special trains with subsidised tickets were arranged. At one such meeting, Gil Robles made some illuminating remarks about his political strategy. Parliament was something which was repugnant but was accepted as a necessary sacrifice to achieve the CEDA's goals. The CEDA was further to the right than any other group, yet could defend its parliamentary tactic by reference to its successes so far in repealing the legislation of the first *bienio*. 'We are going to get power, by whatever means,' he concluded; 'With the Republic? It doesn't matter. To do things otherwise would be senseless and suicidal.'[50] Such admissions could only convince the Left that Gil Robles was exploiting Republican legality as Hitler had used Weimar. The rally's style owed much to Gil Robles's visit to Germany.

Since the rally itself coincided with the political crisis over the amnesty, it naturally had the appearance of an attempt to put pressure on Alcalá Zamora by a show of force. The choice of Philip II's monastery of El Escorial as venue was an obviously anti-Republican gesture. Accordingly, a general strike was called in anticipation of a fascist 'march on Madrid'. Significantly, the lead in organising the strike was taken not by the Caballeristas of the Agrupación Socialista Madrileña but by the Trotskyist Izquierda Comunista, since the Socialists were reluctant to risk a clash with Salazar Alonso's new strike legislation.[51] The rally did little to allay left-wing fears. A crowd of 20,000 gathered in driving sleet in a close replica of the Nazi rallies. They swore loyalty to 'our supreme chief' and chanted, '¡Jefe! ¡Jefe! ¡Jefe!' – the Spanish equivalent of 'Duce'. The JAP's nineteen-point programme was recited, with emphasis on point two, 'Our leaders never make mistakes', a direct borrowing from the Italian Fascist slogan, '*Il Duce sempre ha raggione.*' The general tone was bellicose. Luciano de la Calzada, CEDA deputy for Valladolid, affirmed that 'Spain has to be defended against Jews, heretics, freemasons, liberals and Marxists.' Ramón Serrano Súñer, CEDA deputy for Zaragoza and later architect of Franco's National-Syndicalist state, fulminated against 'degenerate democracy'.

The high point of the rally was naturally a speech by Gil Robles. His aggresive harangue was greeted by delirious applause and prolonged chanting of '¡Jefe!' 'We are an army of citizens ready to give our lives for God and for Spain,' he cried. 'Power will soon be ours ... No one can stop us imposing our ideas on the government of Spain.' He was disparaging about foreign examples, but only because he felt that the same authoritarian and corporativist ideas so admired in Italy and Germany could be found in Spanish tradition.[52] 'I want this Spanish feeling to be exalted to paroxysm,' he declared. This tone, together with the parading, saluting and chanting, led the English correspondent Henry Buckley to see it as the trial for the creation of fascist shock troops. It was, in this sense, something of a failure. A turn-out of 50,000 had been expected, but, despite the transport facilities, the giant publicity campaign and the large sums spent, fewer than half that number arrived. Besides, as Buckley observed, 'There were too many peasants at El Escorial who told reporters quite cheerfully that they had been sent by the local political boss with fare and expenses paid.'[53]

What might have been the outcome had the rally been more of a success is a matter for speculation. Since all the CEDA's propaganda was left in the hands of the JAP, it is not surprising that the Socialists – and indeed the monarchists – took the fascist posturing of the youth as indicative of the predilections of their elders. This was, after all, taking place in the shadow of the widely publicised events in Germany and Austria. Even José Antonio Primo de Rivera, leader of the Falange, described the El Escorial rally as a 'fascist spectacle'.[54]

The immediate outcome of the crisis was that Martínez Barrio left the

Radical Party and Lerroux resigned in protest at Alcalá Zamora's delay in signing the amnesty and was replaced by Ricardo Samper, an ineffective Radical, incapable of independent policies. Lerroux had never considered the possibility that the President would accept his resignation. However, he gave Samper permission to form a government, because he was frightened that, if he did not, the President would dissolve the Cortes and call upon a Socialist to preside over new elections. Cándido Casanueva, the leader of the CEDA parliamentary minority, proposed another solution. This was for the CEDA and the monarchist deputies to join the Radicals in passing a vote of confidence in Lerroux, thereby provoking Alcalá Zamora's resignation. The CEDA's proposed scenario would then be completed by the elevation of Lerroux to the Presidency of the Republic.[55] It was an attempt by Gil Robles to speed his progress to power, since the new President would then have to call on him to form a government. Lerroux was too wily to fall for the manoeuvre. He knew that it was only a matter of time before he would be Prime Minister again. Accordingly, Samper formed a cabinet virtually identical to its predecessor. It continued to pursue a policy agreeable to the CEDA. A decree of 11 February which had evicted thousands of *yunteros* in Extremadura was followed by one on 4 May which annulled the post-10-August expropriations and by one on 28 May which left rural wages to the whim of the owners.[56]

The greatest practical victory for the CEDA's landed backers was the definitive repeal of the law of municipal boundaries. The successful assault on it in the Cortes had been led by the most aggressive of all CEDA deputies, Dimas de Madariaga (Toledo) and Ramón Ruiz Alonso (Granada), both representatives of provinces where the law's application had infuriated the large landowners. The outrage of the Socialists was expressed in a moving speech by María Lejárraga y García de Martínez Sierra, PSOE deputy for Granada. She said:

> We called for a law that would defend the poor against the rich but the rich must realise that a law which defends the poor against the rich is a law which preserves the privilege of the rich. We, to tell the truth, felt considerable qualms of conscience in trying to drag from the privileged some crumbs which would slow down the eventual triumph of our ideals . . . I ask myself, are we doing the right thing in struggling here? Are we doing the right thing in wanting to squeeze out a miserable improvement? Are we doing the right thing in wanting the way things are in Spain to go on even for just a year or two? Are we doing the right thing in

> sustaining the unsustainable? Are we doing the right thing in not precipitating the catastrophe? We the Socialists are not doing the right thing! We are not doing our duty! ... You do not want to concede anything; you do not want to listen to anything; you do not want to hear the voice of misery, the voice of hunger, the voice of those who work and produce.

The law was overthrown after a long and acrimonious debate which finally ended with the application of the guillotine on 23 May.[57]

The repeal of the law of municipal boundaries, just before the harvest was due to start, allowed the owners to bring in Portuguese and Galician labour to the detriment of local workers. The defences of the rural proletariat were falling rapidly before the right-wing onslaught. The last vestige of protection that left-wing workers had for their jobs and their wages was, in the countryside, that afforded them by the Socialist majorities on many town and village councils. Salazar Alonso had already begun to remove most of them, on the flimsiest pretexts. From the moment that he took up office, in response to petitions from local *caciques*, he had been giving orders for the removal of *alcaldes* who 'did not inspire confidence in matters of public order' – that is to say, Socialists. This left workers increasingly at the mercy of the *caciques'* retainers and the Civil Guard.[58]

The situation in the countryside was growing critical, as landowners took advantage of official acquiescence to slash wages and discriminate against union labour. Even *El Debate* commented on the harshness of many landlords, but it still continued to advocate that jobs be given only to affiliates of Catholic unions. In Badajoz starving labourers were begging in the streets of the towns. The monarchist expert on agrarian matters, the Vizconde de Eza, said that in May 1934 over 150,000 families lacked even the bare necessities of life. Workers who refused to rip up their union cards were denied work. The owners' boycott of unionised labour and the notorious '*Comed República*' ('Eat Republic' – or 'Let the Republic feed you') campaign were designed to reassert pre-1931 forms of social control and to ensure that the reformist challenge to the system mounted by the first *bienio* should never be repeated. In many villages, this determination was revealed by physical assaults on the Casa del Pueblo. A typical incident took place at Puebla de Don Fadrique, near Huéscar in the province of Granada. The Socialist *alcalde* was replaced by a retired army officer who was determined to put an end to what he saw as the workers' indiscipline. The Casa del Pueblo was sur-

148

rounded by a detachment of Civil Guard, and as the workers filed out they were beaten by the Guards and by retainers of the local owners.[59]

The response of the FNTT to this challenge was an illuminating example of how the newly revolutionised Socialists were reacting to increased aggression from the employers. The FNTT newspaper, *El Obrero de la Tierra*, had adopted a revolutionary line after the removal of the Besteirista executive on 28 January. The only solution to the misery of the rural working class, it maintained, was the socialisation of the land. In the meanwhile, however, the new executive adopted practical policies indistinguishable from those of their predecessors. They sent to the Ministers of Labour, Agriculture and the Interior a series of reasoned appeals for the application of the law regarding obligatory cultivation, work agreements, strict job rotation and labour exchanges, as well as protests at the systematic closures of the Casas del Pueblo. That was in the third week of March. When no action was taken, and, indeed, the persecution of left-wing workers began to increase prior to the harvest, a polite appeal was sent to Alcalá Zamora – also to no avail. The FNTT declared that thousands were slowly dying of hunger and published interminable lists, with details, of villages where union members were being refused work and physically attacked.[60]

Finally, in a mood of acute exasperation, the FNTT decided on a strike. The decision was not taken lightly. The first announcement of a possible strike was accompanied by an appeal to the authorities to impose respect for the *bases de trabajo* and equitable work-sharing.[61] The UGT executive committee advised the FNTT against calling a general strike of the peasantry and gave several reasons for this advice. In the first place, the harvest was ready at different times in each area, so the selection of a single date for the strike would lead to problems of co-ordination. Secondly, a general strike, as opposed to one limited to large estates, would cause hardship to leaseholders and sharecroppers who needed to hire one or two workers. Thirdly – showing even more strongly than the other two reasons the strength of the UGT's reformist tradition – the provocation offered by the owners and the authorities would be such as to push the peasants into violent confrontations. In a series of meetings between the UGT and the FNTT executives through-out March and April, efforts were made to persuade the peasants' representatives to a narrower strategy of staggered, partial strikes. The UGT pointed out that a general strike would be denounced by the government as revolutionary, that it risked a terrible repression which might in its turn provoke a national general strike, which the UGT was not prepared to call – a further stark illustration of how far the Socialist movement was from being able to launch a revolutionary action. Largo Caballero told the FNTT leaders not to expect any solidarity strikes from industrial workers and rejected an offer from the Partido Comunista de España to prepare a joint revolutionary strike. Moreover, the joint PSOE–UGT committee appointed in January to prepare the revolutionary movement sent messages to its sections in every province informing them that the peasants' strike had nothing to do with any such movement.[62]

The FNTT executive told the UGT that not to go along with their rank and file's demand for action would be to abandon them to hunger wages, political persecution and lock-out. Thus, a strike manifesto announced the beginning of the movement on 5 June. Before resorting to this measure, which was carried through in strict accordance with the law, ten days' notice being given of the strike, the FNTT leaders tried every possible procedure to impel the relevant ministries to apply the remaining social legislation. Yet hundreds of appeals for the payment of the previous year's harvest wages lay unheard at the Ministry of Labour. All over Spain, the work conditions agreed to by the mixed juries were simply being ignored. Protests were met by an intensification of repression. In the province of Badajoz, for instance, there were 20,000 unemployed and 500 workers in prison. In Fuente del Maestre, the Civil Guard met a typical hunger march with violence. Four workers were shot dead and several more wounded. A further forty were imprisoned. In the province of Toledo, FNTT affiliates found it almost impossible to get work. Those who did find a job had to accept the most grinding conditions. The *bases de trabajo* had decreed a wage of 4.50 pesetas for an eight-hour day. The owners were in fact paying 2.50 pesetas for *de sol a sol* (sun-up to sun-down) working. In parts of Salamanca, wages of 75 céntimos were being paid.[63] On 28 April, the FNTT sent an appeal to the Minister of Labour for action to remedy the situation simply by ensuring the implementation of the existing law. When nothing was done, the FNTT National Committee met on 11 and 12 May to decide on strike action. Its manifesto pointed out that 'this extreme measure' was the culmination of a series of useless negotiations and that the preparation of the strike was legal and open.[64]

The ten objectives of the strike could hardly be considered revolutionary. They had two basic objectives: to secure an improvement of the brutal conditions being suffered by rural labourers and to protect unionised labour from the manifest determination of the employer class to destroy the rural unions. The ten demands were (1) application of the *bases de trabajo*; (2) strict work rotation without prejudice of political affiliation; (3) limitation on the use of machinery and outside labour, to ensure forty days' work for the labourers of each province; (4) immediate measures against unemployment; (5) temporary take-over by the Institute of Agrarian Reform of lands scheduled for expropriation under the agrarian reform bill so that they might be rented out to the unemployed; (6) application of the law of collective leases; (7) recognition of the right of workers benefited by the law of obligatory cultivation to work abandoned land; (8) the settlement before the autumn of those peasants for whom the Institute of Agrarian Reform had land available; (9) the creation of a credit fund to help the collective leaseholdings; and (10) the recovery of the common lands. Before the announcement of the strike, the Minister of Labour, the Radical José Estadella Arnó, had denied that hunger wages existed in the countryside and that Socialist workers were being refused work. Now he recognised that something had to be done. He started to make token gestures, calling on the mixed juries to elaborate work contracts and on government labour delegates to report the employers' abuses of the law. Negotiations were also started with FNTT representatives.[65]

Salazar Alonso, however, was not prepared to lose this chance to strike a deadly blow at the largest section of the UGT. He was, after all, the political representative of the Badajoz landowners and a close collaborator of Gil Robles. Just as compromise negotiations between the FNTT and the Ministers of Agriculture and Labour were beginning to make progress, Salazar Alonso issued a decree making the harvest a national public service and the strike a 'revolutionary conflict'. All meetings, demonstrations and propaganda connected with the strike were declared illegal. Draconian press censorship was imposed. *El Obrero de la Tierra* was closed down, not to reopen until 1936. In the Cortes debate on Salazar Alonso's tough line, the CEDA votes, along with those of the Radicals and the monarchists, ensured a majority for the Minister of Interior. Nevertheless, the points raised in the debate starkly illuminated the issues at stake.

José Prat García, PSOE deputy for Albacete, opened with a speech pointing out the anti-constitutional nature of Salazar Alonso's measures. He reiterated that the FNTT had followed due legal process in declaring its strike. The application of existing legislation in a spirit of social justice would be more than sufficient to solve the conflict, claimed Prat in a reasoned appeal to the Cortes's sense of justice. Salazar Alfonso had, despite the availability of a peaceful solution, simply given the government a free hand for repression. The minister replied belligerently

151

that, because its objective was to make the government take action, it was a strike against the government. He said that there could be no question about the strike's revolutionary nature, since the executive of the FNTT were followers of Largo Caballero. Interestingly enough, Largo Caballero sprang to his feet to deny that he had ever rejected legality, confirming that his revolutionary rhetoric was meant to frighten the government and satisfy the impetuous demands of his own militants, without his ever seriously facing the prospect of putting it into practice. Prieto shouted out, 'The fact is that we are seeing an attempt to start a dictatorship.' When Salazar Alonso stated, falsely as it happened, that the government was taking steps against owners who imposed hunger wages, Prat replied that, on the contrary, the minister had frustrated all attempts at conciliation, by overruling the negotiations between the FNTT and the Ministers of Labour and Agriculture. He concluded by stating that the strike aimed only to protect the rural labourers and to end a situation that in Guadix (Granada) had reduced the workers to eating grass. José Antonio Trabal Sanz, Esquerra deputy for Barcelona, pointed out that Salazar Alonso seemed to regard the interests of the plutocracy and the national interest as synonymous. Cayetano Bolívar, Communist deputy for Málaga, claimed that the government's provocation was closing the doors of legality and pushing the workers to revolution. When Bolivar referred to the workers' hunger, a deputy from the right-wing majority shouted that they too were hungry and the debate ended.[66]

In fact, Salazar Alonso had long since been making plans, with the head of the Civil Guard and the Director-General of Security, for the repression of a possible strike. Conciliation had not, therefore, been uppermost in his mind, even before the strike started. His measures were now swift and ruthless. Workers' leaders were rounded up before the strike had started. Other liberal and left-wing individuals in the country districts were arrested wholesale. Even four Socialist deputies, along with numerous school-teachers and lawyers, were arrested – in flagrant violation of articles 55 and 56 of the Constitution. Several thousand peasants were loaded at gunpoint onto lorries and deported hundreds of miles away from their homes and then left to make their own way back penniless and on foot. Workers' centres were closed down and many town councils, especially in Badajoz and Cáceres, were removed, and the mayor and councillors replaced by government nominees. The government claimed that the strike call was not obeyed. The number of arrests and the maintenance of censorship for several weeks suggest otherwise. In fact, the stoppage seems to have been almost complete in Jaén, Granada, Ciudad Real, Badajoz and Cáceres, and substantial elsewhere in the south. In Jaén, there were violent clashes in many villages between strikers and the permanent workers (*fijos* and *pegaos*) and armed guards of the large estates. However, neither there nor in other less conflictive provinces could the strikers stop the owners drafting in outside labour, with Civil Guard protection, from Portugal, Galicia and elsewhere. The army was brought in to use threshing machines and the harvest was collected without serious interruption. Areas of CNT strength did not join in the strike, which limited its impact in Seville and Córdoba. Although most of the labourers arrested on charges of sedition were released by the end of August, emergency courts sentenced prominent workers' leaders to four or more years of imprisonment. The Casas del Pueblo were not reopened and the FNTT was effectively crippled until 1936. In an uneven battle, the FNTT had suffered a terrible defeat. In several provinces, the remaining Socialist *ayuntamientos* were overturned and replaced by town councils made up of the *caciques'* nominees. In one province, Granada, the Civil Governor, Mariano Muñoz Castellanos, was removed at the behest of local landowners because he had made an effort to ensure that the remaining labour legislation was implemented after the strike.[67]

Salazar Alonso had effectively put the clock back to the 1920s. There were no longer any rural unions, social legislation or municipal authorities to challenge the dominance of the caciques. The CEDA could not have been more delighted at this further practical demonstration of the advantages of legalism. Speaking in Badajoz, Gil Robles said that 'As long as the Radicals carry out our programme, there is no reason to change our attitude. Could we ask for more?' Two days later, on 2 June, he said that the government had fully implemented the CEDA's policy. There could be little other reason for the belligerence of Salazar Alonso's attitude than CEDA pressure, and his own authoritarian predilections, since the strike had so evidently not been a revolutionary bid for power. If it had been planned as such, instead of having limited material objectives, it would have been more ambitious and enjoyed the solidarity of the UGT's industrial workers. By choosing to regard the strike as revolutionary, Salazar Alonso was able to justify his attack on Socialist *ayuntamientos*; by the end of the conflict he had removed 193 of them.[68] By his determined and aggressive action during the peasant strike, the Minister of the Interior had inflicted a terrible blow on the largest union within the UGT. He had called Largo Caballero's revolutionary bluff and thereby significantly altered the balance of political power in favour of the Right.

In fact, the stalemate in the construction strike and the defeats suffered in both the printing and peasant strikes posed a major dilemma for the Socialists. The belligerent stance of the minister and the enthusiastic support that he received from Gil Robles confirmed the left-wing conviction that the Radicals were fulfilling the CEDA's authoritarian ambitions. It was the same conviction as had largely fuelled the revolutionary threats of late 1933 and early 1934. In fact, when, by the spring, it had become clear that those threats, far from inhibiting the CEDA and precipitating new elections, were simply justifying a rightwards swing of the government, the revolutionary ardour of Prieto and even of Largo had begun to cool. The one significant move that the Socialist Left had made in the direction of a revolutionary strategy was to adopt the notion of an Alianza Obrera (Workers' Alliance). The Alianza was the brainchild of Joaquín Maurín, leader of the quasi-Trotskyist Bloc Obrer i Camperol (Worker and Peasant Bloc). Foiled in an attempt to infiltrate the CNT and turn it into a bolshevik vanguard, throughout 1933 he advocated the Alianza Obrera as the only valid working-class response to the great advances of the authoritarian Right in Spain and elsewhere. After the electoral defeat in November 1933, the Socialists had started, understandably, to show interest in the notion.[69]

However, from the first it seemed that the Socialists saw the Alianza Obrera as a possible means of dominating the workers' movement in areas where the PSOE and UGT were relatively weak. They viewed the Alianza less as an instrument of rank-and-file working-class unity than as a liaison committee linking existing organisations.[70] In Madrid, the Alianza was dominated by the Socialists, who imposed their own policy. Throughout the spring and into the early part of the summer of 1934, they blocked every revolutionary initiative proposed by the representative of the Izquierda Comunista, Manuel Fernández Grandizo, and did so on the ostensible grounds that the UGT had to avoid partial actions and save itself for the ultimate struggle against fascism. In fact, these arguments reflected the innate caution of both Prieto and Largo Caballero and their desire to rely on revolutionary threats rather than risk revolutionary action. This was undermined even further by the debates over the peasant strike. Once Salazar Alonso had made it clear that there was to be no conciliation and that his objective was to break the FNTT, the only possibility of success for the landworkers' federation – and indeed for the UGT as a whole – was a massive show of solidarity by industrial workers. If such an action had taken place, it would either have brought down the government or have led to a bloody confrontation between the forces of order and the unions. Nevertheless,

154

not to declare industrial solidarity was to condemn the peasants to defeat. Faced with the harsh reality of putting his threats into action, Largo Caballero and the rest of the UGT executive refused to take such a dangerous step and devoted their efforts to a vain attempt to find a peaceful solution to the peasant dispute: before the strike was declared Pascual Tomás and José Díaz Alor had visited the Ministry of Labour and pleaded with the minister to intervene. Disgusted with the UGT's defensive policy which was tantamount to standing as a spectator while union after union – the metalworkers, the building workers, the printers and then the peasants – was drawn into strikes and defeated, the Izquierda Comunista representative ostentatiously withdrew from the Madrid Alianza.[71]

The reasons for Largo's caution were made clear when the UGT National Committee met on 31 July to hold an inquest into the failure of the peasant strike. Ramón Ramírez, the representative of the Federación de Trabajadores de la Enseñanza, the small school-teachers' union, attacked the UGT executive for its failure to go to the aid of the peasants and virtually accused Largo Caballero of being a reformist. Largo pointed out that he had warned Ricardo Zabalza, the FNTT secretary-general, before the strike that there would be no solidarity action. Zabalza claimed that his own rank and file gave him no choice but to go ahead with the strike. When the strike was under way and faced with difficulties, it hardly mattered that the UGT had predicted its defeat. Once Salazar Alonso had forced a major confrontation, the UGT had to face the choice of either watching its most important section broken or risk a major trial of strength with the government and the Right. It was a terrible dilemma. In the event, Largo's reformist background had prevailed. He was not prepared, he said, to see a repeat of the defeat of August 1917. He attacked the frivolous extremism of Ramón Ramírez, and, apparently forgetting his own rhetoric of four months previously and the existence of the joint revolutionary committee, declared that the Socialist movement must abandon its dangerous verbal revolutionism. When Ramírez read some texts of Lenin to the meeting, Largo replied that the UGT was not going to act in every case according to Lenin or any other theorist. With rare but incontrovertible realism, the UGT secretary-general reminded his young comrade that Spain in 1934 was not Russia in 1917. There was no armed proletariat; the bourgeoisie was strong. Under such circumstances, Lenin would not recommend revolutionary adventures. Other interventions at the meeting revealed the strength of reformist pragmatism of the senior union leaders within the UGT.[72]

The only section of the Socialist movement which, after the daunting experiences of the strikes of March to June, still maintained its flow of shrill revolutionary rhetoric was the Juventud Socialista. Although the younger elements acknowledged Largo as their spiritual leader, he seems to have become increasingly annoyed at their facile extremism, complaining that 'they did just what they felt like'.[73] The Socialist Youth were now committed to the idea of an armed insurrection but the activities of the joint PSOE–UGT–FJS revolutionary liaison committee had done little to give such an adventure any hope of success. For Largo Caballero and the other senior union leaders, the only weapon available to the working class was the general strike. August 1917 and December 1930 had shown them that little was to be expected from sympathetic elements in the army. Amaro del Rosal, Santiago Carrillo and Carlos Hernández Zancajo, however, were convinced that it would be possible to create an armed FJS militia which would seize the apparatus of the state when the moment came. However, their efforts to recruit a powerful militia, the accumulation of files of names of willing volunteers and their paper organisation into 'squads' and 'companies', came to little. There was no national organisation and the rank and file consistently failed to appear for dawn manoeuvres and drilling. Their strident publicity facilitated police vigilance. That together with the failure of their feeble efforts to buy arms severely diminished their chances of success. Despite Rosal's claim of 6000 Socialist militiamen in Madrid and 2000 in the Basque country, they probably never had more than a few hundred activists of whom only a handful ever had access to weapons. The FJS militias would be conspicuous by their absence when the revolution finally broke out.[74]

That the belligerent tone with which the Socialists had greeted their departure from power had led to no fundamental change of the UGT's tactics came as no surprise to more genuine revolutionaries. Largo Caballero had gone to Barcelona in February 1934 to negotiate the formation of the Alianza Obrera with the Trotskyist Izquierda Comunista and Bloc Obrer i Camperol, with the dissident anarcho-syndicalists, the Treintistas, and with various Catalanist groups, including the Unió Socialista and the Unió de Rabassaires. The CNT refused to join, on the grounds that 'the entire Socialist campaign for insurrection is a demagogic platform'. The anarchists distrusted the PSOE's revolutionism, especially after the lack of solidarity shown during their December 1933 uprising. They were convinced that the Socialists intended no more than to provoke new elections and return to the government in coalition with the Republicans. An open CNT appeal to the UGT in mid-February to prove its revolutionary sincerity had not elicited any reply. Even those parties which did join the Alianza soon found themselves in the grip of the UGT's cautious domination. Within a month of the creation of the Alianza, the Unió Socialista de Catalunya left in protest at Largo's oppressive tutelage in demanding that the party's leader, Joan Comorera, resign his seat in the Generalitat.[75]

The Izquierda Comunista also regarded the Socialists' revolutionism as fraudulent and were later to break with Trotsky partly because of that belief. They believed that Largo Caballero was only playing at revolution, and that his aim in doing so was to maintain his hold on the militant rank and file and to gain control over other revolutionary groups (in other words, they accused him of the classic sin of 'tailism', the social-democrat tactic of verbally outflanking the vanguard in order to neutralise their militancy).[76] When Manuel Fernández Grandizo temporarily withdrew from the Alianza during the peasant strike, he told the other delegates that the UGT's lack of solidarity with the FNTT revealed 'yet again that the Alianza Obrera is not for the Socialists an organism of the revolutionary united front, but merely an instrument with which to frighten the bourgeoisie'. The Izquierda Comunista had only a small following, but contained a team of highly competent Marxist theorists, headed by Andrés Nin.[77] Trotsky recommended that they follow the tactic of 'entryism' – that is, join the PSOE in the hope of accentuating its revolutionary line. All but a handful of the Izquierda Comunista rejected Trotsky's advice, because they were convinced that Largo Caballero's reformist grip could not be broken. They opted instead for a valid Marxist alternative, hoping that the Socialist rank and file would eventually see how they had been betrayed and then turn their backs on Largo Caballero.[78]

The Trotskyists did, however, agree sufficiently with Trotsky to remain convinced of the need for a united front against fascism. Accordingly they stayed in the Alianza Obrera, as the only potentially revolutionary instrument in Spain. In Madrid the Alianza was never able to overcome the UGT's irresolution, and in Barcelona it faced the almost insuperable obstacle of the CNT's lack of discipline. The one area where the Alianza was a success, uniting discipline and mass support, was Asturias. There were many reasons for this. The Asturian CNT had a long tradition of support for initiatives of working-class unity. The local CNT leaders, Eleuterio Quintanilla and José María Martínez, were sympathetic to the proposals of the Socialists. The high level of maturity that had been attained by the Asturian proletariat through the great mining strikes ensured thorough rank-and-file support for unity. The miners, perhaps more even than the peasants, realised how violently capitalism in crisis could react to the challenge of reformism. They had little doubt that a fascist threat existed. The SOMA newspaper, *Avance*, edited by Javier Bueno, reiterated that threat daily. With their life of brutal conditions and constant risk of violent death, the miners were not afraid to fight to defend what they had gained through years of gradual struggle. The Asturian Alianza Obrera was clinched on 28 March 1934 with the participation of the Socialists, the anarchists, the Izquierda Comunista and the Bloc Obrer i Camperol, only the Communists remaining outside. It maintained tight discipline, avoiding all sporadic strike action in order to conserve its strength for the expected fascist assault.[79]

Fascist or not, Gil Robles's strength seemed to be waxing in the summer of 1934. After defeating the peasants, the government felt sufficiently secure to extend its offensive elsewhere. The new area of operations was to be Catalonia, which, because of its autonomous status, was the area of Spain where the attack on the achievements of the Republic had been least effective. A crisis over Catalan agriculture was provoked in such a way during the summer as to suggest that the last Republican stronghold was now to come under attack. The Generalitat of Catalonia, in the hands of the left Republican Esquerra, had passed a law known as the *ley de contratos de cultivo*, a progressive measure which gave tenants some security of tenure and the right to buy land which they had worked for eighteen years. It was bitterly opposed by the landowners who rented out the plots. The Catalan conservative party, the Lliga, representative of the Catalan landlords and industrialists, protested to the central government with the enthusiastic support of the CEDA. This raised complex constitutional issues over the competence of the central government to intervene in Catalonia. The government, under pressure from the CEDA, handed the question to the Tribunal of Constitutional Guarantees, whose membership was predominantly right-wing.[80]

The Left was outraged when, on 8 June, and by only thirteen votes to ten, the court found in favour of the Lliga and against the Generalitat. Azaña said in parliament that 'the government of Catalonia is the only Republican power left standing in Spain'. The Generalitat replied to the challenge by passing the law again on 12 June, something Azaña considered their 'Republican obligation'. The Prime Minister, Samper, was inclined to negotiate, but the CEDA pressed for a harder line. Gil Robles was even opposed to any discussion of the matter in the Cortes. When a tense and lengthy debate took place over several days, he made two major speeches calling for the sternest application of the law against the Generalitat's 'act of rebellion'. As Samper vacillated, Gil Robles's support for the government began to waver. Throughout the crisis *El Debate* called for the government to make the Catalans submit. This attitude reflected the traditional centralism of the Castilian Right, although it also derived from the fact that the CEDA's landed backers resented any threat to their privileges.[81]

The threat to the Generalitat raised the possibility of the revival of the broad Republican–Socialist solidarity which had characterised the years 1931–3. Profoundly uneasy about the implications of his party's revolutionary rhetoric, Prieto had maintained contact with Azaña and Marcelino Domingo in the conviction that the defence of the Republic was impossible without their collaboration. This had provoked the hostility of Largo Caballero, who, at a joint meeting of the executive committees of the PSOE and the UGT in mid-March 1934, had declared that there would be no collaboration with the Republicans either in the revolutionary movement or in the subsequent provisional government.[82]

As the Catalan crisis blew up into ever more conflictive proportions, there were rumours that Alcalá Zamora might be obliged to resign in protest at the government's treatment of the Generalitat. Azaña sent messages to the Socialist leadership via Prieto to enquire as to what their reaction would be if the President did so and, by implication, suggesting some form of co-ordinated action. On 2 July, a joint meeting of the UGT and PSOE executives debated whether this was the moment to launch the planned revolution and whether, after its triumph, there should be, as Prieto, Fernando de los Ríos and Anastasio de Gracia advocated, a Republican–Socialist coalition or, as the Caballeristas wanted, an exclusively Socialist government. The majority decided against any understanding with the Republicans and Enrique de Francisco was instructed to inform Azaña, and the Catalan leader, Lluis Companys, of that decision.[83]

Nevertheless, given the gravity of the situation, Azaña now requested a meeting with the Socialist leadership to discuss 'a joint political plan'. He did so formally in his capacity as president of Izquierda Republicana, which had been formed on 2 April 1934 from the merger of the left wing of the Partido Radical Socialista under Marcial Domingo, Santiago Casares Quiroga's Organización Regional Gallega Autónoma and his own Acción Republicana. The meeting took place on 14 July at the home of José Salmerón, secretary-general of Azaña's new party. Salmerón, Marcelino Domingo and Azaña represented Izquierda Republicana and were accompanied by Companys's lieutenant, Juan Lluhí i Vallescá, the Generalitat's Minister of Justice. Largo Caballero, Enrique de Francisco and the Caballerista Manuel Lois, leader of the shopworkers' union, represented the PSOE. Azaña spoke for an hour about the need for unity and the profound effect that the announcement of such unity would have on the political situation. He was absolutely right. There was more chance of Alcalá Zamora considering a dissolution of the Cortes and the calling of elections as the best pacific solution to the present crisis, if there had existed a united bloc of left Republican and Socialist forces. Largo Caballero, however, was not interested and said that he had attended the meeting merely 'out of personal deference to those who had called it'. He declared at that meeting that he could not be seen by the Socialist masses to be entering into an agreement with the Republicans for fear of being 'materially and morally diminished'. In the hope that circumstances might change, Azaña concluded the meeting with a formula which left the door open to future contacts: 'Each would develop his thoughts in case circumstances required their modification'.[84] It would require tragic events before the bulk of the Socialist movement would contemplate such contact. As it was, several editorials in El Socialista in the course of July rejected out of hand any possibility of a return to the 1931 Republican–Socialist coalition.[85]

It was a tragically ironic commentary on the confused situation at the top of the Socialist movement that its leaders should thus turn their backs on their greatest potential allies just as their enemies were preparing to strike. Behind the appearance of tight unity, with Caballerista executives in the PSOE, the UGT and the FJS, the movement was severely divided. The brave talk of revolution, like the chaotic attempts at organising it, was no more than a sham. The younger bolshevisers believed firmly in their Leninist dreams of armed insurrection but had little or no idea of how to make it happen. The more experienced trade union followers of Largo Caballero used the same revolutionary phrases but with decreasing conviction. The outrage of November and December 1933 had given way to alarm at the way in which the organised labour movement had been decimated during the strikes of the spring and early summer of 1934. The Right was fully aware of the emptiness of the revolutionary threat, but happy to feign belief in its menace in order to justify a pre-emptive strike.

5

A BLUFF CALLED
The insurrection of 1934

One of the central paradoxes of the Socialist position in 1934 was the role of Indalecio Prieto. Normally a shrewd realist with an acute sense of humour, he was also given to bouts of despair. His dabblings in the revolutionary posturings of the Socialist movement in 1934 were born of that essential despair. Given the ferocity of the rightist attacks on the working class in the wake of the November 1933 elections, he shared the blind outrage which suffused the entire Socialist movement. His case was symptomatic of the senior trade union leadership. In no mood to listen to Azaña's counsels of reason and perhaps, in their desperation, seduced by the possibility that revolutionary action, or at least the threat of it, might reverse the rightist triumph, Prieto and Anastasio de Gracia, Ramón González Peña and others went along with the Caballeristas in January 1934. As his natural pessimism reasserted itself, Prieto was probably the least convinced of the Socialist would-be revolutionaries, yet, ironically, he would be the one to make the most serious efforts to buy arms. While the young Socialists organised their early morning manoeuvres under the eyes of the police, he at least was determined that there should be some substance to the revolutionary threats.

Years later, speaking in the Círculo Pablo Iglesias in Mexico City, he said remorsefully:

> I declare myself guilty before my own conscience, before the Socialist Party and before the whole of Spain, for my participation in that revolutionary movement. I declare it as guilt, as sin, not as glory. I am free of blame for the genesis of that movement, but I must take full responsibility for its preparation and development ... I accepted tasks from which others fled because there hung over them the risk not only of losing their liberty but the more painful shadow of losing their honour. Nevertheless, I

undertook those tasks. I collaborated in that movement heart and soul, I accepted the aforementioned tasks and I found myself violently outraged.[1]

Despite Prieto's efforts, the preparations for revolution were chaotic and ineffectual.

Largo Caballero's PSOE–UGT–FJS liaison committee had built up a large collection of file-cards with details of potential local revolutionary committees and militias. However, the infrastructure of the revolution was more substantial in the committee's filing system than on the street. Each union and party or FJS section made its own exiguous arrangements for creating militias, usually no more than drawing up lists of names of those who might be prepared to 'take to the streets'. There was no central co-ordination. Largo Caballero himself commented that the majority of local party and union leaders thought that

the revolution was inevitable but feared it and just hoped that some initiative or incident might see it avoided and so they invested only the minimum effort in its preparation, not wanting to appear to be hostile to it in order to keep the loyalty of their members.

He might well have been talking about himself.[2]

The Sunday excursions of the young Socialists to practise military manoeuvres in Madrid's Casa del Campo, armed with more enthusiasm than weapons, daunted no one. Indeed, Salazar Alonso had virtually no difficulty in eliminating these activities. Desultory forays into the arms market had seen the Socialists lose some of their scarce funds to unscrupulous arms dealers and had produced only small caches of revolvers and rifles hidden in Casas del Pueblo or private houses on the outskirts of towns. Since the police were fully informed, either by spies or by the arms dealers themselves, about the purchases, their raids on Socialist centres and headquarters were usually uncannily fruitful. They seemed to know exactly where weapons could be found behind false walls, under floorboards or in wells. Various contacts were made with allegedly sympathetic officers in the army, the Civil Guard and the Assault Guard, which could account for leaks to the authorities. The most celebrated arms purchase, of astonishing complexity, was carried out by Prieto. Arms – initially destined for exiled enemies of the Portuguese dictatorship, who had not paid for them, and now allegedly being sent to the Abyssinian government – were shipped to Asturias on the steamer *Turquesa*. In an incident redolent of Ruritanian adventure, the shipment fell partly into the hands of the police but Prieto escaped.

The remainder was not substantial. Only in Asturias, thanks to pilfering from local small-arms factories and dynamite available in the mines, was the local working class armed.[3]

Nothing points more brutally to the lack of conviction behind the Caballeristas' revolutionary rhetoric than the fact that they had taken no steps to harness for the projected revolution the wave of industrial militancy which had swept through the Socialist rank and file throughout 1934. Not only had that militancy been dissipated, but as the printers' and landworkers' strikes had shown, industrial conflicts had been fought at times and on battlefields chosen by the Right.

Similar doubts about the Caballeristas' seriousness are raised by their choice of the strategic moment for the launching of the revolution. That had been linked to the entry of the CEDA into the government. Given Gil Robles's similarity to Dollfuss, the events of Austria in February 1934 had convinced the Socialists that the arrival of the CEDA in power would be the prelude to their annihilation. Accordingly, while the Caballerista leadership of the UGT had presided over the erosion of the trade union movement's strength in one disastrous strike after another, the moment for unleashing the final battle had been left in the hands of others. That alone is sufficient to suggest that for the bulk of the Socialist leadership, if not for the bolshevising youth, there was never any real intention of making a revolution. Largo Caballero was convinced that President Alcalá Zamora would never invite the CEDA to join the government because its leaders had never declared their loyalty to the Republic.[4] If that was an accurate prediction, then the Socialist hope could only have been that eventually the President could be impelled to call new elections. The experience of November 1933 had shown that the Socialists could not win alone. Accordingly, they should have been working towards the re-creation of the Republican–Socialist electoral understanding. However, Largo Caballero was sufficiently carried away by his half-understood Marxist rhetoric to reject any formal link with the 'bourgeois' Left Republicans.

It is hardly surprising then that Prieto had spent much of 1934 in an agonising dilemma. He had undertaken various tasks on behalf of the revolutionary committee not only without conviction but in the belief, shared with Azaña, that the defence of the Republic and its social achievements lay elsewhere – in the rebuilding of the Republican–Socialist coalition. Throughout the year, Azaña had issued both public and private warnings about the dangers of continued left-wing disunity. That had been the theme of a speech he had made to a large crowd at the Barcelona bullring on 7 January 1934. In reply to Prieto's public

163

threat on 4 February of revolutionary action if the Right did not desist from its onslaught on the working class, Azaña, exactly seven days later, also speaking at the Teatro Pardiñas in Madrid, made a monumental speech warning against the frivolous resort to revolutionary solutions. It was a reasoned appeal for unity and moderation, but few Socialists, including even Prieto, were yet ready to pay him heed. Having gone against party policy to include Azaña in the electoral slate for Bilbao, Prieto had needed no such warning, but he seems to have hardened his heart to Azaña's advice.[5] Nevertheless, Azaña had persisted. Even the rebuff from Largo Caballero at the beginning of July had not shaken Azaña's determination to re-establish contact with the Socialists.

Controlling all the major sections of the Socialist movement, Largo Caballero seems to have been pinning his hopes on the threat of revolution both inhibiting the Right and also impelling the President to calling elections which would be won by the Socialists. There is little about his behaviour at any point in 1934 – either in refusing to subject strike declarations to the overall control of the revolutionary committee or immediately before and during the revolutionary crisis of October 1934 – to suggest that Largo Caballero personally ever believed that his bluff would be called. On the other hand, it is clear that the existence of a revolutionary threat, particularly an empty one, played neatly into the hands of the Right. Both Gil Robles and Salazar Alonso were ready to take any advantage of the Socialists' rhetoric to strengthen the position of the Right. That had been illustrated brutally during the printers' and landworkers' strikes. It was also something which underlay the Catalan crisis of the summer months. Both the Left Republicans and many Socialists regarded Catalonia as the last remaining outpost of the 'authentic' Republic. Moreover, the Catalan leader, Lluís Companys, had declared that Catalonia would come to the defence of the Left in Spain if it were threatened by fascism and reaction.[6]

There is little doubt that the Catalan crisis was being manipulated by Gil Robles in such a way as to provoke the Left. This was revealed clearly on 8 September, when the Catalan landowners' federation, the Instituto Agrícola Catalán de San Isidro, organised an assembly in Madrid. The Socialists reluctantly called a general strike.[7] The Bloque Patronal, the employers' bloc, which had recently announced its determination to reduce the unions to submission, issued detailed instructions for blacklegging and reprisals to be taken against the strikers. The assembly was attended by representatives of all the major pressure groups of the rural oligarchy – the Asociación General de Ganaderos (Stockbreeders' Association), the Agrupación de Propietarios de Fincas

Rústicas (Rural Landowners' Group), the Asociación de Olivareros (Olive-growers' Association), the Confederación Española Patronal Agrícola (Spanish Agrarian Employers' Federation) and many regional organisations. The police prepared for the meeting by closing down the Madrid Casa del Pueblo and the UGT offices and by arresting large numbers of Socialists and other leftists. The assembly was indistinguishable from any other held by the agrarian financiers of the CEDA. Its objectives – the limitation of the rights of the unions, the strengthening of the forces of authority and, more specifically, the crushing of the Generalitat's 'rebellion' – were the CEDA's. Addressed by Gil Robles, its tone could be gauged from the frequent ovations for aggressive monarchist leaders like Calvo Sotelo and Goicoechea, as well as for the Catalan Carlist Joaquín Bau.[8]

The Catalan owners' assembly was part of a campaign being orchestrated by Gil Robles to impress upon the President the Right's dissatisfaction with Samper's government and his reluctance to adopt harsher methods. It was part of a steady build-up of pressure to oblige Alcalá Zamora, sooner rather than later, to invite the CEDA to form part of a coalition government. Already, in mid-August, Gil Robles had decided to make it clear to Samper that his cabinet was no longer to the CEDA's liking and could not count on its parliamentary support for much longer. On 5 September he warned both Samper and Salazar Alonso that at a JAP rally to be held on the 9th he would publicly announce his discontent with the government's unsatisfactory approach to public order. That he would do so had been common knowledge throughout the summer. On 21 August, *El Socialista* had reported that Gil Robles intended to withdraw support from Samper and demand participation in the government himself. The site for the JAP rally was to be Covadonga in Asturias, the starting-point for the reconquest of Spain from the Moors – its selection clearly a symbol of belligerence. The rally closely resembled that of El Escorial in organisation and it had a similar purpose, that of mounting a show of strength during a government crisis.

The Asturian Alianza Obrera saw the rally as a fascist provocation by which the CEDA would force its way to power. A general strike was called, roads into the province were blocked, and railway lines were sabotaged. Salazar Alonso arranged two trains with naval personnel and Civil Guard escorts.[9] Thus the rally went on, albeit on a reduced scale. The local CEDA leader, José María Fernández Ladreda, announced threateningly that 'the masses of Acción Popular, irrespective of who stands in the way, will conquer power to bring the reconquest of Spain'. The implication was that the Left was the contemporary equivalent of the foreign infidel and should be swept out of Spain. Gil Robles also spoke in warlike terms of the need to deal with the 'separatist rebellion' of the Catalans and the Basque Nationalists, with whom government mishandling had also caused a conflict. The supreme Jefe of the JAP worked himself up to a frenzy of patriotic rhetoric and demanded that nationalist sentiment be exalted 'with ecstasy, with paroxysms, with anything; I prefer a nation of lunatics to a nation of wretches'. He went on to comment that the CEDA was advancing to power with giant steps.[10]

There was more than a small element of provocation of the Left involved in what was happening. Gil Robles was aware that the Left considered him a fascist. He was also fully aware that the Socialists intended to prevent the CEDA coming to power, something they regarded as synonymous with the establishment of fascism. He knew that the Caballerista leadership of the Socialist movement had linked its threats of revolution specifically to the entry of the CEDA into the cabinet. He was confident that the Left was not in a position to succeed in a revolutionary attempt. Constant police activity throughout the summer had dismantled most of the sporadic preparations made by the revolutionary committee and captured most of the weapons that it had managed to buy. Gil Robles wanted to enter the government because rather than in spite of the fact that it would have serious consequences in terms of the Socialists' reaction. 'Sooner or later,' he wrote afterwards, 'we would have to face a revolutionary coup. It would always be preferable to face it from a position of power before the enemy were better prepared.'[11]

Lerroux was also aware of this argument, since Salazar Alonso had been broadcasting it in more blatant form for some time. If the entry of the CEDA into the government was the necessary pretext which would provoke a revolutionary bid from the Socialists and justify a definite blow against it, then the CEDA must be invited into the government. On 11 September, at a deeply conflictive cabinet meeting, Salazar Alonso proposed the declaration of martial law precisely in order to provoke a premature outbreak of a revolutionary strike. Both the Prime Minister, Ricardo Samper, and the Minister of Agriculture, Cirilo del Río Rodríguez, protested at such irresponsible cynicism. 'The problem', said Salazar Alonso, 'was no less than that of starting the counter-revolutionary offensive to proceed with a work of decisive government to put an end to the evil.' It was not just a question of smashing the revolution but of setting up durable counter-revolutionary barriers against the Left.[12]

The Radical Minister of the Interior, with the collusion of some of his ministerial colleagues, had already cynically tried to provoke a revolutionary strike in order to have a justification for crushing the Left. That may be deduced from his politically provocative measures, culminating in the harvest strike. The President of the Republic was aware of the Socialists' rhetorical preparations for a revolution. He believed, rightly, that they were being made in order to pressure him into calling new elections. He concluded that the best response would be to clamp down on those preparations as soon as possible. Accordingly, on several occasions in the spring and summer of 1934, he offered to sign the necessary decrees suspending constitutional guarantees in several provinces in order to permit searches for, and confiscations of, arms. Salazar Alonso had refused the offers with knowing contempt, presumably in the knowledge that such measures would curtail his plans for a larger-scale repression of the Left.[13] In this context, the possibility arises that military manoeuvres, planned in the late spring and to be held in León in late September, were part of his wider plan.

Gil Robles admitted even at the time that he shared Salazar Alonso's declared provocative intentions. He knew that the Left intended to react violently to what it saw as an attempt to establish a Dollfuss-type regime. He was equally aware that its chances of success were remote. Speaking in the Acción Popular offices in December he said:

I was sure that our arrival in the government would immediately provoke a revolutionary movement . . . and when I considered that blood which was going to be shed, I asked myself this question: 'I can give Spain three months of apparent tranquillity if I do not enter the government. If we enter, will the revolution break out? Better that it do so before it is well prepared, before it defeats us.' This is what Acción Popular did, it precipitated the movement, met it and implacably smashed it from within the government.[14]

The Covadonga meeting suggested that the CEDA was now ready to flex its muscles.

The time was as propitious as it would ever be. In mid-September, the military commander of the Balearic Islands, General Francisco Franco, left his post in Mallorca and travelled to the mainland to take up an invitation from the Minister of War, Diego Hidalgo, to join him as his personal technical adviser during the army manoeuvres that were due to take place in León at the end of the month under the direction of General Eduardo López Ochoa. It is these large-scale manoeuvres which seem to have been part of a wider project by Salazar Alonso, Hidalgo and Gil Robles to crush the Left. The manoeuvres were held in an area contiguous, and of nearly identical terrain, to Asturias where the final left-wing bid to block the CEDA's passage to power was likely to come.[15] In retrospect, it appears more than a coincidence that Salazar Alonso's colleague and fellow deputy for Badajoz, Diego Hidalgo, should have arranged for General Franco to accompany him as his personal adviser on those manoeuvres and thereby have him available to direct repressive operations against the revolutionary strike the provocation of which was the intention, on their own accounts, of both Salazar Alonso and Gil Robles.

It is not clear why the Minister of War should have needed a 'personal technical adviser' on the manoeuvres when López Ochoa, the Chief of the General Staff, and every other senior officer present were under his orders. On the other hand, if the central concern was the ability of the army to crush a left-wing action, Franco was more likely to give firm advice than López Ochoa or General Carlos Masquelet, the Chief of Staff, both of whom were convinced Republicans, freemasons and friends of Azaña. Franco's lifelong friend and first biographer, Joaquín Arrarás, claimed that when Hidalgo invited Franco to leave the Balearics and come to the mainland, 'his real intention was to ensure that the general would be in Madrid at the Minister's side during the hazardous days which were expected'.[16] There can be no doubt that Hidalgo was aware of a possible left-wing insurrection in Asturias. At the end of August, he had named General Fanjul to head an investigation into the loss of weapons from the state small-arms factories in the area.[17] Moreover, in early September, when some members of the cabinet had been in favour of cancelling the manoeuvres, Hidalgo had insisted that they go ahead precisely because of imminent left-wing threats. Once the revolutionary strike did break out in Asturias in early October, the astonishing speed with which Franco was able to order the Spanish Legion from Africa to Asturias suggests some prior consideration of the problem. Three days before the manoeuvres began, Hidalgo ordered the Regiment no.3 from Oviedo which was to have taken part not to leave the Asturian capital also because he expected a revolutionary outbreak.[18]

On the Right, the readiness of the army to deal with a likely leftist initiative seems to have been an issue of frequent discussion. Salazar Alonso raised it at cabinet meetings and in press interviews. At this time, secret contacts between the CEDA and senior military figures had provided assurances that the Army was confident of being able to crush any leftist uprising provoked by CEDA entry into the cabinet.[19]

There was a tremendous air of crisis throughout September. Many on the Left, and not just the Socialists, felt that something had to be done to stop further erosion of the Republic. Azaña made one last try to get the Socialists to see reason. On 26 September 1934, Jaume Carner, the wealthy Catalan Republican who had been Azaña's Minister of Finance, died. Azaña went to the funeral along with numerous other Republican figures. In fact, he had been in Barcelona less than a month previously and had made a speech calling for the reconquest of the Republic. Now, at the end of September, meeting Prieto and De los Ríos in Barcelona, Azaña lamented the lack of agreement between the Socialists and the left Republicans. The realism of what Azaña had to say was particularly painful to Prieto, who agreed with it in its entirety yet found himself irrevocably hitched to the Caballerista leviathan. As Azaña himself noted:

> Prieto maintained a stony silence throughout the entire discussion. All that we said probably seemed otiose to him, and perhaps he was right. I was sure that Prieto did not approve of the plans for armed insurrection but that he was going along with them out of fatalism, out of a belief that they were unstoppable, out of party discipline.[20]

On 30 September, Martínez Barrio made the closing speech at the congress of Unión Republicana – the party he had formed with those liberal elements who had accompanied him when he abandoned the Radicals and the right wing of the Radical Socialist Party under Félix Gordón Ordás. His words were bitter and pessimistic as he made reference to

> this disfigured Republic which is on the way to becoming a debased Republic ... The regime in Spain is still, legally speaking, a Republican one; but in reality, if we are to judge by the political and administrative physiognomy of the towns of Spain, it is no longer a Republican regime but a monarchical and dictatorial one.

The Left – from Martínez Barrio, via Azaña, to Largo Caballero himself – expected the crisis to be resolved by Alcalá Zamora calling elections, and the Socialists began to step up their revolutionary rhetoric as part of their attempt to convince the President of the dangers of letting the CEDA enter the government. The conviction that the threatened revolution would not have to be unleashed is the only plausible explanation for the Socialists' lack of preparation. Genuine revolutionary elements later complained bitterly about the fact that the PSOE had not grasped the revolutionary initiative and had been unwillingly forced into a defensive movement.[21]

The extent to which Largo Caballero was convinced that Niceto

Alcalá-Zamora would never open the doors of power to the enemies of the Republic was starkly illustrated by what, at the time, seemed like a minor dispute within the Socialist Party. On 1 October 1934, exasperated by the radicalised Left's complaints that the so-called *minoría parlamentaria* (the group of PSOE parliamentary deputies in the Cortes) was insufficiently revolutionary, Prieto had proposed at a meeting of the PSOE National Committee that the *minoría* be submitted to the overall authority of the party executive. His aim was to oblige the radicalised executive to stand publicly by its revolutionary commitments. Prieto won the vote. Largo Caballero, who was prevented by illness from attending the meeting, disagreed with the proposal on the procedural grounds that such a decision transgressed articles 26 and 27 of the party statutes and therefore required a decision of the party's full congress. He wrote a letter to this effect to the National Committee in which he denounced the move as a *'pequeño golpe de Estado'* (a little *coup d'état*) and resigned as president of the PSOE. His fastidiousness indicated just how far he was from those who wanted to bolshevise the party at any cost and turn it into a centralised instrument. Resignation as PSOE president implied the abandonment of his position within the revolutionary liaison committee. Unless this was only a subterfuge to bypass his responsibilities just before the revolution broke out, it has to be concluded that he was making his threat in the utter confidence that, in the last resort, it would not be necessary to put the revolutionary threats into action. In the event, his resignation was not accepted.[22]

On 26 September the CEDA opened the crisis by announcing that it could no longer support a minority government. Its communiqué claimed that, in view of the present government's 'weakness' regarding social problems and irrespective of the consequences, a strong government with CEDA participation had to be formed. The resignation of Samper was precipitated, as foreseen, on 1 October. Samper announced to the Cortes that a solution to the Catalan problem was near. Gil Robles responded with an attack on the government's lack of decision and a call for a government which reflected the numerical composition of the chamber. The demand was backed by an unmistakable threat: 'we are conscious of our strength both here and elsewhere'. Alcalá Zamora held the normal consultations on the resolution of the crisis. Moderate Republicans, such as Martínez Barrio and Sánchez Román, advised him not to allow the entry of the CEDA into the government. The Socialists consulted, Julián Besteiro and Fernando de los Ríos, counselled the dissolution of the Cortes and the calling of elections. It was a difficult decision. The CEDA was the largest party in the Cortes, but, as Besteiro pointed out, its programme was clearly in opposition to both the spirit and the letter of the Constitution. Gil Robles's determination to establish a corporative state made his party's inclusion in the government a threat to the regime. Alcalá was told that because of the Right's power of electoral pressure, the number of CEDA deputies in the Cortes was a considerable exaggeration of its popular numerical support. There was, then, a case to be made for a dissolution and elections. The President, however, decided to entrust Lerroux with the task of forming a cabinet, with CEDA participation, hoping that this would be limited to one ministry. Gil Robles insisted on three, despite efforts to persuade him that this was being deliberately provocative. He claimed that the dignity of his party and the need to counteract the 'congenital debility' of the Radicals made three the minimum number acceptable.[23]

The provocation did not end there. The cabinet was announced on 4 October and contained three Cedistas, José Oriol y Anguera de Sojo (Labour), Rafael Aizpún (Justice) and Manuel Giménez Fernández (Agriculture). Anguera de Sojo was a deliberately provocative choice. On the one hand, he had been the public prosecutor responsible for a hundred confiscations and numerous fines suffered by *El Socialista*. Equally, as an extreme ultraist member of the Instituto Agricola Catalán de San Isidro, he was a bitter enemy of the Esquerra, the Catalan Republican party ruling in the Generalitat. As a hard-line Civil Governor of Barcelona in 1931, his uncompromising strike-breaking policies had pushed the CNT towards insurrectionism. The choice was consciously offensive, since the Esquerra sent a deputation to see Alcalá Zamora and plead for his exclusion. Gil Robles refused point-blank the suggestions of the President.[24] Aizpún, CEDA deputy for Pamplona, was anything but a convinced Republican, and made no secret of his strong Traditionalist convictions. Giménez Fernández was, as it happened, to turn out to be one of the more moderate Cedistas. This, however, was an unknown factor and could do nothing to mitigate the Left's unease at the prospect of a CEDA Minister of Agriculture. The harsh policies favoured by the CEDA's landowning supporters were well known and it was felt that a CEDA minister could only intensify the awful repression that had followed the harvest strike. Moreover, Giménez Fernández, as deputy for Badajoz, was inevitably assumed to be as faithful a representative of the aggressive landlords of that province as Salazar Alonso had been. The suppositions about the minister were wrong; those about the Badajoz landlords were right. Because of his relatively liberal policies, he was not accepted as a candidate for Badajoz in the 1936 elections and was forced to run in Segovia. He was one of the very few prominent Cedistas later to oppose the Franco dictatorship.[25]

In the light of the policies followed by the Radicals when the CEDA was not yet in the government, the Socialists were convinced that the new cabinet would consolidate the trend towards authoritarian and reactionary rule. On 1 August the National Committee of the UGT had issued a detailed denunciation of the political situation which had developed since the Radicals had been in power. It pointed out that 222 of the 315 days of Radical government had seen the country submitted to an official *estado de alarma* (state of emergency), which meant the suspension of constitutional guarantees, and that sixty of the ninety-three days on which there was constitutional normality were during the electoral period of late 1933. Press censorship, fines and seizures of newspapers, limitation of the right of meeting and association, declaration of the illegality of almost all strikes, protection for fascist and monarchist activities, reduction of wages and the removal of freely elected Socialist *ayuntamientos* amounted, for the UGT, to the establishment of a 'regime of white terror'. Yet Gil Robles had denounced these policies as weakness and clearly intended to impose more repressive ones. In late September, while there remained a slight hope of persuading the President to resolve the crisis by calling elections, the Socialist press resorted to desperate threats. Talking as if the revolution was highly prepared, *El Socialista* announced that only loose ends remained to be tied up for the workers' army to be mobilised. 'Next month', it cried, 'could be our October.' It is inconceivable that Zugazagoitia, the editor for the PSOE paper, was unaware of the fact that the Socialist movement was anything but ready for a revolutionary confrontation with the state. If his paper's line was not senseless irresponsibility – and Julián Zugazagoitia, despite his annoyance with his own failure to gain a seat in the Cortes in the November 1933 elections, remained a faithful supporter of Prieto and was not an extremist – it can be seen only as a last-ditch threat to the President.[26]

Three days before the new government was announced, Fernando de los Ríos issued a last appeal for a change of direction of Republican politics. He pointed out that, at a time when an increasing number of the workers and the middle classes were turning to the Socialist movement, the persecution of its organisations, the imprisonment of its members, the closure of its societies and the removal of its town councils were part of a deliberate strategy to force it into illegality. It was both a declaration of weakness and a plea for the PSOE's revolutionary bluff not to be called. Alleging that the entry of the CEDA into the government would lead to policies which it had been the purpose of the Republic to avoid, he called on the President to bring the Socialists into the government as a prelude to new elections.[27] These were hardly revolutionary objectives. In fact, although he loyally kept his doubts to himself, De los Ríos disagreed with the revolutionary tactic and had decided that, after the crisis, he would withdraw from politics.

The executives of the PSOE and the UGT met and agreed that, if indeed the President did what they were sure he would not do – invite the CEDA to join the government – then the revolution must be launched. Coded telegrams – with messages like 'I arrive tomorrow', 'Angela is better', 'Pepe's operation went well' – were sent to local committees in every province. However, far from making the final preparations for the seizure of power, Largo Caballero's revolutionary committee spent the next three days 'anxiously awaiting' news of the composition of the cabinet in Prieto's apartment. Largo himself remained totally convinced that Alcalá Zamora would never hand over power to the CEDA. The revolutionary militias had neither leadership nor organisation, and indeed very few members. At 11 p.m. on 3 October, two Socialist journalists, Carlos de Baraibar and José María Aguirre, turned up with the news that a government had been formed with CEDA participation. Although the news was still unofficial several members of the revolutionary committee declared that the time had come to start the movement. Largo, however, stated flatly that 'Until I see it in the *Gaceta* [the government bulletin], I won't believe it.' Only the arrival of some soldiers shortly after announcing that the new cabinet had already declared martial law convinced him. Even then, it seems to have been with reluctance that the Socialists prepared for action. However, they felt that they had no choice. 'The die was cast,' wrote Largo.[28]

The response of all of Spain's Republican forces to the new cabinet was, with the obvious exception of the Radicals, unanimous. They all issued statements declaring that the entry of the CEDA into the government was a direct assault on the essence of the Republic. The Socialists were not alone in their estimate of the CEDA. Azaña's Izquierda Republicana stated that 'the monstrous fact of handing over the government of the Republic to its enemies is treason' and broke with the institutions of the regime. A similar note from Martínez Barrio's Unión Republicana referred to the falsification of the Republic. One of the most significant notes came from Miguel Maura's Partido Republicano Conservador, which was anything but left-wing and had even entered electoral coalitions with the CEDA in the 1933 elections. It stated that the policy of 'surrendering the Republic to its declared and secret enemies was engendering civil war'. The CEDA's public hostility to the essential postulates to which the regime was committed provoked Maura to declare his 'incompatibility with this disfigured Republic'. It is impossible to exaggerate the importance of this moment. Although political differences were to intensify between October 1934 and the outbreak of the Civil War, the basic polarisation of forces would now go no further. Those parties which opposed the entry of the CEDA into the government were those which resisted the military rising of 1936, and vice versa.[29] The division in 1934, as it was to be in 1936, was between those who wanted the Republic to reform the repressive socio-economic structures of the old regime and those who defended those structures.

The determination to defend the concept of the Republic developed between 1931 and 1933 was the motive force behind the events of October 1934. The immediate results of the entry of the CEDA into the cabinet were the existence for ten hours of an independent Catalan Republic; a desultory general strike in Madrid; and the establishment of a workers' commune in Asturias. With the exception of the Asturian revolt, which held out during two weeks of fierce fighting and owed its 'success' to the mountainous terrain and the special skills of the miners, the keynote of the Spanish October was its half-heartedness. There is nothing about the events of that month, even including those in Asturias, to suggest that the Left had prepared a thorough and well-planned rising.[30] In fact, throughout the crisis, Socialist leaders were to be found restraining the revolutionary zeal of their followers. The movement was essentially defensive. The ideal bases for revolutionary local workers' councils had, in most of Spain, been prevented by the caution of the UGT delegates from developing into potential soviets.

After the beginning of the October events, the Socialists actually rejected the participation of anarchist and Trotskyist groups who offered to help make a revolutionary coup in Madrid. The few arms which they had were not distributed. In Madrid, on 4 October, the UGT leadership gave the government twenty-four hours' notice of a pacific general strike, presumably to give the President time to consider changing his mind. In the event, this compromise gesture enabled the government to arrest workers' leaders and take precautions against possible insubordination within the police and the army. Without specific instructions, Socialists and anarchists in Madrid went on strike and simply stayed at home rather than mounting any show of force in the streets. The army took over basic services – conscripts were classified according to their

174

peacetime occupations – and bakeries, right-wing newspapers and public transport were able to function with near normality. Those Social-ist leaders not arrested either went into hiding, as did Largo Caballero, or fled into exile, as did Prieto. The masses were left to dissipate their enthusiasm standing on street corners awaiting instructions and within a week the strike had petered out. Plans for a seizure of power by revolutionary militias came to nothing. Assistance from sympathisers in the army did not materialise and the few militants with arms quickly abandoned them on rubbish heaps. Some scattered sniper fire and many arrests were the sum total of the revolutionary war unleashed.[31]

Asturias was a different matter. There, the rank and file of the UGT, allied in the Alianza Obrera with the rank and file of the CNT and, to a much lesser degree, of the Communist Party, took the lead. It is significant that, even in Asturias, the revolutionary movement did not start in the stronghold of the party bureaucracy, at Oviedo, but was imposed upon it by outlying areas – Mieres, Sama de Langreo and Pola de Lena. Throughout the insurrection, the president of the SOMA, Amador Fernández, was in Madrid, and on 14 October, without the knowledge of the rank and file, he was trying to negotiate a peaceful surrender.[32] Left-wing critics of the PSOE have pointed out that the revolution was strongest where the party bureaucracy was weakest: thus, in the Basque country, for instance, the workers seized power in small towns like Eibar and Mondragón, but Bilbao, the capital, was relatively quiet with the silence broken, as in Madrid, by sporadic sniper fire.[33]

There can be little doubt that it was spontaneous rank-and-file mili-tancy which impelled the local Asturian UGT and PSOE leaders to proceed with the revolutionary movement. They knew that without the solidarity of the rest of Spain it was condemned to defeat, but, unlike the Madrid leadership, they stayed with their followers. Teodomiro Menéndez, Prieto's lieutenant, opposed the movement as suicidal but stayed in Oviedo, being captured and horribly tortured by the govern-ment forces. The miners fought mainly with dynamite, since they had little ammunition for the arms that they captured. They organised trans-port, hospital facilities, food distribution and even telephones within days. Subject to heavy artillery attacks and bombing raids, they fought on with indomitable courage, thinking it was better to die for the ideal of a workers' Republic than down a mine.[34] When four military columns converged on Oviedo, the revolutionary committee of Mieres, under Manuel Grossi of the Bloc Obrer i Camperol, and the Sama committee, under Belarmino Tomás of the SOMA, remained with their men in the hope of negotiating a more favourable surrender.[35]

The defeat of the Asturian commune was inevitable once it became clear that Madrid and Barcelona had not risen. In Catalonia, many of the local Alianza Obrera committees did, in fact, take over their villages. They then waited for instructions from Barcelona, which never came.[36] The initiative in Catalonia remained with the bourgeois politicians of the Esquerra and they were ill-prepared and had little stomach for it. The anarchists took little part in the revolt. On the one hand, the Catalan CNT was opposed to the Alianza Obrera; and, on the other, the anarchists bitterly resented the way in which the Generalitat had followed a repressive policy against them in the previous months. This had been the work of the Generalitat's counsellor for public order, Josep Dencás, leader of the quasi-fascist, ultra-nationalist party Estat Català. Since the Catalan President, Lluís Companys, had 3500 Assault Guards and as many armed Escamots (the Estat Català militia), the Catalan Alianza Obrera decided that the initiative lay with the Generalitat. Accordingly, Companys declared Catalan independence on 6 October in a heroic gesture to meet popular demand for action against the central government and at the same time forestall revolution. Joan Lluhí, the Minister of Justice in the Catalan cabinet, informed Azaña that the Generalitat intended to use its declaration as a bargaining counter in the agrarian dispute with Madrid.[37] A swift and anticipated surrender followed. Although the Generalitat had far more armed men than the 500 mustered by the Barcelona army garrison, Dencàs refused to mobilise them claiming later that they were inadequately armed. Since the working class had also been denied arms the army was able to trundle artillery through the narrow streets and the Generalitat surrendered in the early hours of the 7th.[38]

The lack of resolution shown by the leaders of the Left was in marked contrast to the behaviour of Gil Robles. Indeed, there was little about his policy, both during and immediately after the October revolt, to dispel the suspicion of deliberate provocation. If the Socialists looked for a compromise on 5 October, they found no spirit of conciliation from the new Radical–CEDA government, but rather that same determination to crush their movement which was the favourite theme of CEDA propaganda. Gil Robles told Lerroux that the Chief of the General Staff, General Carlos Masquelet, as a liberal and a military engineer specialised in fortifications, did not inspire his confidence either ideologically or professionally. He had almost as little faith in General López Ochoa who was encharged with restoring order in Asturias. At the cabinet meeting on 6 October, however, Gil Robles's proposal to send Franco to take over operations was overruled and the views of Alcalá Zamora, Lerroux and his more liberal cabinet colleagues prevailed.[39]

Nevertheless, the overall supervision of the repression of the Asturian rising was entrusted to General Franco by the device of his being named technical adviser to the Minister of War. Diego Hidalgo effectively ceded his powers to Franco. One of Franco's first decisions was the order to bomb and shell the working-class districts of the mining towns. With CEDA approval, Franco also insisted on the use of troops from Africa. It is difficult to exaggerate the significance of this. The nationalist values on which the Right claimed to stand rested on the central symbol of the struggle to reconquer Spain from the Moors. Now they shipped Moorish mercenaries to Asturias, the only part of Spain never dominated by the Crescent, to fight against Spanish workers.[40] Such decisions were not unanimously approved within the army and some of the more liberal generals regarded them as excessively brutal.[41]

The losses among women and children, along with the atrocities committed by the Moroccan units under the command of Franco's lifelong crony Colonel Juan Yagüe Blanco, contributed to the demoralisation of the virtually unarmed revolutionaries. There was serious friction between López Ochoa, who conducted his operations with moderation, and the unrestrained Yagüe. Yagüe sent an emissary to Madrid to complain to both Franco and Gil Robles about the humanitarian treatment given by López Ochoa to the miners. On one occasion, their disagreements reached the point of Yagüe threatening López Ochoa with a pistol. It was clear that Yagüe, unlike López Ochoa, enjoyed the confidence of Franco. López Ochoa's pact with the miners' leader Belarmino Tomás, permitting an orderly and bloodless surrender, provoked Franco's suspicions.[42] Franco's mistrust of López Ochoa had been reflected in the confidence which he placed in Yagüe during the active hostilities, in the course of which a savage repression was carried out by the African troops. When Gijón and Oviedo were recaptured by government troops, summary executions took place.[43]

The CEDA insisted on the most severe policy possible against the rebels. On 9 October, Gil Robles rose in the Cortes to express support for the government and to suggest that parliament be closed until the repression was over. Thus, the annihilation of the revolution, which was particularly savage, took place in silence. No questions could be asked in parliament and press censorship was total, although the right-wing press was full of gruesome tales – never substantiated – of leftist barbarism. The new Minister of Agriculture, the social conscience of the CEDA,

Manuel Giménez Fernández, was a lone voice when he told the staff of his ministry on 12 October, 'The disturbances which have taken place against the state have not started on the rebels' side of the street but on ours, because the state itself has created many enemies by consistently neglecting its duties to all citizens.'[44] Remorse had no part to play in CEDA thinking. Of even more interest to the bulk of the party than the military action were the round-ups all over Spain of workers' leaders. Prisons were full in areas where there had been no revolutionary movement, but where landowners had had problems with their *braceros*. Casas del Pueblo were closed down in towns and villages in every part of the country. 1116 Socialist *ayuntamientos* were removed. The Socialist press was banned. In the same session of 9 October, the CEDA voted for an increase in the forces of order and the re-establishment of the death penalty. Arrests were made on a massive scale.[45]

In the immediate aftermath of the victory over the Asturian rebels, Lerroux and Gil Robles wrestled with the problem of the punishment of the revolutionaries in Asturias and the officers who had defended the Generalitat. On 12 October 1934, the commanding officers of the Mossos de l'Escuadra, the forces which had defended the Generalitat during the brief Catalan rebellion, Major Enrique Pérez Farras, Major Ricardo Sala Ginestà, Captain Frederic Escofet Alsina and Captain Francisco López Gatell, were tried and sentenced to death. Sergeant Diego Vázquez Cabacho, who had deserted to join the strikers in Asturias, was tried and sentenced to death on 3 January 1935.[46] The bulk of the Right clamoured for vengeance but Alcalá Zamora favoured clemency for those sentenced to death in mid-October by courts martial and Lerroux was inclined to agree. The extreme Right wanted Gil Robles to threaten to withdraw his ministers and his parliamentary support from the government in order to force the implementation of the death sentences. He refused to do so, for fear of Alcalá Zamora giving power to a more liberal cabinet.

Apologists for Gil Robles have claimed that his failure to seize power following the successful repression illustrates the basic respect he entertained for the parliamentary system.[47] The Socialists, on the other hand, argued that the relative success of the Asturian rising gave him no choice. Four army columns with artillery and air support were held back by poorly armed miners and were defeated by them on two occasions. The difficulty of pacifying one region did not augur well for an attempt to take over the entire country. On the admission of the Minister of War, if there had been a rising elsewhere, the army would have been unable to cope. The army had shown itself sufficiently Republican in spirit for African mercenaries to be necessary. At least one senior officer is reported to have ordered his men not to fire on their proletarian brothers.[48] Nineteen thirty-four had been a year in which the PSOE and CEDA leadership had engaged in a war of manoeuvre. Gil Robles had had the stronger position and he had exploited it with skill and patience. The Socialists were forced by their relative weakness to resort to threats of revolution, and even this they did badly. In the event, and although the fact was hardly apparent during the repression of October, it was the militancy of their own rank and file that saved the Socialists from the CEDA's inexorable progress to the authoritarian state.

6

THE LEGAL ROAD TO THE CORPORATE STATE
The CEDA in power, 1934–5

For Gil Robles the successful repression of the Asturian insurrection was adequate confirmation of the efficacy of his legalist tactic. When the Socialists had formed part of the Republican government, his monarchist allies had tried to destroy the regime with a badly organised military coup in August 1932. That direct assault had, in fact, strengthened the Republic in the same way that the Kapp putsch strengthened the Weimar Republic. Thus Gil Robles, in the aftermath of the abortive 10 August rising, reinforced Acción Popular's commitment to legal tactics. He was confident that skilful propaganda would bring electoral success and eventually power. It clearly made more sense to carry out his party's ambitions – the defence of the pre-1931 social order and the destruction of the Socialist threat – from the government rather than in opposition to the state's repressive apparatus. Having won an electoral success in circumstances not likely to be repeated, he had nursed that success with considerable skill and patience until, in October 1934, three CEDA ministers had joined the government. To his satisfaction, the Socialists had taken the bait and launched a hopeless assault on the state. Now thousands of Socialist cadres were in prison and the Socialist press was silenced – *El Socialista*, like *El Obrero de la Tierra*, was not to reappear for over a year. Apologists for Gil Robles have pointed out that the Cortes continued to meet after 5 November 1934, that the Socialist unions were not destroyed and that the military victory in Asturias was not used to impose the corporative state.[1] There is ample evidence to show that the CEDA was anxious to do all of these things and was held back only by Gil Robles's sense of realism.

The Cortes met, although there was censorship of debates and for some time the Left was not present. It thus became a valuable tribune from which to denounce the Left's insurrectionism uncontested. It also served as an extremely useful legal rubber stamp. In any case, the continued existence of the parliament revealed nothing about Gil Robles's democratic sincerity. Only the Alfonsist monarchists and the Carlists were publicly hostile to parliamentary democracy. It is likely that a substantial number of CEDA deputies would not have objected to the closing of the Cortes, if their public pronouncements mean anything; but that still left a considerable majority of Radicals, Republicans of various sorts and Socialists, as well as those CEDA deputies who were democrats, committed to the existence of the Cortes. Parliament could be overthrown only by military action. Consultation with senior generals showed Gil Robles that there could be no question of that.

Attacks were made on the unions. The CEDA youth newspaper, *JAP*, called shrilly for the destruction of both the UGT and the PSOE. Speaking for more moderate sections of the party, *El Debate* demanded a ban on Marxist unions and the strict regulation and control of other unions. On 5 November, Gil Robles told the Cortes that the country could not permit the existence of unions with revolutionary social aims. Already, on 19 October, Acción Popular and various non-Marxist and patronal unions had united to form the Frente Nacional del Trabajo (National Labour Front). It was to become the CEDA's response to left-wing unionism and developed into the Confederación Española de Sindicatos Obreros (Spanish Confederation of Workingmen's Unions). This coincided with the directive of the Bloque Patronal (Employers' Bloc) to its members advising the dismissal of all workers who had taken part in the October strike and their replacement where possible by those who had acted as strike-breakers then. In Asturias measures were introduced whereby miners had to carry identity cards, with details of their work records.[2]

If unions were not abolished, it was because of Acción Popular's need to proceed always within the letter of the law. No proof could be found of the unions' part in the October rising and their legal abolition was difficult. Gil Robles did, nevertheless, advocate their dissolution and call for the confiscation of their funds to pay for the damage done during the revolutionary events of October. In the following Cortes debate, on 14 November, the militant CEDA deputy Dimas de Madariaga declared that 'the power of socialism derives from the cowardice of employers and the government' and it should be destroyed. In practice, the continued legal existence of unions hardly mattered, since the arrest of union leaders had effectively emasculated the syndical organisations, and employers were able to carry out thorough reprisals against workers. Reprisals were not only directed against the trade unions. *El Debate* called for a purge of 'unreliable' civil servants and school teachers, meaning Republicans appointed during the previous two years. The Catalans' cherished *ley de cultivos* was abolished by military decree. In response to the demands of the CEDA press, and as a gesture of aggressive centralism, a governor-general to assume the functions of the Generalitat was appointed by Madrid on 2 January 1935. It was regarded by the President, Niceto Alcalá Zamora, as an 'excessive and unjust' measure which 'totally strangled' regional liberties.[3]

Throughout October, Gil Robles had manifested his anxiety that nothing should stand in the way of the efficient repression of the revolt. Alcalá Zamora was appalled and anxious to avoid unnecessarily embittering the situation. Supported by Lerroux and the other Radical ministers and opposed by the CEDA ministers, the President, as he had done after 10 August 1932, held out against confirming the death sentences passed against the officers who had supported the rebellion of the Generalitat. Alcalá Zamora was, however, subjected to intense pressure from the CEDA ministers but, to their consternation, he received their threats of resignation with what Giménez Fernández called 'surprising calm' (*asombrosa tranquilidad*). The threats were not implemented but Gil Robles tried to maintain the pressure. On 23 October, he said, 'The horrors of Asturias must be adequately punished.' When the Cortes reopened he demanded the 'inflexible application of the law' and some exemplary bloodshed. On 15 November he called for the chamber to announce its 'moral incompatibility' with the Left, a proposal seen by the Left as the prelude to the outlawing of the Socialist Party. This, together with its accompanying call for the dissolution of unions implicated in the rising, was opposed by the Radicals.[4]

The parties of the extreme Right, and a substantial group of his own supporters, were howling for vengeance and wanted him to threaten to withdraw his ministers from the cabinet and his parliamentary support for any future Radical cabinet. Gil Robles himself was totally opposed to any form of conciliation, but he was worried that, if he pursued such intransigence, the President would resolve the crisis by giving power to a leftist cabinet and dissolving the Cortes. Alcalá Zamora had already demonstrated that he had doubts about the wisdom of bringing the CEDA into government in October. However, right-wing generals like Franco, Fanjul and Goded were outraged at what they saw as the government's weakness in contemplating pardons for those who had taken part in the rebellion in Catalonia.[5]

The tension over the death sentences underlined the extent to which Gil Robles, despite the success of his tactics in provoking a left-wing rising, was still some way from power. He would have liked to resolve the difficulties by turning to the army, but as he wrote afterwards, 'It is doubtful that the armed forces really had the internal unity and necessary force.' Nevertheless, it was quite clear that the firmness of the CEDA position would depend entirely on the extent to which the army was in a position to back it. On 19 October, Fanjul and Goded made a pre-arranged visit to the CEDA deputy Cándido Casanueva, deputy for Salamanca and a close friend of the Jefe in the hope of putting pressure on Gil Robles about the death sentences. On the previous day, Casanueva had checked with Gil Robles about what he should say to the generals. The CEDA leader told him to tell them that his party would not oppose a coup. He justified this with two Jesuitical sophistries. The first was to claim that, if Alcalá Zamora forced through a pardon for the condemned officers, it would violate the Constitution. The second was to argue that, if the CEDA opposed him, the President would give power to a more liberal cabinet, which would constitute a *coup d'état* that only the army could prevent. Accordingly, Casanueva suggested to Fanjul and Goded that the only way in which the CEDA could avoid acquiescing in the pardons was for them to make a coup. He assured them that the CEDA would co-operate in whatever the army wished to do. He suggested that they consult other generals and the commanders of key garrisons to see if it might be possible 'to put Alcalá Zamora over the frontier'. After checking with Franco and others in the provinces, they returned a day later to say that they did not have the force necessary for a coup.[6] The much praised legalism of Gil Robles at this stage was thus the result of the unavailability of an alternative line of action.

With no possibility of taking power by force, Gil Robles now returned to the gradual process of taking it legally. Although the successful repression of the Asturian rising was exactly the scenario which Gil Robles had envisaged, he joined Calvo Sotelo in an onslaught on the alleged weakness of the Radical government. This was consistent with his tactic of consistently weakening the Radicals in order to hasten his own road to power. Calvo Sotelo, for his part, feared that the collaboration between the Radical Party and officers like Franco and López Ochoa might presage the consolidation of a conservative Republic, and so eliminate the need for the authoritarian monarchy which was his aim.[7] In particular, Calvo Sotelo accused Diego Hidalgo of failing to purge the Army of ideologically suspect officers and the Minister of War became one of the sacrificial victims.[8] On 16 November, Hidalgo and Samper, who had become Foreign Minister in the 4 October cabinet changes, were edged out of the government for alleged 'responsibility'

183

in the preparation of the revolt. Hidalgo was replaced by Lerroux and Samper by Juan José Rocha García. The process of eliminating 'liberal' elements and restructuring the government to the CEDA's taste took a further step forward on 21 December. The Minister of Public Instruction, Filiberto Villalobos, of Melquíades Alvarez's Liberal Democrats, had already upset the CEDA by his zeal in building schools. He had already made clear his opposition to the implementation of the death sentences and now he made the mistake of complaining against savage cuts in the education budget and was attacked in debate by the CEDA deputy Jesús Pabón. In reply, Villalobos denounced the CEDA for wishing to undermine public education in favour of a private system and was forced to resign – as Gil Robles put it, 'it was the second crisis that I found myself forced to provoke' – and complained bitterly that he owed his departure to his Republicanism. Together with the forced schism of the Martínez Barrio group nine months previously, it constituted part of an inexorable process whereby liberals were pushed out of the governmental coalition, leaving those who remained increasingly dependent on the CEDA.[9]

It was at this time that the CEDA was able to put into practice its much vaunted aim of beating the revolution through a programme of social reform. This task fell to Giménez Fernández in the Ministry of Agriculture. Yet his mildly reformist plans were to excite such an outburst of embittered opposition within his own party as to confirm leftist fears that no reform could be expected from Spain's conservative classes except by revolution.

Without attacking the agrarian problem at its root, the series of measures which Giménez Fernández tried to introduce between November 1934 and March 1935 did attempt to mitigate with a spirit of social justice some of its more appalling abuses. But he found little solidarity in the CEDA, many of whose deputies regularly voted against him, and he was the object of vicious personal abuse. For instance, in January he introduced a leases bill which would give tenants the chance to buy land they had worked for twelve consecutive years. Mild as it was, the project provoked a coalition of ultra-rightist deputies, led by a traditionalist, José María Lamamié de Clairac, and three CEDA deputies, Mateo Azpeitia (Zaragoza province), Cándido Casanueva (Salamanca) and Adolfo Rodríguez Jurado (Madrid) who was also president of the Agrupación de Propietarios de Fincas Rústicas, the aristocratic union of rural property-owners. Lamamié and Casanueva, like Gil Robles himself, were deputies for Salamanca. They were all three members of the Bloque Agrario of Salamanca, and in February 1935 were to be found addressing meetings together while Giménez Fernández was under attack. This was hardly surprising. *El Debate* had already responded to Giménez Fernández with caution, affirming in December that agrarian reform should not be 'too rapid or extensive in geographical area'. The paper had, moreover, reported with sympathy the meetings of the Agrupación de Propietarios de Fincas Rústicas which had expressed virulent hostility to the principle of allowing peasants access to property.

In session after session in the Cortes, Lamamié and the CEDA ultras stripped Giménez Fernández's work of its progressive features. Minimum leases were reduced from six to four years, access to property was dropped, inspection boards to supervise leasing were abandoned. And clauses were added which permitted a spate of evictions. The minister had even less success with other measures. Gil Robles claimed to be in total agreement with Giménez Fernández's analysis of the need for reform and even admitted publicly that only concessions made in a Christian spirit could hold back the revolution. Yet he stood back and watched his minister insulted and defeated by CEDA votes. Giménez Fernández was called a 'white bolshevik' and 'a Marxist in disguise'. Hostility came from more than a small minority of the party. Gil Robles wrote in his memoirs of a 'grave split' in the CEDA. He was clearly influenced by the strength of reaction provoked by attempts at reform and named Giménez Fernández's fiercest enemies to join the parliamentary committee examining the draft of his law. When he next provoked a cabinet crisis Gil Robles quietly dropped Giménez Fernández. That it was a sacrifice to party unity is made obvious by the CEDA leader's remark that 'I did not dare let Giménez Fernández occupy the Ministry of Agriculture again.' Gil Robles did later insinuate that Giménez Fernández might be offered the Ministry of the Navy, a possibility which was curtailed when he replied that he 'wouldn't know what to do with a fishing-rod'.[10]

The defeat of the small social-Catholic wing of the CEDA at this time was merely one aspect of a general swing to the right by the wealthier supporters of the CEDA, who justified their own inflexibility on the grounds that 'the revolution had to be liquidated'. In industry, many union members found themselves out of work. But it was in the countryside that conditions really grew worse. Many landowners continued to keep land uncultivated out of vindictiveness, and still told workers to let the Republic feed them, using the harsh slogan *'Comed República'*. With union leaders in jail, *jurados mixtos*, if they were not suspended, barely functioned and were heavily weighted in favour of the owners.[11] On 14 December 1934 the Catalan statute was suspended indefinitely.

Yet for all the general intensification of conflict, the CEDA felt that the Radicals had not been decisive enough in exploiting the defeat of the October revolution.

The CEDA dissatisfaction with the 'pace' of politics was expressed in its most extreme form by the JAP. In November its paper called for a purge of Marxists and freemasons, and in February for a new Constitution which banned both. Gil Robles described in its pages his vision of the future state: a stronger executive power, the reduction of elected assemblies to specific legislative functions and the drastic limitation of the right to criticise the work of government. Clearly, for the CEDA, Lerroux's essential liberalism left a lot to be desired. For the JAP, the defects of the liberal and parliamentary state could be remedied only by following the example of Germany, Italy, Austria and Portugal on the road to corporativism. The JAP leitmotiv was 'All power to the Jefe', varied with 'The Jefe is always right'. In his memoirs, Gil Robles made it apparent that he found no fault in the postures of his youthful followers. For him, they represented CEDA ideals untrammelled by compromise with political realities. If he himself had to be more moderate, it was merely a question of tactics.[12] At a meeting in Santiago de Compostela, Gil Robles said that JAP was the vanguard, CEDA the consolidator.[13]

Other sections of the CEDA, even if they did not express their ambitions with the vehemence of the JAP, were little less direct. In December *El Debate* called for a Constitution in tune with the spirit of the times, to reinforce authority, diminish the power of parliament and introduce a corporative system of representation. Gil Robles expressed the same sentiments in a lecture at Acción Popular headquarters, manifesting his dissatisfaction with democracy and his desire for something more 'organic' – Italy and Germany were cited as 'prototypes'.[14]

These desires contrasted with the reality of government in coalition with the Radicals. The cabinet lacked vigorous direction. In fact, Lerroux constantly failed to appear in the Cortes. Gil Robles regularly filled the gap, but he wished to invigorate the government with his ideas on a more formal basis; that is, through greater CEDA representation. Frustrated by the government's lack of decision in the 'liquidation' of the revolution and by Radical inertia in contrast to the CEDA's determination to proceed to an authoritarian state, Gil Robles wrote to Lerroux at the beginning of January calling for a 'change of orientation and of acceleration in the rhythm of government'. On several occasions that month he saw the Prime Minister and recommended to him a 'more intense rhythm of political action', and eventually Lerroux agreed to greater CEDA participation in the government.[15]

What might be signified by a 'more intense rhythm of political action' was suggested by an Acción Popular lecturer who called for the restriction of the right to strike and proclaimed the need to organise all social forces in a corporative organisation as in Italy. This line was echoed by *El Debate* in its Sunday supplement of 20 January, with a feature on the economic triumphs of two years of Nazism in power. And it was taken up again by Gil Robles when he addressed the businessmen of the Circle of the Mercantile Union, on 2 March. The economic problem, he said, was one of authority. Its solution lay in the creation of a corporative council of national economy.[16]

The crisis which was to give the CEDA the increased power with which to push its ideas came out of the question of the execution of Socialists implicated in the October rising. Two of Prieto's followers, Teodomiro Menéndez and Ramón González Peña, were sentenced to death, but to the chagrin of the CEDA, Lerroux, like Alcalá Zamora, was in favour of clemency. Gil Robles called for firmness and *El Debate* declared that pardons would constitute 'a travesty of the law and a mockery of the innocent victims of the October revolution, an undeniable stimulus for the enemies of the social order'. Gil Robles threatened Lerroux with the break-up of the governing coalition, but the Radical leader was adamant. Accordingly, on 29 March, the three CEDA ministers withdrew from the government, because, said Rafael Aizpún, the Minister of Justice, 'Clemency represents a revealing symptom of leniency in the repression of the subversive movement of October.'[17] While the CEDA complained of the cabinet's lack of zeal in repressing the Left, the government had taken an interesting initiative in the area of social control. The Spanish Ambassador in Berlin had been instructed on 14 March to seek formal co-operation between the Gestapo and the Spanish police in the struggle against communism.[18] Nevertheless, Gil Robles still chose to regard the government as 'soft' (*débil*).

Alcalá Zamora hoped to be able to resolve the crisis with a coalition cabinet which would include Republican forces to the left of the Radicals. Gil Robles, of course, indignantly refused to allow CEDA participation in such a scheme, since he had provoked the crisis in order to impose a more rightist, not a more Republican, orientation. He wanted six ministries in the new government, including that of the Interior, and the Ministry of War for himself. In this ambition, he met the strong hostility of the President, who distrusted the CEDA's flimsy loyalty to the regime. The situation was temporarily resolved by a one-month dissolution of parliament and the formation of a government of personal friends of Lerroux and Alcalá Zamora. Gil Robles could afford to wait. With the present Cortes, no government could be formed without his consent. If he did not yet demand to be Prime Minister himself, it was because he was afraid that the President would respond by giving a decree of dissolution of the Cortes to a left Republican cabinet. For the moment, he was content to increase his power slowly, but inexorably, by increasing his control over the government generally and by himself taking command of the Ministry of War. The latter was vital to his policy of strengthening the repressive power of the government, the crucial element of which he saw to be in the army. In December 1934 he had stated publicly that he saw the army as the bulwark against the masses and their social aspirations. However, he had been disturbed by the manifest military difficulties encountered in Asturias and by the generals' inability to support him with a coup in October 1934. During the second half of April 1935, Gil Robles pushed his case in a series of meetings with Lerroux, who did not object to some increase in CEDA ministerial power. Gil Robles organised a series of noisy CEDA rallies, the final show of strength taking place on Sunday 28 April, when 197 meetings (at least two in each province) took place. At last, knowing that the CEDA would eventually bring down the government, and reluctant to call elections, since he could do so only twice during his mandate, Alcalá Zamora gave in and allowed Lerroux to form a government on 6 May containing five Cedistas, with Gil Robles as Minister of War.[19] The most liberal section of the Radicals, those from Valencia, nearly split off from the party because of Lerroux's acquiescence in Gil Robles's plans. However, Alcalá Zamora persuaded Samper against this schism.[20]

Gil Robles's anxiety to take over the Ministry of War as opposed to any other must be seen in the light of what Fanjul had said in October 1934 regarding the army's inability to rise at that time. The Jefe was apparently disturbed by the presence of Republican elements in the forces. Already on two occasions, 15 and 27 February 1935, he had made lengthy speeches in the Cortes on the need to eliminate 'masonic' elements from the army.[21] He claimed that he wanted to make the army 'the adequate instrument of a vigorous national policy'. When the Right said 'national', it normally meant 'right-wing'. And so the army was to be strengthened to face the 'revolution', to fight subversion and to defend the fatherland from external and internal enemies. The political overtones were soon made clear. As soon as he took control, Gil Robles held a meeting with several senior anti-Republican generals, Fanjul, Goded and Franco, and virtually placed himself in their hands.[22] Franco was appointed Chief of the General Staff and thereby chosen as keystone of the reorganisation of the armed forces. Gil Robles did this against the advice of Alcalá Zamora, who said that 'young generals aspire to be fascist *caudillos*'. Gil Robles's other appointments were equally significant. As his under-secretary he chose Fanjul, a rabid monarchist who had left the Agrarian Party when it declared itself Republican. Fanjul had once said, 'All the parliaments of the world are not worth one Spanish soldier.' Goded was named Inspector-General and Director of the Air Force. Like Fanjul, he was involved in the Unión Militar Española, the anti-Republican conspiratorial group, was an untiring plotter and was closely linked with the monarchists of Acción Española, who were working for the overthrow of the Republic. Every act and decree issued by Gil Robles while he was at the ministry was examined by a committee including all three. The American Ambassador commented that, in upper-class circles, 'There was open jubilation at the expected shifting of monarchistic or fascist-minded generals to the strategic positions.'[23]

Not surprisingly then, the main preoccupation at the Ministry of War was the purging of 'undesirable elements'. Franco worked ceaselessly to 'correct the reforms of Azaña and return to the armed forces the internal satisfaction which had been lost with the coming of the Republic'.[24] Socialists and Communists were systematically weeded out. Even Alcalá Zamora was shocked by the progressive elimination of liberal and Republican officers and their replacement by fierce nationalists and Africanistas. Many loyal Republican officers, who were extremely able professionals, such as Juan Hernández Saravia, José Riquelme, Felipe Díaz Sandino and Ignacio Hidalgo de Cisneros, were removed from their posts on the grounds of their 'undesirable ideology'. Others known to be enemies of the Republic were promoted.[25] Emilio Mola was put in charge of all military forces in Morocco and given the task of keeping the colonial army in readiness to repress working-class unrest.[26] At the same time, Gil Robles cannot have been unaware of the spread of conspiratorial juntas of the anti-Republican Unión Militar Española throughout the officer corps.[27] A series of practical reforms was made with a view to pleasing the more conservative and militarist sections of the army. Regiments were reorganised; motorisation was begun; the General Military Academy, considered by Republicans to be the cradle of reactionary officers, was re-established. Arms factories were to be militarised in the event of a 'conflagration', a clear response to the

Asturian workers' take-over of such factories. Manoeuvres were held in Asturias to study means of combating a future rebellion. When Gil Robles was forced to leave the ministry, a major rearmament had just begun. Gil Robles tried unsuccessfully to have control of the police and the Civil Guard transferred from the Ministry of the Interior to his own Ministry of War. Without accepting the more extreme leftist accusations, it would seem reasonable to suggest that, not least in his choice of staff, Gil Robles did as much as possible to prepare the army for a potential rising.[28] Indeed, a recent apologist for Gil Robles has claimed that the CEDA leader made possible the 1936 rising.[29]

The circumstances of the proposed rearmament, which were kept scrupulously secret within Spain, are extremely illuminating. The five CEDA ministers met in San Sebastián in August 1935 to discuss the political situation. They were intensely worried that Moscow's recent adoption of the Popular Front line would lead to Communist collaboration with other left-wing forces in Spain and a revolutionary threat to the government. On the grounds that only the army could meet this alleged revolutionary challenge, which he must have known was beyond the resources of the defeated Left, Gil Robles was anxious to increase military striking power. The Minister of War also justified his desire for arms purchases by claims that the Balearic Islands were threatened by Italy during the Abyssinian crises. Mussolini certainly had designs on the islands and the Spanish Foreign Ministry supported the League of Nations line on sanctions. However, *El Debate*, perhaps under pressure from the Vatican, opposed sanctions against Italy and Gil Robles massed troops on the border with Gibraltar while the British cabinet debated the issue. Whatever his motive, the CEDA leader turned to Germany as a potential supplier. There was a case for importing German manufactured goods, since Spanish fruit and ore exports had produced a favourable trade balance with the Reich. Accordingly, Cándido Casanueva, Gil Robles's second-in-command in the CEDA who became Minister of Justice in the May 1935 reshuffle, arranged for an agent for the party, a certain Eduardo de Laiglesia, to make contact with the German Federation of Industry. On 14 September, Laiglesia sent a letter, believed by the Germans to have been drafted by Casanueva, to the German Ambassador in Madrid, Count Welczeck. The letter stated that the army could be equipped on the necessary scale only over a period of three years. In order to assure the continued presence of the CEDA in the government, the Germans were asked to make a substantial contribution to party election funds. Efforts were made to force the issue on the other ministers in the government by the provocation of a strike in some Basque ore mines. As part of the same deal, the Germans temporarily banned the import of Basque ore, enabling the CEDA to present the arms purchases as an essential way of securing continued ore sales. Throughout the entire operation, considerable efforts were made to prevent the Radicals from finding out what was going on. Senior military staff, including General Franco, were completely in on the secret. The arrangement was going ahead until the German firms began to find Laiglesia's demands for commission rather extravagant. Before alternative arrangements could be made, the government had fallen and new elections were on the horizon.[30]

The attempt to strengthen the army as a force of domestic repression was entirely in keeping with the reactionary tone of the cabinet formed on 6 May. The five Cedistas included Rafael Aizpún Santafé, traditionalist vice-president of the CEDA, who left the Ministry of Justice to become Minister of Industry and Commerce. The relatively liberal Manuel Giménez Fernández was dropped as Minister of Agriculture, and his arch-opponent, Cándido Casanueva, leader of the CEDA's parliamentary group (minoría), joined the government as Minister of Justice. The cabinet included four ex-members of the old monarchist Liberal Party, including Nicasio Velayos y Velayos, one of the more reactionary Agrarians, as Minister of Agriculture. The social orientation of Velayos was made clear when he allowed a meeting of the Confederación Española Patronal Agrícola, the right-wing rural employers' pressure group, to be held within the ministry itself. El Debate crowed triumphantly that the agricultores had finally conquered the ministry. The pace with which workers were being sacked and wages reduced was now stepped up.[31]

After the fall of Giménez Fernández, the landowners' offensive against day-labourers and leaseholders alike reached proportions described by a Francoist historian as 'not only anti-Christian, remembering that Spanish landowners never behaved collectively like Christians either before or after 1935, but of an authentic ferocity'. Clauses were added to Giménez Fernández's reforms which made them means of attacking the small peasants. Evictions arose at an astonishing rate. The persecution of the Left in the countryside continued unabated. In Don Benito, a small town in Badajoz notorious for the bitterness of local class hatred, two Socialists were murdered. The Socialist deputy for Badajoz, Pedro Rubio Heredia, who was particularly hated by local owners and who had been illegally arrested during the 1934 peasant strike, was assassinated in a restaurant in Badajoz itself.[32] Giménez Fernández was appalled by the enthusiasm with which Velayos set out to create a thorough counter-reform in opposition to the spirit of everything that he had tried to do in the countryside. The new agriculture minister's reform of the existing agrarian reform bill even aroused the hostility of the Falange leader, José Antonio Primo de Rivera.[33]

The new Minister of Labour, Federico Salmón Amorín, was secretary of the CEDA and belonged to the party's social-Catholic wing. He made some attempt to promote housing projects and a show of trying to curb the enormities of the employers. *El Debate* boasted of his efforts, but the picture inadvertently painted by the CEDA organ was one of the minister buried under a mountain of complaints about employers' abuses. Even those complaints could not have come from any but a tiny minority of workers familiar with the necessary procedures and not frightened to complain. *El Debate* was still outraged by the fact that union dues were being collected and that workers affiliated to the anarcho-syndicalist CNT could on occasions find work. The *jurados mixtos* had virtually ceased to function, few owners ever being sanctioned for infractions of the law.[34]

When Salmón took over the Ministry of Labour, unemployment was up to 732,034. Although it dropped somewhat during the summer harvest, by the end of November it had risen again to 806,221. In the light of this situation, the Left regarded Gil Robles's continuing protestations of social concern with some contempt. The much vaunted plans to beat unemployment with public works were shelved for budgetary reasons, although financial stringency was not allowed to hold up Gil Robles's extensive plans for rearmament.[35] Thus, constant propaganda about the CEDA's 'deep Christian sense of social justice' appeared to be little more than hypocrisy. Gil Robles effectively exposed the shallowness of his own pious posturing when he replied to Juan Antonio Irazusta, a Basque Nationalist who protested in the Cortes against evictions which were contrary to the spirit of the law of rural leases. Although the CEDA leader condemned unjust evictions in general terms, he took any sting out of his remarks by defending Nicasio Velayos, the reactionary Agrarian Minister of Agriculture. After his empty rhetorical denunciation of rural injustice, Gil Robles ruled out any sanction against evictions by stating that the minister could not be expected to define an 'unjust' case.[36] The overall impression left by the reality of CEDA policy was of untrammelled economic egoism hidden behind a facade of social-Catholic verbiage. This was emphasised by the reform of the agrarian reform, which was passed in July. Among a series of amendments was one which destroyed any possibility of fundamental change. This was the abandonment of the Inventory of Expropriable Property. Henceforth there was nothing to prevent owners from simply declaring their lands to be smaller than the size at which they became eligible for expropriation. Of 900,000 estates marked for reform, 800,000 were removed from the list.[37]

While Gil Robles prepared the army to 'fulfil its mission' and the practical social advances of the Republic were dismantled in the country-side, both the CEDA and the JAP were looking to the future. The gradual break-up of the Radical Party and the CEDA's seemingly inexorable increase in power necessitated preparation for the time when Gil Robles would take over the government. A flurry of meetings elaborated and publicised the details of the 'new state' which would then be installed. The vocabulary with which this was done was as ambiguous as ever, although what caught the attention of the Left was the constant recurrence of fascist terminology. Talk of the growing threat from free-masonry and Judaism was, if anything, more prevalent. At a JAP rally held at Uclés (Cuenca) and organised with the usual scramble of pre-paratory meetings, special trains and buses, Dimas de Madariaga announced that the 'new state' would not be based on 'decadent liberal-ism in which there circulates the poison of Marxism and separatism and which is infiltrated by freemasons, Jews and Judaisers'. At this meeting the JAP leader, Pérez Laborda, demanded all power for Gil Robles.[38] On returning to Madrid, CEDA militants chanting anti-Republican slogans were jeered by leftists shouting, '¡Viva la República!' Apoplectic with fury, Gil Robles telephoned the Minister of the Interior, Manuel Portela Valladares, a centrist Republican from Lugo in Galicia currently without a parliamentary seat. The Jefe disclaimed any responsibility for violence which might be committed by his supporters in self-defence.[39]

The wave of CEDA propaganda meetings and rallies coincided with early preparations for the reform of the Constitution. While the CEDA's plans were being discussed by the cabinet and being prepared for parliamentary discussion, monster concentrations of the Right's masses were being staged. On 30 June, Gil Robles addressed 50,000 people at Medina del Campo (Valladolid) in the morning and flew to Valencia to speak to 20,000 more in the afternoon.[40] Below the surface of Gil Robles's apparent respect for democratic norms, there was always the threat of using his power if he did not get what he wanted. At a JAP meeting in Santiago de Compostela, he played on the Radicals' fear of a disso-lution by proclaiming that, 'If the present Cortes does not want to proceed to constitutional reform, we will make the life of parliament impossible.'[41]

The vehemence of certain CEDA orators was taken to extremes by those of the JAP. Rather than reform of the existing Constitution, the

JAP, like most groups of the extreme Right, wanted a new Constitution altogether. The 'new state' envisaged by the JAP would see a drastic reduction in the power of parliament. The executive power would be free of parliamentary control, as would the economic council which was to direct the new corporativist economy. The corporativism so insistently held up by all sections of the Spanish Right as the model for the country's political future was not notably different from fascism as it was perceived at that time.[42] The Left regarded the use of the term 'corporativism' as no more than a pious euphemism for fascism. Even more characteristic of the JAP than its authoritarian ambitions for a 'new state' was the virulence with which it reacted to the existing situation. Gil Robles's tactical notion of slowly but surely exploiting the system to attain concrete objectives met with some impatience within his youth movement. In issue after issue of its newspaper, a welter of provocative slogans announced the need to prepare the CEDA for the great struggle which awaited it, the war to clean Marxists and freemasons out of Spain. There was to be no dialogue with the Left:

> Either Acción Popular smashes Marxism or Marxism will destroy Spain. With the Jefe or against the Jefe. There can be no dialogue with anti-Spain. Us and not them. Let us annihilate Marxism, freemasonry and separatism so that Spain may continue her immortal road.

This language was more violent even than that being employed by the radicalised Socialist Youth of the FJS in 1934. Indeed, it was the same language as was to be used by the Falange during the Civil War, after the majority of the JAP's members had migrated to the fascist organisation. With five CEDA ministers in the government, such rhetoric was bound to frighten the Left and the Centre. Gil Robles was aware that the JAP was undermining his long-term plans and tried to restrain some of its virulence. He prevented the ex-JAP president, José María Valiente, who had been deposed because of his open contacts with Alfonso XIII, from speaking at the great JAP rally at Uclés. Valiente resigned from the CEDA and joined the Carlists. Gil Robles held back the week's issue of the JAP bulletin, 15 June, but the following week it was on sale again, with an unchanged line, declaring enthusiastically that 'the Jefe is always right'.[43]

Gil Robles never effectively dissociated himself from the excesses of his youth movement. Inevitably, the Left took the slogans of the JAP to be indicative of what the CEDA was merely too devious to say openly. In fact, when the CEDA discontinued its own party bulletin, it clearly associated itself with the JAP. In its last number, *CEDA* carried an appeal for every member of Acción Popular to transfer his subscription to *JAP*, 'a vibrant publication in which he will find audaciousness, faith, enthusiasm, fearlessness, austerity and discipline'. Since Gil Robles regularly stated at meetings that the CEDA and the JAP were totally identified, the Left assumed him to be implicated in the latter's demands for him to take all power in a dictatorial regime and smash the Left.[44] The fact that Gil Robles aimed to advance slowly and legally to power in no way mitigated what the JAP intended him to do with it once it was acquired.

The reckoning for the CEDA was nearer than even Gil Robles suspected. In June, he had concluded the so-called Pact of Salamanca with the Radicals, an act seen, by the monarchists of the Acción Española group at the time and by his apologists since, as evidence of his Republican faith. There can be no doubt of the cynicism behind the step. Gil Robles told the crowd at the Valencia meeting on 30 June that, just as they did not question who put money into their businesses when profits were at stake, so too he did not question whom he used for his political ends. José Antonio Primo de Rivera commented wryly, 'That is to say, he puts up with the Radicals as undesirable, but for the moment indispensable, partners.'[45] The extent to which the Radicals were the essential vehicle of the CEDA's approach to power was shown when their political effectiveness was shattered by revelations of their corruption. Thereafter, the legalist tactic could not be followed by the CEDA alone.

In mid-September, there arose a crisis which was not of Gil Robles's making. Its *dénouement* illustrated the fragility of his plans to use the Radicals to leapfrog his way to power without risking elections. The crisis was provoked in September by the resignation of Antonio Royo Villanova, the Agrarian Minister of the Navy, a fierce centralist who was outraged because the government of Catalonia had been ceded control of its own roads. He was joined by his fellow Agrarian Velayos. The crisis coincided with impending ministerial changes imposed by a scheme, devised by the Minister of Finance, Joaquín Chapaprieta, for reducing government expenditure by reducing the number of ministries. To complicate matters further, the President's decision regarding the resolution of the crisis had to be taken in the knowledge that a giant financial scandal, the so-called Estraperlo affair, was about to be exposed, to the very considerable detriment of the Radicals. After various consultations with prominent members of the political élite, Alcalá Zamora decided to offer the premiership to Chapaprieta, who managed to secure the collaboration of both Gil Robles and Lerroux. Both were prepared to accept the situation because they knew that, if they did not, the President would dissolve the Cortes. And neither was prepared to face elections at a time when the Left was gradually beginning to repair some of the cracks in its unity. Chapaprieta was very much the lesser evil.[46]

By dint of Chapaprieta's austerity plan, the cabinet was reduced in size from thirteen to nine, with CEDA participation down to three. This represented no loss of power for Gil Robles. He kept the Ministry of War, Luis Lucia held the combined ministries of Public Works and Communications, and Federico Salmón received the combined portfolios of Labour and Justice. The CEDA had the same number of ministers as the Radicals, and, in fact, controlled what had previously been five ministries. The composition of the cabinet also represented a minor triumph for Gil Robles, in that the centre-Republican Interior Minister, Manuel Portela Valladares, whom he distrusted as a liberal, was replaced by a Radical, Joaquín de Pablo-Blanco. Portela had pursued a fairly hard but neutral law-and-order line. Nevertheless, he had permitted the reopening of the Republican cultural club, the Madrid Ateneo, and had allowed Azaña to address a number of gigantic public rallies. He had even unsuccessfully suggested, to the disgust of the CEDA members of the cabinet, re-opening the Socialist Casas del Pueblo and permitting the publication of *El Socialista*. Portela had also opposed the Jefe's insistent demands that the command of the Civil Guard pass from the Ministry of the Interior to that of War. This manifest desire for the monopoly of the state's apparatus of violence had disturbed others among Gil Robles's cabinet allies and his request had been refused. However, he had successfully pressed for Portela's removal. The CEDA leader remained the government's dominant figure in the Cortes. Moreover, since he was aware from his vantage point in the Ministry of War that the condition of the army was still such as to give him no viable alternative to following the legalist tactic, he can have been little less than satisfied with the outcome of the crisis. In particular, there was advantage to be derived from the fact that Chapaprieta was something of a nonentity and was willing for Gil Robles virtually to take control of the cabinet. As he himself put it, 'To Señor Gil Robles, for whom I felt a great liking and with whom I was always in agreement, I expressed my desire that we should continue in collaboration in all government business.' In fact, Gil Robles used to arrive at cabinet meetings half an hour before the other ministers for a prior discussion about the agenda. Chapaprieta regularly dropped in at the Ministry of War to inform the Jefe of any new developments. Moreover, for all his concern with financial austerity, Chapaprieta, who remained as Minister of Finance, gave the Minister of War every assistance in budgeting for his programme of rearmament.[47]

The Left continued to be uneasy about Gil Robles's intentions. Both Martínez Barrio and Félix Gordón Ordás, united since September 1934 in Unión Republicana, expressed concern in the Cortes regarding rumours of an imminent rightist coup.[48] In fact, a coup was unlikely, since at that time Gil Robles was more concerned about maintaining what power he already had. On 9 October, aware that a scandal was brewing, even if he did not realise its magnitude, he took part in a banquet in honour of Lerroux. In his speech, he reaffirmed the CEDA alliance with the Radicals, an alliance which was now the central bulwark against the dissolution of the Cortes, an event that he dreaded. The Jefe also declared his opinion that the President could dissolve the Cortes only once in his mandate. The precariousness of the situation was soon revealed. Accusations concerning the Radicals' implication in the Estraperlo gambling fraud were placed in the hands of the government, and on 22 October the matter was debated in the Cortes.[49]

Chapaprieta and Gil Robles had visited Lerroux and asked him to resign as Foreign Minister, but he refused to do so until the whole business had been discussed in parliament. It was a difficult situation for Gil Robles. After all, his own party was involved in negotiations with the German government for donations of electoral funds in return for a monopoly of arms sales to Spain. This affair was not only every bit as illegal as the Estraperlo roulette swindle, but it also involved national security. Gil Robles managed the crisis with some panache. Determined not to be implicated in the Radicals' downfall, he took a prominent role in demanding that the whole affair be thoroughly examined. When he called for the most energetic sanctions, it looked to the Left in general, and to Gordón Ordás especially, as if Gil Robles, having seen that the Radicals could no longer serve him, aimed to gain the fullest advantage from their destruction. They were, in any case, mortally wounded. José Antonio Primo de Rivera declared that they were disqualified from public life. He claimed that the entire Radical Party should suffer as the CEDA had made the whole of the Socialist movement suffer after Asturias. On 29 October, Lerroux and his crony, Juan José Rocha, the Minister of Education, resigned. They were replaced by two more Radical men of straw, Luis Bardají López at Education, and Juan Usabiaga Lasquivar at Agriculture. The Agrarian Martínez de Velasco passed from the Ministry of Agriculture to that of Foreign Affairs. Now more than ever, Gil Robles was the effective leader of the government. In their death agony, the Radicals did not even bother to turn up for debates.[50]

All things considered, the CEDA leader had come out of the cabinet crisis very well. He was in a strong position to renew his gradual climb to supreme power. For the moment, however, the main political interest of the day was centred on Chapaprieta's schemes for fiscal reform. He wanted to extend the incidence of death duties, which were the lowest in Europe, and to subject company funds to taxation. Inevitably, this aroused the hostility of the classes who constituted much of the CEDA's, and also the Radicals', financial support.

On Gil Robles's own admission, the most tenacious opponents in parliament to Chapaprieta's reforms were to be found in the CEDA. In fact, Chapaprieta was subjected to violent attacks by the Cedistas Casanueva and Azpeitia, who had opposed Giménez Fernández with such success. As before, they used the tactic of overloading bills with amendments. They were seconded in their delaying tactics by other CEDA deputies, who stayed away from the Cortes and thereby prevented the passing of any clauses at all. On 2 November, Chapaprieta announced to the press that he would resign if he could not fulfil his plans in their entirety. Gil Robles assured him CEDA votes, but they never materialised. When Chapaprieta finally raised the matter at a cabinet meeting, Gil Robles informed him that he was impotent to oblige his deputies to vote for the reforms. This seems highly unlikely, given the adulation to which the Jefe was subjected by all sections of the CEDA. Moreover, Casanueva was Gil Robles's second-in-command, a loyal collaborator, who had once said publicly that, 'With a chief like Gil Robles, even cleaning out latrines is fun.'[51] Ramón Serrano Suñer, at the time CEDA deputy for Zaragoza and a prominent figure within the JAP, spoke of the 'machine-like discipline' of the CEDA parliamentary minority.[52] What seems more probable, and this was Chapaprieta's view, is that Gil Robles was using the CEDA's sincere opposition to fiscal reform to time the next government crisis. He knew that another scandal on the scale of Estraperlo was brewing. Known as the Nombela scandal, it concerned illegal payments made by the Radicals from government funds. The continuance of the Radicals in power would be impossible and so Gil Robles was confident that a crisis would result in his being made Prime Minister. He asked Chapaprieta that he drop his reforms from the budget, knowing that this suggestion would provoke his resignation. It did. Chapaprieta resigned on 9 December.[53]

Under the circumstances, Alcalá Zamora could only choose between offering the government to Gil Robles and dissolving the Cortes. The

The only choice open to Gil Robles was between staging a *coup d'état* and taking some backward step which would enable the CEDA to carry on in the government. He essayed both solutions at once. On the same evening a messenger was sent to Cambó, head of the Catalan Lliga, to ask him to join the CEDA and the Radicals in a government which would preclude the President's needing to dissolve the Cortes. Cambó refused. Meanwhile, in the Ministry of War, Gil Robles was discussing the situation with Fanjul, who said that he and General Varela, a close crony of General Franco, were prepared to rise with the Madrid garrison to prevent the President from going through with his plans for a dissolution. Gil Robles tried to justify his inclination towards such a proposal by replying, as he had done in October 1934, that Alcalá Zamora's action in itself constituted a coup. There was no shortage of officers, particularly members of the Unión Militar Española, who would enthusiastically join in a movement led by Fanjul, particularly if it had the backing of the Minister of War and therefore were not strictly a mutiny. However, Gil Robles was worried that such a rising might fail, since it would have to face the determined resistance of the Socialist and anarchist masses. Nevertheless, he told Fanjul that, if the army felt that its duty lay in a coup, he would not stand in its way and, indeed, would do all that he could to maintain the continuity of administration while it took place. Only practical doubts disturbed him and so he suggested that Fanjul check the opinion of Franco before making a definite decision. He then passed a sleepless night while Fanjul weighed up the chances of success with Goded, Varela and Franco. They concluded that the army was not yet ready for a coup since its raw conscripts might have to face the hardened professionals of the Civil Guard.[57] So, on 12 December, Gil Robles had to abandon the Ministry of War. The military staff of the ministry assembled to bid him farewell and a weeping General Franco said, on their behalf:

> the army has never felt itself better led than in this period. Honour, discipline, the basics have been re-established and have been personified by your Excellency. I can say no more in these moments in which emotion prevents me from speaking.

The Jefe was not consoled by this recital of his achievements. He left with 'infinite bitterness' because he had overreached himself. Unable to take power by force, he had also lost his grip on the situation whereby he could edge towards power legally.[58]

Now the legalist tactic would again have to pass the test of elections. After tentative attempts by both Chapaprieta and Miguel Maura to form governments, the President gave power on 13 December to Portela Valladares, in the hope that he could form a wide coalition. Spurned by Gil Robles, he formed a government of the old coalition forces minus the CEDA. Considered a magician of electoral management, he hoped to manage the elections so as to create a new party of the Centre which would be the arbiter of the Cortes. This could be done only at the expense of the CEDA and Gil Robles was determined to prevent it. Already the monarchist press was joyfully claiming that the legalist tactic had failed. There existed the strong possibility that the substantial right wing of the CEDA, which had accepted legalism for as long as the party was able to pass on to it the material benefits of power, might now go over to those who proposed less dilatory solutions to their problems. So Gil Robles set about bringing down the Portela government. On 16 December he announced his determination to prevent the parties of the old governmental bloc from being attracted to Portela by the temptation of electoral success through official manipulation of the elections. On the following day he wrote to Alcalá Zamora to demand that the government extend the present budget only with parliamentary approval. Either Portela would have to appear in the Cortes, where the CEDA would bring him down, or else Alcalá Zamora would have to speed up the calling of elections. While the President hesitated the CEDA issued a note, on 28 December, saying that it would make no electoral alliances with any groups in the government. This provoked a disintegration of the cabinet, since all its component groups were aware that to go to the polls in opposition to the CEDA would be to hand electoral victory to the Left. The cabinet resigned on 30 December and was replaced by another made up of Portela's friends, without parliamentary support and aiming only at organising the next elections.[59]

On the question of electoral alliances, the CEDA held all the cards as far as the Right was concerned. Coalitions were mutually beneficial, but the CEDA as the largest party still had the most to offer. From the first, Gil Robles made it clear that he aimed to win regardless of what alliances he had to form. As early as 14 December, he had called for the widest possible counter-revolutionary national front. To gain victory, he was prepared to include in that front both Radicals and extreme monarchists. The front's appeal was to be to the 'employer, mercantile and industrialist class'. That political ideals would not be allowed to stand in the way of the protection of these social interests was revealed when Gil Robles overrode pressure from the CEDA liberals Lucia and Giménez Fernández to avoid alliances with the extreme conspiratorial Right and to join only with conservative Republicans.[60]

Throughout December and January, negotiations were carried out with all groups. In this, Gil Robles enjoyed the active support of the Church. A delegation of the leaders of the Partido Nacionalista Vasco was in Rome to discuss with the Vatican Church–state relations in the Basque country. Archbishop Pizzardo, Cardinal Pacelli's secretary, told them that they must join Gil Robles's coalition, since a victory for the CEDA was a victory for the Church over Lenin. When the Basques replied that the Church should not pin its future on transitory electoral results, Pizzardo replied that, if they did not sign an undertaking to ally with Gil Robles, they would not be received by either Pacelli or the Pope. José Antonio Aguirre, the Basque Nationalist leader, was confident that all the Cortes seats for the Basque region would go to Catholics of his party and therefore refused to join unnecessarily with what he saw as Gil Robles's extremist right-wing coalition. When the Basques were ostracised by the Pope, presumably on Pacelli's advice, the ACNP press network tried to make political capital out of it.[61] Although agreeing with the Popular Front's aim of political amnesty, the Basques did not want to be instrumental in electing a Communist and they went into the elections alone.

With the exception of the Basques, only the monarchists represented any problem. They demanded a broad maximalist programme which would be binding after the election, and a numerous representation in the joint candidacies. Gil Robles stood firm. He realised that, in the event of victory, a sizeable Renovación Española group would be able to do to the CEDA what the CEDA had done to the Radicals. In any case, he felt that a national agreement on the basis of an alliance would be counter-productive, since in many areas either the Republican Right or the ultra-monarchists would be repelled by a joint candidacy. Therefore he insisted that alliances be made locally. In areas of considerable left-wing strength, like Badajoz, Jaén, Córdoba and Asturias, where the victory had been very narrow in 1933, the CEDA was willing to ally with anyone who did not belong to the Popular Front. On the other hand, in Salamanca, Navarre and most of Castile, the areas of strongest reactionary sentiment, Gil Robles felt that contact with groups not of extreme rightist character would lose votes. Thus, alliances came to depend on local circumstances, with the CEDA standing on its professed ideals only when it could afford it. In Badajoz, Giménez Fernández was dropped as a candidate because the local Right regarded his social Catholicism as dangerous leftism. In Salamanca, the alliance was with Carlists and Agrarians only; in Asturias, with the local Liberal Democrats of Melquíades Alvarez; in Pontevedra, with the Radicals; in

Navarre, with the Carlists; in the Balearic Islands, with the all-powerful local boss, Juan March. In the great Republican strongholds of Catalonia there emerged a highly implausible coalition of the CEDA, the Radicals, the Carlists and the Lliga, united in a 'law-and-order' front.[62]

The intense cynicism of the CEDA's approach to the elections was illustrated by Gil Robles's contacts with Portela Valladares, whom he despised and had tried so hard to have removed as Minister of the Interior during the previous autumn. Faced with the virtual impossibility of creating a Centre party without popular support, Portela had proposed an electoral alliance with the Left. His offer was roundly rejected in most provinces except Lugo and Alicante. In Lugo, Portela's personal machinery of electoral falsification made it virtually impossible for anyone to prevail against him. The special circumstances of Alicante are described below. It was an immensely valuable offer that Portela was making – the government had at its disposal a massive apparatus of electoral influence, the control of town councils, of the forces of order, of the mechanisms of electoral scrutiny. The Left's refusal spoke volumes about its attitude to the democratic process as a means of expressing the popular will. In the light of the refusal, Portela announced on 7 February that candidates sponsored by him would ally with the Right in areas where there was no agreement to be had with the Left. The offer was accepted and in many provinces the Right went to the elections in coalition with Portela's candidates.[63]

In his memoirs, Gil Robles describes Portela's men as turncoats and parasites. He professes to have been disgusted by the idea of using the mechanism of corruption: 'My repugnance to the idea of an agreement with the government forces was infinite. But how else could we prevent our defeat in constituencies with high numbers of voters?' It is a penetrating commentary on the sincerity of Gil Robles's democratic convictions. He was interested in the power that an electoral victory might bring and had no concern with the pronouncement being made by the electorate.[64] He had already made publicly clear his agreement with the JAP's contention that democracy should be used to bring about its own destruction. Accordingly, he was not above indulging in electoral manipulation to acquire the necessary results. Because of his party's deal with Portela, the CEDA enjoyed government support in most of Extremadura and Andalucía, areas of left-wing rural strength, where the behaviour of the Civil Guard would be crucial in deciding results. An illuminating example of the Right's electoral morality took place in the province of Alicante. There Portela had begun negotiations with the local Right, but, when they had refused to offer him what he considered a satisfactory number of seats in the coalition, he made a proposition to the Left. He placed the control of the province and most town councils in the hands of Republicans and Socialists. Chapaprieta has shown in his memoirs the righteous indignation and disgust with which the province's rightists witnessed this corruption. Nevertheless, the Right's negotiations with Portela continued, and, when Gil Robles made an acceptable offer of seats in the candidacy, the left-wing appointees were unceremoniously thrown out and replaced by rightists. Neither Gil Robles nor Chapaprieta appears to have found this situation, morally identical with the first, in any way reprehensible.[65]

Nothing more clearly demonstrated the CEDA's determination to win the election at any cost than the nature of its campaign. Huge funds were available for propaganda, provided by wealthy backers such as Juan March.[66] Already, in late October, Gil Robles had requested the German Ambassador, Count Welczeck, for a complete range of Nazi anti-Marxist propaganda pamphlets and posters, to be used as a model for CEDA publicity material.[67] In practical terms, the Right enjoyed an enormous advantage over the Left. Ten thousand posters and 50 million leaflets were printed. They presented the elections in terms of an apocalyptic struggle between good and evil, survival and destruction. CEDA propaganda was often printed with a hammer-and-sickle motif or the letters 'CNT', to capture the attention of working-class voters.[68] The content was as virulent as in the majority of cases it was untrue. In Seville, for instance, pamphlets distributed to women claimed that the Republic intended to take away their children and destroy their families. Another leaflet alleged that, if the Left won the elections, the consequences would be 'the arming of the rabble; burnings of private houses and banks; distribution of private goods and lands; wild looting and the common ownership of women'. Rightist defeat was presented as an awful catastrophe. It was claimed that the Republic signified increased crime, with robbery, arson and murder topping the list.[69] This kind of propaganda was distributed by the ton. Lorries carried it to small villages and aeroplanes dropped it on farms. This saturation propaganda was crucial in the northern countryside. It was thereby able to reach the uneducated rural population, for whom the printed word commanded tremendous respect. In Madrid, half a million leaflets were sent by ordinary post – an indication of the Right's access to ready money. A three-storey-high portrait of Gil Robles dominated the Puerta del Sol. Although there was a ban on radio transmissions, Acción Popular could afford to have a Gil Robles speech broadcast privately on 9 February to twenty-six towns, and on the eve of the election to have one relayed to some 400 places. Also in February, ten theatres were hired in Madrid and a speech by the Jefe was relayed to them.[70]

The intensity and malevolence of the CEDA campaign were developed in both the public meetings and the massive Catholic press network. Indeed, the CEDA press, especially in the provinces, despite its declared 'accidentalism', was at least as truculent as that of the monarchists and Carlists who were declared enemies of the Republic. El Debate saw the election as an irreconcilable conflict between Spain and anti-Spain, between civilisation and barbarism. The JAP, which took the lead in the CEDA campaign, was more explicit and declared that the battle was between Gil Robles and the triangle (freemasonry – a symbol of Republicanism), the sickle and the solitary star (of David). The JAP conducted the campaign in an atmosphere of frenetic adulation for Gil Robles.[71] Chants of '¡Jefe! ¡Jefe! ¡Jefe!' resounded throughout meetings, often mixed with vivas for the army. At one point, after a JAP meeting in Soria, Pérez Laborda was arrested because of the viciousness of his attack on the President of the Republic. Gil Robles was hardly less vehement. On a tour of Galicia, he repeatedly railed against a Constitution which, he claimed, united the worst aspects of parliamentarism and the presidential system. In Toledo, he attacked the moderation of the President regarding the repression of Asturias. And it was an echo of an earlier Gil Robles speech that sounded in Pérez Laborda's words at the close of a meeting in Madrid: 'Exaltation of Spain! Think of Spain! Work for Spain! Die for Spain! Exaltation of the fatherland with ecstasy, with frenzy.'[72]

The CEDA press all over the country was characterised by a relentless hatred of the Left, which was accordingly much preoccupied with what a rightist victory would mean for it. The belligerence of El Debate belied its claims to legalism: 'Between the ruin and the salvation of Spain there is no middle way'; 'Spain is threatened in its very being by the Marxist hordes determined to fulfil the promise of red October.' It was alleged that a political amnesty would release 'the murderers, the thieves, the pyromaniacs of socialism, syndicalism and communism'. Detailed graphs were printed to prove that socialism was tantamount to gangsterism.[73] The provincial press was, if anything, more bellicose. In Almería, La Independencia called on voters to rescue Spain from Jews and freemasons. The choice was between God and anarchy. Crude appeals were made to landowners: 'Your property will disappear if they triumph.' The tone of CEDA propaganda contrasted with the moderation of the rival Republican newspaper, El Diario de Almería. An even more striking contrast was to be found in Granada, between Acción Popular's strident *Ideal* and the more reasoned *El Defensor*.[74]

Inevitably, it was upon the utterances of CEDA propagandists and newspapers that the Left based its accusations of fascism. The Left's concern is understandable. *JAP* summed up the CEDA programme in the event of victory: deposition of the President, full powers to the government, dissolution of the Socialist Party, annihilation of the revolution, the silencing of the 'rabble press', a new Constitution. These were not just the verbal excesses of youth. Gil Robles himself was still toying with the idea of dictatorship. He knew that, even if the CEDA, which had 178 candidates, scored a rousing victory, it could not count on more than 140 seats in the Cortes. This would mean more coalition governments. On 5 February he announced ominously, 'Spain can no longer put up with a sterile Cortes. There has been enough already.' Many of his followers were urging him towards a civilian dictatorship. He, of course, remembered his consultations with the generals in October 1934 and December 1935. Araquistain, the Socialist theoretician, suggested with some plausibility that Gil Robles was not of the stuff of which dictators are made. But the fact remains that many Cedistas took up the idea.[75] The most extreme statement of the possibility came from the JAP in as fascistic a manifesto as ever emanated from the Spanish Right. After the triumph, there would be energy, the repudiation of liberalism, a young and virile policy. Twenty-seven reasons were given as to why Gil Robles should be given full power, and among these were the need to crush the revolutionary spirit, to limit liberties (seen as 'criminal'), to prohibit the organisations which preached the class struggle, to put an end to laicism, to put an end to the vices of parliamentarism, to strengthen the executive power, to realise an energetic policy of public order and to create a strong army, navy and air force.[76]

Just how determined the CEDA was to gain the power which would have made all this possible was shown by the extent to which propaganda and electoral alliances were augmented in the field by all kinds of pressures and the use of force. The evidence for this is necessarily anecdotal, but is, nevertheless, overwhelming. Electoral pressures in the towns were various, but were largely variations on the theme of vote-buying. In both urban and rural areas of unemployment, Acción Popular began to open soup-kitchens and to distribute blankets to the poor. *El Socialista* made accusations of the direct purchase of votes. Economic hardship was sufficient to make it possible to do so quite cheaply. The American Ambassador recounts that 'An agent, canvassing the apartment house in which Constancia de la Mora lived . . . , thought that he

207

had bought her Andalusian maid for 25 pesetas, but she promptly reported to her mistress.' The English journalist Henry Buckley goes into more detail:

> I knew of one landlord owning seven houses who warned the concièrges of the houses that he would call for them with a car in order to take them and such of their families as had votes to the polling station. This meant, of course, that at the door of the booth he would hand them a voting paper for the Right and watch from the door to make sure that they dropped it into the box. And various women of the Right whom I knew had made arrangements to take their servants to the polling booths with them, just as they had done last time.

In Madrid offices, pressure was put on employees to vote for the Right. Those who wanted to act as scrutineers for the Left were told that they would get trouble if they did. At the same time, rightist employees were given every facility, time off and the train fare to their provincial homes, to help them cast their votes.[77]

The situation in rural areas was much more violent and the Right had far more facilities to influence results. An extreme example of the Right's behaviour was in Granada, where a particularly reactionary landowning class saw a CEDA victory as the only chance of protecting its privileges. The Casas del Pueblo were still closed after the October revolution. The Republican press mysteriously disappeared somewhere en route between Granada and outlying districts, in contrast to the CEDA paper *Ideal*, which always got through. *Ideal* called on right-wingers to abandon their 'suicidal inertia' (*inercias suicidas*), an appeal which was extended to 'Christian women who fear for the peace of hearth and home' (*las mujeres cristianas que temen por el sosiego de su hogar*). All the social problems of the province were blamed on the Left in general and Fernando de los Ríos in particular. *Ideal* set the tone when it said that a few beatings would keep the Left quiet, since all leftists were cowards. Local *caciques* seem to have taken it at its word, for they hired gangs of thugs who, often with the assistance of the Civil Guard, prevented the dissemination of left-wing propaganda. Republican posters were ripped down at gun-point; Republican orators were turned away from villages by road-blocks; rumours were spread that the peasants could not vote unless they had special documentation. Known Republicans were illegally arrested and the Left's scrutineers were prevented from exercising their functions. During the actual voting, pressures grew more varied. In some villages, groceries were issued to the unemployed before they voted; in others, with only armed right-wing scrutineers present, glass ballot boxes were used. In Loja, the town council, having previously forbidden all left-wing propaganda including posters, requisitioned all cars, taxis, buses and lorries for the day so that workers could not come in to vote. In Chite, all Republicans were kept in jail for the day. In Fonelas, peasants arriving to vote found that the *alcalde* had put his watch forward and closed the voting station an hour and a half before time. Even after all this, the *caciques* had to alter the returns, and they did not scruple to keep up appearances. In Hués-car, gunmen led by the *cacique*'s foreman seized the urns and stuffed them with votes for the Right. In twenty villages the Popular Front candidates did not receive a single vote – though this was an area of great left-wing strength.[78]

Granada may have been an extreme case, but it was by no means atypical. In Badajoz, for example, the authorities also kept the Casas del Pueblo closed, in direct contravention of government orders. At the same time, the Civil Guard co-operated with local rightists to hinder the electoral preparations of Socialists and Republicans. In Huelva, right-ist *alcaldes* forbade all Popular Front meetings. The few eyewitness accounts that have been published tell the same story. In Mijas (Málaga) the *cacique* deployed his retainers and the Civil Guard to prevent any leftist propaganda. They also took steps to stop the Left from getting its voters to the polls. In Novés (Toledo) the *cacique*, a Cedista who had tried to dominate the local peasantry by refusing to cultivate his lands, received full co-operation from the Civil Guard in his efforts to stop the Popular Front electoral campaign. After the elections the Left made accusations of rightist malpractice in several provinces. There seems to have been evidence of vote-buying in Salamanca, but it was difficult to establish conclusive proof, and the Right had its counter-accusations. However, if the Left had been prepared to pervert the popular will at any cost, it had only to have accepted Portela's offer of a coalition with the government candidates. Yet it did not; it was the CEDA which availed itself of the machinery of falsification.[79]

The elections held on 16 February resulted in victory for the Popular Front. In fact, the parties of the Right increased their vote by more than three-quarters of a million votes, largely as a result of the disappearance of the Radical Party and the probable transfer of most of its votes to the CEDA.[80] In that sense, Gil Robles's immensely expensive electoral campaign had been a success. However, the parties of the Left increased their vote by about 1 million. Rightist policies during the *bienio negro* had ensured that the two vital conditions of the 1933 election result, leftist division and anarchist abstention, were not repeated. The consequent recriminations from monarchists and the more extreme Cedistas were directed at Gil Robles for having wasted valuable time and money on an ultimately unsuccessful legalist tactic. In fact, it was not until the final stages of the Civil War that, almost as an afterthought, the validity of the election results was impugned, as part of an attempt to legitimise the military rising of July 1936.[81]

However, it was precisely because the election results did represent a statement of the popular will that the Right so willingly turned to more violent tactics. Already the propaganda campaign of the anti-Marxist front had described defeat as the beginning of the holocaust. To a large extent, Gil Robles had staked the existence of his legalism on victory in the elections. Inevitably, after the apocalyptic tone of the electoral campaign, the results produced a feeling of despair within the CEDA. The youth movement and many of the movement's wealthy backers were immediately convinced of the necessity of securing by violence what was unobtainable by persuasion. By dint of massive expenditure and helped by leftist tactical folly, the Right had managed to gain victory in the 1933 elections. The vindictive use made of that triumph reunited the Left. Now, in 1936, an even greater amount had been spent on propaganda; thousands of Socialist, Communist and anarchist cadres were in jail; the machinery of electoral falsification had been at the disposal of the Right; every form of economic blandishment and threat had been used against voters. And still the Left had won. The October insurrection had prevented the peaceful establishment of the corporative state and the Popular Front elections postponed the possibility indefinitely. The elections marked the culmination of the CEDA attempt to use democracy against itself. This meant that henceforth the Right would be more concerned with destroying the Republic than with taking it over. In the course of the CEDA's gradual undermining of the regime, sufficient dissatisfaction with bourgeois democracy had been spread to ensure that the Socialist movement would not be prepared to sacrifice itself for the Republic as it had done between 1931 and 1933. To that extent, for all its apparent failure, the CEDA had considerably eased the task of its more violent allies.

7

SOCIALISM UNDER STRESS
Repression, radicalisation and the Popular Front

In the widest perspective, the Spanish Left did not view the Asturian rising of 1934 as a defeat. The conviction that Gil Robles had intended to establish fascism in Spain coloured all later leftist judgements of the revolutionary movement. The overall balance, it was felt, had been positive in that Gil Robles had been shown that the peaceful establishment of fascism would not be permitted by the working class. For many on the Left, the words with which Belarmino Tomás had explained the need for surrender to the Asturian miners became symbolic. The surrender was merely 'a halt on the road'.[1] The view that Asturias pointed the way to a revolutionary working-class unity was adopted, with variations, by the Trotskyists, the orthodox Communist Party (the PCE) and the FJS.

The Bloc Obrer i Camperol denounced the Socialists for permitting a premature insurrection but still proclaimed Asturias as 'a magnificent starting point for the future'. For Joaquín Maurín, Asturias 'was the work of the Alianza Obrera'.[2] After criticising the Socialists for the poor timing and the lack of preparation of the rising, the PCE leadership, now committed to the policy of the united front, publicly claimed responsibility for Asturias. With the Socialist organisation in disarray, the PCE's seizure of the banner of Asturias boosted the party's calls for proletarian unity. The claim was largely false. The Communists had joined the Alianza Obrera in Asturias only at the last minute, deciding to do so on 11 September and actually securing entry into the revolutionary committee on 4 October. Nevertheless, with the PSOE reluctant to accept responsibility, in the course of 1935 the speeches of the party's secretary-general José Díaz and the PCE's network of clandestine press had some success with its claim.[3]

The Socialist movement was, in fact, badly scarred by the events of October. The insurrection may have been an 'objective victory', but it remained a terrible immediate defeat. Most prominent Socialists were either in prison or else in exile, mostly in France or Russia. Prieto hid in the apartment of a family friend known for her Catholic piety. Then he managed to escape from Madrid – astonishingly, given his substantial girth – hidden in the boot of a Renault car guided through police checkpoints by the Spanish air attaché in Rome, Ignacio Hidalgo de Cisneros. In contrast, after fleeing to Portugal, the pugnacious Amaro del Rosal was arrested in Lisbon and sent back to Spain by Salazar's police. Largo Caballero and most of the leadership of the revolutionary committee – Enrique de Francisco, Pascual Tomás, Carlos Hernández Zancajo, Santiago Carrillo, José Díaz Alor – and many more, found themselves in the *cárcel modelo* in Madrid. In Asturias a desultory guerrilla struggle carried on until early 1935, but in the rest of Spain the movement was cowed.[4] Police vigilance was stepped up. In Asturias, under the direction of Franco's friend Major Lisardo Doval, torture was used in interrogations. Courts martial passed out many death sentences against miners' leaders in Asturias. All over Spain, Socialist *ayuntamientos* were replaced by government nominees. The Casas del Pueblo were closed. The unions, if not formally dismantled, were unable to carry on their syndical functions. Since the entire UGT executive – except for the president, Anastasio de Gracia, and Manuel Lois – was in jail, the clandestine life of the movement was, in fact, directed from the *cárcel modelo*. The editor of *El Socialista*, Julián Zugazagoitia, was also imprisoned and the entire Socialist press was silenced.[5]

Largo Caballero told the military judge investigating his case that he had taken no part in the organisation of the rising:

> I was in my house . . . and I issued an instruction that anyone who came looking for me be told that I was not there. I gave that order, as I had done in the past, because I was playing no part in what was going on, I was having nothing to do with anything that might happen; I did not want to have any contact with anyone, with anyone at all.

These were completely plausible claims in the light of the total failure of the movement in Madrid. Nevertheless, they came ill from the man soon to be hailed as 'the Spanish Lenin' and played directly into the hands of the Communists, who were only too glad to assume the responsibility. José Díaz, the PCE secretary-general, visited Largo Caballero in prison and suggested that the PCE and the PSOE jointly claim to have organised the revolution. Largo refused. Prieto from his exile urged that the PSOE openly declare its responsibility, which infuriated Largo

Caballero. It was later claimed that the Socialist leader had denied his participation to prevent an admission of guilt being used by the CEDA to justify carrying through its determination to smash both the PSOE and the UGT.[6]

It may well have been the case that to admit responsibility would have been a futile romantic gesture and would simply have played into the hands of bourgeois justice. However, in the political context of 1935, it was a potentially counter-productive tactic for the Caballerista wing of the Socialist movement. In the first place, it gave credibility to the Communist allegation that the events of October showed that the PSOE was not a revolutionary party and that Largo Caballero was incapable of leading a revolution. Moreover, the denial of participation greatly strengthened the Prieto wing of the party. The only parts of Spain where there had been effective action by the workers in October 1934 – that is to say, Asturias and part of Vizcaya – were those where the Socialist movement was dominated by followers of Prieto. The influence of Prieto was clearly not the only one which dictated the course of events, and indeed, the Prietista leaders had at first been reluctant to proceed to an insurrection. However, once the rank and file had shown their determination, Ramón González Peña, Belarmino Tomás and the other SOMA leaders had stuck by their men. This contrasted starkly with the pathetic showing made in Madrid by Largo Caballero and the Socialist Youth. There, once it was clear that revolutionary threats had not diverted Alcalá Zamora from bringing the CEDA into the cabinet, the Socialist leaders went to ground. No arms were distributed and the masses were left without instructions. No serious plans for a rising had been made, and the Alianza Obrera had been prevented from forming an armed militia. Amaro del Rosal, one of the more extremist young Socialists and one of the supposed leaders of the projected revolution, denied participation. In a sense, he was telling the truth. When Manuel Fernández Grandizo of the Izquierda Comunista asked Del Rosal on 5 October what the plans of the revolutionary committee were, he is reported to have replied, 'If the masses want arms, they can go and look for them and they can do what they like.'[7] The events of October 1934 were to become the central myth of the Socialist movement and the behaviour of the Caballeristas was effectively handing the monopoly of that myth to Prieto.

After being resoundingly defeated within the UGT and many affiliated trade union federations in January 1934, the reformist faction which followed Besteiro had ever less influence within the Socialist movement. Only the railway workers' union, led by Trifón Gómez, remained a

Besteirista stronghold. At a time when the vindictive policies of the CEDA–Radical coalition were provoking rank-and-file militancy, the Besteiristas' known hostility to revolutionary tactics had tended to leave them isolated. An indication of the distance separating the right and left wings of the Socialist movement was provided when, during the October events, a group of extremists from the FJS attacked Besteiro's home. Understandably saddened by this, in early 1935 the professor virtually withdrew from the political stage for a time.[8] In fact, renewed attacks on Besteiro's revisionist position and calls for his expulsion from the party finally provoked his followers to take up his defence against the youthful bolshevisers. That was not to be until June 1935, and in the immediate aftermath of the insurrection the crucial division among the Socialists was between Largo Caballero and Prieto.

Although both had adopted a more or less revolutionary stance after the electoral defeat of 1933, it is far from paradoxical that 1935 should have found them locked in a struggle for the legacy of the October rising. Ever since the disastrous general strike of 1917, the various factions of the Socialist movement had usually reverted to certain basic patterns of behaviour at moments of crisis. Besteiro's long-term orthodox Marxist projections consistently resulted in his advocating that the working class abstain from bourgeois politics. Prieto and Largo Caballero had always been more pragmatic, albeit in different ways. Prieto valued democracy as an end in itself and favoured a gradual road to socialism in Spain, given the objective strength of the bourgeoisie. Largo had a much narrower view, favouring always whatever seemed most advantageous to the trade union movement. Concrete benefits for the UGT had led him to collaborate with Primo de Rivera and a drift of militants away from the union had impelled him to join Prieto in the Republican camp. While social advances were possible, there was no more fervent advocate of the Republic than Largo Caballero. Only when the total opposition of the Right began to make reform impossible did Largo's attitude change. He started to adopt a revolutionary stance for two reasons. To begin with, he had hoped to frighten the Right into a more pliant attitude. Then he had discovered that his new line found a sympathetic echo among the masses. Rather than risk losing their support to the CNT or the Communists, he gave them what they wanted to hear. Thus in 1934 he came to coincide with Prieto, who was advocating revolution because he believed that the Republic was threatened by an attempt at dictatorship by Gil Robles.

After the Asturian rising, with the more far-reaching rightist ambitions momentarily checked, Prieto, backed by the Asturian miners and the

Basque metalworkers, and with a majority in both the executive and national committees of the PSOE, hoped to rebuild the Republic along the lines set down between 1931 and 1933. Largo Caballero, however, for all his vacillations in October, began to manifest an increased commitment to a revolutionary position, in rhetorical terms at least. There were several reasons for this, not least of which was an acute personal resentment of Prieto.[9] Largo is also reputed to have read for the first time many basic Marxist-Leninist texts during his sojourn in prison.[10] If he was influenced by his reading, he was equally impressed by the fact that the aggressive policies being carried out by the Radical–CEDA cabinet had seriously undermined working-class faith in the reforming possibilities of the Republic.

The first initiatives in the struggle within the Socialist movement came from Prieto. Aware that the vindictive policies of the Radical–CEDA coalition were inadvertently provoking a great national resurgence of support for the Republic, he made no secret of his conviction that the immediate goal for the Left had to be the recapture of state power by means of a broad coalition to ensure future electoral success and so bring working-class suffering to a speedy end. Prieto's views were shared by Azaña who had himself become the focus of popular Republicanism. He had been arrested in Barcelona at the beginning of the October events and imprisoned on a prison-ship until the end of December 1934. Despite, or perhaps because of, the abuse to which he was subjected by the right-wing press, he became a symbol for all the victims of the authoritarian politics of the Radical–CEDA coalition. Intensely embittered by the experience – which he recounted in his book *Mi rebelión en Barcelona* – Azaña was moved by the popular solidarity that was generated during his persecution to redouble his efforts for the recuperation of the Republic. In prison, he received large numbers of letters of support from intellectuals and politicians and collective letters signed by hundreds of ordinary Spaniards. One, which was published, was signed by eighty-seven leading personalities from the literary and academic worlds including Fernando de los Ríos, the doctor and writer Gregorio Marañón, the left-wing Catholic writer José Bergamín, the historians Américo Castro and Manuel Núñez de Arce, the poets Federico García Lorca, Juan Ramón Jiménez and León Felipe, and the novelist Ramón del Valle Inclán.[11] Azaña wrote to Prieto from prison on 25 December 1934:

I get hundreds and hundreds of letters, in which the recurrent theme is 'now more than ever' ... And everyone speaks of 'a left-wing reaction which is every day more powerful' ... They also say that there is more Azañismo than ever, 'even among people who are not of the Left'.[12]

Azaña had committed no crimes and eventually the charges against him were dropped. His release from prison coincided with his saint's day and Izquierda Republicana invited all those who sympathised with him to send a card or telegram of congratulation. The messages of support arrived at the party's Madrid headquarters by the thousands. A member of the Izquierda Republicana Youth described the scenes:

the postmen could not cope with the delivery of the cards and telegrams, bearing bulging postal sacks for which there was soon no room in the party's branch offices. An endless queue of citizens, both men and women, endlessly delivered their personal congratulations and wound around the block, through the Puerta del Sol and down the Calle del Arenal. That spontaneous demonstration of hope by the Madrileños and from Spaniards from the furthest confines of the country was a surprise for all of us, even the initiators of the idea.

In total, 146,000 letters were received in Izquierda Republicana offices throughout Spain.[13] Azaña was deeply moved by this further demonstration of popular esteem and enthusiasm for a return to the Republic of 1931-3. He wrote again to Prieto on 16 January 1935:

a movement of optimism and hope has been produced here, simply by the fact of my liberation, and for that reason I have been the object of an almost plebiscitary demonstration by all the forces and organizations of the left in Spain.[14]

Prieto replied from Paris with an undertaking to throw his efforts into overcoming the radicalism and consequent isolationist trend within the Socialist movement.[15]

While Prieto assumed the job of neutralising the hostility to the Left Republicans manifested by the young radicals imprisoned with Largo Caballero, Azaña himself worked to consolidate the Republican unification begun in the previous spring. In the late summer of 1934, he had used his influence to ensure that the new party Unión Republicana would drop its anti-Socialist leanings. Immediately, after his release from prison, he renewed his contacts with Diego Martínez Barrio and Félix Gordón Ordás of Unión Republicana and also with the conservative Felipe Sánchez Román of the Partido Nacional Republicano.[16]

Prieto's tentative views on the need for broad coalition were already being favourably examined by those members of the executive committee of the PSOE who were not in prison – Juan Simeón Vidarte, Fernando de los Ríos, Anastasio de Gracia, Manuel Cordero and Remigio Cabello, who was prevented by illness from playing an active role. On 20 March, Vidarte wrote to Prieto inviting him to submit his ideas on the subject to the committee.[17] This he did on 23 March. He placed much emphasis on the need for a wide alliance with forces both to the right and to the left of the Socialist movement. Not unnaturally, in the light of the Asturian experience, several militants were enthusiastic about the idea of an exclusively proletarian bloc. Prieto, however, pointed out that it would be difficult to arrive at an agreement with both anarchists and Communists. He also showed that not to include the Republicans would result in three-sided electoral contests, which would inevitably involve the loss of parliamentary seats. With the possible exception of anarchist electoral participation as opposed to abstention, the failure to ally with the Left Republicans would lead to the next elections' being fought in identical conditions to those of 1933. Prieto's letter also revealed a determination not to let the party fall into the hands of the extremist youth, which he discreetly hinted would lead to a non-Socialist, and presumably Communist, preponderance. The Federación de Juventudes Socialistas, he said, would have to be disciplined. Prieto was clearly disturbed by the effect that the Communists' attempt to claim a revolutionary monopoly was having on the youth movement. Instead of following the FJS's negative rejection of the Republic Prieto proposed the recovery of the Republic by means of an electoral coalition bound by the ten-point reforming programme which he had elaborated in January 1934 and by an undertaking to introduce an amnesty for political prisoners.[18]

This was a realistic proposition based on an awareness of the strength and ruthlessness of the landed and industrial oligarchies. Its weakness lay in the fact that it had been precisely those mild reformist policies of the first *bienio* which had provoked the belligerence of the Right. Yet, even if that suggested that Spain's structural problems required a revolutionary solution, it did not invalidate Prieto's basic point. Most of the Socialists' problems derived from the tactical error of 1933. Out of the government, they could introduce no change, reformist or revolutionary. October may have served as a defensive movement to check the CEDA's dictatorial ambitions, but it had revealed the Socialists' incapacity to organise a revolution. In the objective circumstances, there were two valid positions open to the Left: the one suggested by Prieto, the return to power and the gradualist road to socialism; and the one advocated by the Trotskyists, which recognised the revolutionary incompetence of both the PSOE and the PCE and aimed at the long-term construction of a genuine bolshevik party. Both of these analyses coincided in the need for a prior electoral victory.[19] Although contradictory, they were both coherent policies and more realistic than the FJS's utopian revolutionism.

Prieto's 23 March letter was duplicated and distributed throughout the Socialist movement. It met a sympathetic response from moderate militants and infuriated the left wing of the party, which began to prepare replies. In the meanwhile, Prieto's follower Vidarte, who as vice-secretary of the PSOE and in the absence of other leaders was virtually running the party, issued an important party circular on 30 March. The draft was cobbled together from Prieto's letter with additions from Vidarte and Fernando de los Ríos. Vidarte and De los Ríos took the draft to the *cárcel modelo* and submitted it to Largo Caballero, who, after discussing it with the other imprisoned members of the executive, Pascual Tomás, Wenceslao Carrillo and the party's secretary-general Enrique de Francisco, made no objection to its being published. The circular set out to show how the Republic had signified considerable progress over the monarchy. It also argued that the October rising had been a popular attempt to defend the legislation of the Republic, threatened by the oligarchy. The Socialist Party, said the text of the circular, was not 'demagogic, nor rabble-rousing, nor terrorist, nor adventurist'. Since the Right would certainly go into the next elections united, the excutive committee of the PSOE recommended that local Socialist organisations maintain good relations with Republican and other leftist groups. The circular was an intelligent plea for the use of legal possibilities to defend the Socialist movement and the working class.[20]

Much as it infuriated the Socialist Left, Prieto's line delighted many moderate PSOE and UGT members as well as Republicans of Left and Centre. The virulent and clumsy attacks by Gil Robles and Lerroux on Azaña had, by March 1935, impelled the non-government Republican forces to think about their future survival. By the end of the month, Azaña's Izquierda Republicana, Martínez Barrio's Unión Republicana and the conservative Partido Nacional Republicano of Felipe Sánchez Román had arrived at an agreement. On 12 April, the fourth anniversary of the fall of the monarchy, they issued a joint declaration of the minimum conditions that they regarded as essential for the reconstruction of political coexistence in Spain. The seven conditions were: the prevention of torture of political prisoners; the re-establishment of constitutional guarantees, especially those concerning personal liberties; the release of prisoners arrested during the events of October; an end to discrimination against liberal and leftist state employees; the readmission to their jobs of workers sacked because of the October 1934 strike; the legal existence of trade unions; and the reinstatement of the freely elected town councils which had been overthrown by the government.[21] This programme was not so ambitious as Prieto's January 1934 plan, but it was none the less acceptable to the Socialist moderates and was a potential basis for a renewal of the Republican–Socialist coalition.

Already, on 31 March, Prieto had received a letter from Ramón González Peña, the Socialist national hero of October, endorsing his position. Peña lamented the fact that Largo Caballero and his imprisoned comrades had denied any participation in the events of October. In outraged terms, he condemned demands of the *niños* (children) of the FJS who were demanding that the PSOE be bolshevised and Besteiro and his followers expelled. He ended with a call for a wide anti-fascist front for the next elections.[22] Copies of the letter, along with a similar letter from young Asturian Socialists imprisoned in Oviedo, were circulated throughout the Socialist Party, much to the chagrin of the Caballeristas.[23] Confident that he enjoyed the backing of the prestigious Asturian section of the movement, as well as that of the Basque country and of the moderates currently running the PSOE executive, Prieto made public his basic agreement with the manifesto of the Azaña–Sánchez Román–Martínez Barrio alliance. On 14 April both Sánchez Román and Prieto published in Prieto's Bilbao newspaper, *El Liberal*, articles on the need for a wide coalition. Above all, Prieto condemned the suicidal tactic that had been adopted in 1933, when, despite the fact that the electoral law had been specifically designed to derive maximum benefit from Socialist–Republican co-operation, the Socialists had gone alone into the elections. In the light of what Gil Robles had done with his exiguous victory, there could be little doubt that another leftist defeat would be the end of democracy in Spain. Even if an electoral union were achieved, victory was far from assured, wrote Prieto, given the Right's massive propaganda apparatus and the fact that the unemployment crisis made it easy for the votes of the hungry to be bought. Quoting from his letter to the PSOE executive, Prieto made an appeal for realism and a wide alliance for the defence of the Republic and the Socialist movement and for the release of thousands of political prisoners.[24]

A few days after Prieto's article, the radical youth launched a major counter-attack. This took the form of a long pamphlet, signed by the FJS president, Carlos Hernández Zancajo, entitled *Octubre – segunda etapa*. In fact, it had been written, in prison, by Hernández Zancajo, Santiago Carrillo and Amaro del Rosal.[25] The publication had three main objectives: to cover up the fiasco of the FJS's participation in the October events in Madrid; to combat Prieto's interpretation of the Asturian rising as an attempt to defend the Republic; and to eradicate the influence of both Besteiro and Prieto from the Socialist movement as a prelude to its 'bolshevisation'. The first part of the pamphlet consisted of a largely mendacious interpretation of the activities of the Socialists during 1934. It was alleged that strikes like those of the printers, the construction workers, the metalworkers and the peasants had dissipated working-class energies. This was true, but what the pamphlet failed to mention was that the 'union organisation' blamed for these tactical errors was dominated at the time by members of the FJS. The responsibility for the immediate defeat of October was placed firmly on Besteiro's reformists. This was used to justify the 'second stage' announced in the pamphlet's title, the expulsion of the reformists and the 'bolshevisation' of the PSOE. Such a process would involve the adoption of a rigidly centralised command structure and the creation of an illegal apparatus to prepare for an armed insurrection. This never took place, partly because the strength of Prieto's and Besteiro's support prevented it and more so because many of its advocates had joined the Communist Party before they were in a position to try. Conscious of Asturian backing for Prieto, the FJS did not dare call for his expulsion but did demand the abandonment of his 'centrist' line in favour of a revolutionary one.[26]

Octubre – segunda etapa was not nearly so central to the great Socialist debate of 1935 as has been claimed.[27] Largo Caballero, despite being the subject of rapturous praise in the pamphlet, claimed to have been annoyed by its publication, which had been arranged without his permission, and protested to Santiago Carrillo, then secretary-general of the FJS. Carrillo himself admitted later that the youth acted in total independence of the PSOE.[28] Few references were made to the pamphlet during the debate, except to admonish the youth for their temerity in daring to dictate to their elders and, above all, in trying to silence inner-party democracy. Within days of the pamphlet's publication, Manuel Cordero, who had lined up with Prieto, publicly disowned the ideas contained in it. In an interview widely publicised in the Republican press, Cordero reaffirmed the PSOE's commitment to democracy. He also stated that there was room in the party for all kinds of doctrinal tendencies and for constant ideological revision and debate, a clear rejection of the kind of narrow exclusivism advocated by the bolshevisers.[29]

Prieto's advocacy of an understanding with the Republicans and the continued Caballerista commitment to revolutionism were the two main poles of Socialist thought in the spring of 1935. However, at much the same time as the pamphlet on October was being published by the FJS, Besteiro was emerging from his silence. His group had opposed the rising, but they had since tried to help the imprisoned Socialists. Nevertheless, they had been the object of insulting attacks from the FJS's clandestine news-sheet, *UHP*, and the bolshevisers' call for their purging from the party was growing more strident.[30] It was largely in reaction to the youth movement's demands for their expulsion that the Besteirists were impelled to found a publication to defend their ideas. Called *Democracia*, it appeared weekly from 15 June to 13 December. Given its moderate line and the fact that it was largely concerned with internal PSOE matters, the Minister of the Interior, Manuel Portela Valladares, permitted its appearance. This was taken by the 'bolshevisers' as proof of the Besteirist treachery to the Socialist cause.[31]

Six weeks before the appearance of the first issue of *Democracia*, Besteiro himself had entered the fray. On 28 April he had given his inaugural lecture (*discurso de ingreso*) as a member of the Academy of Political and Moral Sciences, taking as his subject 'Marxism and Anti-Marxism'. Unfortunately for him, he had been elected to the academy as the replacement for Gabino Bugallal, one-time head of the old monarchist Conservative Party, who had been renowned for the severity he had brought to bear against the Socialists after 1917. Protocol demanded that Besteiro make a formal eulogy of his predecessor. That eulogy, together with the content of his discourse on Marxism, earned him intensified hostility from the PSOE leftists. That was hardly surprising, since his speech constituted an almost direct critique of the 'bolshevisers'. Besteiro set out to prove that Marxism justified democratic socialism and that Marx had been hostile to the notion of the dictatorship of the proletariat. Although Besteiro was reputed to be the PSOE's most sophisticated theorist, his Marxism did not go much beyond the position of Kautsky. He rejected the thought of Lenin and Trotsky with peremptory haste and his analysis of the phenomenon of fascism was extremely slight. His insinuations that the violence of the Socialist Left was hardly distinguishable from fascism did not endear him to the Caballeristas.[32]

A reply was undertaken by Largo's most competent theoretical adviser, Luis Araquistain, in the doctrinal journal *Leviatán*, which had survived the repression of the Socialist media. In a series of three long articles, Araquistain demolished Besteiro's arguments with energetic sarcasm. Besteiro had defended socialists who had become bourgeois politicians – such as Millerand, Briand, Ramsay MacDonald, Philip Snowden and even Mussolini. This formed part of his gradualist theory of socialism, whereby bourgeois society was 'impregnated'. A successful example of the impregnation of bourgeois society by socialist ideas was Roosevelt's New Deal. Araquistain pointed out that this was Fabianism and that there was little valid Marxism in Besteiro's thought. The fact that Besteiro seemed unaware of the close relationship between bourgeois capitalism and fascism proved to Araquistain that the professor's Marxism was of the flimsiest kind. Largo's adviser reasserted the revolutionary nature of Marxism and the temporary need for the dictatorship of the proletariat, while he rejected the 'pseudo-Marxism' of Bernstein and Kautsky, with whom he associated Besteiro.[33] The two articles written in reply by Besteiro protested at the vehemence of Araquistain's tone, but they did not seriously contest the issues raised in Leviatán.[34]

Araquistain's articles were of a notably higher level of theoretical competence than the inflammatory tract produced by the FJS in April. To a great extent, Araquistain's victory confirmed Besteiro's withdrawal from the leadership stakes within the PSOE. Despite the continued existence of Democracia, Besteiro was no longer a serious contender for the direction of Spanish socialism. He did not re-emerge as a major figure until his participation in Colonel Casado's attempt to end the Civil War in March 1939, although that did not save him from a harsh death in a Francoist prison. Throughout 1935, Besteiro's lieutenants tended to align with Prieto. Oddly enough, Leviatán, although closely associated with the Socialist Left, never really made an all-out attack on Prieto. There were two reasons for that. On the one hand, Araquistain was a rather more responsible figure than the FJS leaders who had produced Octubre – segunda etapa. On the other, since the fundamental preoccupation of his journal was the analysis of fascism and the search for a valid leftist response to it, Araquistain could not ignore the basic common sense of Prieto's appeal for unity.[35]

In fact, just as the polemic between Araquistain and Besteiro was getting under way, Prieto made a highly influential statement of his views. This took the form of five articles published in late May in El Liberal of Bilbao, La Libertad of Madrid and several other Republican newspapers in the provinces. Collectively titled 'Posiciones socialistas', the articles were published shortly afterwards as a book.[36] They were concerned to reaffirm the need to avoid the great tactical error of 1933 and to answer some of the more offensive accusations of Octubre –

segunda etapa. In the first, he rejected the FJS executive's claim that he should remain silent, and gave as his reasons that the executive had not scrupled to break Socialist ranks with its pamphlet and that there was reason to believe that, in areas like Asturias, it did not enjoy the backing of its rank and file. In the second article, he showed how the proposed electoral alliance would be mutually beneficial to Socialists and Republicans. He also rejected criticisms of the electoral law which favoured such coalitions, and in so doing made a veiled reference to the fact that Largo Caballero had been one of the most fervent advocates of the law when it was first introduced.[37] Finally, Prieto pointed out that, since the Right would be united at the next elections and an exclusively workers' coalition would be the victim of anarchist indiscipline, there was no method other than a Republican–Socialist coalition to guarantee an amnesty for political prisoners. The last three articles set out, in mild yet firm language, to expose some of the more absurd contradictions of *Octubre*. He rejected the right of untried youngsters to call for the expulsion of militants who had dedicated their lives to the PSOE. With some distaste, he pointed out that the accusations made against various sections of the Socialist movement by the pamphlet were most applicable to the FJS itself. Above all, he denounced the dictatorial tendencies of the FJS and proposed a party congress to settle the direction that the movement was to take.

This was a condemnation of youthful extremism which contrasted starkly with Gil Robles's complicity with the strident ambitions of the JAP. Not surprisingly, it provoked the indignation of the PSOE Left. *Octubre* was reissued with a reply to Prieto. However, a popular edition of the five articles by Prieto was distributed in large numbers.[38] As a result, Enrique de Francisco wrote in friendly terms to Prieto protesting that he had no right to make party policy in bourgeois newspapers and that the party's electoral strategy remained formally that which had been agreed in November 1933. Prieto replied, equally cordially, to De Francisco pointing out that it was odd that the same rigid view had not inhibited the Socialist Youth from advocating bolshevisation. More stridently, the reply of the young bolshevisers was undertaken by the Catholic journalist Carlos de Baraibar, one of Largo Caballero's closest collaborators. Baraibar rapidly prepared, with Largo's knowledge, a book attacking the 'false socialist positions' of Prieto.[39] From a self-proclaimed position of 'the principles of pure Marxism', Baraibar denounced Prieto's arguments as 'puerile and premature'. His main objections were to the fact that Prieto had broken party discipline in publicising his ideas and had done so in the bourgeois press. This was a somewhat specious argument, since the FJS, whose position was approved by Baraibar, had equally made its views public in its clandestine press and in *Octubre*. Moreover, the papers in which Prieto had written were the most left-wing being published legally. Baraibar's points were laboured in the extreme. He opposed Prieto's advocacy of a wide electoral coalition to secure a political amnesty, and gave two reasons for his opposition. On the one hand he claimed that the CEDA would probably change the electoral law, and on the other he declared that amnesty was a short-sighted objective and that the Socialists' aim should be to destroy the system which took political prisoners.[40]

There was more theoretical consistency than practical realism in Baraibar's book – and little enough of either. Already the Left of the PSOE had recognised, particularly in the pages of *Leviatán*, that the Republic was not synonymous with a classic bourgeois revolution. The Spanish bourgeoisie had shown by its reaction to the reforming legislation of 1931–3 that its position was anything but progressive. If the realisation of this had pushed some members of the PSOE into believing that only revolution could change Spain's regressive structures, it had convinced others, like Prieto, that the oligarchy's strength was such as to oblige the Left to seek governmental power through the medium of elections. To the Caballeristas, it seemed as if Prieto was uselessly pinning his hopes on a discredited bourgeois democracy. There was much to be said for the validity of the revolutionary analysis. However, that did not undermine the accuracy of Prieto's belief in the need for control of the apparatus of the state. Moreover, although the activities of the revolutionists in the PSOE were never to go beyond rhetorical extremism, they were still far more counter-productive than Prieto's modest objectives could ever be.

The fact that the revolutionism of the Caballeristas was largely verbal could not alter the fact that, in the upper reaches of the movement at least, Spanish socialism was seriously divided. In early May, appalled by the depth of the divisions, Fernando de los Ríos had proposed that a meeting of the PSOE's National Committee be convened to resolve the differences. There were several issues that De los Ríos wanted discussed by the National Committee. In particular, since a new Radical—CEDA cabinet, with five CEDA ministers, had been formed on 6 May, he wanted policy guidelines to be laid down for the PSOE's *minoría parlamentaria* in the Cortes. He also wanted discussion of whether the Socialist Youth should be subjected to tighter party discipline. Above all, he wanted consideration of future party electoral policy. The four imprisoned Caballerista members of the PSOE executive – Largo

Caballero, Enrique de Francisco, Pascual Tomás and Wenceslao Carrillo – opposed the idea on the spurious grounds that it should wait until after their trials. Three of the four belonged to the National Committee of the UGT which met without difficulty. Their statement, dated 12 May, also claimed speciously that the FJS was not subject to party discipline. Privately, Largo Caballero was keen to avoid any progress towards an electoral alliance with the Republicans. Fernando de los Ríos concluded that the depth of division within the PSOE was such that he had no choice but to resign from the executive, which he did in a letter to Vidarte on 16 May.[41]

It is extremely difficult to estimate with any numerical accuracy how the division was reflected at rank-and-file level. The repressive policies of the CEDA–Radical government certainly intensified militancy and made the Socialist masses more open to revolutionary propaganda. On the other hand, the memory of the Asturian October, the continued existence of thousands of political prisoners and the vindictive behaviour of the Right all ensured a sympathetic mass response to Prieto's call for unity and a return to the progressive Republic of the first *bienio*. In August, Azaña wrote to Prieto saying, 'I am sure that you have won the battle, not only in the eyes of the public, but also within the mass of your own party. This is not just my assessment but that of many people, Socialists and non-Socialists.' The polemic continued between *Democracia* and the weekly *Claridad*, which the Caballeristas had managed to bring out on 13 July using money initially collected for the 1934 revolution. Azaña believed that, since the majority of ordinary militants accepted Prieto's point of view, they saw the polemic only as boring irrelevance, although they were shocked by some of the personal insults used. He had been told that in Madrid the average Socialist was just not bothering to read either of the sides in the polemic.[42] This was, of course, only Azaña's opinion, and he was committed to Prieto.

Nevertheless, Azaña's point was supported by the popular response that greeted a series of open-air speeches – the so-called *discursos en campo abierto* – which he made between May and October. His campaign in favour of unity began on 26 May at the Campo de Mestalla in Valencia. Before an audience of more than 100,000, he announced that Izquierda Republicana was working with other parties on an electoral platform and a future plan of government which would eventually be submitted to the approval of groups further to the left. Then on 14 July, he spoke to an even larger crowd at the Campo de Lasesarre in Baracaldo near Bilbao, provoking intense enthusiasm when he called for new elections and defended the necessity of an electoral coalition. The crowd, which must have contained many thousands of workers, frequently broke out into spontaneous cheers for Prieto. However, the culmination and the most spectacular event of his campaign came on 20 October 1935 on a huge area of waste ground at Comillas, in what in those days were the outskirts of Madrid.

Azaña was thoroughly aware of what was at stake in his campaign. On the day before he was due to speak, he visited Comillas by car and somewhat daunted by the size of the venue asked the members of the organising committee, 'Do you really think that this will be filled? Because if not, we are going to look ridiculous.' In the event nearly half a million arrived to hear him elaborate his projected programme of government.[43]

The Comillas meeting was a remarkable occasion. For millions of Spaniards Azaña had become the very symbol of the Republic. Hundreds of thousands put up with considerable hardship in order to be present at a speech which most of them must have found hardgoing. Azaña was not a populist orator but a reasoned intellectual debater. It did not matter. Those who went to Comillas on that day did so as a gesture of outrage and rejection of the Radical–CEDA government and to demonstrate their support for the task of 'reconquering' the Republic undertaken by Azaña and Prieto. The English journalist Henry Buckley wrote of the occasion:

> More than half the spectators could not even see the stand from which the former Prime Minister addressed them. The loudspeakers functioned only partially and therefore tens of thousands not only saw nothing but they heard nothing either. This meeting had not been widely advertised. It was frowned upon by the authorities and in some cases the Civil Guard turned back convoys of trucks carrying spectators. All vehicles bringing people from afar were stopped some miles outside Madrid, thus causing endless confusion and forcing weary men and women to trudge a long distance after a tiring ride. Admission was by payment. The front seats cost twelve shillings and sixpence and the cheaper ones ten shillings and half a crown. Standing room at the back cost sixpence. No one was forced to go to that meeting. Presence there, in fact, was much more likely to bring the displeasure of employer or landlord ... From the furthest points of Spain there were groups who had travelled in some cases six hundred miles in rainy cold weather in open motor lorries.[44]

At the end of his speech, Azaña called the huge crowd to total silence and ended with the moving words:

> The silence of the people declares its grief and indignation; but the voice of the people can sound as terrifying as the trumpets of the day of judgement. Let my words not rebound against frivolous hearts but penetrate yours like darts of fire. People, for Spain and for the Republic, unite!

His listeners burst into a frenetic ovation and thousands of clenched fists flowered. Not only did the display of discipline by those who attended seriously disturb the Right, but the sheer size of the crowd and its enthusiasm helped resolve remaining doubts among those who still opposed the creation of the electoral front.

The Socialist masses almost certainly did not divide over the bolshevisation issue in the way that their leaders did. Mass militancy, which favoured Largo, was balanced by a desire for unity, which favoured Prieto. In any case, Prieto ignored the leftist criticisms to which he was being subjected and continued to work for unity with the Republicans. Throughout the summer of 1935, Azaña, Martínez Barrio and Sánchez Román worked on a manifesto. On 27 August, Martínez Barrio announced that the document was being submitted for the approval of the PSOE and was soon to be published. Two days later, an anonymous editorialist, presumably Prieto himself, wrote in *El Liberal* that it would benefit the Right immensely if the PSOE adopted a long-term revolutionary strategy to the exclusion of immediate necessities such as an electoral agreement with the Republicans. In mid-September, he met Azaña in Belgium to discuss the programme of the projected coalition.[45]

In the meanwhile, the battle between *Democracia* and *Claridad* grew more heated. Under the editorship of Andrés Saborit, *Democracia* advocated party unity and showed a reluctance to enter into a polemic. This did not save it from a fierce denunciation in the form of a PSOE executive committee circular signed by Largo Caballero. When Saborit visited the prisoners in the *cárcel modelo*, Largo Caballero ostentatiously refused to shake his hand or even speak to him.[46] *Claridad* accepted the FJS call for the expulsion of the Besteiristas and the removal of the Prietistas from positions of power within the movement. Each side regularly claimed the support of various provincial organisations, but no definite picture of the rank-and-file attitude to the polemic emerged. *Claridad* claimed to be backed by the Socialist Federations of Valencia, Salamanca and Alicante. The Agrupación Socialista de Alicante even expelled Manuel González Ramos, one of its Cortes deputies, for the crime of writing in *Democracia*. In its turn, Saborit's weekly printed declarations of support from the Socialist organisations of Asturias, Badajoz and Albacete. For what such declarations were worth, the pro-*Democracia* groups were more important by a considerable margin. Equally, *Claridad* claimed that its circulation was rising dramatically while *Democracia* was losing sales at an alarming rate.[47]

The most telling point made in the pages of *Democracia*, by an anonymous Asturian and in a letter from Amador Fernández, president of the SOMA, was that the whole bolshevisation campaign was simply a manoeuvre to divert attention from the fiasco created by the FJS in Madrid in October 1934. The unknown Asturian said that the bolshevisers were in no position to call other party members traitors. Amador Fernández pointed out that, since the Caballeristas had had exclusive control of the movement in Madrid, they could not throw the blame for its failure on either the reformists or the centrists of the party. He went on to accuse Baraibar in particular of an action tantamount to betraying the movement to government spies, without actually specifying whether that action had been the result of incompetence or of disloyalty.[48] The fact that *Claridad* could never find a satisfactory answer to criticisms from the proven revolutionaries of Asturias tended to lend credibility to their accusations against the bolshevisers.

In fact, given the indisputable realism of Prieto's analysis of the Left's electoral needs, it is difficult to see how *Claridad* could have maintained its opposition to his views. As it turned out, the Caballeristas were saved from an awkward situation by the Communists. Already, as part of their plans for the bolshevisation of the PSOE, some of the younger revolutionaries were toying with the idea of unity with the PCE. On 2 June 1935 the PCE secretary-general, José Díaz, had made a speech in the Cine Pardiñas in Madrid calling for the creation of a 'popular anti-fascist concentration'. Then in August, at the Seventh Congress of the Comintern, Dimitrov had launched the call for a united front of the proletariat and a wide popular front of all anti-fascist forces. Soon the Spanish Communists were openly calling for union with the PSOE.[49]

This change of tack by the PCE had a twofold effect on the left wing of the PSOE. The FJS maximalists were delighted, but Araquistain and Largo Caballero remained suspicious. The FJS representative at the Moscow congress, José Lain Entralgo, reported back enthusiastically that the Communist union, the Confederación General de Trabajo Unitaria, would incorporate with the UGT. He also claimed that the switch of tactics implied that Moscow had now returned sovereignty to the various national parties and that there was therefore no longer any reason why the FJS should not join the Comintern.[50] Santiago Carrillo, already well on the way to becoming a Communist, was trying to arrange the incorporation of the Trotskyist Bloc Obrer i Camperol and the Communist Youth into the PSOE as part of the process of bolshevising the party. Neither Largo nor Araquistain shared this enthusiasm, instinctively suspecting that the Communists wanted to take over the workers' movement, which was, of course, Largo's own ambition. Writing in *Leviatán*, Araquistain suggested the new Comintern policy simply served the interests of Russian foreign policy. He pointed out that the fundamental objective behind the Popular Front tactic was the Russians' desire to ensure that liberal and left-wing governments would be in power should war break out with Germany. Far from breaking with the old Comintern habit of dictating the same policy for each country, as the FJS fondly thought, the new tactic confirmed the dictatorial customs of the Third International. While Araquistain accepted the need for proletarian unity, he rejected the notion of alliance with the bourgeois Left.[51] Largo Caballero, while maintaining his enthusiasm for working-class unity and for the absorption of the Communist working-class rank and file into the UGT, opposed the idea of the PSOE joining the Comintern. And, like Araquistain, he was not favourable to an electoral coalition with the Left Republicans.[52]

There was a large degree of personal animosity in Largo's attitude. The fact that Prieto favoured alliance with the bourgeoisie was probably sufficient to guarantee Largo's hostility. He was not of a forgiving nature. Thus, having convinced himself in 1933 that the PSOE had been betrayed by the Republicans, he opposed a new alliance with them. Even in that there was an element of personal resentment. One of Azaña's senior lieutenants, Claudio Sánchez Albornoz, was always conscious of Largo's enmity without ever finding out the cause.[53] In addition, Largo Caballero bitterly resented the insinuations that he and the Madrid leadership had acted in a cowardly faction either during the events of October 1934 or in their declarations at their trials. Although such accusations had emerged spontaneously among the rank and file in Asturias, Largo was convinced that Prieto had stirred them up.[54] Above all, anxious to maintain his far-from-warranted reputation as a revolutionary, Largo was frightened to disappoint the militancy of fellow prisoners in the *cárcel modelo*.

However, the resonance of Azaña's Comillas speech had already had its effect on the Caballeristas.[55] By late October, the Radical Party, mortally wounded by Lerroux's involvement in the Estraperlo and Nombela scandals, was forced out of government. Since Alcalá Zamora refused to ask Gil Robles to form a government, general elections became inevitable. On 14 November, Azaña made the PSOE executive a formal proposal of electoral alliance. Faced with a dramatic choice, Largo Caballero quickly convoked a session of the PSOE executive for 16 November. The PSOE leadership was shortly afterwards joined by the UGT and FJS executives for a joint meeting. Recognising the absurdity of repeating the error of 1933, Largo Caballero himself spoke in favour of Azaña's proposal and it was decided with little debate to accept it. Two of the three great 'bolshevisers' of the FJS, those closest to the Communist Party, Santiago Carrillo and Amaro del Rosal, followed the Comintern line and spoke strongly in favour of the electoral alliance. The third, Carlos Hernández Zancajo, opposed it – and thereby anticipated divisions among the Caballeristas that would not be fully consummated until the Civil War. Largo Caballero, however, insisted that any coalition should extend to other working-class organisations including the Communist Party. He was determined that a readiness to deal with the bourgeois Republicans should not strengthen the Prietista wing of the Socialist movement. Accordingly, the Caballeristas swiftly abandoned their opposition to alliance with the Communists. The UGT executive decided on the same day as it accepted Azaña's proposal to open negotiations with the PCE for the incorporation of the Confederación General de Trabajo Unitaria into the UGT. Moreover, Largo Caballero insisted that the electoral programme to be elaborated should be submitted to the approval of the PCE and the CGTU as well as to the FJS, the PSOE and the UGT.[56]

Prieto and Azaña were not pleased by a set of moves which were clearly aimed at ensuring that the Caballerista wing would be able to dictate the terms of the electoral programme of the proposed alliance. Their intention had been that the Popular Front programme would be the exclusive work of the PSOE and the Left Republican parties. Enrique de Francisco wrote to Azaña on the same day and a cordial correspondence began in which Azaña was careful not to raise any objection to the inclusion of the FJS and the CGTU in any negotiations lest it undermine the process before it had properly begun. Vidarte wrote on 20 November to Prieto who was still exiled in Brussels informing him of the decisions taken four days earlier. Prieto wrote back in strong terms pointing out that the disproportionate weight to be given to the Communist Party was likely to be damaging to the interests of the PSOE and that to consider the FJS as an autonomous organisation was entirely contrary to the traditions of the movement.[57]

The Secretariat of the Comintern was sufficiently concerned about

Prieto's hostility to the inclusion of the Communists in the electoral coalition to dispatch, in early December, an emissary to Madrid in the form of Jacques Duclos. A meeting in the *cárcel modelo* was arranged by Largo's pro-Communist adviser, Julio Alvarez del Vayo. Thirty years later, Duclos claimed that, for three days, he had had to use subtle arguments and flattery on a tight-lipped Largo Caballero in order to break down his opposition to the Popular Front. According to Duclos, when he told him that a broad front of workers, peasants and intellectuals in France had successfully combated fascism, Largo quoted Marx and Lenin at him to prove that the working class was the only revolutionary class. Since Largo had already accepted the principle of an electoral alliance and, for his own purposes, was keen on collaboration with the Communists, Duclos's claim that his visit made possible the Popular Front in Spain is a gross exaggeration. Largo's churlish response was almost certainly a reflection of his distrust of the Comintern and resentment of what he saw as unwanted and patronising interference.[58]

The outstanding problem which still remained concerned the programme to be elaborated for the electoral coalition. However, before further progress could be made towards its composition, there occurred a dramatic development in the internal struggle for the control of the PSOE. On 16 December 1935 there was a meeting of the party's National Committee, which was attended secretly by Prieto, who had returned clandestinely from exile and was living in hiding. At the meeting, Largo Caballero made it clear that, in his view, any electoral coalition should be dominated by the workers' organisations. Before a full-scale discussion could blow up, Prieto proposed, as he had on 1 October 1934, that the PSOE executive committee take responsibility for the activities of the parliamentary minority. The proposal was approved by nine votes to five with two abstentions, and Largo Caballero, who had been one of the five, resigned as president of the party. It seemed a simple issue and not one to provoke Largo's resignation, especially as the parliamentary group's submission to the executive was one of the objectives of the bolshevisers. The reaction of the Socialist rank and file to the consequences of the meeting was one of stupefaction. This was understandable, since the average militant was not familiar with the background to the meeting. In fact, the origins of this clash over an apparent technicality went back to the National Committee's meeting fourteen months earlier.

In 1934, Largo had played a double game of verbal extremism and practical moderation or inactivity. As part of his revolutionary image-building, he had attacked Prieto, the de facto leader of the PSOE parliamentary minority, for allegedly pursuing an insufficiently revolutionary line. This infuriated Prieto for a variety of reasons. On the one hand, the minority's activities in the Cortes had strictly followed the agreements of the executive, and, on the other, Prieto had done more than Largo to put the PSOE's revolutionary rhetoric into practice. Moreover, Largo's performance in the Cortes had been anything but that of a revolutionary. Accordingly, at the PSOE National Committee meeting of 1 October 1934, Prieto set about calling Largo's bluff. He proposed that the parliamentary minority be subject to the authority of the executive committee, which would then have to stand by its own orders. The voting went in favour of Prieto. Largo, who was not present at the meeting, had naturally opposed the proposal, as he had done before. As a notorious stickler for the party statutes, he had alleged in a letter to the National Committee that the proposal transgressed articles 26 and 27 of the statutes and that therefore only a party congress could determine such a matter. He had also resigned. Given the tense political context in which the meeting was taking place, the members of the National Committee were horrified by the possible consequences of the president's resignation. It was decided to scrub the entire debate from the records and Largo withdrew his resignation.[59]

When the National Committee next met, on 16 December 1935, Prieto tabled the same proposition. His objective may well have been to exploit Largo Caballero's obsession with procedural niceties in order to provoke his resignation and thus ease the path to negotiations with the Republicans. Contrary to his own published advocacy of the parliamentary group's submission to the executive, Largo again voted against the proposal, basing his objections on the same technicality from the party's statutes. Of the fourteen members present, nine, including Prieto and Cordero, voted against the president. The vice-president, the veteran Remigio Cabello, was one of two who abstained, the other being the Asturian Prietista, Ramón Lamoneda. Prieto's lieutenant, Juan Simeón Vidarte, and his fellow 'centrist' Anastasio de Gracia, voted with Caballero. The line-up of the vote is itself sufficient to throw doubt on Largo's contention that the whole thing had been a plot to remove him from the party leadership. In fact, when he resigned, Vidarte tried hard to dissuade him. Nevertheless, once Largo Caballero had left the meeting, Prieto expounded his moderate vision of the Republican–Socialist electoral coalition. Effectively, Largo Caballero's proposal that any negotiations with the Republicans should be carried out by a workers' bloc including the PCE and the CGTU was dead. His resignation was quickly followed by those of Enrique de Francisco, the PSOE secretary-general,

Wenceslao Carrillo and Pascual Tomás but the committee refused to ratify the resignations. When Vidarte, as vice-secretary, and Remigio Cabello, as vice-president, convoked an election for the vacant presidency, their letter made it clear that the National Committee was recommending the re-election of Largo Caballero.[60]

The resignation of the four Caballeristas broke the control of both the party and the union which had been established after the defeat of the Besteiristas in January 1934. These new resignations were clearly conceived as the first step to clearing out the centrists from the party although in immediate terms they left the UGT in the hands of the Caballeristas and the PSOE in the hands of the Prietistas. Largo Caballero made no secret of his reasons for resigning. He told Vidarte that the executive should always be unanimous, as the 'homogeneous organ of an iron leadership'. This was entirely consistent with his new bolshevising advocacy of a centralised party hierarchy. There was also an element of personal disgust at Prieto's manoeuvre. The moderates, however, being concerned with party unity, were not out to secure the expulsion of their opponents, but rather to make them see reason. This became very apparent in the immediate aftermath of the president's resignation. The National Committee requested that, in view of the reappearance of El Socialista on 18 December, both Claridad and Democracia should cease publication. Saborit complied, but the Caballeristas ignored the call. They began a ferocious campaign against the Prietista leadership of the party, calling for its resignation. Hoping to see the imposition of an entirely Caballerista National Committee, Claridad organised an unofficial plebiscite within the party. The new line-up favoured by the leftists was Largo Caballero as president, Julio Alvarez del Vayo as vice-president, Enrique de Francisco as secretary, Wenceslao Carrillo as vice-secretary, Pascual Tomás as minutes secretary, and Luis Araquistain, Ricardo Zabalza, Carlos Hernández Zancajo, Rodolfo Llopis and two others as ordinary members.[61]

The official leadership mildly condemned this fractional activity and raised the banner of unity, claiming that, with or without Largo, the PSOE was still the same party which had made the October rising. While Claridad published declarations of support for an apparently victimised Largo Caballero, El Socialista, the official party newspaper, edited by Prieto's follower, Julián Zugazagoitia, tried to paper over the cracks. On 4 January 1936, Zugazagoitia published a letter to the party's vice-president, Remigio Cabello, signed by himself, González Peña, Luis Jiménez de Asúa, Juan Negrín and many other prominent Socialists. The letter appealed for party unity and discipline, and pointing out that revolution and reform, or legal and illegal tactics, were not incompatible, presented a more democratic alternative than the Caballeristas' monolithic ambitions for the party. Four days later Cabello replied, lamenting the divisive language used so far and declaring his commitment to a broadly based party unity. With his letter were printed declarations of support, mainly from Socialist sections in the north, including those of Guipúzcoa and Teruel. *El Socialista* then began to publish a long series of reports about the events of October 1934, and some spine-chilling, and verifiable, accounts of the repression. These articles have usually been considered as part of the election campaign, but it is more likely that part of their function was to keep the Prietistas in the running with the militant rank and file.[62]

It is impossible to state with total precision how support for Prieto and Caballero was divided among the Socialist masses, or even to what extent the polemic was followed by the rank and file. There can be no doubt that the bolshevisers made more noise, and it is probably this which has led some writers to assume that the masses were completely convinced of Caballero's position.[63] Since the Caballeristas aimed at splitting the party, they had no reason to be inhibited about their language. Given the conflictive policies of the *bienio negro*, the Socialist masses were certainly more susceptible to revolutionary rhetoric, but they were not unaware of the need for unity. As it was, both sides published lists of the sections which supported them, but they were contradictory. A given local executive did not necessarily reflect the views of its rank and file. It is almost certain that all local sections contained not only devotees of both sides but also Socialists who could see merit in the positions of both sides. The Agrupación Socialista Madrileña, for instance, was alleged by the Caballeristas to have voted by 1800 votes to 600 in favour of the *Claridad* committee. Equally, the Basque country and Asturias were strongly in favour of Prieto.

The selection of candidates for the February elections by local constituency parties indicated that the bolshevisers enjoyed less support than they claimed. The north was solidly pro-Prieto in its choice. Vizcaya's two candidates were Prieto and Zugazagoitia. Asturias chose the Prietista heroes of October, Belarmino Tomás, Graciano Antuña and the SOMA president, Amador Fernández, among its seven candidates. The Levante was ambiguous. Alicante, for instance, had dropped Manuel González Ramos as a reprisal for his collaboration in *Democracia*. Valencia, on the other hand, chose Manuel Molina Conejero (in the capital) and Pedro García y García (for the province), both of whom had voted against Largo Caballero in the 16 December meeting which had provoked his resignation. The south showed growing support for the party maximalists, but they were still far from in total control. Andrés Saborit did not run for Ciudad Real as he had done in 1933. Córdoba dropped Francisco Azorín, who had voted against Largo on 16 December. Equally, Seville did choose Victor Carretero, who had also voted against Largo. Huelva, with a strong contingent of Socialist miners, was an interesting case. The local section did not choose Ramón González Peña as part of the Popular Front candidacy, but he ran alone and was elected with as many votes as the coalition. Jaén dropped the Besteirista veteran, Lucio Martínez Gil, but kept the moderates Jerónimo Bugeda, Juan Lozano and Tomás Alvarez Angulo. Granada retained Fernando de los Ríos. Valladolid, however, seems to have been solidly Caballerista. Manuel Cordero and Eusebio González Suárez, who had both voted against Largo, and Remigio Cabello, who had abstained but shown his hostility to bolshevisation, were all three dropped.[64]

There is evidence to suggest that the Caballeristas, as budding Leninists, were extremely active and vocal in local party politics. They seem thereby to have attained a level of dominance of certain local party organisations which was disproportionate to their actual degree of rank-and-file support. This is illustrated by an examination of the two Caballerista strongholds of Madrid and Badajoz. The Agrupación Socialista Madrileña voted a candidacy which included the more significant leftists, who also figured in *Claridad*'s suggested executive committee. However, alongside Largo Caballero, Alvarez del Vayo, Araquistain, Hernández Zancajo and Enrique de Francisco, both Julián Besteiro and Luis Jiménez de Asúa, were chosen as candidates. There were 3039 voting members of the Agrupación. As might have been expected, Largo came top of their list, with 2886 votes; Besteiro only just made it, with 1157 votes in the second round. What was surprising was that Jiménez de Asúa, who had lined up with Prieto, came second. Even more of a shock to the Caballeristas were the actual election results. There were thirteen Popular Front candidates, including the seven Socialists. Azaña came top, with 224,928 votes, followed by Besteiro, with 224,875. The next highest Socialist was Jiménez de Asúa, in sixth place. Alvarez del Vayo, Araquistain, de Francisco and Hernández Zancajo came respectively eighth, ninth, tenth and eleventh. Largo Caballero was twelfth, with 220,981 votes, beating only the Communist, José Díaz. The triumph of Besteiro cannot be explained by the claim that he received more middle-class votes. The same working-class districts which voted for Largo gave more votes to Besteiro; the upper-class districts gave few votes to either of them.[65] In fact, there was not that much difference in numerical terms, but the success of Besteiro and Jiménez de Asúa gave the lie to some of *Claridad*'s more extreme claims.

Badajoz also presented a fascinating picture. The local Popular Front candidacy consisted of six Socialists, four Republicans and a Communist. The Republican representation was disproportionate, since in 1933 the Socialists had gained 139,000 votes to the Republicans' 8000. Vidarte, Prieto's lieutenant from Badajoz, felt that two places would be sufficient for the Republicans, one each for Izquierda Republicana and Unión Republicana. However, the local Socialist federation had included two more Republicans, in order to exclude the two Besteiristas, Narciso Vázquez, the pioneer of socialism in Extremadura, and Anselmo Trejo Gallardo, who had, with Vidarte, taken part in the defence of the villages of Castilblanco – for which he was later shot by the Francoists. The Socialist candidacy included three Caballeristas, Ricardo Zabalza, Margarita Nelken and Nicolás de Pablo, and three Prietistas, Vidarte, José Aliseda Olivares and José Sosa Hormigo. The Caballeristas seemed to have most strength in the provincial capital, while Vidarte and Aliseda apparently enjoyed loyal support in the country towns, such as Don Benito and Llerena. This was illustrated by the fact that they managed to get their supporters to cast tactical votes for centre candidates, thereby ensuring the defeat of the rightist candidacy, even in the contest for the minority allocation of seats.[66] Although an intelligent move, it would not have been approved by the Caballeristas.

The PSOE's internal power struggle continued through the selection of candidates for the Popular Front, but the very fact of the Caballeristas' participation in the coalition was a victory for Prieto and Azaña. The two main conceptions of an electoral alliance, that of Prieto and Azaña, and that of the Comintern, had thus been brought together although not without sacrifices on the part of the working-class groups. Negotiations for a joint programme were continued between the representatives of Izquierda Republicana (Amos Salvador), of Unión Republicana (Bernardo Giner de los Ríos) and of the PSOE (Vidarte and Cordero). In fact, the two Socialists were also representing the Left as a whole, the Communists, the break-away syndicalists of Angle Pestaña and the POUM (Partido Obrero de Unificación Marxista), as well as the UGT and the FJS. The Republicans and Prieto had always wanted the negotiations to be limited to the PSOE and the Left Republican parties. In the aftermath of Largo Caballero's resignation as PSOE president and the defeat of his scheme for the UGT, the PCE and the CGTU also to be represented, Vidarte and Cordero had demanded that the UGT at least be represented. In the end, it was Largo Caballero who reluctantly prevented total deadlock by suggesting that the two PSOE delegates should represent all the working-class groups.[67]

There was basic agreement on the need for political amnesty, the restoration of civil liberties and the re-establishment of the social legislation of the Constituent Cortes. The Socialists would have liked a programme like that drawn up by Prieto in January 1934, but the Republicans refused to accept workers' control of industry and the nationalisation of land and the banks. In fact, it seems to have been the Communists, already attempting to appeal to the petty bourgeoisie, who overcame Largo Caballero's reluctance to accept these limitations. The PCE was anxious lest Largo's intransigence provoke the departure of one of the Republican groups left in the coalition. Sánchez Román had already refused to participate in an alliance with the Communists. However, the pact signed on 15 January could hardly have been vaguer or more mildly reformist. Indeed, it infuriated the Trotskyists who had not entered the POUM as much as it appeased Miguel Maura and Manuel Portela Valladares.[68]

Since Prieto had to maintain the fiction of being in exile, the Socialists' election campaign was dominated by Largo Caballero. His two main themes were the need for proletarian unity and for the transformation of capitalist society. Wrapped up in an apparently revolutionary rhetoric, they delighted his working-class audiences all over Spain. At one point, on 11 February, he spoke with José Díaz at a joint PSOE–PCE meeting on the subject of unity. In fact, by unity both orators meant the take-over of the entire working-class movement by their own organisations. Moreover, when Largo declared his commitment to thorough social change, he made it clear that he saw revolution as a thing of the future. Thus, while he emphasised that capitalist society could hardly be fundamentally changed by capitalist democracy, he also underlined that this did not mean immediate revolution but simply pointed out the need for the long-term preparation of the working-class for the future revolutionary moment. Although he reiterated that the Socialists did not forgo their determination to introduce radical social change, he also declared that they would stick by their undertaking to support a Republican government until the fulfilment of the minimum programme of 15 January.[69]

The Left scored a notable triumph in the elections of 16 February. The way in which the Socialist selected their candidates for the elections, the nature of Largo Caballero's propaganda campaign and the success achieved at the polls suggest some important points about the Socialist movement at the beginning of 1936. Above all, the belligerent and vengeful policies followed by the CEDA–Radical coalition had considerably accelerated the leftward trend of the PSOE. The candidacy for the election showed that, while Besteiro seemed to have retained his tremendous personal popularity in Madrid, his reformist section of the party had dramatically lost support, especially in the rural south. However, even if the most rightist section of the PSOE was in decline, the party seemed to be inconclusively divided between the supporters of Prieto and those of Largo Caballero.[70] Indeed, the Socialist rank and file gave little indication of being aware of the polemic which was sundering its leadership. The future was thus problematic. Prieto was committed to an attempt at rebuilding the progressive Republic of the first *bienio*. Even Largo had expressed a hope that electoral victory would herald a period of social peace. Whether the militant radicalisation of the Socialist masses could be halted by intelligent and forward-looking policies depended on the reaction of the Right. There was little about their behaviour between 1931 and 1935 to suggest that they would adopt the tolerant stance which might have permitted Largo Caballero to risk losing popularity by preaching moderation to his followers.

8

THE ABANDONMENT OF LEGALISM

The PSOE, the CEDA and the coming of war in 1936

The events of October 1934 and the result of the 1936 elections shattered CEDA dreams of being able to impose an authoritarian, corporative state without having to fight a civil war. Two years of aggressive rightist government had left the working masses, especially in the countryside, in a far from conciliatory mood. Having been thwarted once in its reforming ambitions, the Left was now determined to proceed rapidly with meaningful agrarian change, which would directly challenge the economic interests of the CEDA's backers. Having predicted that left-wing electoral success would be the prelude to the most spine-chilling social disasters, the CEDA had undermined its own *raison d'être*, the legal defence of landed and religious interests. The small section of the CEDA leadership, around Manuel Giménez Fernández and Luis Lucia, which believed that the party should now fully accept the Republic was unable to influence policy. It was rather late to attempt to reverse the cumulative effects of CEDA propaganda and already the rural and industrial oligarchies were switching their financial support to the conspiratorial Right. Gil Robles seems to have accepted that the legalist tactic had now outlived its usefulness. He was briefly involved in efforts to prevent a hand-over of power to the Left after the Popular Front elections. When this failed, he did not try to stem the flow of CEDA members to more extremist organisations. At the same time, he played an active, and indeed crucial, role, in parliament and the press, in creating the atmosphere which made a military rising appear to the middle classes as the only alternative to catastrophe.

This is not to say that Gil Robles would not have preferred to see a socially conservative, corporative state introduced by legal means. However, his readiness to turn to the military in October 1934, December 1935 and February 1936 revealed that the end was more important than the means. Once convinced that the legal road to corporativism was blocked, he did everything possible to help those who were committed to violence. He had already made two crucial contributions to the success of the 1936 rising. The first, of which he was later to boast, was to have fomented mass right-wing militancy. The other was the undermining of Socialist faith in the possibilities of bourgeois democracy. The success of the CEDA, both in and out of power, in defending the pre-1931 social structure had diminished the readiness of important sections of the PSOE to defend the Republican regime.

In a very real sense, the ambiguity of the Socialist attitude to the Republic was to be the crucial factor of 1936. Prieto remained as convinced as ever of the need for Socialist collaboration in the government, not least because of his awareness of the strength and determination of the Right. However, despite controlling the PSOE executive, Prieto still faced the opposition of Largo Caballero and his revolutionary entourage. A series of factors influenced Largo's attitude – resentment of Prieto, a delight in the flattering attentions of the Communists and the PSOE leftists who hailed him as the 'Spanish Lenin' and, above all, the militancy of the Socialist rank and file. A combination of the economic crisis and the vindictive policies of landowners towards labour saw unemployment reach 843,872, or 17 per cent of the working population, by the end of February 1936.[1] The election results signalled an almost immediate return to the rural lock-out of 1933 and new aggression from urban employers. As far from being convinced of the need for revolution as he had been in October 1934, Largo Caballero was motivated by fear of a rank-and-file drift into the CNT or the PCE if he did not hold out hopes of a revolutionary future to the Socialist masses. Moreover, his most revolutionary proposal, the call for proletarian unity, merely concealed the desire to aggrandise the UGT by taking over both the anarchist and Communist movements. It suited the Communists to indulge his conviction that he was a real revolutionary, since they were confident of being able to dominate the united working class in the event of Largo achieving a proletarian merger.

The anarchists and the Trotskyists remained distrustful. They believed that, although Largo accepted in theory that the working class had little to hope for from a bourgeois regime, in practice he could never break away from his reformist habits.[2] Thus, as far as they were concerned, Largo was doing no more than mouthing revolutionary platitudes. Their analysis was almost certainly correct, but the counterfeit nature of Largo's revolutionism did nothing to allay the fears of a middle class already terrified by rightist propaganda. Embittered by his experience of co-operation with the bourgeois regime between 1931 and 1933, and determined never again to suffer the opprobrium of another Casas Viejas, the UGT president hoped that the Republicans would carry out the electoral programme and then make way for an all-Socialist government. Largo talked of getting into power 'by any means', but it seems unlikely that he ever considered insurrectionary action, since he was confident of ultimately being able to introduce sweeping social reform from the government once it was in the exclusive hands of the Socialists. Thus, he opposed any interim PSOE participation in the government and continued to talk of revolutionary social change as being imminent.

In so far as he had any strategy, it was based on two related scenarios. In the first, the Republicans would be permitted to govern. Having gone as far as their bourgeois limitations would permit, and by then exhausted, they would hand over their votes in parliament and power to the Socialists, who would then make the revolution. In the second, a fascist or military coup would be made to prevent the transition from Republicans to Socialists. Largo Caballero was confident that it would be defeated by working-class action, thereby accelerating both the collapse of the bourgeois state and the making of the proletarian revolution. By thinking in this way, Largo Caballero fell between two stools. The threat of a right-wing military or fascist coup might have been averted by immediate revolutionary action, although the objective conditions were hardly conducive. Equally, a strong Socialist presence in the government might have curtailed fascist provocation before it created the necessary context for a coup. A Republican–Socialist coalition cabinet was Prieto's hope. Largo's policy prevented either revolution or strong government and ensured rather that an ineffectual Republican government would be in power while the military conspiracy was prepared.

Apart from preventing the PSOE from joining the government, Largo Caballero did nothing in the course of the spring of 1936 to hinder the work of the Republican government. However, moderately to stand aside was not enough. The Socialist and Republican leaderships were fully aware of the intensity of the rightist determination to prevent the Popular Front from enjoying its victory. Shortly before handing over power to Azaña, on 19 February, Portela Valladares had told the PSOE's acting secretary, Juan Simeón Vidarte, that there had been a serious threat of a military coup. Azaña had been fully informed by loyal Republican officers in the Ministry of War. Subsequent revelations – by Portela, Franco and Gil Robles – have confirmed what both were told.[3]

In the early hours of Monday 17 February, the results were coming through. All the indications were of a small numerical victory for the

Popular Front, which because of the electoral arithmetic in a system which favoured coalition, would be converted into a substantial triumph in terms of *escaños* (Cortes seats). With jubilant crowds on the streets, right-wing circles were prey to ever-intensifying panic. Gil Robles and General Franco, in a co-ordinated fashion, entirely understandable given their recent relationship as Minister of War and Chief of the General Staff, acted frantically to neutralise the inexorable outcome of the elections. The focus of their efforts was Portela Valladares, who was Minister of the Interior as well as Prime Minister. Their intention was to get him to stay in post and thereby ensure that the Civil Guard and the Assault Guard would not oppose any military schemes to reimpose order.

At about 3.15 a.m., Gil Robles, accompanied by his private secretary, the Conde de Peña Castillo, had gone to the Ministry of the Interior and demanded to see Portela, who had already left the ministry and retired to bed in his suite at the Hotel Palace. Woken to be told that the CEDA leader was waiting to see him, Portela hastened back to his office. At about 4.00 a.m., Gil Robles, declaring that he spoke for the entire spectrum of right-wing parties, told the Prime Minister that the Popular Front triumph meant anarchy, and asked him to declare martial law. Portela replied that his task had been to preside over the elections and nothing more. However, he was sufficiently alarmed by Gil Robles to agree to the declaration of a state of alert (*estado de alarma* – a stage prior to the declaration of martial law). Portela also telephoned Alcalá Zamora and asked him to sign decrees suspending constitutional guarantees and imposing martial law. Alcalá Zamora promised to sign the decrees at the next cabinet meeting but advised him to calm down.[4]

This was not enough for Gil Robles. Accordingly, while Portela was on the telephone to the President, he sent Peña Castillo to instruct his one-time military aide, Major Manuel Carrasco Verde, to make contact with General Franco. Franco was not only still Chief of the General Staff but, given the ineffectiveness of General Nicolás Molero, Gil Robles's successor as Minister of War, was virtually running the ministry. Carrasco was to inform Franco of the likely electoral results and of Gil Robles's encounter with Portela and to get him to add his own influence to persuade the Prime Minister not to resign and to implement the decree of martial law. Convinced that the Popular Front victory meant the triumph of communism in Spain, Franco sent Carrasco to warn Colonel Valentín Galarza Morante, head of the conspiratorial Unión Militar Española, to alert key officers in the organisation. He also telephoned General Sebastián Pozas Perea, the Director-General of the Civil

Guard, and, in typically oblique style, proposed that he bring out his forces to impose order:

> It would be more efficacious if persons with responsibility and those of us who occupy certain posts in the service of the state and of the constituted system were to establish the necessary contact in order that the masses do not get out of control.

A loyal Republican, Pozas dismissed Franco's fears of the celebrating crowds in the street. Franco then went to try to persuade the minister, General Molero, to do something to get martial law declared. With a speech scripted by Franco, Molero persuaded a now exhausted Portela to discuss the matter at the cabinet meeting scheduled for later that morning.[5]

When the cabinet met, it was decided only to declare a state of alert although Alcalá Zamora, who chaired the session, agreed to sign a decree of martial law to be kept in reserve and used only in the event of a major emergency. Informed by Molero of the existence of this document, Franco made frantic efforts to see Portela to get him to use it. At the same time, he renewed his pressure on Pozas as well as other efforts to organise military intervention. He spoke with Generals Manuel Goded and Angel Rodríguez del Barrio to see if they could bring out their troops in Madrid and, from his office in the Ministry of War, tried to implement the blank decree of martial law which Portela had been granted earlier in the day. He cited its existence to get local commanders to declare martial law. A state of war was actually declared in Zaragoza, Valencia, Oviedo and Alicante and arrangements were made for such a declaration in Huesca, Córdoba and Granada. However, not enough local commanders responded, not least because Pozas surrounded all suspect garrisons with detachments of the Civil Guard.[6]

Franco finally saw Portela on the evening of 17 February and offered military support if he would stay in power to help hold back the communist hordes of the Popular Front. While careful to obscure his own illegal initiatives of the afternoon, he made clear that the would-be plotters needed Portela's constitutional authority to neutralise the Civil Guard, which remained an effective obstacle to any army takeover. As Prime Minister and Minister of the Interior, Portela could overrule Pozas, who had refused to join in a movement to nullify the election results. Portela refused outright.[7] Accordingly, following on from his conversation with Franco earlier in the day, Goded tried to bring out the troops of Madrid's Montaña barracks. However, the officers of the capital and of other garrisons refused to rebel without a guarantee that the Civil Guard would not oppose them. General Pozas, backed up by General Miguel Núñez de Prado, head of the police, knew that Franco was conspiring and they reassured Portela that the forces of order would oppose any coup. Pozas surrounded all suspect garrisons with units of the Civil Guard.[8]

Had the coup worked, Gil Robles would have been made Prime Minister. Knowing that they had failed, Gil Robles made a last effort to persuade Portela to stay on. He met him secretly on the outskirts of Madrid at 8.30 a.m. on 19 February. It was to no avail and, indeed, the main consequence of these incidents was to frighten Portela and the rest of his cabinet into accelerating their resignations and handing over power to Azaña immediately, instead of waiting for the opening of the Cortes in order to do so.[9] To his annoyance, Azaña was forced to accept power prematurely from a broken Portela, on the afternoon of 19 February. With Largo Caballero adamant that the Socialists should play no part in the cabinet, Azaña assembled in a matter of hours a ministerial team consisting exclusively of left Republicans. Among other problems bequeathed Azaña by the hasty and panic-stricken way in which Portela handed over power was the fact that the outgoing Prime Minister did not inform him of the full extent of his conversations with Franco until well after the outbreak of the Civil War. Accordingly, Franco was not punished for transgressing his authority and was in a position to play a crucial role in the military rebellion of July 1936.[10]

For the moment, the CEDA had no choice but to accept the election results. It was a great blow. Deprived of the benefits of legalism, the Catholic party seemed stunned. Rumours flew around that Gil Robles was about to abandon politics. He seems to have toyed with the idea of retiring from politics and handing leadership of the CEDA to Giménez Fernández. However, the virulently hostile reaction of the party's most prominent backers led him to change his mind and simply to take a short break for two days.[11] For a while too, it seemed that defeat had moderated CEDA spirits, that the pre-electoral demagogy was a thing of the past and that the party was ready to take part in an effort to tranquillise the political situation. The impression was illusory. Giménez Fernández visited Azaña on 20 February in a state of some agitation to inform him that the CEDA was prepared to vote for the amnesty of those imprisoned for political reasons since October 1934. It seemed to the Prime Minister that this was merely an attempt to avoid the consequences of the CEDA's aggressive policies during the previous eighteen months. 'If they had won the elections,' he wrote bitterly in his diary, 'they would not have bothered about pacifying things and, far from granting an amnesty, they would have thrown into prison those who still had their freedom.'[12]

After the acute polarisation of the previous two years, Azaña faced an awsome task of pacification and reconciliation. The simmering divisions within the Socialist Party had serious implications for his own government since they cast considerable doubt on the stability of its parliamentary backing. At the same time, military plotters had already begun to prepare for the July rising and their work would be greatly facilitated by any sign of government uncertainty or a breakdown of law and order. Left-wing joy at the election victory and sporadic manifestations of a desire for revenge for the sufferings of the *bienio negro* sowed panic on the Right.

In the large towns, relative tranquillity was quickly restored after the elections. However, in much of the southern countryside, where rightist persecution had gone furthest, the turning of the tables was manifested in innumerable ways which provoked in equal measure the fury and alarm of the Right. The most extreme case was the anarchist-inspired incidents in Palma del Río in the province of Córdoba where Acción Popular headquarters, the magnificent parish church of La Asunción, two convents and the homes of the town's eleven richest citizens were vandalised. (One of those citizens – the *latifundista* Féliz Moreno – later wreaked a terrible vengeance, having three hundred workers shot when the Nationalists recaptured the village.) Azaña wrote of his 'black despair' (*negra desesperación*) at church burnings and attacks on right-wingers. In small rural towns elsewhere, popular jubilation at the victory spilled over into demonstrations in favour of the amnesty of those arrested after the 1934 landworkers' strike. In the course of these demonstrations, some *casinos* (the clubs of the rich) and local headquarters of Acción Popular were invaded and windows and furniture broken. The *caciques* were further provoked by the flying of red flags from workers' clubs and civic buildings and by the newly confident attitudes of the *braceros*. More substantially, the right-wing *ayuntamientos* imposed in 1934 were overthrown and the nominees of the *caciques* replaced by the Socialists and others elected during the April 1931 municipal elections. Their most urgent task was the unemployment consequent upon the four months of heavy rain since December which had flooded the fields and made it impossible to work. To the outrage of the local *latifundistas*, the Socialist councillors re-established *jurados mixtos* and *bases de trabajo* and levied informal local taxes to provide work for the unemployed. Some also prohibited religious festivals. There were cases of demonstrators burning deeds to property in municipal land registries. There also took place, egged on by a newly resurgent FNTT, occupations of lands in private ownership which were claimed to be former common lands illegally enclosed.[13]

For the moment, however, moderation was ostensibly the order of the day for the CEDA at least, if not for the unashamedly 'catastrophist' Right. Gil Robles, in an interview for *Le Petit Parisien*, said that opposition to the government would not be systematically destructive but prudent, intelligent and moderate. The CEDA National Committee met on 4 March to examine its position in the aftermath of the electoral defeat. A statement was issued reaffirming the party's commitment to the legalist tactic and claiming that it did not 'think remotely of solutions of force'. Given that Gil Robles had twice since mid-December been involved in attempts to organise a coup, the statement may be seen less as a declaration of intent and more as a defensive ploy to mitigate leftist hostility and suspicion. CEDA support was offered to the government for the maintenance of public order, which, it was claimed, was seriously endangered by the supporters of the Popular Front.[14] Such support was clearly worthless to a government committed more to fulfilling the aspirations of the masses and not to their indiscriminate repression.

The Left was not impressed by Gil Robles's protestations of moderation or by his insinuations that all threats to order came from those who had voted for the Popular Front. During the period of CEDA dominance, over 270,000 gun licences had been issued to rightists. Now, in the first half of March, armed attacks on prominent left-wing and liberal politicians were beginning. The Left did not accept that the CEDA was free of implication in the terrorism of action squads manned by Falangists and financed by the monarchists of Acción Española. *El Socialista* alleged that the CEDA was also organising motorised machine-gun assault groups. As the spring wore on, increasing numbers of the rightist youths arrested for acts of violence were members of the JAP.[15] The Left did not feel that Gil Robles's concern for public order distinguished him from other rightist groups. Rather, it was seen, along with the Falangist provocations, as part of an attempt to discredit the government and prove the need for a dictatorial regime of the Right. The CEDA, Renovación Española, the Carlists and the Falange were regarded by the Left as specialised units of the same army. Only their tactics differed. They shared the same determination to establish a corporative state and to destroy the effective forces of the Left. Leaders of each group addressed the meetings of the others and were usually cheered. Space was regularly available in the CEDA press for favourable reports on the activities of its more violent rivals. Divisions between them never went beyond tactical criticisms of the CEDA's legalism. There is considerable evidence to support this interpretation of the parties of the Right. They were all the servants of the landed and industrial oligarchy in so far as they depended on it for their finance and all their political activities were directed towards the protection of its interests. They rarely broke unity in parliament, at election times or during the Civil War – a stark contrast with the divisions which split the Left, both in peace and in war.

The leftist press consistently warned its readers, albeit with varying success, not to respond to fascist provocation. On 12 March, Falangists tried to kill Luis Jiménez Asúa. Despite the fact that Jiménez Asúa had been his defending lawyer after the October events, Largo Caballero did not deign to visit him to enquire about his condition after an attack in which he had nearly lost his life. Four days later, it was Largo Caballero's turn when his house was fired upon by a rightist terror squad. It thus infuriated the Left when Gil Robles went to see the Minister of the Interior, Amós Salvador, on 17 March to protest about disorder. A prosperous and likeable architect, Amós Salvador, had neither the spirit nor the skill to control the situation. The CEDA also tabled a debate on the subject in the Cortes. Omitting to mention that the Falange and probably the JAP were implicated in the violence, CEDA protests declared that the government and the Left were responsible.[16] This emphasised the entirely propagandist nature of the CEDA's new-found moderation. Gil Robles was forced to tread delicately. He knew that the army was not yet ready to seize power. Equally, he was aware that all-out obstruction of Azaña's government could only lead to a completely Socialist government, which would have given short shrift to the extreme Right. Accordingly, he devoted his energies to creating the atmosphere in which the middle classes, terrified by the spectre of disorder, would eventually turn to the army as their only saviour.

In the meanwhile, the CEDA leader was kept fully informed of the development of the conspiracy. Some of the key liaison officers between the military and civilian elements were Cedistas. On 8 March a crucial meeting of Generals Franco, Orgaz, Villegas, Fanjul and Varela took place in the home of the prominent stockbroker José Delgado who had been an unsuccessful CEDA candidate for Madrid in the February elections. Given the ambiguity of the CEDA's public position and the growing extremism of important sectors of the party, Gil Robles was deeply annoyed when, on 19 March, Manuel Giménez Fernández called for the CEDA to make its position clear. Faced by his demand for a choice between the monarchy and the Republic, the members of the party's parliamentary minority decided that it was not 'opportune' to modify their position of Republican legality. Asked to choose between democracy and fascism, the CEDA deputies expressed a preference for the former, but announced ominously that, if democracy were not possible, the party would be dissolved and each member would join the group nearest to his own ideology. On debating whether or not to remain in parliament, the deputies decided to stay, in order to use the Cortes as a tribune of propaganda. An open declaration of Republicanism by the CEDA at this time would have strengthened the regime considerably against extremists of both Right and Left. However, the party's backers, and, indeed, most of its members, were not interested in consolidating the regime.[17] In the Cortes, CEDA deputies provocatively challenged the Socialists to abandon their speechmaking and to make a revolution. At the beginning of April, Largo Caballero revealed a similar provocation. Apparently, the Right was printing leaflets, supposedly issued by the UGT, containing detailed plans for revolution and black lists of the Left's enemies. Without renouncing his long-term objectives, the UGT president declared that the Socialists had no intention of disturbing public order.[18]

The way in which the Right in general, and the CEDA in particular, simply used parliament for its propaganda value was clearly established during the debates held to examine the validity of the recent elections. The Francoist commission set up to prove the illegitimacy of the Republican government alleged that the Popular Front used its majority on the committee for examining electoral validity, the Comisión de Actas, to inflate the number of its deputies by more than fifty.[19] This was the reverse of the truth, since the committee acted with a punctilious legalism which, by excluding much evidence of falsification, frequently favoured the Right. In Santander, for instance, allegations of intimidation of Republicans were ignored for lack of proofs witnessed by notaries, and the rightist victory was confirmed. Other decisions went in favour of the Right in the provinces of Ciudad Real, Toledo and Avila, for similar reasons. In Zaragoza province, evidence of intimidation aside, the results for seventy-eight villages were simply made up by the civil governor. Nevertheless, the rightist victory was approved because of a lack of legally acceptable documentary proofs. The results in the Balearic Islands, the fief of Juan March, were not even questioned. In Albacete there had been villages where more votes were cast than there were voters. The secret vote had also been transgressed. Yet, because the Left had not been able to afford to have a notary present during the election, insufficient acceptable evidence could be gathered to impugn the Albacete results.[20]

Despite the relative impartiality with which the Comisión de Actas carried out its functions, the CEDA contrived to cover up its own involvement in electoral malpractice and also to give the impression that it was being persecuted. This was a crucial part of the process whereby right-wing opinion was being convinced that democratic coexistence was no longer possible. Several of the constituencies whose results were being challenged were represented by senior rightist leaders. Gil Robles and Cándido Casanueva in Salamanca, Calvo Sotelo in Orense and Goicoechea in Cuenca were all in danger of losing their seats. If the most flagrantly dishonest elections of all, those of Granada, were invalidated, the CEDA stood to lose five deputies. Accordingly, Giménez Fernández, the CEDA representative on the Comisión de Actas, declared the Comisión partisan and claimed that it was creating a parliament to be the instrument of a totalitarian regime. He then led a withdrawal of the CEDA deputies from the Cortes after a menacing speech which ended with the words, 'We leave the fate of the parliamentary system in your hands.' This simple manoeuvre was designed to allow the CEDA to denounce the composition of parliament as abitrary and undemocratic. ABC claimed that the Right had been expelled from parliament. Giménez Fernández favoured only a short absence from the Cortes but the more extreme members of the CEDA, especially Cándido Casanueva and Ramón Ruiz Alonso who were both in danger of losing their seats, were pushing for a definitive withdrawal.[21]

It was precisely to prevent the Right from being able to discredit the Cortes in this way that Prieto, the chairman of the Comisión, had been prepared to come to an agreement with the CEDA representatives. They demanded more than he was prepared to concede. When he resigned the chairmanship for other reasons, the Right claimed it as proof that he, as an honest Socialist, was disgusted with the dishonest activities of the Comisión. Prieto seems to have resigned partly out of a feeling that it would have been politically more prudent not to pursue the expulsion of senior right-wing figures, however justified it might have been. He felt that it was safer to have them in parliament than conspiring elsewhere. He is also alleged to have resented pressure from Alcalá Zamora to approve the especially shady election of Portela Valladares in Pontevedra and from Azaña to turn a blind eye to corruption in La Coruña, examination of which would have endangered the seat of his Minister of Public Works, Santiago Casares Quiroga. Prieto considered it wrong to ignore evidence of malpractice in Pontevedra and not to do the same in Orense or La Coruña. However, he made it quite clear in the Cortes on 7 April that he had not resigned because he felt that the Right was being swindled out of parliamentary seats.[22]

Prieto was replaced by Jerónimo Gomariz, the Unión Republicana deputy from Alicante. The results of Pontevedra, La Coruña and Orense were approved but otherwise the findings of the Comisión continued to be along the reasonable lines established by Prieto. The results of Cuenca were annulled for two reasons. To begin with, there had been falsification of votes, and then, once the defective votes were discounted, no candidate reached the minimum 40 per cent of the votes required for election. There was overwhelming proof that in Granada the legal representatives of the Popular Front had been imprisoned during the elections, that armed gangs had controlled voting booths and that people had been forced at gun-point to vote for the Right. Accordingly, the Granada elections were also annulled. The situation regarding the Sala-manca results was rather more complex. All six of the victorious right-wing candidates, Gil Robles, Cándido Casanueva, Ernesto Castaño and José Cimas Leal of the CEDA, together with two Carlists, José María Lamamié de Clairac and Ramón Olleros, were implicated in improperly soliciting the votes of the province's wheat-growers by offering to buy up their surplus stocks. Eventually the elections of Lamamié, Castaño and Olleros were declared void and they were replaced as deputies by the candidates with the next highest number of votes.[23]

With his own seat now secure, Gil Robles led the CEDA back into the chamber on 3 April, albeit at a price. Azaña, like Prieto, realised that there was little hope for Spanish democracy if the Right could claim through its massive press network that it was being excluded from the Cortes. Accordingly, partly in compensation for the CEDA return to parliament, Azaña postponed the municipal elections which had been due to take place on 14 April. In the current atmosphere, these would almost certainly have led to a massive victory for Popular Front candi-dates and to the elimination of right-wing *alcaldes* throughout most of Spain. The Left was bitterly disappointed.[24] Gil Robles did little to earn his prize and exploited every opportunity to misrepresent the work of the Comisión de Actas. On 7 April, he claimed in the Cortes that the CEDA had been cheated out of forty seats. He then protested about the electoral malpractice in Granada and Cuenca as if it had been the fault of the Left. Needless to say, the right-wing press, on reporting his speech, did nothing to clarify this cunning confusion of the issues.[25]

The Cortes session of 7 April was intensely dramatic for reasons other than the heated debate over the Comisión de Actas. Article 81 of the

Republican Constitution gave a President the power to dissolve the Cortes twice during his mandate. To avoid then having a President deprived of the crucial capacity to call new elections, article 81 further required that, in the case of a second dissolution during the mandate of a single President, the newly elected Cortes ascertain the necessity and validity of the decree whereby its predecessor was dissolved. In the event of the Cortes deciding that the previous decree of dissolution had not been necessary, the President would be obliged to resign. A broad majority of the Cortes welcomed this opportunity to get rid of Alcalá Zamora. The parties of the Left had never forgiven him for permitting the entry of the CEDA into the government in October 1934 and the parties of the Right were furious that he had not handed power to Gil Robles in December 1935. Indeed, had they won the elections, the parties of the Right had intended to use article 81 to replace Alcalá Zamora with General Sanjurjo. Accordingly, the President's days were numbered since he had little parliamentary backing other than that from the twenty-odd centrist deputies gathered around Portela Valladares.[26]

Both Azaña and Prieto distrusted Alcalá Zamora and saw in this technicality an opportunity to remove him and so consolidate the new government. Azaña, in particular, was exasperated by the President's constant interference in cabinet meetings and his barely concealed hostility. The exchanges between them had become increasingly acerbic. Azaña had begun to refer to Alcalá Zamora, who was from Priego in Córdoba, as 'the curse of Priego' (el maleficio de Priego). Azaña had in any case never forgiven the President for acquiescing in his persecution after October 1934. Now, well-founded rumours had given him reason to fear that Alcalá Zamora hoped to avoid his fate by forcing the resignation of Azaña's cabinet before article 81 was discussed, thereby permitting him to call new elections.[27] Initially, however, Azaña, Prieto and many other leftist Republicans and Socialists were inhibited by the apparent contradiction of impeaching the President or doing precisely what they had been clamouring for him to do since shortly after the 1933 elections. Others, including Fernando de los Ríos, advised against deposing Alcalá Zamora for fear it might provoke a military intervention. Nevertheless, after lengthy deliberations, Azaña concluded that he

> could not bear the responsibility of leaving the Republic's worst enemy in the Presidency. And, if everyone regretted having voted for him in 1931, I did not want to have to regret electing him again in April 1936 which, if we missed the opportunity of Tuesday, is effectively what would happen.

251

Prieto undertook the task of overcoming the doubts of the predominantly leftist PSOE *minoría parlamentaria*.[28]

With a resolution drafted by Azaña, Prieto, seconded by his lieutenant Vidarte, raised the issue of the validity of Alcalá Zamora's dissolution of the previous Cortes as a ploy to provoke his resignation. Since he could not resist the temptation to cite the many occasions during the recent election campaign in which Gil Robles had demanded the removal of the President, the CEDA abstained from the final vote. Alcalá Zamora gained only five votes with 238 against. Once the President was impeached, the interim Headship of State was assumed by the President of the Cortes, Diego Martínez Barrio. The transition to a new President seemed to open up opportunities to strengthen the Republic. Azaña was delighted by the speed and efficiency of the operation but seems not to have given much thought to the consequences. His only doubts centred on the divisions in the PSOE: 'Everything could work out well if Araquistainism had not poisoned the Socialist Party, as a result of which the Front will be broken.'[29]

Although intended to strengthen the regime, the decision to depose Alcalá Zamora was to have serious consequences for the Republic.[30] The Constitution required that a new President be elected within thirty days. Azaña wrote to his brother-in-law, 'Once the Presidency was vacant, I thought that there would be no other solution than for me to occupy it.' He had long thought that it would benefit the Republic more if the enormous popularity that he had enjoyed since 1935 were used to strengthen the Presidency rather than worn away by the attrition to which the Prime Minister was subjected. He was anxious too to escape from the exhausting daily round of politics. There was public and private discussion of the merits of Besteiro, Sánchez Román and Martínez Barrio as candidates. Prieto was convinced that Azaña was the only plausible candidate and did more than anyone to ensure that he would be Alcalá Zamora's replacement. He rejected Vidarte's suggestion of Besteiro, on the grounds that Largo Caballero would never agree. When Vidarte mentioned De los Ríos, Prieto replied that the Republicans would never agree to a Socialist. He argued Azaña's case in his newspaper *El Liberal*. The idea was widely welcomed.[31]

Neither Izquierda Republicana nor the PSOE Left favoured Azaña's candidacy. The bulk of Azaña's colleagues in the leadership of his party were appalled at the thought of losing him as Prime Minister and of Izquierda Republicana being decapitated. Largo himself told Vidarte that he considered it ludicrous to transfer Azaña from where he was doing an essential job to the 'guilded cage' (*jaula dorada*) of the

Presidency. Araquistain's mouthpiece *Claridad* wanted Azaña left as Prime Minister because it was hoped that he could carry out the bourgeois Republican reform programme quickly and so make way for an exclusively Socialist government. *Claridad* and the UGT leader preferred the Left Republican Alvaro de Albornoz but, when Vidarte suggested Albornoz to the PSOE executive, Prieto objected and ensured that the Socialist Party would not put forward any candidate. When Izquierda Republicana proposed Azaña, Prieto insisted that the PSOE throw its weight behind his candidacy. Curiously, although *Claridad* railed against Azaña and Prieto, the PSOE Left did not produce its own candidate.[32] Prieto was gambling – rashly in view of what he knew of the stance of the Caballeristas – on being able to follow Azaña as Prime Minister. If he failed, there would be no one else capable of leading the government at a time of intensifying rightist hostility.

Prieto and Azaña were probably the only two politicians with the skill and popularity to stabilise the tense situation of the spring of 1936. Working together as President and Prime Minister, they might have been able to keep up the pace of reform to a level which could have satisfied the militant Left, with an increasingly militant trade union movement ready to declare political strikes. They might have shown the determination to crack down on the extreme Right, and might possibly have revealed the statemanship to have attracted the moderate Right. However, in view of the fact that the CEDA had shown that it could accept only a Republic committed to social conservatism, it is unlikely that significant numbers of its members would have been converted to Republican loyalty by strong liberal government. However, Prieto and Azaña might have been able to stop the fascist provocations and the leftist responses to them which were preparing the ground for a military coup. That required Azaña in the Presidency and Prieto as Prime Minister. However, neither seem seriously to have considered what would happen if Azaña was removed as Prime Minister and *not* replaced by Prieto. As things turned out, the deposition of the President and his replacement by Azaña ensured that neither could lead the cabinet.

The need for determined leadership had been revealed on 15 April, when Azaña presented his programme of government to the Cortes. He made an extremely moderate speech and undertook to fulfil the electoral programme of the Popular Front. Calvo Sotelo replied belligerently that any government which relied on PSOE votes was only a step away from Russian dominance. Gil Robles, speaking with less virulence, took up Calvo Sotelo's theme that the country was in the grip of left-wing anarchy and the government was impotent. The clear implication was that only solutions of force remained. Already, he said, his followers were turning to paths of violence. He claimed that the time was rapidly approaching when he would have to inform CEDA members that they had nothing to hope for from legality. Speaking in apocalyptic terms which hardly corresponded to the contemporary situation and which completely ignored the rightist contribution to political violence, he issued a dire warning:

> Half the nation will not resign itself to die. If it cannot defend itself by one path, it will defend itself by another ... Civil war is being brought by those who seek the revolutionary conquest of power and it is being sustained and weaned by the apathy of a government which does not turn on its supporters ... when civil war breaks out in Spain, let it be known that the weapons have been loaded by the negligence of a government which has not been able to fulfil its duty towards groups which have stayed within the strictest legality.

This was an extremely partial interpretation of a situation which had largely been created by the Right during the CEDA's sojourn in power. Gil Robles's speech ended with a prophetic battle-cry which closely prefigured what was to happen to the CEDA when the military rising took place:

> For the fatherland, whatever is necessary, even our disappearance if great national interests demand it. But it will not be a cowardly disappearance, offering our necks to the enemy. It is better to know how to die in the street than to be trampled on as a coward.

This speech has been interpreted as a sincere plea for order.[33] However, it is clear that the only order acceptable to the Right was one which did not challenge 'national interests'. In the vocabulary of the Right, such interests tended to be identical with those of the oligarchy. Gil Robles was effectively threatening war if the government's commitment to thorough reform of the social and economic structure were not dropped.

It is in this context that the growth of disorder during the spring of 1936 must be seen. That there was disorder is clear, but its scale was immensely exaggerated by the right-wing press and in the parliamentary speeches of Gil Robles and Calvo Sotelo. Moreover, it is impossible to apportion responsibility with the certainty that both sides enjoyed at the time. One factor cannot be ignored. Only two groups stood to benefit, even in theory, from the proliferation of indiscriminate lawlessness – the extreme Left and the 'catastrophist' Right. The Communists were overwhelmingly concerned during 1936 to broaden their support among the middle classes as part of the Popular Front tactic imposed by Moscow. They also hoped to take over much of the Socialist movement through unification with the PSOE Left. It was far from their intentions to seize power in the midst of a total breakdown of law and order. The anarchists were readier to use random violence, but it was not part of their overall strategy. In the Socialist movement, both *El Socialista* and *Claridad* constantly warned their readers to ignore rightist provocation. Having won the elections, none of the components of the Popular Front had any need to provoke violence in order to take power. The creation of an atmosphere of turmoil and disorder could, on the other hand, justify the resort to force to establish a dictatorship of the Right. Nevertheless, it remains almost impossible to say of street fights between Falangists and Communists or Japistas and Socialists what was provocation and what reprisal.

True as that may have been of individual incidents, a wider perspective confirms that it was the Right which benefited from the violence. If any of the main leftist groups hoped to use the breakdown of law and order, it remains to be explained why they consistently urged their followers not to get involved in reprisal/provocation spirals and why they stood by the Republican government as the basis of order.[34] It is significant that wealthy conservatives who had previously financed Gil Robles as the most effective defender of their interests were now switching funds to the Falange and the strike-breakers of the Sindicatos Libres. At the beginning of March, *ABC* opened a subscription in favour of a little known Federación Española de Trabajadores, behind which could be discerned the figure of Ramón Sales, the self-styled fascist *agent provocateur* who had become famous in the political gangsterism of 1919–23. By the end of April the fund had reached 350,000 pesetas, donated by aristocrats, landowners, industrialists and many anonymous 'fascists' and Falangists. Since the money was never used for syndical purposes and an alarming number of individuals arrested for acts of violence were found to be members of the Sindicatos Libres, the Left had no doubts that this was a fund to finance *agents provocateurs*. Professional gunmen were being hired by the Right and their operations were designed to provoke the widest repercussions.[35]

The attacks on Socialist leaders such as Jiménez de Asúa and Largo Caballero were clearly aimed at provoking reprisals. The most successful operation of this kind was carried out in Granada on 9–10 March. A squad of Falangist gunmen fired on a group of workers and their families, wounding many women and children. The local unions called a general strike in the course of which there was widespread violence. Falange and Acción Popular offices were set on fire, the ACNP newspaper, *Ideal*, was destroyed, and two churches were burned. In Granada and elsewhere, incidents were often caused by strangers who disappeared as quickly as they had appeared. The most vociferous anarchists and Communists in Granada later revealed themselves as Falangists when the Nationalists took power. Given the thorough repression of the Left taking place during the war, it is highly unlikely that they were just turncoats. Throughout Spain, leftist municipal authorities went to considerable trouble to maintain order against possible disturbances. They were not helped by the fact that conservative members of the judiciary sympathised with Falangist activities. Judges who did take a strong line against rightist gunmen were, in their turn, selected as targets.[36]

The rightist press magnified every incident and, by the simple device of grouping on one page, devoted to 'social disorders', all brawls, fights and strikes, however insignificant, painted a picture of overwhelming anarchy. Inflated statistics of the alleged anarchy were then cited in the Cortes by Calvo Sotelo and Gil Robles as justification for a military rising. Calvo Sotelo actually made public invitations to the army to stage a coup, but both he and Gil Robles knew that a rising was already being prepared. Falangist violence and the leftist responses to it provided material for speeches which placed the entire responsibility on the Left. Unhindered by censorship and fully reported, these speeches created an atmosphere of terror among large sectors of the middle and upper classes, who increasingly looked to the army for salvation.

Gil Robles's attitude to violence was more ambiguous than that of Calvo Sotelo. In the rightist division of labour, his function seems to have been to persuade more moderate middle-class opinion that the government was impotent and that the only hope was the army and the Falange. His remarks in the Cortes of 15 April and his assiduous attendance at the funerals of Falangist gunmen strengthened the desired impression that political violence was the exclusive province of the Left. He seems to have been remarkably unpreoccupied by the growing taste for the use of force within the CEDA. Nothing was done to stop the drift of members to the Falange and no recruiting took place to replace those who left. It appeared that, in fulfilment of the decisions taken on 19 March, members were being allowed to join the group they found most congenial. Gil Robles implied in his memoirs that the CEDA was kept in being in order to make propaganda in parliament and to act as a shield for more violent groups. In the celebrated interview which he conceded to *El Defensor de Cuenca*, he virtually announced his approval for those 'who take the path of violence, believing that national problems can be solved in this way', condemning only those who left the CEDA because the party, out of power, could no longer provide sinecures.[37] Almost immediately after the elections, the majority of the DRV (Derecha Regional Valenciana) rejected the moderation of their leader, Luis Lucia, in favour of direct action. Under the leadership of the party's secretary-general, José María Costa Serrano, the DRV was collecting arms and organising its own clandestine militia. Liaison was established with the local Falange, Renovación Española and the military conspirators of the Unión Militar Española. The DRV's youth section drilled and held shooting practice. Throughout the spring, at least 15,000 members of the JAP joined the Falange. Many of those remaining with the CEDA were in active contact with groups committed to violence. Calvo Sotelo enjoyed some sympathy in Acción Popular. And, when the war broke out, thousands of Cedistas joined the Carlists.[38]

Even officially, the CEDA's links with the Falange were growing. At the beginning of May there were repeats of the disputed elections of Granada and Cuenca. In Granada the CEDA campaigned in exclusive alliance with the Falange. Local Socialists offered to let the CEDA win three seats if the name of the hated Ramon Ruiz Alonso were withdrawn from the right-wing list. Gil Robles refused and the Popular Front put up candidates for all the Granada seats. After the scandal of the previous elections, the masses were determined that they would not be swindled of their victory again. There appears to have been some harassment of rightist candidates, which, paradoxically, enabled the Right to derive benefit from almost certain defeat. Convinced that they could not win, the rightist candidates declared that they had been prevented from campaigning and simply withdrew from the contest, thereby impugning the validity of the elections.[39] In the re-run elections in Cuenca scheduled for the beginning of May 1936, the right-wing slate included both José Antonio Primo de Rivera and General Franco. The Falange leader was included in the hope of securing for him the parliamentary immunity which would ensure his release from jail where he had been since 17 March. With the enthusiastic approval of Gil Robles, negotiations to this effect were carried out in mid-April by the monarchist leader, Antonio Goicoechea, and the CEDA deputy for Zaragoza and close friend of José Antonio Primo de Rivera, Ramón Serrano Suñer. General Fanjul, who had stood successfully in the original elections and lost his post of military commander in the Canary Islands for so doing, stood down in favour of the Falangist leader.[40]

Serrano Suñer was also behind the late inclusion of his brother-in-law, General Franco, in the right-wing list announced on 23 April.[41] On 20 April, a letter from Franco was delivered by Serrano Suñer to Gemini-ano Carrascal, the secretary of the CEDA. In it, Franco expressed his interest in being a candidate in one of the forthcoming re-run elections, preferably in Cuenca. His choice was perhaps inspired by the earlier success there of General Fanjul. Carrascal, in the absence of Gil Robles, told Serrano Suñer that he thought that the party would be happy to endorse Franco's inclusion as a candidate in the right-wing list. When the Jefe returned, he discussed the matter himself with Serrano Suñer and expressed his approval for the scheme and Serrano Suñer set off immediately for the Canary Islands to inform his brother-in-law. Antonio Goicoechea was as enthusiastic as Gil Robles and even offered to give up his place in the right-wing list. His sacrifice was not needed since Gil Robles instructed the CEDA provincial chief, Manuel Cas-anova, to stand down.

The support for Franco manifested by Gil Robles and Goicoechea was not matched by the leader of the third political party involved in Cuenca, the Falange. When the revised list of right-wing candidates was published, Gil Robles received a visit from Miguel Primo de Rivera who came to inform him that his brother was firmly opposed to the list, regarding the inclusion of Franco as a 'crass error'. Since General Varela was also standing in the simultaneous re-run at Granada, José Antonio Primo de Rivera shrewdly wished to avoid his chances of election being diminished if the rightist eagerness for military candidates were too transparent. He also feared that Franco would be a hopeless parliamen-tary speaker and threatened to withdraw from the Cuenca list if Franco's name was not removed, something which Gil Robles felt unable to do. After Gil Robles had informed the other right-wing leaders of this complication, Goicoechea visited the Falange leader in prison and tried unsuccessfully to get him to withdraw his opposition to Franco. Carras-cal recalled Serrano Suñer from the Canary Islands and he too visited José Antonio in vain. Serrano was then faced with the difficult job of returning to the Canaries to inform Franco. He managed to persuade his brother-in-law that he would not take well to the cut-and-thrust of parliamentary debate. The argument that Franco would be risking public humiliation did the trick. At that point, on 27 April, Franco withdrew and Manuel Casanova returned to the list.[42] Since the Cuenca election was technically a re-run, on the grounds that no candidate had obtained

40 per cent of the vote in February, new candidates could not be admitted, much to the chagrin of the CEDA deputies, who argued vainly in favour of the fascist leader.

The CEDA leadership's acquiescence in the growth of right-wing violence was a consequence of the realisation that legal methods could no longer keep inviolate the material interests of the landed oligarchy. The rightist obstruction of reform in the Constituent Cortes and the behaviour of the landowners while the CEDA was in power had hardened the Left's determination to secure fast and effective reforms. Soon after Azaña's government was formed, his new Minister of Agriculture, Mariano Ruiz Funes, announced his commitment to rapid agrarian reform. The resurgent Landworkers' Federation intended to make him keep his word. After the harsh rural repression of the previous two years, in 1936, the FNTT began to expand at a vertiginous rate. Its militant leadership was in no mood to tolerate delays from the government or obstruction from the big landowners.

Immediately after the elections, Ricardo Zabalza, the dynamic secretary-general of the FNTT, had written to Ruiz Funes urging him to expedite the return to their lands of the leaseholders evicted in 1935. He also called for the re-establishment of the *jurados mixtos*, as well as the application of the decree on obligatory cultivation. In a letter to the Minister of Labour, Enrique Ramos, Zabalza demanded the introduction of a scheme for placing unemployed workers with landowners. A third letter, to Amós Salvador, Minister of the Interior, called for the disarming of the *caciques*. Seriously alarmed by the quantity of weapons at the disposal of landowners and their retainers, and by the fact that the rural upper classes still enjoyed the sympathy of the Civil Guard, the FNTT soon began to recommend that its members form popular militias, to prevent a repetition of the persecution of 1934 and 1935. Before the Cortes opened in mid-March, there were peasant demonstrations all over Spain calling for the implementation of Zabalza's requests.[43] The FNTT's demands were not revolutionary but they still constituted a major challenge to the balance of rural economic power. Moreover, the events of the previous two years had exacerbated class tensions to a point which rendered the pacific application of the desired social legislation highly unlikely. Even leaving aside the bitter class hatred now prevailing in the countryside, economic circumstances ensured that the reforms, which were essential to alleviate the misery of the landless peasants, could not be absorbed by the owners without a significant redistribution of rural wealth. The constant rains between December 1935 and March 1936 had seriously damaged the grain harvest and reduced the profit margins of growers large and small. This natural disaster simply clinched the reluctance of owners and workers alike to be conciliatory.

Throughout March the FNTT encouraged its members to take the law into their own hands, particularly where they had been the victims of eviction. In Salamanca and Toledo there were small-scale invasions of estates. Only in Badajoz were there mass land seizures. After the government legalised these land invasions, many landowners either abandoned their estates or else adopted highly belligerent stances. Confrontation did not start on a major scale until after the negotiation of work contracts (*bases de trabajo*) in April, after which time it became clear that the mixed juries intended to implement the contracts by means of substantial fines.[44] There were attacks on local FNTT sections in Cuenca and Ciudad Real. In Castellón, the owners refused to give work to men during the orange harvest. The *bases de trabajo* were virtually ignored in Badajoz, Córdoba, Ciudad Real, Málaga and Toledo. In Badajoz the owners refused work by day and used machinery to bring in the harvest by night. Faced with a virtual rural lock-out, the FNTT resorted to strike action in Málaga and Badajoz. It was remarkable that the FNTT managed to maintain the discipline of its members, even after an incident reminiscent of Casas Viejas. This took place at the end of May at Yeste (Albacete). The peasants of the village had lost their livelihood when large tracts of fertile land were taken over to make a reservoir in 1932. The efforts of the newly restored Republican–Socialist *ayuntamiento* to place (*colocar*) unemployed workers with landowners had infuriated the local Right. Out cutting down trees and ploughing land once common, but now in private hands, unemployed labourers were obliged by the Civil Guard to return to the hamlet of Graya where, after a disturbance, six young workers were arrested. On 29 May, when the prisoners were being taken to the nearby town of Yeste, a crowd tried to free them. A Civil Guard was killed; his companions opened fire on the crowd and then pursued fleeing peasants into the surrounding hills, killing a total of seventeen people and wounding many more. Fifty FNTT members were arrested.[45] Yeste and other clashes could have led to bloodshed on a large scale. However, the FNTT leadership restrained its rank and file because of its faith in the advanced agrarian policy being pursued by the government. That policy represented precisely the challenge to their social hegemony which the large landowners had struggled to resist since 1931. No longer able to put their hopes in the CEDA as their first line of defence, they began to look to the military for their protection.

At no time during the Second Republic was there a greater need for strong and determined government than in the spring of 1936. Military conspirators were plotting the overthrow of the regime. The youthful activists of Right and Left were clashing in the streets. Unemployment was rising and social reforms were meeting dogged resistance from the landowners. The problem had become particularly acute after the elevation of Azaña to the Presidency on 10 May. The new President immediately asked Prieto to form a government. Prieto had already advertised his suitability for the job by an extremely statesmanlike speech in Cuenca on 1 May. In that speech he had exposed the danger of a military rising under the leadership of General Franco, spoken of the need to remedy social injustice, denounced the provocations of those on the Right who rejected the election results, and criticised the revolutionary maximalists who were playing into their hands.[46] When summoned by Azaña on 11 May, he told him of his plans to restore order and accelerate reform. He intended to remove unreliable military commanders, reduce the power of the Civil Guard and disarm the fascist action squads. He also planned to promote massive public works, irrigation and housing schemes, as well as speeding up agrarian reform. It is possible that such a programme of government, carried through with determination, might have prevented civil war. It was a project which would certainly have infuriated the Right and therefore required the unstinting support of leftist forces. Prieto was, however, doubtful that he could count on the votes of the left wing of the PSOE.[47]

Prieto had good reason to anticipate the hostility of the supporters of Largo Caballero. Determined never again to carry out bourgeois policies in a coalition government with Republicans, Largo was waiting for the fulfilment of the Popular Front programme before pushing for an all-Socialist cabinet. He was in a strong position within the PSOE to impose his views. On 8 March, Caballeristas had won all the senior posts in the Agrupación Socialista Madrileña, the strongest section of the PSOE. The Caballerista candidacy – Largo as president, Alvarez del Vayo as vice-president, Enrique de Francisco as secretary, Wenceslao Carrillo as vice-secretary, Pascual Tomás as administrative secretary and a committee including Rodolfo Llopis, Díaz Alor, Araquistain, Hernández Zancajo and Zabalza – was the same as that which hoped to wrest the PSOE executive from the Prietistas. The ASM now became the centre of the Caballerista struggle for the party leadership. Indeed, *Claridad* declared that the new ASM executive would become the PSOE executive at the next congress.[48] Moreover, on 16 March, Largo had been elected as president of the PSOE parliamentary minority. He ruled it with a rod of iron – even prescribing where each deputy sat in the Cortes.[49] The Caballerista grip on the party appeared unshakable.

Ironically, however, an apparent victory for Largo on 5 April did much to redress the balance. As part of their revolutionary policy, the Caballeristas were anxious to create a single party of the proletariat. Since the anarcho-syndicalists and the POUM were not interested, the policy could progress only with the Communists, with the PSOE Left naïvely assuming that the Socialist movement would simply absorb the rank and file of the Communist Party. The fusion of the CGTU and the UGT had already taken place. In Catalonia, the small Communist and Socialist parties merged to form the Partit Socialista Unificat de Catalunya. Its name aside, the PSUC was effectively the Communist Party of Catalonia.[50] For the moment, Prietista control of the party executive prevented any move to merge the PSOE and the PCE. However, the young 'bolshevisers' of the FJS had forged ahead in negotiations with their Communist counterparts – talks which were masterminded by the Comintern's delegate in Spain, Vitorio Codovila.

In March 1936, a joint delegation of the FJS and the Unión de Juventudes Comunistas went to Moscow to discuss details of the unification with the Communist Youth International. On their return, the FJS and UJC executives agreed that the UJC's rank and file would simply enter the existing Socialist federations. The unification was made public at a joint rally in the Madrid bullring on 5 April. This seemed to fulfil part of Largo Caballero's ambition of uniting the working class, but in reality it simply meant the loss of about 40,000 young Socialists to the PCE. The FJS leader, Santiago Carrillo, already attended meetings of the central committee of the Communist Party and the JSU (Juventudes Socialistas Unificadas) were swiftly to become an adjunct of the PCE.[51] Nevertheless, at the time the creation of the JSU seemed a triumph for Largo, and Prieto had cause to be unsure of his own position.

Throughout the spring, the PSOE Left subjected the Prietistas to a constant stream of verbal abuse. There was fury when Prieto skilfully responded to their demands for a party congress by proposing that it take place in Asturias. Asturias was his fortress and there the empty verbal revolutionism of the Caballeristas would get short shrift. The Prietista executive tried to load things further in their favour by suggestions that only fully paid-up sections of the PSOE would be permitted to attend – which, together with the expense of a journey to the north, would exclude delegates from the poorer southern *agrupaciones*, many of whom might be supposed to belong to the Caballerista FNTT. The ASM mounted a noisy campaign among the rank and file which forced the party executive to back down and agree to a congress in Madrid in the summer. The Caballeristas were also furious during the first half of May at what they presented as the undemocratic way in which Prieto had ensured the support of the Socialist *minoría parlamentaria* for Azaña's candidacy. From their stronghold in the Agrupación Socialista Madrileña, they issued a protest which had less to do with any theoretical objection to any possible Republican–Socialist coalition than with the mere involvement of Prieto.[52] They conveniently forgot that the parliamentary group which voted for Azaña was overwhelmingly Caballerista in composition and presided over by Largo Caballero himself.

On 12 May, Prieto informed the PSOE parliamentary minority that Azaña had asked him to form a government. He had little hope of receiving assurances of its support. Already on 13 April, Largo Caballero had declared his outright hostility to 'injections of socialism' into the government. On 6 May, to emphasise the point, the Caballero-controlled UGT executive had issued a note threatening to break with the Popular Front if a government were formed including any Socialists. On 11 May, the PSOE's parliamentary minority had met under the chairmanship of Largo Caballero to discuss the party's reply to the Presidential request for its advice on the formation of a government. Opposition within the PSOE to Prieto's becoming Prime Minister was generated by the *Claridad* group of Araquistain, Baraibar and Amaro del Rosal. It was feared within the group that Prieto might become 'the Noske of the Spanish revolution'. Accordingly, at the 11 May meeting of the parliamentary minority, when Prieto proposed that the PSOE recommend a broad Popular Front government including Socialists, he was defeated, forty-nine votes to nineteen, by Alvarez del Vayo's counter-proposal for an all-Republican cabinet. After Azaña had consulted all the parties, he made a formal offer to Prieto, who faced the minority again. When Largo Caballero argued against his acceptance, he conceded defeat without a fight.

The victim of his own fatal tendency towards pessimistic defeatism, Prieto neither defended his own proposed government programme and the need for a strong, broadly based administration nor pressed on despite the parliamentary group's opposition. That opposition was reason sound enough for Prieto's surrender but he knew all about it before enthusiastically backing Azaña's elevation to the Presidency. The vehemence of the hostility displayed towards him by *Claridad* and, above all, by Largo Caballero himself had left him in no doubt that, if he formed a government, the deputies of the PSOE Left would oppose him in the Cortes. Nevertheless, even after Largo Caballero had carried the hostile vote in the minority meeting, Prieto could probably still have formed a government since he could count on the support of the Republican parties and about a third of PSOE deputies. However, as he declared in 1940, that would have meant splitting the PSOE and he was not prepared to do that. If he had been, he would then have had to seek parliamentary support further to the Right and he was not prepared to be called a traitor to his own party.

Vidarte urged him to accept Azaña's proposal in the hope that, when the time came, Largo would not vote against him in the Cortes. Prieto was, understandably, not convinced and, when Vidarte offered to arrange a meeting between the executive and the UGT president, away from the pressures of his radical followers, he replied bitterly, 'Let Caballero go to hell.' The rest of the executive believed that he should take the issue to the PSOE National Committee on which he had the majority and which had the statutory power to resolve any dispute between the executive and the *minoría parlamentaria*. It is possible that, had he done so, the PSOE would have split, although Largo Caballero himself would always have opposed all-out schism. When the crunch came, Prieto could not bring himself to take the risk. His comrades on the executive wanted him to go ahead, form a government and then face a full party congress confident of gaining its approval.[53] Not to do so was a grave act of at best weakness, at worst irresponsibility, the more so since he had already played such a key role in removing Azaña from the government. At the same time, the Caballeristas, having blocked the Prietista option to consolidate the Republic, had done nothing to advance their own plans. It was, after all, inconceivable that Azaña would ever invite Largo Caballero to form a government.

Azaña's offer to Prieto on 11 May was not the only attempt during the spring to form a strong government. Throughout April and May, desultory negotiations were taking place between Azaña, Miguel Maura, Claudio Sánchez Albornoz, Prieto, Besteiro, Giménez Fernández and Luis Lucia. Gil Robles was aware of Giménez Fernández's involvement in these conversations. He knew that they could have little chance of success. It was inconceivable that Prieto, having failed to get PSOE support for a coalition with the left Republicans, would get it for a government including the CEDA. Moreover, since most CEDA deputies opposed Giménez Fernández, they were hardly likely to endorse a link with Prieto. Gil Robles was fully aware of the plans being made for a military rising and was involved in them. He would not have tolerated a government of national concentration which attempted to take action against the army. Thus, as his own account implies, he probably only tolerated Giménez Fernández's negotiations out of a hope of splitting the Socialist Party.[54]

Azaña was replaced as Prime Minister by the consumptive Santiago Casares Quiroga, who was no match for the problems that he was called upon to solve. The men he chose for key posts symbolised the inadequacy of his cabinet. Neither his Minister of the Interior, Juan Moles, nor his Minister of Labour, Juan Lluhí Vallescá, fully appreciated the seriousness of the crisis. Casares himself consistently refused to believe reliable reports of military conspiracy. Both Casares and Moles failed to take action, despite repeated visits from Prieto and Largo Caballero. Prieto was deeply hurt when Casares, in reply to a warning about the plotters, said, 'I will not tolerate your menopausic outbursts.' He told Largo Caballero that he paid too much attention to the stories of bored and embittered officers.[55] Azaña too was accused by the PSOE Left of simply fleeing from his responsibilities. Certainly, once he became President, he took immense delight in his ceremonial functions, in the restoration of official buildings, in the decoration of his apartments in the old Palacio Real and in becoming a patron of the arts.[56] The euphoria of the President and his Prime Minister was entirely misplaced. By May 1936, the military conspiracy, the ramifications of which went back to 1931, was well under way.

Gil Robles stayed in the background of the preparations for war – as did Calvo Sotelo – but he was fully aware of what was happening. At the end of May, Gil Robles warned a friend, the American journalist H. Edward Knoblaugh, against taking his holidays in the summer, darkly hinting at the plot in the making.[57] Party members who asked the Jefe for instructions were told to place themselves under the orders of the army as soon as the rising began. In a declaration made in 1942, Gil Robles stated that he co-operated in the rising with advice, 'with moral stimulus, with secret orders for collaboration, and even with economic assistance, taken in appreciable quantities from the party's electoral funds'. This last was a reference to 500,000 pesetas which Gil Robles gave to General Mola, confident that its original donors would have approved of his action.[58]

Throughout June and July, Gil Robles issued instructions to provincial CEDA leaders. On the outbreak of the rising, all party members were to join the military immediately and publicly, party organisations were to offer full collaboration without seeking benefit for the CEDA, youth sections were to join the army and not form separate militias, party members were not to take part in reprisals against the Left, power struggles with other rightist groups were to be avoided, and the maximum financial aid was to be given to the authorities. Only the instruction about reprisals was ignored, and Cedistas were prominent in the Nationalist repression in Granada and Valladolid. The first section of the CEDA to join the rising was the DRV. Lucia was fully informed of what was happening but he left the operational details to the DRV secretary-general, José María Costa Serrano. When General Mola was finalising civilian participation in June, Costa Serrano offered 1250 men for the early moments of this rising and promised 10,000 after five hours and 50,000 after five days. Along with the Valencian sections of the Falange, Renovación Española and the Carlists, the DRV placed itself unconditionally under the orders of the military junta.[59]

Gil Robles was extremely discreet. Nevertheless, he did several useful services for the conspirators. In early July he accompanied the owner of *ABC*, Juan Ignacio Luca de Tena, on a mission to the Carlist leader, Manuel Fal Conde. They were sent by Mola to persuade Fal Conde to ease his conditions for Carlist participation in the rising.[60] Gil Robles's link with Mola was through the CEDA deputy Francisco Herrera Oria, brother of Angel and managing director of the Editorial Católica. Francisco Herrera, a close friend of Gil Robles, had concluded that military intervention was the only solution to Spain's problems. Accordingly, he negotiated financial support for the conspiracy with Juan March and he planned with Colonel Juan Yagüe to resolve the hesitations of Franco by presenting him with a *fait accompli* in the form of an aircraft sent to take him on the 1200 kilometre journey from the Canary Islands to Morocco. Herrera had got in touch with Colonel Valentín Galarza, the co-ordinator of the Unión Militar Española and known within the conspiratorial organisation as *'el técnico'*. Galarza introduced him to General Mola. He was given the job of liaising with Morocco, hence his contacts with Yagüe.[61]

Arrangements for civilian participation were to have been made by Gil Robles, the Carlist Conde de Rodezno and Calvo Sotelo, but were frustrated by the assassination of the monarchist chief on 13 July. Gil Robles was determined not to be publicly compromised. It was through his intermediary, Herrera, that he discussed with Mola his future role in the post-war state. When Mola asked him to attend a meeting of rightist deputies in Burgos on 17 July to declare the government and the Cortes illegal, and to make a public appeal for military intervention, he refused. After five years of propounding legalism, he felt that it would be 'indecorous'.[62]

It is in the light of Gil Robles's clandestine activities that his public pronouncements should be seen. Ambiguous speeches, which were ostensibly appeals for moderation, were also justifications of violence. On 19 May the CEDA leader replied in the Cortes to Casares Quiroga's presentation of his programme of government. Trying to drive a wedge between the components of the Popular Front, he claimed that the Republican government was the servant, and would soon be the victim, of the Socialists. He also alleged that growing disorder was increasing the relevance of fascist solutions. If he was critical of fascism, it was only because of its foreign origins, its philosophical pantheism and its elements of state socialism. He claimed that people were being forced to turn to fascism because there was no other way for them to defend their interests. In identifying democracy and disorder, he made no mention of the way in which the present political violence had been fomented by the repressive and vindictive policies carried out while he was in power nor of the activities of fascist provocateurs. Indeed, he claimed that the arrest of Falangists was unjust. Declaring that democracy was now dead, he praised the trend to fascism as the result of 'a sense of patriotism ... profoundly wounded to see that the rhythm of politics is not planned in accord with great national interests, but is controlled by you [turning to the Socialist deputies] with orders from Moscow'. He was effectively endorsing the flight of the JAP masses into the Falange. With a provocative challenge to the Left's revolutionary ardour, he made a slighting reference to 'you ferocious revolutionaries who do nothing but talk'.[63] At the end of May the CEDA leader stated, in an interview given to an Argentinian daily, that democracy in Spain led inevitably to anarchy. He also spoke highly of Italian Fascism, which he said had cured Italy of disorder and restored her international prestige.[64]

The picture painted by Gil Robles and Calvo Sotelo of disorder and impending Communist revolution was exaggerated. In fact, the last thing that Moscow or the PCE wanted was revolution in Spain, for fear of unfavourable repercussions on Russian foreign policy. Seeking alliances with the Western democracies, the Kremlin did not want to frighten them into the arms of Hitler. Accordingly, the Communist leadership regularly denounced church-burnings and other manifestations of disorder.[65] Ironically, it would be the military rising which would precipitate revolution and the rise of the Communist Party to a position of dominance. The Socialists too, for all their internal divisions, went to great lengths to maintain order. However, disorder aside, two factors contributed to the credibility of the rightist view of the situation: the continued verbal revolutionism of the Caballerista wing of the PSOE and the high level of strike action, particularly where the CNT was involved, throughout the spring of 1936. Behind both the strikes and Largo Caballero's revolutionary rhetoric was a mounting tide of working-class militancy. This was a consequence, in the first instance, of a backlog of grievances dating from the two years of untrammelled aggression by the employers when strikes had been virtually impossible. The situation was then exacerbated by the employers' refusal, sometimes out of economic necessity and sometimes out of tactical intransigence, to readmit workers who had been jailed after the Asturian rising.

After the election victory of February, workers had simply showed up at building sites, factories and shops demanding their jobs back and the expulsion of the non-union labour which had replaced them. In a context of economic crisis, employers were unable to absorb the costs and, after two years of right-wing government, were appalled by the change in the balance of power. The UGT tried to maintain discipline but, in Madrid, for instance, it was increasingly challenged by the greater militancy of the CNT. In the capital, where the biggest sector of unionised labour was to be found in the construction industry, skilled craftsmen of the UGT could defend their living standards. Unskilled labourers, who lived on the outskirts of the city and belonged to the CNT, were easily mobilised for strikes and street demonstrations. In Madrid, the UGT was confused, using revolutionary rhetoric to keep up with the CNT, yet instinctively trying to control a process which permitted the Right to denounce a breakdown of law and order. The situation in the capital was replicated in Granada and Sevilla albeit not generalised across Spain. In Zaragoza, the UGT and the CNT collaborated with the new Republican Civil Governor, Angel Vera Coronel, in establishing public works schemes to absorb the unemployed. Their efforts were not, however, sufficient to calm the fears of the local employers.[66]

The main strike wave got under way in late May, long after the Right had begun denouncing industrial and rural anarchy. By then there was evidence of deliberate patronal intransigence in the form of lock-outs and the refusal to accept the decisions of arbitration committees. Many industrialists, out of either panic or knowledge of the imminent military rising, abandoned their enterprises and smuggled their capital abroad. The UGT and the Communists appear to have done everything possible to restrain their own militants and to persuade the CNT to do the same. Socialists came to blows with anarchists in Madrid over the UGT's attempts to end the major construction strike which took place in June and July. Communists also fought with anarchists in Málaga. The Caballerista newspaper, *Claridad*, regularly called upon the government to resolve social conflicts so that the rightist press would not be able to use them to foment middle-class terror. The worst strikes took place in Madrid in June among building workers, central-heating and lift engineers, clothing workers and woodworkers. By the middle of the month there were over 110,000 men on strike. The UGT tried to restrain the strikers and pushed for a rapid return to work after the mixed juries had found in favour of workers' demands for wage increases and shorter hours. The tailoring employers refused for several weeks to accept arbitration. The construction site owners withdrew from the juries, declared a lock-out and later boasted how their attitude had favoured the creation of a suitable atmosphere for a military rising. Throughout the crisis the Socialist and Communist press denounced the conflictive stance of the CNT.

Yet the fact remains that the employers provoked strikes in Barcelona by refusing to return to the forty-four-hour week, which had been lost after October 1934, and in Badajoz, Málaga and other southern provinces by rejecting the *bases de trabajo* worked out by the mixed juries. Equally, the workers, embittered by the treatment they had received in 1934 and 1935, and intoxicated by the election victory of the Popular Front, were in a determined and aggressive mood.[67]

It was largely a perennial fear of losing his increasingly militant followers which lay behind Largo Caballero's continued predictions of the impending doom of the capitalist system. It is true that his experience of the rightist obstruction of reform between 1931 and 1933, together with his prison reading in 1935, had convinced him of the futility of reformism. However, between the theory and the practice stood a lifetime of pragmatic gradualism. In 1936 Largo Caballero continued to act very much as he had always done, concerned above all with consolidating the UGT. In speeches about the revolutionary road to socialism, he gave the workers what they wanted to hear. The fact that Largo was not seriously propagating immediate revolution was hardly appreciated by the middle classes who read his speeches. In that sense his attempts to maintain the allegiance of the Socialist rank and file were playing into the hands of Gil Robles and Calvo Sotelo.

The anarcho-syndicalists were highly suspicious of Largo Caballero's verbal revolutionism. In fact, the most revolutionary thing that the UGT president proposed was the unification of the proletariat. The anarcho-syndicalists suspected, with good reason, that Largo's proposal aimed simply at the take-over of the CNT masses by the UGT. After all, during the early spring the Socialists had made little secret of their conviction that they should have exclusive control of the revolutionary working class. On 18 April, the Agrupación Socialista Madrileña had held a meeting to elaborate a new programme to be presented for discussion at the next PSOE congress. In view of the rising threat of fascism and the increasing radicalisation of the working class, the proposed new programme aimed at the elimination of reformist illusions from Socialist thinking. In the course of the discussion, in which Besteiro and Trifón Gómez defended the existing programme, a militant, Antonio Muñoz Lizcano, suggested the addition of a clause emphasising that the leadership of the revolution was the task of the Alianzas Obreras. Largo argued vehemently that the PSOE could and should do the job itself. He stated that the achievement of syndical unity would eliminate the need for the Alianzas. This was typical of Largo's attitude to working-class unity. Throughout 1935, he had prohibited local UGT organisations taking part in joint activities with the Alianzas Obreras. The clear implication was that proletarian unification meant Socialist take-over. Indeed, in the spring of 1936, Araquistain was involved in a polemic with the Communists over which workers' party should lead the revolution.[68] Accordingly, at the CNT congress held at Zaragoza in early May, the Socialists' bluff was called. The CNT rejected the notion of union with the UGT, but offered instead a revolutionary pact with certain conditions. These included the UGT's public rejection not only of the Socialist policy of parliamentary collaboration with the Republic but of the existing political and social regime, as well as the libertarian notion that the future organisation of society could be freely decided upon by the working class. Not surprisingly, Largo did not take up the CNT's invitation. Moreover, within a couple of days, he resuscitated the idea of the Alianzas Obreras, as a means of disciplining the CNT.[69] If the use that he made of the Alianzas in 1934 had revealed anything, it was that the domination of the working-class movement by the UGT meant far more to Largo Caballero than any future prospect of revolution.

Socialist behaviour throughout 1936 belied the rhetoric even of the Caballeristas. All sections of the PSOE were aware that a military rising was being prepared. Casares Quiroga's optimism that it could be crushed at will was not shared by the Socialists, nor by the PCE. Nevertheless, the only weapon at the Left's disposal, the revolutionary general strike, was never used. The spontaneous and unsynchronised character of the working-class resistance to the rising in July demonstrated that there had been little preparation or revolutionary action in the preceding months. Indeed, when serious proposals for revolution were made in April by Joaquín Maurín, one of the leaders of the POUM, there were howls of protest. The recently formed POUM, based on an alliance between the Bloc Obrer i Camperol and the Izquierda Comunista, was branded by the PCE as a renegade enemy of the Popular Front.[70] Much has been made of the divisions within the PSOE as a symptom of the party's revolutionary drift. Certainly the left wing of the party made regular statements – about the death agony of capitalism and the inevitable triumph of socialism – which Prieto, with some cause, regarded as dangerously provocative. Yet party discipline was maintained in such a way as to contribute to the stability of the Republican government. The Caballeristas, despite their reservations, joined the Prietists in voting for the nomination of Martínez Barrio as president of the Cortes and for the elevation of Azaña to the Presidency of the Republic. The PSOE consistently supported the government, and often, at the request of Casares Quiroga, held back awkward questions in the Cortes about military conspirators and the provocation of disorder.[71]

The Socialists were caught in a terrible dilemma. Prieto believed that strong reforming government was the only answer to the dangers threatening the Republic. However, there was nothing about the behaviour of the Right at the time to suggest that conspiratorial plans would have been voluntarily abandoned for anything less than policies like those which had been the norm during the *bienio negro*. Largo Caballero was convinced, after the experience of the Constituent Cortes, that a Republican–Socialist coalition such as Prieto advocated would be incapable of carrying out adequate measures. The UGT president aimed at an all-Socialist government, in much the same way as he aimed at an all-UGT labour movement. This division of opinion, exacerbated by personal resentments, paralysed the political initiative of the Socialist movement. In fact, Largo Caballero and many of his closest associates – Carlos de Baraibar, Luis Araquistain, Carlos Hernández Zancajo and Wenceslao Carrillo – never favoured the idea of splitting the party. They hoped to impose their more revolutionary programme on the rest of the PSOE by means of a party congress. Initiatives to break up the party as a prelude to the unification of schismatic Socialists with the PCE came from fellow travellers like Alvarez del Vayo and Margarita Nelken and JSU leaders Santiago Carrillo and Federico Melchor.[72]

The behaviour of the radicalised Socialist Youth was a surrogate for revolution. Largo Caballero's own plans were as negative as those he had nurtured in 1934. Then he had hoped that revolutionary threats would induce Alcalá Zamora to call elections; now he hoped that revolutionary posturing would lead to Azaña asking him to form a government. Accordingly, the two main consequences of the Socialist divisions were the abortion of Prieto's attempt to create strong government and

271

the fomenting of middle-class fears of revolution by the demagogic behaviour of the pro-Communist left wing of the PSOE. The fact that the Communists themselves, for all their demagogy, did not aim at revolution, and that Largo Caballero's rhetoric was directed primarily at the aggrandisement of the UGT, meant little to the middle classes. After all, leftist demagogy, combined with visible evidence of strikes and politically motivated disorder, simply seemed to verify the exaggerated picture of unmitigated chaos being painted by Calvo Sotelo and Gil Robles.

The readiness of the JSU to become involved in street clashes with Falangists, under the misguided impression that they were undertaking revolutionary activities, and the CNT's maintenance of a hard line during the strikes of June and July obscured an important internal development within the PSOE. In some respects, the obstacles placed in the way of Prieto in May constituted the low point of Socialist paralysis. If the post-election euphoria had favoured the PSOE Left, the subsequent strikes and church-burnings, the intensifying air of political crisis and the deafening rumours of military conspiracy were gradually persuading many Socialists that Prieto's realistic stance made much more sense than the revolutionary Utopias of Largo Caballero. At the end of May, therefore, Prieto began to fight to recover the initiative within the PSOE.

On 25 May, a meeting of the PSOE National Committee, on which he had the majority, decided to purge the Left while it still had control of the levers of power. In the event, this process did not get under way fully until well into the Civil War. However, a determination to establish a firm grip on party institutions was manifest in the convocation of elections to cover six vacancies on the eleven-man executive committee elected at the PSOE's Thirteenth Congress in October 1932. The vacancies had been created by the resignation of Fernando de los Ríos on 16 May 1935, that of Largo Caballero and his three lieutenants, Enrique de Francisco, Pascual Tomás and Wenceslao Carrillo, on 16 December 1935 and the death of the party vice-president, Remigio Cabello, in April 1936. The same meeting of the National Committee authorised the executive to expel local *agrupaciones* which did not obey the executive's instructions. The *agrupaciones* were required to provide an explanation of their role in the events of October 1934 and a new party programme was drawn up to be placed before a full party congress. *Claridad* was denounced for fostering division in the party.

The partial elections for the PSOE executive were held at the end of June. The executive proposed a list of well-known and respected candidates headed by Ramón González Peña. As a hero of the Asturian

272

rising, for his part in which he had been sentenced to death, and leader of the Sindicato de Obreros Mineros Asturianos, he was an ideal candidate to run against Largo Caballero. The candidacy also included the distinguished jurist Luis Jiménez Asúa, who had been defending lawyer at the trial in which Largo Caballero had denied any participation in the October events, and Ramón Lamoneda, leader of the UGT printers' union, the Federación de Artes Gráficas, and a convert from the Left. The Caballeristas proposed instead a candidacy for the entire PSOE executive consisting of the executive of the Agrupación Socialista Madrileña elected on 8 March. The National Committee had made it clear that only votes for candidates for the six places on the executive would be valid and that votes for an entire executive would be considered null and void.[73] The most vicious propaganda war now erupted within the PSOE. On two occasions, meetings addressed by Prieto and González Peña, at Egea de los Caballeros (Aragón) and Écija (Seville), were disrupted by JSU squads and they were lucky to escape with their lives.[74]

Figures for the voting differed widely in the versions published by El Socialista and Claridad. Many of the votes claimed by the Caballeristas were not from fully paid-up members of the party, but from JSU militants and union activists who were not party members. Figures published by El Socialista claimed that González Peña had defeated Largo Caballero by 10,933 valid votes against 2876. Irregularities over membership status or non-payment of dues were used to discount large numbers of votes. Largo Caballero had had 7442 invalid votes cast for him against González Peña's 1155. The Prietista candidacy was declared to have won. Feeble protests from Claridad that the Caballerista line had carried the day in Cádiz, an anarchist stronghold, and Jaén reinforced the impression that the tide was turning in favour of Prieto. The immediate result was an intensification of the verbal battle which was silenced briefly by the military coup of 18 July.[75]

The victory of the PSOE moderates did not go undisputed within the Socialist movement. Even if it had, it seems unlikely that the Right would have been sufficiently impressed to have changed its tactics. In fact, rightist militants made no secret of their delight at the Socialists' internecine squabbles.[76] The army's preparations were well advanced. Strikes and disorder, whatever their origin, had convinced much middle-class opinion that Gil Robles and Calvo Sotelo were right when they asserted that nothing could be expected from the democratic regime. On 16 June, in the Cortes, Gil Robles delivered his last great denunciation of the Popular Front government. Superficially couched as an appeal for moderation, it was more of a lengthy justification of the rising that was under way. The CEDA leader read out a long list of murders, beatings, robberies, church-burnings and strikes, a catalogue of disorder for which he placed the responsibility on the government. Some of it was true, some of it blood-curdling exaggeration. He gave no indication that the Right had had any participation in what he described. Indeed, he protested about the imprisonment of Falangist and JAP terrorists and the imposition of fines on recalcitrant employers. The blame for disorder was put firmly on the fact that the government relied on the votes of Socialists and Communists. As long as that remained the case, thundered Gil Robles, there could never be peace in Spain.[77] Since Gil Robles was far from being the most extreme figure on the Right, his attitude indicated that even a moderate government presided over by Prieto would have found little tolerance outside the Popular Front.

By the spring of 1936, coexistence was impossible unless the Left relinquished its aspirations of structural reform or the Right dropped its opposition to such reform. A Republican–Socialist coalition under Prieto would have been committed to a rhythm of social change which had been shown to be intolerable to the rural upper classes. In 1936, after five years of accelerating social misery, the left-wing masses looked for reform more advanced than that which had been possible between 1931 and 1933. The legalist Right's obstructionist tactics then and its social policies when in power together revealed the profound incompatibility between the two views of social organisation which were in conflict. On 1 July the Agrarian José María Cid attacked the situation which was developing in the countryside under the Republican Minister of Agriculture, Mariano Ruiz Funes.[78] Yet the Left regarded what the minister was doing as the minimum acceptable. Given the Right's determination to concede nothing, civil war could have been avoided only if the Left had been prepared to accept the pre-1931 social structure.

Gil Robles's speech on 16 June was an *a priori* attribution of responsibility for the war to the Left. The accusation was repeated after the murder of Calvo Sotelo by Assault Guards in reprisal for the killing of two of their number by rightist gunmen.[79] Two days after the discovery of Calvo Sotelo's body on 13 July, Gil Robles spoke again at a meeting of the standing committee of the Cortes, the so-called Diputatión Permanente. He accused the government of criminal, political and moral responsibility for the assassination. He reiterated his claim that the Left had ensured that nothing could be achieved by democratic methods and that it must take the blame for the growth of a movement of violence in Spain.[80] He did not recall that preparations for a military rising had been under way, with his knowledge, since the February elections.

EPILOGUE

The Socialists were defeated along with the rest of the Republican forces in 1939, their internal divisions of 1935 and 1936 bitterly exacerbated during the Civil War. Just as the CEDA was to be eclipsed by the Falange, the PSOE was overshadowed by the burgeoning influence of the Communist Party. That reflected the contrasts both between the flaccid response of the Socialist International and the dynamic reaction of the Comintern to events in Spain and between Anglo-French non-intervention policies and the material help provided by the Soviet Union.[1] In the spring of 1936, the Caballeristas had assumed the Communists to be their natural allies. However, the need to win the support of the Western democracies ensured that Communists and Prietistas would soon be allied in a determination to stifle the forces of popular revolution.

It was symptomatic of the extent to which the PSOE Left underestimated the likelihood of military rebellion that Largo Caballero and the bulk of the UGT executive went to a congress of the International Federation of Trade Unions, returning only on 16 July.[2] As a further indication of misplaced confidence, when war broke out on the night of 17 July, Largo Caballero ordered the declaration of an indefinite general strike. It was a suicidal conclusion to the antics of the radical Left of the PSOE and in the towns of Castile and the south, in Salamanca and Granada, in Valladolid and Seville, it was a mistake paid for by the blood of the Socialist rank and file. In the areas where the military rising was not initially successful, the scenario prophesied by the Caballeristas became a reality in that the Republican authorities collapsed and the workers filled the vacuum by creating their own instruments of power.

A Republican government under José Giral uneasily took power, with Prieto acting as its behind-the-scenes strategist. However, Prieto's hopes of finally forming the wide Republican–Socialist cabinet planned in May were aborted by the strength of spontaneous popular revolutionism. It seemed the fulfilment of the Caballerista prophesies and the logical continuation of their scenario that, on 4 September 1936, a government of working-class unity should be headed by Largo Caballero himself.[3] However, with Franco's African columns nearing Madrid, the exigencies of co-ordinating the war effort within a hostile international environment ensured that Largo Caballero soon found himself obliged to rebuild the bourgeois state which had collapsed after the military uprising and to use that state to contain popular revolutionary spontaneity. Largo Caballero, who did not bother to seek ratification of his appointment from the PSOE executive, effectively put into practice the broad Popular Front strategy of Prieto which he had blocked in May 1936. Both that usurpation of their policies and the destructive six-month delay in their implementation increased the bitterness of the PSOE's reformist centre.[4]

Having succeeded in retrieving the bourgeois state from the revolutionary masses, Largo Caballero was himself swept aside in May 1937 by a circumstantial alliance of bourgeois Republicans, Prietista Socialists and the Communists. All three were motivated by a sense of Largo Caballero's inadequacy as a wartime leader and by a fear that his reputation as the 'Spanish Lenin' was off-putting to the Western democracies. The Communists were also driven by impatience with his objections to the unification of the PSOE and the PCE. The Prietista right wing of the PSOE was out for revenge, and once Largo Caballero was replaced by Juan Negrín, a thorough-going purge of the Socialist movement began, whose legacy of bitterness would reverberate on into the 1960s.[5]

After the Civil War, Prieto escaped into exile in Mexico and Largo Caballero to France where he was captured in 1943 by the Germans and put into a concentration camp. He ended the Second World War a broken man and died on 23 March 1946. Before dying, he had returned to his reformist origins and had overcome his resentment of Prieto sufficently to accept the idea that the restoration of the Republic should not necessarily be the immediate goal of the struggle against the Franco dictatorship.[6] Prieto's pragmatism reached its apogee in September 1947 when he found himself in London negotiating with Gil Robles for the creation of a broad anti-Franco front.[7] In the event, they were both out-manoeuvred by Franco. Prieto, however, despite his Latin American exile, travelled, in political terms at least, a shorter road from Madrid 1936 to London 1947 than did Gil Robles.

On 18 July 1936, the CEDA rank and file joined the rebels wherever they could. A number of CEDA deputies unlucky enough to find themselves in the Republican zone were killed, including Federico Salmón and Dimas de Madariaga. Gil Robles himself, anxious that no blood should be seen to be on his hands, went to Biarritz in the south of France. He resisted the encouragement of monarchist friends to accept General Mola's call for prominent politicians of the Right to go to Burgos to add their support to the rising. He told them that he was totally committed to the rising but felt that he could help it more from abroad. It was a political error from which he was never to recover.[8] Given forty-eight hours by the Blum government within which time he had to leave France, he was advised by Juan March, the Marqués de Luca de Tena and the Conde de los Andes that his help could be invaluable in securing the assistance of Oliveira Salazar. Accordingly, he proceeded to Portugal, where he helped Franco's brother Nicolás to establish a Nationalist unofficial embassy or 'Agency of the Burgos Junta' in the Hotel Aviz in Lisbon. Together with a motley band of aristocrats, rightist diplomats and politicians, including the Marqués de la Vega de Anzó and the Carlist Joaquín Bau, both of whom were also friends of Franco, Gil Robles played a vital role in organising the purchase of arms and other supplies, propaganda and financial assistance for the rebel cause.[9] By the beginning of August 1936, he was in a position to inform a delighted Franco that he had raised foreign currency worth eight million pesetas. So close a relationship did he establish with Oliveira Salazar that he became his regular intermediary with Franco.[10]

These activities on behalf of the military rebels were conducted by Gil Robles in the shadows, with considerable discretion. As the autumn wore on, he was obliged to give some consideration to his own political future. The military uprising constituted as big a change for the civilian Right as it did for the Left and, despite his pre-eminence before 18 July 1936, Gil Robles's status was now far from clear. Queipo de Llano predicted to Arthur Koestler in late August 1936 that Gil Robles would play no part in the future government of Spain.[11] Anxious to play a more prominent role, in October, he publicly praised the JAP for their patriotism in joining the rising.[12]

The Jefe visited rebel Spain on several occasions, notably at the end of July, in late August and in mid-September 1936 and in May and July 1937, but met an increasingly hostile reception. In Pamplona on 28 July, where he had gone to collect his wife and son, he was insulted in his hotel by several aristocratic ladies and accused of being responsible for what was happening in Spain, an accusation which was to be made with increasing frequency.[13] After passing through Salamanca, he arrived in Burgos on 2 September 1936 and, within a matter of hours, a group of Falangists had tried to beat him up and arrest him. General Fidel Dávila, the Civil Governor of Burgos, sought instructions from the President of the Junta de Burgos, General Cabanellas, who ordered that the CEDA chief be given protection.[14] On one subsequent visit to Salamanca, the palpable enmity that he found obliged him to remain hidden in the house of a friend. On another, he wandered alone and incognito around the deserted university.[15]

Franco's personal hostility to Gil Robles can be deduced from a paranoid and clearly apocryphal story that he told a Mexican journalist to the effect that some members of the JAP had asked the Jefe for advice at the beginning of the war only to be told that they should stand aside and let the Republicans and the military rebels tear each other apart until the CEDA could step in and take over. To establish his own benevolence, Franco then alleged that, when Gil Robles visited Burgos in the early spring of 1937 (perhaps confusing this with the September 1936 incident with Dávila), Mola had telephoned him for instructions because Falangists held Gil Robles responsible for the outbreak of the war and wanted to kill him. The Generalísimo claimed that he told Mola to 'take the necessary forces, save Gil Robles but tell him to be more discreet'. Thereafter, Gil Robles went back to Lisbon where, in the words of Franco, 'he helped us greatly because of his excellent contacts'.[16]

Once Franco was made Chief of State on 1 October 1936, there was little political future for Gil Robles. He was the object of popular hostility in the Nationalist zone for what, in the heated atmosphere of the war, was regarded as the accidentalist betrayal of right-wing interests. Franco had no interest in revindicating the Jefe's position. Given his own ambiguous commitment to the conspiracy during the spring of 1936, Franco wanted to wipe out memories of his own links with the CEDA. Moreover, as he concentrated on building up his own political power, he had no reason to encourage the presence of a strong personality of the enormous political talent of Gil Robles. Gil Robles himself believed that Franco could not tolerate having around someone who had been his superior. Certainly, remarks made many years later by Franco to Manuel Fraga show that the Caudillo harboured deep-rooted resentments from their time together in the Ministry of War.[17]

In fact, Gil Robles did nothing that even remotely suggested that he might ever challenge Franco's leadership. Throughout the war, his public statements were those of an eager subordinate. On 10 February

1937, he was interviewed by the newspaper *Arriba España* and declared that:

> The Movement which began on 17 July marks a new direction for the *Patria*. Once victory is achieved, political parties should disappear and be integrated into a single, broad national movement. When this happy moment arrives, Acción Popular, far from being an obstacle or a stumbling block, will be proud to facilitate the process. How could it be otherwise, if it means the fulfilment of one of its supreme aspirations.[18]

He wrote to *The Universe* in early 1937 a vehement defence of the military rebellion and Acción Popular's support for it:

> From the first instant of the present military revolt, it is true to say that Acción Popular has united itself in its entirety with the Revolution, has given thousands upon thousands of soldiers to the army, and is ready to support the national cause with all its moral strength, with all its financial resources, and with the life of every one of its members. The Acción Popular is with the Nationalists in the fullness of its character as a Catholic party.[19]

In April 1937, when General Franco forcibly united the various political forces of the Nationalist zone, Gil Robles wrote to him to place the entire organisation of Acción Popular at his disposal for its incorporation in the new single party. In his letter of 22 April, the Jefe wrote:

> My dear and respected friend, I have just read in the Portuguese press the text of your broadcast speech in which you call, in the name of Spain, for the union of all her children. In the name of Acción Popular, I am pleased to accept your call and to tell you that I put into your hands the entire organisation, both of the party which is already suspended and of the militias, already militarily organised, so that you may adopt whatever measures you consider convenient for this unification. The Command Council (*Junta de Mando*) of the militias, the only official section of Acción Popular which is now functioning, receives today the peremptory order to present itself at your headquarters to receive orders for their dissolution, their obligatory fusion with another or other organisations or their incorporation pure and simple into the army. In doing so, I hope to interpret faithfully the spirit of those who since 1931 have died in the civic struggle which is the precursor of the present epic and of those who, when this Movement of salvation

broke out, renounced their party interests to join the army as volunteers and of those who, with the emblem of Acción Popular on their chests, know how to fight and die without expecting a mention or a reward. With the greatest emotion on making this sacrifice for Spain, in your hands, of something so dear to me, I plead to God to guide your steps to lead us all to the certain victory and the salvation of the beloved Patria.[20]

The CEDA itself was dissolved, its leadership and middle-rank functionaries absorbed into the Francoist *movimiento*. Several of the CEDA's leaders found preferment under Franco but Gil Robles was not one of them. He was still derided in the Nationalist zone as having delayed the inevitable war against corrupt democracy. It served for nothing that he accepted the unification. In the scramble for posts in the post-war polity, there were many close to the Caudillo who were glad to see Gil Robles removed as a competitor. If he expected a call from Franco, he was to be disappointed.[21]

Even leaving aside personal jealousies, in the charged atmosphere of war, the Jefe's legalist stance had no place. Indeed, as the catastrophist groups which had worked to overthrow the Republic became more enmeshed in the killing, they were less inclined to see Gil Robles and accidentalism as anything other than treachery. This accounts for the fact that, after the Civil War, *El Debate* was never permitted to reappear. It was also reflected both in Francoist historiography and also in subsequent pro-Gil-Robles literature in terms of an exaggeration of the Jefe's democratic credentials. It accounts for his own schizoid attempts in his memoirs simultaneously to present himself as a democrat – which he had indeed become by the time of their composition – and, in reply to Nationalist criticisms, to show how much he had done to make the *movimiento* possible. After all, the Francoist war effort was devoted to achieving many of the goals to which the CEDA had aspired. Throughout the Nationalist zone, and in all of Spain after 1939, a corporative state was established. Trade unions were abolished, the left-wing press was destroyed. Socialist and other leftist cadres who survived the war but could not escape into exile were subjected to long terms of imprisonment, if not executed. The pre-1931 social structure was re-established. The Republic's social legislation disappeared. The rural domination of the *caciques* and the Civil Guard was consolidated.

Despite its use of a radical fascist party, the Falange, to mobilise the population of the Nationalist zone during the war, the Francoist state remained the instrument of the traditional oligarchy. The veneer of antioligarchical novelty adopted by Hitler and Mussolini was eschewed by Franco. His corporate state jealously guarded the traditional agrarian structure at least until the mid-1950s. Only while an Axis victory in the world war seemed likely did Falangist counsels carry more weight than those of Carlists, orthodox monarchists and Cedistas.

Francoist links with the old order made the Republic appear as a mere interlude. In that interlude, a challenge had been mounted to the existing balance of social and economic power. The most effective part of that challenge was constituted by the reforming programme of the Socialists, because it had the legal sanction of parliament. The response of the traditional Right was twofold – the violence of the self-styled 'catastrophists' and the 'accidentalism' of Acción Popular. The resort to violence had little possibility of success in the early years of the Republic and the defence of the old social order was assumed by the legalists. So successful were the tactics of the CEDA and the Agrarians in blocking reform and building up a mass party that the optimistic reformism of the Socialists was hardened into a more aggressive and apparently revolutionary stance. The rising of October 1934 and the election results of 1936 signalled the impossibility of defending traditional structures by means of the legal imposition of a corporative state. Given the apparent determination of the working class to introduce major reforms and of the oligarchy to resist them, the failure of legalist tactics could not but lead to a resurgence of the 'catastrophist' Right and the imposition of a corporative state by force of arms.

NOTES

1 THE ORIGINS OF THE SOCIALIST SCHISM: 1917–31

1 Regarding the 1934 insurrection, Richard A.H. Robinson, *The Origins of Franco's Spain* (Newton Abbot, 1970), p. 12, has alleged that, 'given that the future of the Republic depended on the Socialist movement and the Catholic party, it is important to recognise that it was the former and not the latter which abandoned democratic methods and appealed to violence'.

2 Salvador de Madariaga, *Spain: A Modern History* (London, 1961), p. 455. A more sophisticated version of the same thesis is to be found in Guillermo Díaz Doin, *Como llegó Falange al poder* (Buenos Aires, 1940), pp. 63–74.

3 See also Paul Preston, 'The Agrarian War in the South', in Paul Preston, editor, *Revolution and War in Spain 1931–1939* (London, 1984); José Manuel Macarro Vera, 'Causas de la radicalización socialista en la II República', *Revista de Historia Contemporánea* (Sevilla), no. 1, December 1982; and Santos Juliá Díaz, *La izquierda del PSOE (1935–1936)* (Madrid, 1977), *Madrid, 1931–1934: de la fiesta popular a la lucha de clases* (Madrid, 1984); and 'Corporativistas obreros y reformadores políticos: crisis e escisión del PSOE en la II República', *Studia Historica*, vol. 1, no. 4, 1983.

4 Andrés Saborit, *Julián Besteiro*, 2nd edition (Buenos Aires, 1967), p. 250; Luis Romero Solano, *Vísperas de la guerra de España* (Mexico City, n.d. [1947]), pp. 176–7; Carlos de Baraibar, 'La traición del Stalinismo', *Timón* (Buenos Aires), no. 7, June 1940; speech of Luis Araquistain in Toulouse on 24 January 1947, quoted in Saborit, *Besteiro*, p. 262; and remarks by Araquistain to Juan Marichal quoted in the latter's introduction to Manuel Azaña, *Obras completas*, 4 vols (Mexico City, 1966–8), vol. III, pp. xxxi–xxxii.

5 This has been noted by critics of both Right and Left. See Ricardo de la Cierva, 'Marxismo en España, hoy', *ABC*, 8 June 1973; Juan Andrade, *La burocracia reformista en el movimiento obrero* (Madrid, 1935), an acute critique; Fernando Claudín, 'Dos concepciones de la vía española al socialismo', in *Horizonte español 1966*, 2 vols (Paris, 1966), vol. II, p. 60. For more systematic recent studies, see Paul Heywood, 'De las dificultades para ser marxista: el PSOE, 1879–1921', *Sistema*, no. 74, September 1986; Eusebio Fernández, *Marxismo y positivismo en el socialismo español* (Madrid, 1981), pp. 94–148; José R. Gómez Nazabal, *Consideraciones en torno al ideario y la praxis del socialismo español 1879–1921* (San Sebastián, 1981), pp. 111–71; Pedro Ribas Ribas, *La introducción del marxismo en España (1869–1939)* (Madrid, 1981),

pp. 13–76; Paul Heywood, *Marxism and the Failure of Organised Socialism in Spain 1879–1936* (Cambridge, 1990), pp. 1–58.
6 Gerald Brenan, *The Spanish Labyrinth*, 2nd edition (Cambridge, 1950), p. 218; Grandizo Munis, *Jalones de derrota, promesa de victoria* (Mexico City, 1948), p. 50; Gerald H. Meaker, *The Revolutionary Left in Spain, 1914–1923* (Stanford, Calif., 1974), pp. 10–14, 196–7; Manuel Pérez Ledesma, *El obrero consciente: dirigentes, partidos y sindicatos en la II Internacional* (Madrid, 1987), pp. 142–53.
7 *El Socialista*, 9, 10 November 1917.
8 Heywood, *Marxism*, pp. 1–28; Juan Pablo Fusi Aizpurua, 'El movimiento obrero en España, 1876–1914', *Revista de Occidente* (Madrid), no. 131, February 1974; Meaker, *Revolutionary Left*, p. 4.
9 Juan Antonio Lacomba, *La crisis española de 1917* (Madrid, 1970), pp. 213–55; Carlos Forcadell, *Parlementarismo y bolchevización: el movimiento obrero español 1914–1918* (Barcelona, 1978), pp. 237–50; Manuel Tuñón de Lara, *El movimiento obrero en la historia de España* (Madrid, 1972), ch. 10.
10 Francisco Largo Caballero, *Mis recuerdos: cartas a un amigo* (Mexico City, 1954), pp. 55–8; Julián Besteiro, *Cartas desde la prisión* (Madrid, 1988), pp. 29–113.
11 Juan Díaz del Moral, *Historia de las agitaciones campesinas andaluzas*, 3rd edition (Madrid, 1973), pp. 265–360; Antonio Barragán Moriana, *Conflictividad social y desarticulación política en la provincia de Córdoba 1918–1920* (Córdoba, 1990), pp. 98–165; Alberto Balcells, *El sindicalismo en Barcelona 1916–1923* (Barcelona, 1965), pp. 73–129; Antonio Bar, *La CNT en los años rojos (del sindicalismo revolucionario al anarcosindicalismo 1910–1926)* (Madrid, 1981), pp. 557–628.
12 Juan Pablo Fusi Aizpurua, *Política obrera en al país vasco 1880–1923* (Madrid, 1975), ch. 8. David Ruiz, *El movimiento obrero en Asturias* (Oviedo, 1968), pp. 162–81, and Enrique Moradiellos, *El Sindicato de los Obreros Mineros de Asturias 1910–1930* (Oviedo, 1986), pp. 56–78, indicate the bitterness of social conflict in the region.
13 The best accounts are Meaker, *Revolutionary Left*, pp. 225–384; Heywood, *Marxism*, pp. 62–83; and Tuñón, *Movimiento obrero*, pp. 681–717.
14 Gabriel Morón, *El Partido Socialista ante la realidad política española* (Madrid, 1929), pp. 109–14.
15 *El Socialista*, 14, 22 September 1923. Cf. Heywood, *Marxism*, pp. 88–90.
16 This position is fervently stated in Francisco Largo Caballero, *Presente y futuro de la Unión General de Trabajadores de España* (Madrid, 1925), *passim*.
17 Luis Araquistain, '¿Qué hacen los socialistas?', *El Socialista*, 1 May 1929; Enrique de Santiago, *La Unión General de Trabajadores ante la revolución* (Madrid, 1932), pp. 21, 22, 25, 44; Manuel Cordero, *Los socialistas y la revolución* (Madrid, 1932) pp. 43–51, 60–7. Largo Caballero's *Mis recuerdos: cartas a un amigo* (Mexico City, 1954) is strangely uninformative on the issue, but is vituperative (see esp. pp. 90–1) against those who opposed the passive tactic adopted by the PSOE and UGT.
18 The anarchists were attacked from the first moment; see José Peirats, *La CNT en la revolución española*, 2nd edition, 3 vols (Paris, 1971), vol. I, pp. 37–8. The Dictator offered to tolerate the Communists if they would undertake to abandon their agitation. When the leadership refused, the arrests began; see José Bullejos, *La Comintern en España* (Mexico City, 1972), p. 54.
19 Joaquín Maurín, *Los hombres de la Dictadura* (Madrid, 1930), pp. 153–6.
20 Morón, *Partido Socialista*, pp. 78–85.
21 Antonio Ramos Oliveira, *Politics, Economics and Men of Modern Spain* (London, 1946), p. 205.

22 The thought of Besteiro has received considerable attention of late in Spain. See Alberto Míguez, *El pensamiento filosófico de Julián Besteiro* (Madrid, 1971); Andrés Saborit, *El pensamiento político de Julián Besteiro* (Madrid, 1974); Emilio Lamo de Espinosa, *Filosofía y política en Julián Besteiro* (Madrid, 1973), which contains a detailed account of the positivism and neo-Kantianism which always pervaded Besteiro's Marxism. Besteiro provided the introduction to a translation of Kautsky's *El programa de Erfurt* (Madrid, 1933). See Julián Besteiro, *Obras completas*, edited by Emilio Lamo de Espinosa, 3 vols (Madrid, 1983), and the second edition of Lamo's book, Emilio Lamo de Espinosa and Manuel Contreras, *Filosofía y política en Julián Besteiro* (Madrid, 1990).

23 Lamo, *Besteiro*, pp. 302–7.

24 *El Socialista*, 5 February, 14 November 1924; Besteiro, *Obras*, vol. II, pp. 17–20; Heywood, *Marxism*, pp. 90–1.

25 Largo Caballero, *Mis recuerdos*, p. 37, and *Presente y futuro*, p. 7.

26 Largo Caballero, *Presente y futuro*, pp. 42–3; Santiago, *UGT*, pp. 24–5.

27 This rivalry is apparent in many Socialist writings of the time. See Largo Caballero, *Presente y futuro*, passim; Santiago, *UGT*, p. 44; Cordero, *Socialistas*, p. 64; PSOE, *Convocatoria y orden del día para el XII congreso ordinario* (Madrid, 1927), p. 91. It is expressed most openly by Antonio Ramos Oliveira, who in *Nosotros los marxistas: Lenin contra Marx* (Madrid, 1932) accepts the persecution of the anarchists and Communists by the Dictator on the grounds that such groups are incompatible with any regime.

28 PSOE, *Convocatoria . . . XII congreso*, p. 89.

29 *ABC*, 29 September 1929.

30 *El Socialista*, 2 October, 1 November 1923; Ruiz, *Asturias*, pp. 188–9.

31 Llaneza, letters from prison, published in *El Minero de la Hulla*, August and September 1917, reprinted in Manuel Llaneza, *Escritos y discursos* (Oviedo, 1985), pp. 206–14.

32 Ruiz, *Asturias*, p. 189.

33 Tuñón, *Movimiento obrero*, p. 721. See ibid., p. 776 for evidence of strike action.

34 PSOE, *Convocatoria . . . XII congreso*, p. 96.

35 Largo Caballero and Cordero on the Junta de Abastos, in Santiago, *UGT*, p. 39. Lucio Martínez and other members of the executive were on various other committees; see Tuñón, *Movimiento obrero*, p. 776.

36 PSOE, *Convocatoria . . . XII congreso*, pp. 101–2.

37 Manuel Tuñón de Lara, *La España del siglo XX*, 2nd edition (Paris, 1973), p. 151.

38 PSOE, *Convocatoria . . . XII congreso*, p. 103.

39 *El Socialista*, 11 December 1923; Virgilio Zapatero, *Fernando de los Ríos: los problemas del socialismo democrático* (Madrid, 1974), p. 77.

40 *El Socialista*, 13 December 1923; Largo Caballero, *Presente y futuro*, pp. 42–7, and *Mis recuerdos*, pp. 90–2.

41 Ruiz, *Asturias*, pp. 190–1.

42 Vicente Marco Miranda, *Las conspiraciones contra la Dictadura* (Madrid, 1930), p. 61; Cordero, *Socialistas*, p. 74; Ramos Oliveira, *Nosotros*, pp. 182–3; *El Socialista*, 12 May 1925, 26 February 1926.

43 Eduardo Aunós, *La política social de la Dictadura* (Madrid, 1944), pp. 46–63.

44 Santiago, *UGT*, pp. 25–7, 32–3.

45 Santiago, *UGT*, ibid.; Cordero, *Socialistas*, p. 63; Ramos Oliveira, *Nosotros*, pp. 186, 193. Cf. Maurín, *Hombres de la Dictadura*, p. 189.

46 Tuñón, *Movimiento obrero*, p. 780.

47 Alberto Balcells, *Crisis económica y agitación social en Cataluña* (Barcelona, 1971), p. 34.
48 For an analysis of wages and prices, see Tuñón, *Movimiento obrero*, pp. 755–73. Cf. Joaquín Maurín, *La revolución española* (Madrid, 1932), p. 51.
49 Moradiellos, *SOMA*, pp. 64, 110; Ruiz, *Asturias*, pp. 191–5.
50 Edward E. Malefakis, *Agrarian Reform and Peasant Revolution in Spain* (New Haven, Conn., 1970), p. 159. PSOE, *Convocatoria . . . XII congreso*, pp. 11–12, reprints demands from Socialist organisations in Asturias, Andalusia and Aragón for the PSOE to adopt a more coherent and dynamic agrarian policy.
51 Eduardo Aunós, *Itinerario histórica de la España contemporánea* (Barcelona, 1940), pp. 377–9.
52 Santiago, *UGT*, p. 45.
53 Morón, *Partido Socialista*, pp. 124–35.
54 Saborit, *Besteiro*, pp. 169–70; PSOE, *Convocatoria . . . XII congreso*, p. 121.
55 Maurín, *Hombres de la Dictadura*, pp. 188–9; Andrade, *Burocracia reformista*, *passim*; Ricardo Sanz, *El sindicalismo y la política* (Toulouse, 1966), p. 149; Alvaro de Albornoz, prologue to Morón, *Partido Socialista*, p. 25.
56 Santiago, *UGT*, pp. 44–5.
57 S.G. Checkland, *The Mines of Tharsis* (London, 1967), pp. 212–14.
58 Tuñón, *Movimiento obrero*, pp. 721, 775, 784; Santiago, *UGT*, p. 45; Maurín, *Hombres de la Dictadura*, pp. 197–8.
59 Renée Lamberet, *Mouvements ouvriers et socialistes: l'Espagne* (Paris, 1953), p. 146.
60 Maurín, *Hombres de la Dictadura*, p. 200.
61 Morón, *Partido Socialista*, pp. 182–5; *El Socialista*, 10 July 1928.
62 Tuñón, *Movimiento obrero*, p. 784.
63 Morón, *Partido Socialista*, pp. 189–90.
64 Lamberet, *Mouvements ouvriers*, pp. 146–7.
65 Moradiellos, *SOMA*, pp. 102–13; Ruiz, *Asturias*, pp. 195–7; Gabriel Santullano, 'Las organizaciones obreras asturianas en los comienzos de la segunda República', in M. Tuñón de Lara, editor, *Sociedad, política y cultura en la España de los siglos XIX-XX* (Madrid, 1973), p. 257.
66 *El Socialista*, 3 January 1929.
67 Santiago, *UGT*, p. 54
68 Saborit, *Besteiro*, p. 172.
69 *Boletín de la Unión General de Trabajadores de España* (*BUGT*), August 1929; *El Socialista*, 1 September 1929.
70 Santiago, *UGT*, p. 47.
71 The text of Besteiro's manifesto is reprinted in Saborit, *Besteiro*, pp. 175–80.
72 *BUGT*, September 1929; *El Sol*, 17 September 1929 (emphasis added).
73 Santiago, *UGT*, p. 54.
74 *El Socialista*, 14 January 1930.
75 *El Socialista*, 5, 13 February 1924.
76 *El Sol*, 6, 13 and 17 February 1924.
77 Lamo, *Besteiro*, pp. 57–8, 310–12; Stafford Cripps et al., *Problemas de gobierno socialista* (Madrid, 1934); P. Heywood, *Marxism 1879–1936* (Cambridge, 1990), pp. 89–92.
78 Zapatero, *De los Ríos*, p. 71. Fernando de los Ríos, in his *El sentido humanista del socialismo* (Madrid, 1926), gives an idea of his notion of the pre-eminence of democratic socialism. See also Elías Díaz, 'Fernando de los Rios: socialismo humanista y socialismo marxista', *Sistema* (Madrid), no. 10, July 1975, pp. 115–25.

79 Lamo, *Besteiro*, p. 70.
80 The complete text is reprinted in Saborit, *Besteiro*, pp. 188–90.
81 Dámaso Berenguer, *De la Dictadura a la República* (Madrid, 1946), pp. 51–2.
82 Emilio Mola Vidal, *Obras completas* (Valladolid, 1940), pp. 351–3.
83 Lamo, *Besteiro*, pp. 72–3.
84 Miguel Maura, *Así cayó Alfonso XIII*, 2nd edition (Barcelona, 1966), pp. 50–9; José Sánchez Guerra, *Al servicio de España* (Madrid 1930); Angel Ossorio y Gallardo, *Mis memorias* (Buenos Aires, 1946), pp. 165–6; Gabriel Mario de Coca, *Anti-Caballero* (Madrid, 1936), p. 18; PSOE, *Convocatoria y orden del dia para el XIII congreso ordinario* (Madrid, 1932), pp. 68–9.
85 Ruiz, *Asturias*, pp. 214–17.
86 Tuñón, *Movimiento obrero*, p. 790, gives the following figures: (1929) strikes 96, strikers 55,576, days lost 313,065; (1930) strikes 402, strikers 247,460, days lost 3,747,360.
87 Mola, *Obras*, pp. 352–3; Andrade, *Burocracia*, pp. 204–20.
88 Bullejos, *Comintern*, pp. 100–1; José Peirats, *Los anarquistas en la crisis política española* (Buenos Aires, 1964), pp. 60–4; Mola, *Obras*, p. 353; Tuñón, *Movimiento obrero*, p. 792; Lamberet, *Mouvements ouvriers*, pp. 146–7.
89 Mola, *Obras*, pp. 352–3; Andrade, *Burocracia*, pp. 204–20.
90 Many anarchist, and even Socialist, militants interviewed by the author recalled with bitterness or amusement the great collection of sinecures accumulated by Cordero. For lists, see Andrade, *Burocracia*, pp. 242, 245; Joaquín del Moral, *Oligarquía y 'enchufismo'* (Madrid, 1933), pp. 80–1.
91 Cordero, *Socialistas*, p. 88.
92 Mola, *Obras*, pp. 353–4, 373, 394, 399, 404, 421, 437–46.
93 *Anuario estadístico de España, 1931* (Madrid, 1931), p. 606; *El Obrero de la Tierra*, 17 September 1932. This still did not bring the FNTT back to pre-Dictatorship levels. In August 1922 the UGT had 510 agrarian sections, with 65,405 members – *Anuario estadístico, 1923* (Madrid, 1923), pp. 308–9. *BUGT*, November 1931, complained that one section which had 80,000 received subscriptions from only 21,000.
94 Constancio Bernaldo de Quirós, 'Informe acerca del paro de los jornaleros del campo de Andalucía durante el otoño de 1930', in Ministerio de Trabajo y Previsión Social, *La crisis andaluza de 1930–1931* (Madrid 1931), pp. 8–35.
95 Cordero, *Socialistas*, pp. 93–4.
96 Maura, *Así cayó*, pp. 71–3; Saborit, *Besteiro*, p. 191; Largo Caballero, *Mis recuerdos*, p. 107; Zapatero, *De los Ríos*, pp. 82–3; Lamo, *Besteiro*, p. 72. The best account of the forging of the Pact of San Sebastián is Shlomo Ben-Ami, *The Origins of the Second Republic in Spain* (Oxford, 1978), pp. 68–141.
97 Saborit, *Besteiro*, p. 194; Lamo, *Besteiro*, p. 74; Zapatero, *De los Ríos*, pp. 84–5; Coca, *Anti-Caballero*, p. 11; Largo Caballero, *Mis recuerdos*, p. 108.
98 The Agrupaciones Socialistas of Bilbao, Valladolid and San Sebastián had already ignored a National Committee instruction to send councillors to the re-established town councils; see Saborit, *Besteiro*, p. 194.
99 Maura, *Así cayó*, p. 83.
100 Saborit, *Besteiro*, p. 191.
101 Indalecio Prieto, *Convulsiones de España*, 3 vols (Mexico City, 1967–9), vol. I, p. 61.
102 Largo Caballero, *Mis recuerdos*, pp. 113–14; Saborit, *Besteiro*, pp. 194–5.
103 Ignacio Hidalgo de Cisneros, *Cambio de rumbo*, 2 vols (Bucharest, 1964), vol. I, pp. 221–4. Hidalgo says that the local tramway workers were extremely enthusiastic regarding the revolutionary movement.
104 *El Socialista*, 8–13 October 1932.

105 Julio Alvarez del Vayo, *The Last Optimist* (London, 1950), p. 198. He was already using his position as *Guardian* correspondent to smuggle in small arms for the revolutionary committee (see ibid., pp. 193–6). In his memoirs, Saborit does not mention his lack of co-operation.
106 Mola, *Obras*, p. 543.
107 Largo Caballero, *Mis recuerdos*, pp. 111–12. Saborit (*Besteiro*, p. 196) admits that Largo passed the information to Muiño, then rather disingenuously asks why he did not also speak with Besteiro and Trifón Gómez.
108 The debates are reported in *El Socialista*, 8, 9 October 1932. See also the excellent Besteirist apologia, Mario de Coca, *Anti-Caballero*, p. 63; Saborit, *Besteiro*, p. 197; Cordero, *Socialistas*, pp.84–5. A list of places affected by strikes is given in Tuñón, *Siglo XX*, pp. 210–11. See also Maura, *Así cayó*, p. 75; Ruiz, *Asturias*, p. 215.
109 *Diario de sesiones de las Cortes* (henceforth DSC), 11 April 1934.
110 *El Socialista*, 24 February 1931; Saborit, *Besteiro*, pp. 201–2; Santiago, *UGT*, pp. 86–8; Coca, *Anti-Caballero*, pp. 23–4.
111 See Barrington Moore Jr, *Social Origins of Dictatorship and Democracy* (London, 1967), esp. ch. 8. Cf. Leon Trotsky, letter to the editors of *Contra la Corriente*, 13 June 1930, reprinted in *Escritos sobre España* (Paris, 1971), pp. 1–6, and his pamphlet *The Revolution in Spain* (New York, 1931), reprinted in *The Spanish Revolution (1931–1939)* (New York, 1973), pp. 67–88, where he condemns as pedantic the Spanish Socialists' interpretation of the role of the bourgeoisie.
112 Josep Fontana, 'Transformaciones agrarias y crecimiento económico en la España contemporáneo', in Josep Fontana, *Cambio económico y actitudes políticas en la España del siglo XIX* (Barcelona, 1973), pp. 149–96; Gonzalo Anes, 'La agricultura española desde comienzos del siglo XIX hasta 1868', in Banco de España, *Ensayos sobre la economía española a mediados del siglo XIX* (Barcelona, 1970), pp. 235–63; Jordi Nadal, 'Spain 1830–1914', in Carlo M. Cipolla, editor, *The Emergence of Industrial Society*, 2 vols (London, 1973), vol. II, p. 2; Antonio Miguel Bernal, 'Formación y desarrollo de la burguesía agraria sevillana', in Antonio Miguel Bernal, *La propiedad de la tierra y las luchas agrarias andaluzas* (Barcelona, 1974), pp. 13–49; Miguel Viñas, 'Franquismo y revolución burguesa', in *Horizonte español 1972*, 3 vols (Paris, 1972), vol. III, pp. xv–xxxix; Nicolás Sánchez Albornoz, *España hace un siglo* (Barcelona, 1968), p. 190. For the debate on the bourgeois revolution in Spain, see especially Juan Sisinio Pérez Garzón, 'La revolución burguesa en España: los inicios de un debate científico 1966–1979', in Manuel Tuñón de Lara, editor, *Historiografía española contemporánea* (Madrid, 1980); Manuel Tuñón de Lara et al., *Crisis del antiguo régimen e industrialización en la España del siglo XIX* (Madrid, 1977); Alberto Gil Novales, editor, *La revolución burguesa en España* (Madrid, 1985); and Bartolomé Clavera et al., *Estudios sobre la revolución burguesa en España* (Madrid, 1979).
113 F. G. Bruguera, *Histoire contemporaine d'Espagne 1789–1950* (Paris, 1953), pp. 259–92; Manuel Tuñón de Lara, *La España del siglo XIX 1808–1914* (Paris, 1961), pp. 156–202; C. A. M. Hennessy, *The Federal Republic in Spain 1968–74* (Oxford, 1962), *passim*; Lacomba, *Crisis española*, *passim*.
114 Jesús Pabón, *Cambó*, 3 vols, vol. III (Barcelona, 1952), ch. 10.

2 BUILDING BARRICADES AGAINST REFORM

1 For the ACNP, see A. Sáez Alba, *La otra 'cosa nostra': la Asociación Católica Nacional de Propagandistas* (Paris, 1974), pp. ix–xxii; José R. Montero, *La CEDA: el catolicismo social y político en la II República*, 2 vols (Madrid, 1977), vol. I, pp. 99–100, vol. II, pp.440–508; José María García Escudero, *Conversaciones sobre Angel Herrera* (Madrid, 1986), pp. 16–20. For the CNCA, see Juan José Castillo, *Propietarios muy pobres: sobre la subordinación política del pequeño campesino* (Madrid, 1979), *passim*; Montero, *La CEDA*, vol. I, pp. 83–8.

2 *El Debate*, 7 April 1931; *La Época*, 6 April 1931.

3 The genesis and development of this 'catastrophist' response to the Republic are described in Martin Blinkhorn, 'Carlism and the Spanish Crisis of the 1930s', and Paul Preston, 'Alfonsist Monarchism and the Coming of the Spanish Civil War', both in *Journal of Contemporary History*, vol. 7, nos 3–4, 1972; Raúl Morodo, *Los orígenes ideólogicos del franquismo: Acción Española* (Madrid, 1985), pp. 59–85; Julio Gil Pecharromán, 'Renovación Española: una alternativa monárquica a la segunda República', unpublished Ph.D thesis, Universidad Complutense de Madrid, 2 vols, 1983, vol. I, pp. 119–48, 160–71.

4 Rafael Sánchez Guerra, *Dictadura, indiferencia, República* (Madrid, 1931), p. 137. On Angel Herrera, see García Escudero, *Herrera*, pp. 3–5 and *passim*.

5 José Monge Bernal, *Acción Popular* (Madrid, 1936), pp. 114–15, 122.

6 Gil Robles, *No fue posible la paz* (Barcelona, 1968), pp. 33–4.

7 Monge, *Acción Popular*, pp. 128–9.

8 José María Gil Robles, *No fue posible*, p. 35. (Emphasis added.)

9 Javier Tusell, *Historia de la democracia cristiana en España*, 2 vols (Madrid, 1974), vol. I, p. 59; Manuel Azaña, diary entry for 18 October 1931, *Obras*, vol. IV, p. 189.

10 Telegram from Pacelli to Vidal, 29 April 1931, in Arxiu Vidal i Barraquer, *Esglesia i Estat durant la segona República espanyola*, 4 vols (Monestir de Montserrat, 1971–90), vol. I, pp. 27–9.

11 Arxiu Vidal i Barraquer, *Esglesia i Estat*, vol. I, pp. 36–7.

12 Cf. Henry Buckley, *Life and Death of the Spanish Republic* (London, 1940), p. 58; Constancia de la Mora, *In Place of Splendour* (London, 1940), p. 32.

13 *El Debate*, 28 April 1931.

14 Letter of Cardinal-Archbishop of Seville to Cardinal Vidal i Barraquer, 28 November 1931, in Vidal i Barraquer Archives, *Esglesia i Estat*, vol. II, p. 169; José Ramón Montero Gibert, 'La CEDA: el partido contrarrevolucionario hegemónico de la II República', in Manuel Ramírez Jiménez, (editor), *Estudios sobre la II República española* (Madrid, 1975), p. 99.

15 Carmen Díaz, *Mi vida con Ramón Franco* (Barcelona, 1981), p. 159; Vidal i Barraquer Archives, *Esglesia i Estat*, vol. I, p. 85; Ramón Garriga, *Ramón Franco, el hermano maldito* (Barcelona, 1978), p. 232.

16 Francisco Franco Bahamonde, *'Apuntes' personales sobre la República y la guerra civil* (Madrid, 1987), p. 4.

17 Interview with Miguel Maura in Gabriel Jackson, *Historian's Quest* (New York, 1969), pp. 114–15; evidence of witness no. 30 in the Basque Clergy's compilation *El pueblo vasco frente a la cruzada franquista* (Toulouse, 1966), pp. 23–4. Henry Buckley, an English Catholic journalist who was present, wrote, 'Hence the explosion of rage and violence among the Madrid crowds when they found that even the one limb of the octopus of feudalism which had been cut off was beginning to grow again' (*Life and Death*, p. 64). According to Ricardo de la Cierva, in his *Historia de la guerra civil española*,

vol. I (Madrid, 1969), p. 172, Gil Robles was present at the CMI meeting. Gil Robles himself, in an interview with the author, denied this strongly. Ricardo de la Cierva, in *ABC*, 7 September 1978, quoted an eyewitness, Javier Artiñano, who recalled having seen Gil Robles at the meeting.

18 Monge, *Acción Popular*, pp. 130–2; *ABC*, 10 May 1931; Gil Robles, *No fue posible*, pp. 77–8, 84; Montero, *La CEDA*, vol. I, pp. 97–9.
19 *El Debate*, 5 and 6 May 1931.
20 *El Siglo Futuro*, 5 May 1931.
21 Julián Cortés Cavanillas, *Gil Robles ¿monárquico?* (Madrid, 1935), p. 91.
22 *El Debate*, 8 May 1931.
23 Antonio Monedero Martín, *La Confederación Nacional Católico-Agraria en 1920: su espíritu, su organización, su porvenir* (Madrid, 1921), pp. 22–33; Juan José Castillo, 'Orígenes y primeros años de la CNCA: planteamientos básicos de análisis del catolicismo social en España', paper read at a conference entitled 'La Societé rurale espagnole depuis la crise de l'ancien régime jusque à celle des années trentes' held at the University of Pau, 21–2 March 1975, reprinted in José Luis García Delgado, editor, *La cuestión agraria en la España contemporánea* (Madrid, 1976); Jean Bécarud, *La segunda República española* (Madrid, 1967), pp. 58–63.
24 Rafael Valls, *La Derecha Regional Valenciana 1930–1936* (Valencia, 1992), pp. 95–172.
25 *El Debate*, 9, 30 May, 17 June 1931; a series of interviews conducted by the author in Madrid during the winter of 1970–1 with the Marqués de Gracia Real, a Salamanca landowner, who had been a member of both Acción Nacional and Acción Española during the Republic, as well as having connections with both the Comunión Tradicionalista and the Falange.
26 Monge, *Acción Popular*, pp. 136–8. There is a trend which sees the essential cause of the Civil War as the failure of the 'moderate' Right to achieve its objectives within the Republic. This view argues that the egoism of the Left forced the Right to abandon legalism and defend its interests by other means. Notable works from this school are Robinson, *Origins*, and Carlos Seco Serrano, *Época contemporánea* (Barcelona, 1971) and, above all, Gil Robles, *No fue posible*. There is, however, considerable evidence to suggest that the aims of the 'moderate' Right were incompatible with the meaningful existence of the Republic. See, for example, Ramón Serrano Súñer, *Entre el silencio y la propaganda, la historia como fue: memorias* (Barcelona, 1977), pp. 24–6. The retrospective construction of a democratic CEDA draws its most substantial justification from the denunciation of 'accidentalism', as encouraging democracy and therefore making the Civil War inevitable, made by the Falangists and others. Ironically, Gil Robles in his memoirs endeavoured to placate two opposing audiences. On the one hand, he presented himself as a frustrated democrat during the Republic. On the other, in a tone of hurt at the lack of gratitude which he received from Franco, he also portrays himself as the man who helped make the Francoist victory possible by generating the popular right-wing militancy which underlay the Nationalist war effort. See Chapter 7.
27 *El Debate*, 2 June 1931.
28 *El Debate*, 11, 28 June 1931.
29 *El Debate*, 8 July 1931; Montero, *La CEDA*, vol. I, pp. 152–6.
30 Ramón Salas Larrazábal, *Historia del ejército popular de la República*, 4 vols (Madrid, 1973), vol. I, pp. 7, 14, 22–3; Santos Juliá Díaz, *Manuel Azaña: una biografía política, del Ateneo al Palacio Nacional* (Madrid, 1990), pp. 98–106.

31 Antonio Cordón, *Trayectoria (recuerdos de un artillero)* (Paris, 1971), p. 196; Salas Larrazábal, *Ejército popular*, vol. I, pp. 5–6; Juliá, *Azaña*, p. 106.
32 Michael Alpert, *La reforma militar de Azaña (1931–1933)* (Madrid, 1982), pp. 125–31; ABC, 24 April; *La Época*, 24 April 1931.
33 Mola, *Obras*, pp. 1056–8; Alpert, *La reforma militar*, pp. 133–50; Mariano Aguilar Olivencia, *El ejército español durante la segunda República* (Madrid, 1986), pp. 65–75.
34 Berenguer, *De la Dictadura a la República*, p. 407.
35 Mola, *Obras*, pp. 879–80; José María Iribarren, *Mola, datos para una biografía y para la historia del alzamiento nacional* (Zaragoza, 1938), pp. 39–40.
36 Carolyn P. Boyd, ' "Responsibilities" and the Second Republic, 1931–1936', in Martin Blinkhorn, editor, *Spain in Conflict 1931–1939: Democracy and its Enemies* (London, 1986), pp. 14–39.
37 Boyd, ' "Responsibilities" ', pp. 22–3.
38 Azaña, diary entry for 2 September 1931, *Obras*, vol. IV, pp. 115–16.
39 Alpert, *La reforma militar*, pp. 216–28; Azaña, diary entry for 20 July 1931, *Obras*, vol. IV, p. 35.
40 *La Correspondencia Militar*, 18 June, 17, 31 July 1931; Mola, *Obras*, pp. 1045–65. Cf. Cordón, *Trayectoria*, p. 194.
41 The speech is reproduced in full in Eduardo Espín, *Azaña en el poder: el partido de Acción Republicana* (Madrid, 1980), pp. 323–34. See p. 330. On the injustice of the accusation, see Alpert, *La reforma militar*, pp. 293–7, whose account is slightly flawed by his acceptance of the misquoted version of the speech given in Maura, *Así cayó*, p. 227. Stanley G. Payne, *Politics and the Military in Modern Spain* (Stanford, Calif., 1967), p. 275, accepts that Azaña said the offending phrase. Hugh Thomas, *The Spanish Civil War*, 3rd edition (London, 1977), p. 92, accepts Maura's version.
42 Cordón, *Trayectoria*, pp. 192–3, 197; Juliá, *Azaña*, pp. 101–2.
43 'Discurso de despedida en el cierre de la Academia General Militar', *Revista de Historia Militar*, Año XX, no. 40, 1976, pp. 335–7.
44 Azaña, diary entries for 16, 22 July 1931, *Obras*, vol. IV, pp. 33, 39. See also 9 December 1932, *Memorias íntimas de Azaña* (Madrid, 1939), pp. 307–8. Franco's service record in *Hoja de servicios*, pp. 82–3.
45 Garriga, *Ramón Franco*, p. 155.
46 Azaña, diary entries for 19 April, 25 June 1932, *Obras*, vol. IV, pp. 374, 411–13.
47 *Diario de sesiones de las Cortes Constituyentes*, 28 June 1931; Azaña, diary entry for 19 April, 27, 28 June, *Obras*, vol. IV, pp. 374, 413–18.
48 *El Debate*, 22, 28 July 1931.
49 *Diario de sesiones de las Cortes Constituyentes* (Henceforth *DSCC*), 8, 9 October 1931; Luis Jiménez de Asúa, *Anécdotas de las Constituyentes* (Buenos Aires, 1942), pp. 61–3; Gil Robles *No fue posible*, pp. 51–5; Robinson, *Origins*, pp. 60–8; Joaquín Arrarás, *Historia de la segunda República española*, 4 vols (Madrid 1956–68), vol. I, pp. 181–203.
50 Exchange of letters between Cardinal Vidal i Barraquer and Luis Nicolau d'Olwer on 22 November 1931, between Cardinal Vidal and Manual Azaña on 24, 25 November 1931, and between Cardinal Vidal and Cardinal Pacelli, recounting a conversation with Azaña, on 28 November 1931, Vidal i Barraquer Archives, *Esglesia i Estat*, vol. II, pp. 48–9, 158–63, 168, 179–80.
51 Monge, *Acción Popular*, p. 436.
52 Gil Robles, *No fue posible*, pp. 64–5.
53 *El Debate*, 18 October 1931; *El Sol*, 15 October 1931. For 'accidentalist' hostility to Miguel Maura, see *El Debate*, 27 October 1931.

54 *El Debate*, 20, 23 October 1931.
55 Buckley, *Life and Death*, pp. 66–7.
56 *El Debate*, 1, 3, 10, 12 November 1931; *El Socialista*, 2 November 1931.
57 Martin Blinkhorn, *Carlism and Crisis in Spain 1931–1939* (Cambridge, 1975), pp. 68–9; Montero, *La CEDA*, pp. 246–9.
58 *Acción Española*, no. 1, 16 December 1931, and no. 10, 1 May 1932; Preston, 'Alfonsist Monarchism', pp. 95 ff.
59 For the full text, see Monge, *Acción Popular*, pp. 170–83; *El Debate*, 6 December 1931.
60 *La Época*, 24 February 1932; Monge, *Acción Popular*, pp. 223–5.
61 *La Época*, 2 January 1932; Domingo de Arrese, *Bajo la ley de defensa de la República* (Madrid, 1933), p. 68.
62 *La Época*, 5 January 1932.
63 Gil Robles, *No fue posible*, pp. 67–76; letter of 25 April 1937 from Gil Robles to Luciano de la Calzada, regarding the dissolution of Acción Popular by Franco and its incorporation into the new one-party state. Gil Robles portrayed this 'splendid harvest' as the fruit of his propaganda efforts during the Republic. *Sur* (Málaga) 28 April 1937; cf. José Gutiérrez Ravé, *Gil Robles, caudillo frustrado* (Madrid, 1967), pp. 198–9.
64 Monge, *Acción Popular*, pp. 941, 953, 965, 991. The change was a response to a government ban on use of the word 'national' by non-state entities (see ibid., p. 183).
65 On the daily life of the peasant smallholder, see Manuel Sánchez, *Maurín, gran enigma de la guerra civil y otros recuerdos* (Madrid, 1976), pp. 21–4, 27–8. On the wheat-price agitation, see *El Socialista*, 6 August 1931.
66 *DSCC*, 7 August, 1 September 1931; *El Debate*, 1 December 1931; Marcelina Domingo, *La experiencia del poder* (Madrid, 1934), pp. 240–2.
67 Domingo, *La experiencia*, pp. 243–8; Gabriel Jackson, *The Spanish Republic and the Civil War* (Princeton, NJ, 1965), pp. 86–7. See also Mercedes Cabrera Calvo-Sotelo,'La estrategia patronal en la segunda República', *Estudios de Historia Social*, no. 7, October–December 1978.
68 Juan Antonio Ansaldo, *¿Para qué . . . ? De Alfonso XIII a Juan III* (Buenos Aires, 1951), p. 23; Juan-Simeón Vidarte, *Las Cortes Constituyentes de 1931–1933* (Barcelona, 1976), pp. 252–3.
69 Gil Robles, *No fue posible*, p. 79.
70 Gil Robles, *No fue posible*, p. 79.
71 Malefakis, *Agrarian Reform*, pp. 197–9.
72 Gil Robles, *No fue posible*, pp. 60, 235.
73 *El Debate*, 8 October 1932; Cortés Cavanillas, *Gil Robles*, pp. 138, 144–6.
74 *El Debate*, 21, 23, 25 October 1932; Montero, *La CEDA*, vol. I, 259–71; Robinson, *Origins*, pp. 107–9; Salvador Canals, *El bienio estéril* (Madrid, 1936), pp. 12–13.
75 Gil Robles, *No fue possible*, p. 84.
76 *El Debate*, 11 January 1933; *ABC*, 11 January 1933; Arrarás, *República*, vol. II, p. 137.
77 *El Debate*, 1, 9, 10, 15, 25 November 1932.
78 *El Socialista*, 29, 30 October 1932.
79 *El Debate*, 13 November 1932. See also the editorial on 16 December 1932, 'Towards a Fascist Democracy', and the article on 17 January 1933 on the advantages of a fascist economy.
80 *El Debate*, 26, 30 November 1932; Valls, *DRV*, pp. 167–70; Montero, *La CEDA*, vol. I, pp. 282–3.
81 *El Debate*, 23 December 1932.

82 *El Debate*, 27 December 1932.
83 Arrarás, *Republica*, vol. II, pp. 137–8; Montero, *La CEDA*, vol. I, pp. 283–90.
84 *El Debate*, 1, 2, 3, 5, 7 March 1933; *CEDA*, 1 May 1933; Arrarás, *República*, vol. II, pp. 144–8.
85 *El Socialista*, 8 March 1933.
86 *El Socialista*, 31 January, 5, 10, 11 February, 10 March, 2, 21 April 1933.
87 *El Socialista*, 1 May 1933; the May Day supplement was entitled 'Lessons of the German Counter-Revolution', the 4 May issue carried an appeal for the victims of fascism, and the 6 May issue had a full report on Hitler's destruction of the German unions.
88 *El Debate*, 8, 22 March 1933; Gil Robles, *No fue posible*, pp. 205–7.
89 *El Debate*, 1 January 1933.
90 *El Debate*, 9 May 1933. This was a considerable exaggeration; cf. Jackson, *Historian's Quest*, pp. 152–3.
91 *El Debate*, 18 May 1933.
92 *El Socialista*, 10 May, 20 August 1933.
93 *El Socialista*, 20 June 1933; for examples of deliberate provocation by the Right, see *El Socialista*, 23, 29 June.
94 Claude G. Bowers, *My Mission to Spain* (London, 1954), p. 33.
95 *El Debate*, 16 May 1933. For an account of the CEDA's claims to be socially aware and reform-oriented, see Robinson, *Origins*, pp. 114–16.
96 *El Debate*, 19, 23 May, 16 June, 17, 29 August 1933.
97 *El Debate*, 10 August 1933; Malefakis, *Agrarian Reform*, pp. 268–73; Robinson, *Origins*, pp. 127–8; José María Gil Robles, *Discursos parlamentarios* (Madrid, 1971), pp. 263–7.
98 Gil Robles, *No fue posible*, pp. 87–9; Cortés Cavanillas, *Gil Robles*, pp. 143–4; Julián Cortés Cavanillas, *Vida, confesiones y muerte de Alfonso XIII* (Madrid, 1956), pp. 426–7.
99 Juan Arrabal, *José María Gil Robles* (Madrid, 1933), pp. 9–13; Monge, *Acción Popular*, p. 378; Gil Robles, *No fue posible*, p. 48; *El Debate*, 27 December 1932; Blinkhorn, *Carlism and Crisis*, pp. 100–3, 158–62.
100 *El Socialista*, 2, 4, 11, 18, 21 July 1933.
101 See Angel Viñas, *La Alemania nazi y el 18 de julio* (Madrid, 1974), p. 149.
102 *El Debate*, 28 June, 16, 25 July 1933; *El Socialista*, 21 July, 7 September 1933.
103 *El Debate*, 4, 17, 25 August 1933; *El Pueblo Católico*, 29 March 1933.
104 Antonio Ramos Oliveira, *Alemania: ayer y hoy* (Madrid, 1933), p. 257; *El Debate*, 30 June; *El Socialista*, 2 July 1933.
105 Juan Velarde Fuertes, *El Nacional-Sindicalismo cuarenta años después* (Madrid, 1972), pp. 131–4.
106 For the background to the calling of elections, see Juliá, *Azaña*, pp. 282–300; Jackson, *Republic*, chs 4–6.
107 *CEDA*, 30 September 1933; *El Debate*, 2 September 1933. Gil Robles told the author in February 1973 that he went to Nuremberg as the guest of Von Papen.
108 *El Debate*, 15 September 1933.
109 *El Debate*, 10 October 1933.
110 Gil Robles, *No fue posible*, p. 94; *El Debate*, 12 October 1933.
111 *El Debate*, 17 October 1933. (Emphasis added.)
112 *El Socialista*, 17 October 1933. Gil Robles's visit to Germany had not gone unnoticed (see *El Socialista*, 14 October 1933). For the gloss by De los Ríos, see *El Socialista*, 21 October 1933.
113 *CEDA*, 31 October 1933. Primo de Rivera's remarks in de la Cierva, *La guerra civil*, p. 509.

114 Gil Robles, *No fue posible*, p. 100; *El Debate*, 27 October, 3, 7, 8, 15, 16, 18 November 1933.
115 Buckley, *Life and Death*, pp. 115, 120, 125; Bowers, *My Mission*, p. 55. Cf. the letter from Gil Robles to fund-donors in *CEDA*, 30 December 1933.
116 *El Debate*, 3 November 1933.
117 Bécarud, *La segunda República*, pp. 120–4; Gil Robles, *No fue posible*, pp. 102–5; Ronald Fraser, *In Hiding* (London, 1972), p. 114; *El Socialista*, 25 November 1933.
118 *El Socialista*, 26, 28 November, 1 December 1933; José Tomás Valverde, *Memorias de un alcalde* (Madrid, 1961), pp. 139–47.

3 SOCIAL DEMOCRACY AND SOCIAL CONFLICT

1 *El Socialista*, 31 March 1931; Zapatero, *De los Ríos*, p. 89.
2 Nigel Townson, 'The Collapse of the Centre: The Radical Republican Party during the Spanish Second Republic', unpublished Ph.D thesis, University of London, 1991, pp. 5–13.
3 Zapatero, *De los Ríos*, p. 90.
4 Largo Caballero, *Mis recuerdos*, p. 117; Vidarte, *Cortes Constituyentes*, p. 22.
5 *El Sol*, 24 May 1931.
6 Coca, *Anti-Caballero*, p. 31; Cordero, *Socialistas*, pp. 93–6.
7 Coca, *Anti-Caballero*, pp. 31–2; Juan-Simeón Vidarte, *El bienio negro y la insurrección de Asturias* (Barcelona, 1978), p. 112.
8 Javier Bueno, *El Estado socialista: nueva interpretación del comunismo* (Madrid, 1931), pp. 9–13.
9 Gabriel Morón, *La ruta del socialismo en España* (Madrid, 1932), pp. 24–35.
10 UGT, *Memoria y orden del día del XVII congreso, que se celebrará en Madrid los días 14 y siguientes de octubre de 1932* (Madrid, 1932), p. 61; *El Obrero de la Tierra*, 10, 17 September 1932; Malefakis, *Agrarian Reform*, p. 292.
11 Franciso Largo Caballero, *Posibilismo socialista en la democracia* (Madrid, 1933), p. 16.
12 Cordero, *Socialista*, pp. 343–5; Besteiro, interview in *El Sol*, 3 June 1931.
13 Enrique López Sevilla, *El Partido Socialista Obrero Español en las Cortes Constituyentes de la Segunda República* (Mexico City, 1969), pp. 12–14.
14 *El Debate*, 22 April 1931.
15 Ministerio de Trabajo y Previsión Social, *La crisis agraria andaluza de 1930–31* (Madrid, 1931).
16 Ramón Tamames, *La República, la era de Franco* (Madrid, 1973), pp. 56–66; *BUGT*, December 1931. On the structural deflationary process in Spanish agriculture, Juan Hernández Andreu, *Depresión económica en España, 1925–1934* (Madrid, 1980), ch. 2; Alejandro López López, *El boicot de las derechas a las reformas de la segunda República* (Madrid, 1984), pp. 67–87.
17 Malefakis, *Agrarian Reform*, pp. 166–71; *BUGT*, May, June 1931.
18 Azaña, diary entries for 4, 21 July 1932, *Obras*, vol. IV, pp. 10, 36.
19 *El Sol*, 30 July 1931.
20 Manuel Ramírez Jiménez, *Los grupos de presión en la segunda República española* (Madrid, 1969), pp. 118–24; Mercedes Cabrera, *La patronal ante la II República: organizaciones y estrategia (1931–1936)* (Madrid, 1983), pp. 33–71, 152–65.
21 Extremely detailed tables are provided by Pascual Carrión, *Los latifundios en España* (Madrid, 1932), esp. facing p. 324.
22 *El Debate*, 8 May, 3 October, 1 December 1931; Azaña, diary entries for 5

August, 22 September 1931, *Obras*, vol. IV, pp. 63, 140; the speeches by PSOE deputies Antonio Marcos Escudero (Huelva), Antonio García Prieto (Málaga), Tomás Alvarez Angulo (Jaén) and Juan-Simeón Vidarte (Badajoz) in *DSCC*, 11, 24 September, 1, 23 October, 4 November 1931.

23 *El Debate*, 22 July, 23 September, 1 November 1931; *El Pueblo Católico* (Jaén), 27, 28 July 1931; Azaña, diary entry for 28 October 1931, *Obras*, vol. IV, p. 203.

24 *El Debate*, 23, 24 June; *ABC*, 12, 24, 28 June 1931; Townson, 'Collapse', pp. 30–7; Octavio Ruiz Manjón, *El Partido Republicano Radical 1908–1936* (Madrid, 1976), pp. 186–91.

25 *El Debate*, 26 June 1931.

26 Coca, *Anti-Caballero*, p. 44.

27 *El Sol*, 1 July 1931; *El Socialista*, 12 July 1931; PSOE, *Convocatoria . . . XIII congreso*, pp. 126–35; López Sevilla, *PSOE*, pp. 20–1; Morón, *Ruta del socialismo*, pp. 39–48; Juliá, pp. 111–21.

28 Azaña, in his diary entry for 4 August 1931 (*Obras*, vol. IV, p. 60), was worried that 400 million pesetas had been withdrawn from the Banco Hispano-Americano and that the stock exchange was being artificially maintained. See also *El Liberal*, 2 June 1931.

29 *El Socialista*, 13 June 1931.

30 Cf. Luis Araquistain, 'Los socialistas en el primer bienio', *Leviatán*, no. 18, October–November 1935, p. 25, where he emphasises the difficulty they found in putting reforms into practice.

31 Santullano, 'Las organizaciones', p. 261.

32 *El Socialista*, 9 July 1931; Coca, *Anti-Caballero*, pp. 41–2; Munis, *Jalones*, pp. 73–5.

33 The best account of the strike is by José Manuel Macarro Vera, *La utopía revolucionaria: Sevilla en la segunda República* (Seville, 1985), pp. 147–60; Maura, *Así cayó*, pp. 278–87; Azaña, diary entry for 21 July 1931, *Obras*, vol. IV, p. 37.

34 *DSCC*, 28, 29 July 1931.

35 'El Anticristo sindicalista', '¿Porqué hay tantas huelgas?' and 'Contra el abuso de la huelga', in *El Sol*, 18, 21, 24 July 1931; each reprinted the following day in *El Socialista*. On the strike-breaking role of the UGT, see L. Nicolas, 'L'Union Générale des Travailleurs', *La Révolution Proletarienne*, no. 120, October 1931, reprinted in L. Nicolas, *A travers les révolutions espagnoles* (Paris, 1972), pp. 59–60.

36 Azaña, diary entries for 4, 7 August, 22 September 1931, *Obras*, vol. IV, pp. 60–2, 68–70, 140–5; Prieto, *Convulsiones*, vol. I, pp. 101–6; Morón, *Ruta del socialismo*, pp. 136–41; Marta Bizcarrondo, 'La crisis socialista en la segunda República', *Revista del Instituto de Ciencias Sociales*, no. 21 (1973), p. 74; *DSCC*, 5, 26 August 1931.

37 Manuel Buenacasa, *La CNT, los 'treinta' y la FAI* (Barcelona, 1933), pp. 20–32; John Brademas, *Anarco-sindicalismo y revolución en España 1930–1937* (Barcelona, 1974), pp. 70–86; Eulalia Vega, *Anarquistas y sindicalistas durante la segunda República: la CNT y los sindicatos de oposición en el país valenciano* (Valencia, 1987), pp. 88–95, 145–8.

38 *DSCC*, 27 August, 3, 8, 16 September, 1, 6, 13, 14 October 1931; Jiménez de Asúa, *Anécdotas de las Constituyentes*, pp. 30–8.

39 *El Socialista*, 8 August, 18, 19, 23 November 1931; *El Sol*, 8, 12, 15 September 1931.

40 *El Socialista*, 17 November 1931; Andrade, *Burocracia*, pp. 244–7; declarations

by Largo in *Avance* (Oviedo), the newly founded SOMA daily, 24 November 1931.

41 Coca, *Anti-Caballero*, pp. 52–3; Vidarte, *Cortes Constituyentes*, pp. 235–45.

42 Azaña, diary entries for 30 October, 16, 17, 21, 30 November, 4 December 1931, *Obras*, vol. IV, pp. 207, 231–3, 240–2, 251, 260.

43 *Avance*, 6, 8, 10, 15, 16 December 1931.

44 Actas de la Comisión Ejecutiva del PSOE, 12 November 1931; *El Socialista*, 17, 25 November; Juliá, *Azaña*, pp. 143–4.

45 *El Socialista*, 5, 11, 13 December 1931; *Avance*, 25 November, 27 December 1931.

46 *El Pueblo Católico*, 21 August 1931. For a recent account of patronal reaction in Jaén, see Francisco Cobo Romero, *Labradores, campesinos y jornaleros: protesta social y diferenciación interna del campesinado jiennense en los orígenes de la guerra civil (1931–1936)* (Cordoba, 1992), pp. 295–310.

47 This account is based on the transcript of the trial of the villagers, Luis Jiménez de Asúa et al., *Castilblanco* (Madrid, 1933). See also Vidarte, *Cortes Constituyentes*, pp. 294–308. For a recent reconstruction, see Jesús Vicente Chamorro, *Año nuevo, año viejo en Castilblanco* (Madrid, 1985), pp. 49–74.

48 *El Socialista*, 2, 5 January 1932; *Avance*, 3, 5 January 1932; *ABC*, 1, 2, 3, 5 January 1932; *DSCC*, 5 January 1931; Arrarás, *República*, vol. I, pp. 287–9.

49 Azaña, diary entries for 30 November, 14 December 1931, 5 January 1932, *Obras*, vol. IV, pp. 251, 275, 294–5.

50 *El Socialista*, 6, 7, 13 January 1932; *Avance*, 6, 7, 12, 13, 19 January 1932; *DSCC*, 6 January 1932; Vidarte, *Cortes Constituyentes*, pp. 306, 601; Francisco Bermejo Martín, *La IIª República en Logroño: elecciones y contexto político* (Logroño, 1984), pp. 255–6.

51 *El Socialista*, 23 January 1932; *Avance* 23, 24, 26 January, 12 February 1932; *El Obrero de la Tierra*, 23 January 1932.

52 *Avance*, 5 April 1931; Mariano Pérez Galán, *La enseñanza en la segunda República española* (Madrid, 1975), pp. 332–3.

53 *BUGT*, January 1932.

54 *BUGT*, May 1932.

55 *El Obrero de la Tierra*, 30 January 1932; *La Mañana* (Jaén), 1, 6, 7 April 1932.

56 *El Obrero de la Tierra*, 5, 13, 20 February, 5, 12, 26 March 1932.

57 *El Obrero de la Tierra*, 2 April 1932.

58 *La Mañana*, 12 April 1932.

59 *La Mañana*, 9 July 1932; *El Socialista*, 15 July 1932; Ramos Oliveira, *Nosotros*, p. 68.

60 *Boletín de Ministerio de Trabajo y Previsión Social*, April 1933; Bizcarrondo, 'La crisis socialista', p. 63.

61 It would be superfluous to discuss the delays in the elaboration of the agrarian reform, since the subject is fully dealt with in the admirable study of Malefakis (*Agrarian Reform*, ch. 7). See also *El Obrero de la Tierra*, 11, 25 June 1932.

62 *Avance*, 6, 16 April, 1, 12, 13 May, 12 June 1932.

63 *BUGT*, July 1932.

64 *El Socialista*, 11 November 1931, 15 July 1932.

65 *El Pueblo Católico*, 4 May 1933.

66 Azaña, diary entries for 11, 12, 17, 20 July 1932, *Obras*, vol. IV, pp. 435–43; *DSCC*, 20 July 1932.

67 *El Obrero de la Tierra*, 24 September, 1 October 1932.

68 *El Adelanto* (Salamanca), 1, 4 October 1932.

69 *DSCC*, 18, 21 October 1932; *El Adelanto*, 8 October 1932, reprints the full *bases de trabajo* which provoked the Bloque's circular.

70 *El Obrero de la Tierra*, 8 October 1932.

71 This estimate of living standards is based on the monthly indexes published throughout the Republic in the *Boletín del Ministerio de Trabajo y Previsión Social*. Figures are remarkably stable for the entire period; they are not coloured by the presence of a Socialist at the head of the ministry. The figure of thirty-five pesetas allows nothing for clothing, housing or household requisites, and is calculated on the basis of just one meal per day.

72 This was the belief of the Bloque Agrario of Jaén; see *La Mañana*, 1 October 1932. See also *El Adelanto*, 19 October 1932.

73 *DSCC*, 20 October 1932; a series of interviews held by the author in Madrid in the winter of 1970–1 with the Marqués de Gracia Real, a landowner from Ledesma (Salamanca).

74 *Avance*, 2, 6, 8, 13, 15, 17, 18 September 1932.

75 *El Socialista*, 8, 9 October 1932; Lamo, *Besteiro*, pp. 86–7; Saborit, *Besteiro*, pp. 227–8; Vidarte, *Cortes Constituyentes*, pp. 485–93; Coca, *Anti-Caballero*, pp. 62–5.

76 Andrade, *Burocracia*, pp. 102, 159.

77 *El Sol*, 23 October 1932; *El Socialista*, 23, 25 October 1932; Coca, *Anti-Caballero*, pp. 66–70; Lamo, *Besteiro*, pp. 87–8; Vidarte, *Cortes Constituyentes*, pp. 495–7; Amaro del Rosal, *Historia de la UGT de España 1901–1939*, 2 vols (Barcelona 1977), vol. I, pp. 350–2.

78 *Avance*, 26 January, 27 February, 10 March, 19 April, 2, 3, 7 August 1932. On this point, see also Macarro Vera, 'Causas de la radicalización socialista'.

79 *El Obrero de la Tierra*, 15, 22 October 1932.

80 *Tierra y Trabajo* (Salamanca), 30 November 1932. Manso was to be horribly murdered by local rightists in the early days of the Civil War. Playing on the double meaning of his name (*manso* means tame bull), they killed him using the ritual of the bullring. Sánchez, *Maurín*, pp. 44, 93; Guillermo Cabanellas, *La guerra de los mil días*, 2 vols (Buenos Aires, 1973), vol. II, pp. 860, 1227.

81 Azaña, diary entry for 4 December 1931, *Obras*, vol. IV, p. 260.

82 *Tierra y Trabajo*, 9, 20 December 1932; Arrarás, *República*, vol. II, p. 76.

83 *Avance*, 11, 14, 18, 19, 23 October, 14, 15, 20 November, 8, 9, 10, 11, 13, 14, 15, 16 December 1932.

84 Coca, *Anti-Caballero*, pp. 71–2; Arrarás, *República*, vol. II. p. 77–8.

85 Ramón J. Sender, *Viaje a la aldea del crimen* (Madrid, 1934), pp. 33–42, 70–130; Francisco Guerra, *Casas Viejas: apuntes de la tragedia* (Jerez, 1933); Gérald Brey and Jacques Maurice, *Historia y leyenda de Casas Viejas* (Bilbao, 1976), pp. 65–75; Jerome R. Mintz, *The Anarchists of Casas Viejas* (Chicago, 1982), pp. 189–225; Antonio Ramos Espejo, *Después de Casas Viejas* (Barcelona, 1984), pp. 11–25.

86 *El Debate*, 15 January 1932.

87 Azaña, diary entry for 13 January 1933, *Memorias*, p. 208.

88 *DSCC*, 3, 23, 24 February, 2, 3 March 1933; *El Debate*, 24 February 1933.

89 Azaña, diary entries for 19, 21 February, 1, 3 March 1933, *Memorias*, p. 210, and *Obras*, vol. IV, pp. 447–55.

90 Azaña, diary entry for 6 March 1933, *Obras*, vol. IV, p. 460.

91 Azaña, diary entry for 14 April 1933, *Obras*, vol. IV, pp. 484–5; Vidarte, *Cortes Constituyentes*, pp. 522, 532.

92 There is considerable debate over the interpretation of these figures. See *El Debate*, 25 April 1933; *El Socialista*, 26, 27 April 1933; Azaña, diary entry for

30 April 1933, *Obras*, vol. IV, pp. 501–3; *DSCC*, 25, 26, 28 April 1933; Montero, *La CEDA*, vol. II, pp. 279–85; Arrarás, *República*, vol. II, pp. 116–17; Jackson, *Republic*, p. 104.
93 Azaña, diary entry for 16 May 1933, *Obras*, vol. IV, p. 530.
94 *ABC*, 26 January 1933; *El Obrero de la Tierra*, 19 November 1932, 14, January 1933.
95 *Boletín del Instituto de Reforma Agraria*, March 1933; *El Obrero de la Tierra*, 28 January 1933.
96 *Región* (Cáceres), 24 February 1933; *El Pueblo Católico*, 14 March 1933; *ABC*, 26 March 1933; *La Mañana*, 21, 27 January, 3, 18 February, 5 April 1933; *El Obrero de la Tierra*, 14 January, 4 March 1933; *El Socialista*, 21 January, 20 April, 1 July 1933.
97 See above, Chapter 2.
98 *El Socialista*, 26 March, 4 July 1933; *La Unión Ferroviaria*, August 1933; Rosal, *Historia de la UGT*, vol. I, p. 291.
99 *El Sol*, 15, 19 July 1933. Bizcarrondo, in 'La crisis socialista', pp. 64–5, points out that the high point of the employers' mobilisation was only a few days before Largo publicly demonstrated his adoption of a radical line. Vidarte, *El bienio negro*, p. 188, comments on the Araquistain–Largo Caballero correspondence.
100 *El Socialista*, 25 July 1933.
101 Saborit, *Besteiro*, pp. 237–40; Coca, *Anti-Caballero*, p. 101.
102 Indalecio Prieto, *Discursos fundamentales* (Madrid, 1975), pp. 160–80, and *Convulsiones*, vol. III, pp. 160–5.
103 *El Socialista*, 13 August 1933. The complete text was published as *Posibilismo socialista en la democracia*. Cf. *El Debate*, 15 August 1933.
104 *BUGT*, August–September 1933; *El Obrero de la Tierra*, 12, 20 August, 9 September 1933; *El Debate*, 22, 23, 29 August 1933.
105 Cf. the editorial comment on Largo's Torrelodones speech in *El Debate*, 15 August 1933. For a different interpretation of the radicalisation of Largo Caballero, see Aviva and Isaac Aviv, 'Ideology and Political Patronage: Workers and Working Class Movements in Republican Madrid, 1931–4', *European Studies Review*, vol. 11, no. 4, October 1981; and Marta Bizcarrondo, 'Democracia y revolución en la estrategia socialista de la II República', *Estudios de Historia Social*, nos 16–17, January–June 1981, esp. pp. 255–9.
106 Malefakis, *Agrarian Reform*, pp. 268–73; Madariaga, *Spain*, pp. 418–20.
107 *El Debate*, 19 September 1933; *El Obrero de la Tierra*, 16, 23, 30 September 1933; *BUGT*, November 1933.
108 *El Debate*, 4, 17, 25 August, 2, 15 September; *El Pueblo Católico*, 29 March 1933.
109 *BUGT*, November 1933.
110 *El Socialista*, 3 October 1933.
111 *DSCC*, 2, 3 October 1933.
112 *El Socialista*, 8 October 1933; Marcelino Domingo, *La revolución de octubre* (Barcelona, 1935), pp. 54–8; Vidarte, *Cortes Constituyentes*, pp. 662–73; Azaña, diary entry for 1 July 1937, *Obras*, vol. IV, 646–8. The technicality hinged on the fact that the Socialists had previously moved a motion of censure against other members of the cabinet, something they felt precluded their joining it. On the reactions of the local PSOE organisations, see Vidarte, *El bienio negro*, p. 21, and the Actas de la Comisión Ejecutiva del PSOE, 24, 25, 27, 31 October, 22, 29 November 1933.
113 Bowers, *My Mission*, p. 42.
114 Domingo, *La revolución*, p. 9.

115 *El Debate*, 12, 17, 18, 24 October, 7, 17, 18 November 1933.

116 *El Socialista*, 7, 14, 15 November 1933.

117 *BUGT*, December 1933; *El Obrero de la Tierra*, 30 September, 7, 14 October, 2, 23 December 1933; Ramos Oliveira, *Politics*, pp. 490–1; Joaquín Maurín, *Hacia la segunda revolución* (Barcelona, 1935), pp. 32, 52–3; Bécarud, *La segunda República*, pp. 124–5; Zapatero, *De los Ríos*, p. 105.

118 Prieto, *Discursos fundamentales*, pp. 168–9; Bécarud, *La segunda República*, pp. 123–4; Brenan, *Labyrinth*, p. 266. For a feminist view on this question, see Clara Campoamor, *El voto femenino y yo* (Madrid, 1936), pp. 245–64.

119 Domingo, *La revolución*, pp. 95–7; Bécarud, *La segunda República*, pp. 125–8, 136–7. The composition of the Cortes was as follows: PSOE, 58; left republicans, 38; Radicals, 104; Lliga, 24; Basque Nationalists, 12; conservative Republicans, 41; CEDA, 115; Agrarians, 32; Carlists, 21; Renovación Española and other monarchists, 23. The distribution of votes is discussed in Chapter 4.

4 THE POLITICS OF REPRISAL

1 In a speech on 14 January 1934, Largo Caballero adopted some of the ideas of Otto Bauer; see Francisco Largo Caballero, *Discursos a los trabajadores* (Madrid, 1934), p. 144. On the influence of Bauer, see also Marta Bizcarrondo, 'Análisis económico y socialismo en la segunda República', *Estudios de Historia Social*, no. 14, July–September 1980, p. 242.

2 Unemployment figures up to the end of 1934 are as follows: June 1932, 446, 263; August 1933, 588,174; December 1933, 618,947; April 1934, 703,814; December 1934, 667,898 (*Boletín del Ministerio de Trabajo y Provisión Social*, January 1935). See also Malefakis, *Agrarian Reform*, p. 288; Balcells, *Crisis económica*, pp. 52–63.

3 Figures for union membership refer to June 1932 (*BUGT*, July 1932, supplement). The factional loyalty of the various union presidents has been assessed from their statements at the meetings of the National Committee of the UGT, reported in *BUGT*.

4 Vidarte, *El bienio negro*, pp. 109–10; appendix to Largo Caballero, *Discursos*, pp. 163–6. It is difficult to determine with complete certainty the party loyalties of individual deputies in the Republican Cortes. Cf. Juan J. Linz, 'The Party System of Spain: Past and Future', in Seymour M. Lipset and Stein Rokkan, editors, *Party Systems and Voter Alignments* (New York, 1976), p. 260; Jesús Lozano, *La segunda República: imágenes, cronología y documentos* (Barcelona, 1973), pp. 445–62; Gil Robles, *Discursos*, appendix VI, pp. 789–834.

5 Ramos Oliveira, *Politics*, pp. 489–91; Vidarte, *El bienio negro*, p. 32; Margarita Nelken, *Porqué hicimos la revolución* (Barcelona, 1936), pp. 67–9.

6 See *El Debate*, 21, 22 November, 5 December 1933; Gil Robles, *No fue posible*, pp. 102–5. On Asturias, see Bernardo Díaz Nosty, *La comuna asturiana* (Bilbao, 1974), pp. 52–60.

7 *DSC*, 19 December 1933. The Socialist Youth regarded this as a fascist speech; see *Renovación*, 23 December 1933.

8 *DSC*, 20 December 1933.

9 Cortés Cavanillas, *Gil Robles*, pp. 139–41.

10 Alejandro Lerroux, *La pequeña historia* (Buenos Aires, 1945), p. 212; Robinson, *Origins*, p. 152; Pabón, *Cambó*, vol. II, part 2, p. 290. This compares strangely

with Gil Robles's own open admission of his tactical aims in *No fue posible*, pp. 106–7.

11 *El Debate*, 25 August 1931; *El Socialista*, 26, 28 November, 1 December 1933; *El Pueblo Católico*, 4 May 1933. The other rightist daily in Jaén, *La Mañana*, indiscriminately supported both the Radicals and the CEDA.

12 *El Socialista*, 11 November 1931, 9 May 1934; José Rodríguez de la Peña, *Los aventureros de la política; Alejandro Lerroux* (Madrid, n.d. [1916]), *passim*; Largo Caballero, *Discursos*, pp. 54–5, and *Mis recuerdos*, p. 121.

13 Jesús Pabón, *Palabras en la oposición* (Seville, 1935), p. 196.

14 Azaña, diary entry for 12 July 1932, *Obras*, vol. IV, p. 435.

15 Azaña, diary entry for 29 January 1932, *Obras*, vol. IV, p. 318; Pabón, *Cambó*, vol. II, part 2, p. 297.

16 Azaña, diary entry for 28 June 1937, *Obras*, vol. IV, pp. 635–6; Buckley, *Life and Death*, pp. 186–7. The level of venality was eventually to cause some unease within the Radical Party. Cf. the two letters reprinted in César Jalón, *Memorias políticas* (Madrid, 1973), pp. 214–18.

17 *El Debate*, 6, 7, 22 December 1933; *DSC*, 19 December 1933.

18 Actas de la Comisión Ejecutiva del PSOE, 22 November 1933, Fundación Pablo Iglesias, (henceforth FPI) AH–20–2; Francisco Largo Caballero, *Escritos de la República*, edited by Santos Juliá Díaz (Madrid, 1985), pp. 40–3. In his earlier text, written without access to documents, *Mis recuerdos*, p. 133, Largo Caballero places this plot in the home of the exiled Calvo Sotelo and so confuses it with one in late 1934. Cf. José Bullejos, *España en la segunda República* (Mexico City, 1967), p. 143.

19 *BUGT*, December 1933; *El Obrero de la Tierra*, 23, 30 December 1933, 6, 13 January 1934; *El Socialista*, 14, 23 January 1934. Cf. Vidarte, *El bienio negro*, p. 110.

20 *El Socialista*, 26, 28, 30 November, 1, 2, 8, 19, 21 December 1933, 13, 14 January 1934.

21 Luis Araquistain, *El derrumbamiento del socialismo alemán* (Madrid, n.d. [1933]).

22 María Teresa de León, *Memoria de la melancolía* (Buenos Aires, 1970), p. 266.

23 Actas de la Comisión Ejecutiva del PSOE, 25 November 1933, FPI/AH–20–2; *BUGT*, December 1933, January 1934; Largo Caballero, *Escritos*, pp. 42–8, and *Mis recuerdos*, pp. 131–3. Cf. Vidarte, *El bienio negro*, pp. 110–11.

24 A point made by Gil Robles, in an interview with the author in Madrid in February 1973, in defence of his own admiration for fascism. See also Javier Jiménez Campo, *El fascismo en la crisis de la II República* (Madrid, 1979), pp. 70–84; and Montero, *La CEDA*, vol. II, pp. 241–68.

25 Enrique Montañés, *Anarcosindicalismo y cambio político: Zaragoza, 1930–1936* (Zaragoza, 1989), pp. 98–100; José María Azpíroz Pascual, *Poder político y conflictividad social en Huesca durante la II República* (Huesca, 1993), pp. 161–9; Enrique Pradas Martínez, *La segunda República y La Rioja (1931–1936)* (Logroño, 1982), pp. 139–54; Enrique Pradas Martínez, editor, *8 de diciembre de 1933: insurrección anarquista en La Rioja* (Logroño, 1983), *passim*; Salvador Forner Muñoz, *Industrialización y movimiento obrero: Alicante 1923–1936* (Valencia, 1982), pp. 354–7; Manuel Pérez Yruela, *La conflictividad campesina en la provincia de Córdoba 1931–1936* (Madrid, 1979), pp. 169–71; Francisco Moreno Gómez, *La República y la guerra civil en Córdoba*, vol. I (Córdoba, 1982), pp. 244–8; Macarro, *La utopía*, p. 368; Arrarás, *República*, vol. II, pp. 251–7; Peirats, *CNT*, vol. I, pp. 77–80; César M. Lorenzo, *Les Anarchistes espagnols et le pouvoir* (Paris, 1969), pp. 79–80.

26 *El Socialista*, 12 December 1933; Largo Caballero, *Escritos*, pp. 48–50. The

minutes of the session of the National Committee of the UGT are reprinted in full in Amaro del Rosal, *1934: el movimiento revolucionario de octubre* (Madrid, 1983), pp. 35–93. Besteiro's report on the joint meeting is on pp. 35–6. Prieto's speech in the Cortes, *DSC*, 12 December 1933.

27 Rosal, *1934*, pp. 36–93.

28 *BUGT*, January 1934; Rosal, *1934*, pp. 93–150.

29 Azaña, diary entry for 1 July 1937, *Obras*, vol. IV, pp. 649–50; Vidarte, *El bienio negro*, p. 97; Cipriano de Rivas-Cherif, *Retrato de un desconocido: vida de Manuel Azaña (seguido por el epistolario de Manuel Azaña con Cipriano de Rivas Cherif de 1921 a 1937)* (Barcelona, 1980), p. 294.

30 *Renovación*, 20 January 1934; *El Obrero de la Tierra*, 6, 13, 20 January 1934.

31 For short biographies of Martínez de Velasco and Cid Ruiz Zorrilla, see Lozano, *República*, pp. 420, 431–2. On the Agrarian Party, see Montero, *La CEDA*, vol. I, pp. 158, 182–5, 387–91, 418; Alfred Mendizábal, *Aux origines d'une tragédie: la politique espagnole de 1923 à 1936* (Paris, n.d. [1937?]) p. 191.

32 *El Debate*, 27 December 1933, 26 January 1934; *El Socialista*, 23, 25 January 1934.

33 *El Debate*, 27 January, 8, 25 February 1934; *Renovación*, 6 January 1934; *El Socialista*, 26 January, 2 February 1934; *La Mañana*, 17, 19, 20 January 1934.

34 Largo Caballero, *Discursos*, pp. 134–62.

35 Rosal, *1934*, pp. 151–87; Largo Caballero, *Mis recuerdos*, pp. 134–5; Coca, *Anti-Caballero*, p. 133.

36 Largo Caballero, *Escritos*, pp. 64–75; Dolores Ibárruri et al., *Guerra y revolución en España*, 4 vols (Moscow, 1967–77), vol. I, pp. 52–7, reprints all three projects in full; Ramos Oliveira, *Politics*, pp. 507–8; Santos Juliá Díaz, 'Los socialistas y el escenario de la futura revolución', in Germán Ojeda, editor, *Octubre 1934: cincuenta años para la reflexión* (Madrid, 1985), p. 122.

37 Largo Caballero, *Escritos*, pp. 76–141; *El Socialista*, 25, 26, 28, 30 January 1934; *BUGT*, February 1934; *El Obrero de la Tierra*, 3 February 1934; Rosal, *1934*, pp. 188–200; Coca, *Anti-Caballero*, pp. 137–42; Juliá, 'Los socialistas y el escenario de la futura revolución', pp. 123–7. Rosal, *1934*, p. 200, and Largo Caballero, *Escritos*, p. 86, give slightly differing compositions of the revolutionary liaison committee. For the reasons for considering Rosal to be more accurate, see Santos Juliá Díaz, *Historia del socialismo español (1931–1939)* (Barcelona, 1989) pp. 101–2.

38 Rosal, *1934*, pp. 200–56.

39 *DSC*, 7 February 1934; *La Mañana*, 16 January 1934, had denounced such robberies as 'collective kleptomania'.

40 *El Debate*, 14–17 February 1934; *El Socialista*, 13, 18, 20 February, 4, 7 March 1934; *BUGT*, February, March 1934; *Leviatán*, no. 2, June 1934, was entirely devoted to contemporary fascism and included articles by Austrian socialist survivors. On Largo's conversations, Vidarte, *El bienio negro*, p. 111.

41 *DSC*, 4 January 1934; Gil Robles, *No fue posible*, pp. 111–12; Mendizábal, *Aux origines*, pp. 214–15; *El Socialista*, 2 January 1934; *El Sol*, 23 March 1934. Cambó complained of Gil Robles's doubtful republicanism; see Pabón, *Cambó*, pp. 307–8.

42 *El Debate*, 20, 21, 22 February 1934.

43 *El Debate*, 20, 28 February, 2 March 1934; Lerroux, *La pequeña historia*, pp. 216–38; Diego Martínez Barrio, *Memorias* (Barcelona, 1983) pp. 217–28; Juan Avilés Farré, *La izquierda burguesa en la II República* (Madrid, 1985), pp. 237–9; Manuel Ramírez Jiménez, 'La formación de la Unión Republicana y su papel en las elecciones de 1936', in Manuel Ramírez Jiménez, *Las reformas de la IIª República* (Madrid, 1977), pp. 127–8; Gil Robles, *No fue*

posible, pp. 116–19. Monge, *Acción Popular*, p. 898, shows that the breaking up of the Radical Party was a deliberate CEDA tactic.

44 Azaña, *Obras*, vol. II, pp. 911–44.

45 *El Liberal*, 6 February 1934.

46 *Renovación*, 10, 17 February, 8 March 1934; *El Sol*, 20, 21 April 1934.

47 *El Debate*, 8 March 1934; *El Socialista*, 11, 13, 14, 15 March 1934; *ABC*, 14, 15, 16 March 1934; Rafael Salazar Alonso, *Bajo el signo de la revolución* (Madrid, 1935), pp. 50–73; Torcuato Luca de Tena, *Papeles para la pequeña y la gran historia: memorias de mi padre y mías* (Barcelona, 1991), pp. 167–72. On the changing nature of strikes and CNT–UGT rivalry, see Juliá, *Madrid, 1931–1934*, pp. 191–381.

48 *El Debate*, 2, 8, 10, 11, 22, 27 March 1934; *El Socialista*, 29 March 1934; *DSC*, 8 March 1934; Lerroux, *La pequeña historia*, pp. 235–9.

49 Gil Robles, *No fue posible*, pp. 119–22; Lerroux, *La pequeña historia*, pp. 247–57; *DSC*, 20 April 1934; *El Debate*, 12, 21 April 1934; *El Socialista*, 12 April 1934. *Leviatán*, no. 1, May 1934, saw it as the official glorification of 10 August. The American Ambassador thought that the amnesty legalised treason (Bowers, *My Mission*, p. 74).

50 *El Debate*, 3, 10, 17 April 1934; Arrarás, *República*, vol. II, pp. 305–6.

51 Munis, *Jalones*, p. 114.

52 Cf. Blinkhorn, *Carlism*, p. 158.

53 *El Debate*, 21, 22, 24 April 1934; *El Socialista*, 22, 24 April 1934; Monge, *Acción Popular*, pp. 253–304; Buckley, *Life and Death*, pp. 126–7.

54 Herbert R. Southworth, *Antifalange* (Paris, 1967), p. 78; Gil Robles, *No fue posible*, pp. 190–1; Cortés Cavanillas, *Gil Robles*, pp. 143, 180; José Antonio Primo de Rivera, *Obras*, 4th edition (Madrid, 1966), p. 124.

55 Lerroux, *La pequeña historia*, pp. 256–61; Azaña, *Obras*, vol. IV, p. 717; Ruiz Manjón, *El Partido*, pp. 424–38.

56 De la Cierva, *La guerra civil*, p. 483.

57 *DSC*, 17, 23 May 1934. Ruiz Alonso was later to play a key role in the Nationalist repression of Granada. See Ian Gibson, *The Death of Lorca* (London, 1973), *passim*.

58 *El Debate*, 26 May 1934; *El Socialista*, 24, 25 May 1934; Salazar Alonso, *Bajo el signo*, pp. 122–7; Cobo Romero, *Labradores*, pp. 410–20.

59 *El Debate*, 6, 10 May 1934; *El Obrero de la Tierra*, 17 February 1934; Brenan, *Labyrinth*, p. 275.

60 *El Obrero de la Tierra*, 24 February, 3, 24, 31 March, 14 April 1934.

61 *El Obrero de la Tierra*, 31 March 1934.

62 On 31 July 1934 the National Committee of the UGT met to hold a post-mortem on the defeated strike. The above account derives from the proceedings of the meeting (*BUGT*, August 1934). On the Communist offer, see Vidarte, *El bienio negro*, pp. 152–4.

63 *El Socialista*, 6 May 1934; *ABC*, 2 May 1934; *El Sol*, 2 May 1934; *El Obrero de la Tierra*, 21 April, 5 May 1934.

64 *El Obrero de la Tierra*, 19 May 1934.

65 *El Obrero de la Tierra*, 26 May 1934; Vidarte, *El bienio negro*, p. 155.

66 *DSC*, 30 May 1934. Cf. Vidarte, *El bienio negro*, pp. 156–9.

67 *La Mañana*, 6, 8–12 June 1934, shows the thoroughness of the stoppage. See also *El Socialista*, 31 May, 1, 2, 3, 7, 8, 13, 28, 29, 30 June 1934; *El Debate*, 30, 31 May, 6, 7, 10 June 1934; *DSC*, 7, 14 June 1934; Cobo Romero, *Labradores*, pp. 421–34; Pérez Yruela, *La conflictividad*, pp. 190–6; Moreno Gómez, *Córdoba*, pp. 268–79; José Antonio Alarcón Caballero, *El movimiento obrero en Granada en la II República (1931–1936)* (Granada, 1990), pp. 409–12; Macarro,

La utopía, pp. 388–93; Fernando Pascual Cevallos, *Luchas agrarias en Sevilla durante la segunda República* (Seville, 1983), pp. 91–3; Paloma Biglino Campos, *El socialismo español y la cuestión agraria 1890–1936* (Madrid, 1986), pp. 442–67; Jackson, *Republic*, pp. 134–9. More critical accounts of the FNTT are to be found in Malefakis, *Agrarian Reform*, pp. 335–40, and Salazar Alonso, *Bajo el signo*, p. 141 ff.

68 Salazar Alonso admired Gil Robles and was enthusiastic about CEDA plans. The admiration was mutual. See Salazar Alonso, *Bajo el signo*, pp. 75–7; Gil Robles, *No fue posible*, pp. 120–3.

69 Francesc Bonamusa, *El Bloc Obrer i Camperol (1930–1932)* (Barcelona, 1974), pp. 275–82, 341–2; Victor Alba, *La Alianza Obrera: historia y análisis de una táctica de unidad en España* (Gijón, 1977), pp. 83–131; Antoni Monreal, *El pensamiento político de Joaquín Maurín* (Barcelona, 1984), pp. 159–77.

70 *El Socialista*, 29 December 1933. Cf. Marta Bizcarrondo, 'De las Alianzas Obreras al Frente Popular', *Estudios de Historia Social*, nos 16–17, January–June 1981, pp. 83–7.

71 Grandizo Munis, 'Hace falta una dirección', *Comunismo*, May 1934; Munis, *Jalones*, pp. 116–24. Socialist hesitancy was justified by Largo Caballero in *BUGT*, June–July 1934.

72 *BUGT*, August 1934.

73 Largo Caballero, *Mis recuerdos*, p. 141.

74 Rosal, *1934*, pp. 207–9; Manuel Tagüeña Lacorte, *Testimonio de dos guerras* (Mexico City, 1973), pp. 61–6; Santos Juliá Díaz, *Historia del socialismo español (1931–1933)* (Barcelona, 1989), pp. 105–6.

75 Peirats, *CNT*, vol. I, pp. 81–9; 'Ignotus' (Manuel Villar), *El anarquismo en la insurreccion de Asturias* (Valencia, 1935), pp. 23–7; Arrarás, *República*, vol. II, pp. 298–9; *Avance*, 1 May 1934. The Caballerista desire to take over the workers' movement through the Alianzas Obreras is evident in Segundo Serrano Poncela, *El Partido Socialista y la conquista del poder* (Barcelona, 1935), as the editorial introduction (pp.xi–xii) points out (see also pp. 149, 193). On the Unió Socialista, see Josep Lluís Martíni Ramos, *Els orígens del Partit Socialista Unificat de Catalunya (1930–1936)* (Barcelona, 1977), pp. 118–29.

76 Leon Trotsky, *The Struggle against Fascism in Germany* (New York, 1971), p. 56. Largo Caballero commented to Vidarte that it was difficult to keep control of the rank and file: Vidarte, *El bienio negro*, p. 111.

77 Pelai Pagés, *El movimiento trotskista en España (1930–1935)* (Barcelona, 1977), *passim*.

78 *Comunismo*, March, September 1934; Leon Trotsky, *La révolution espagnole 1930–1940*, edited by Pierre Broué (Paris, 1975), pp. 252–9; Munis, *Jalones*, p. 122.

79 'Ignotus', *Anarquismo*, pp. 31–9; Maurín, *Segunda revolución*, pp. 145–7; Ramón Alvarez, *Eleuterio Quintanilla* (Mexico City, 1973), pp. 336–7; *Avance*, 15 May 1934. On the long-term formation of class consciousness in Asturias, see Adrian Shubert, *The Road to Revolution in Spain: The Coal Miners of Asturias 1860–1934* (Urbana, Ill., and Chicago, 1987), *passim*.

80 Joaquín Maurín, 'El problema agrario en Cataluña', *Leviatán*, no. 4, August 1934; Alberto Balcells, *El problema agrari a Catalunya* (Barcelona, 1968) pp. 135–214; Pabón, *Cambó*, pp. 340–75.

81 Azaña, *Obras*, vol. II, pp. 902, 977–98; Gil Robles, *No fue posible*, pp. 124–6; *DSC*, 25 June, 4 July 1934; *El Debate*, 13, 19 June, 8 July 1934; *El Socialista*, 2 May, 9, 13, 17 June, 3 July 1934.

82 Vidarte, *El bienio negro*, pp. 113–14, 141, 184–5, 210.

83 Minutes of joint meeting of PSOE and UGT executives, 2 July 1934, reprinted in Largo Caballero, *Escritos*, pp. 111–14.
84 Azaña to Cipriano de Rivas Cherif, 23 July 1934, reprinted in Rivas Cherif, *Retrato de un desconocido*, pp. 647–9; Azaña, *Obras*, vol. IV, pp. 653–4 (where, in his wartime diary, Azaña erroneously gives the date of the meeting as 14 June); Largo Caballero, *Escritos*, pp. 114–15.
85 *El Socialista*, 19, 25, 26, 28 July; Juliá, *Azaña*, p. 339.

5 A BLUFF CALLED

1 Indalecio Prieto, *Discursos en América con el pensamiento puesto en España* (Mexico City, 1944), pp. 102–3.
2 Largo Caballero, *Escritos*, pp. 86–110, 115–41; Rosal, *1934*, pp. 207–33.
3 Largo Caballero, *Escritos*, pp. 143–9; Rosal, *1934*, pp. 233–49; Díaz Nosty, *La comuna asturiana*, pp. 105–7; Indalecio Prieto, 'La noche del Turquesa', in Prieto, *Convulsiones*, vol. I, pp. 109–11; Manuel Grossi, *L'insurrection des Asturies*, 2nd edition (Paris, 1972), p. 57; Salazar Alonso, *Bajo el signo*, pp. 226–7. Manuel Benavides, *La revolución fue así* (Barcelona, 1935), pp. 9–20, gives a vivid picture of the earnest naïvety with which the Socialist Youth went about their preparations.
4 Vidarte, *El bienio negro*, p. 231; speech of Largo Caballero in Barcelona, *El Socialista*, 24 February 1934, cited by Juliá in annotations to Largo Caballero, *Escritos*, p. 150; Juliá, *Historia del socialismo*, pp. 120–1.
5 Azaña, *Obras*, vol. IV, pp. 659–60, and vol. II, pp. 901–44; Vidarte, *El bienio negro*, pp. 98–100.
6 Norman Jones, 'Regionalism and revolution in Catalonia', in Preston, *Revolution and War in Spain*, pp. 102–3.
7 Munis, *Jalones*, p. 129; Serrano Poncela, *El Partido Socialista*, pp. 119–20.
8 *El Debate*, 7–9 September 1934; *El Socialista*, 7 September 1934.
9 Alejandro Valdés, *¡Asturias!* (Valencia, n.d. [1935?]), pp. 16–17; Juan Antonio Sánchez y García Saúco, *La revolución de 1934 en Asturias* (Madrid, 1974), pp. 39–40.
10 *El Debate*, 11 September 1934; *CEDA*, 15 September 1934; *El Socialista*, 11, 20 September 1934; Gil Robles, *No fue posible*, pp. 127–30; Cortés Cavanillas, *Gil Robles*, p. 180.
11 *El Debate*, 28 September 1934; Gil Robles, *No fue posible*, p. 131.
12 *El Sol*, 12 September 1934; Salazar Alonso, *Bajo el signo*, pp. 316–20; Jackson, *Republic*, p. 146.
13 Niceto Alcalá Zamora, *Memorias* (Barcelona, 1977), pp. 519–20; Manuel Ballbé, *Orden público y militarismo en la España contemporánea (1812–1983)* (Madrid, 1983), p. 374.
14 *CEDA*, nos 36–7, December 1934.
15 *El Carbayón*, 18, 23, 29 September 1934.
16 Diego Hidalgo, *¿Por qué fui lanzado del Ministerio de la Guerra? Diez meses de actuación ministerial* (Madrid, 1934), pp. 79–81; Arrarás, *República*, vol. II, pp. 440–1; Ballbé, *Orden público*, p. 374. On the relationship between Diego Hidalgo and Franco, see Paul Preston, *Franco: A Biography* (London, 1993), pp. 96–102.
17 Maximiano García Venero, *El general Fanjul: Madrid en el alzamiento nacional* (Madrid, 1967), p. 196.
18 *DSC*, 4, 7 November 1934.

19 De la Cierva, *La guerra civil*, pp. 302–3, a view apparently based on researches in restricted military archives.

20 Azaña, *Obras*, vol. IV, pp. 667–8.

21 Martínez Barrio, *Memorias*, pp. 249–50; *El Socialista*, 1 August, 2 October 1934; Buckley, *Life and Death*, p. 133. For leftist complaints, see Munis, *Jalones*, pp. 130–3; Andrade, *Burocracia*, pp. 250–63.

22 Largo Caballero to Comité Nacional del PSOE, 1 October 1934, FPI/ AH–22–23; Largo Caballero, *Mis recuerdos*, pp. 146–7; Coca, *Anti-Caballero*, pp. 152–4; Juliá, *Historia del socialismo*, p. 125.

23 *El Debate*, 26, 27, 28 September 1934; *El Socialista*, 3, 4 October 1934; Gil Robles, *Discursos*, pp. 338–43; Gil Robles, *No fue posible*, pp. 134–9; Alcalá Zamora, *Memorias*, pp. 285–6.

24 Coca, *Anti-Caballero*, p. 107, makes the remarkable claim that Anguera's mother was a canonised saint. Cf. Vidarte, *El bienio negro*, p. 233. On Anguera in Barcelona, see Jones, 'Regionalism and revolution', p. 91.

25 On Giménez Fernández, see Javier Tusell and José Calvo, *Giménez Fernández: precursor de la democracia española* (Seville, 1990), *passim*, and, on the crisis of October 1934, pp. 52–6.

26 *El Socialista*, 1 August, 27 September 1934. Cf. Vidarte, *El bienio negro*, p. 238.

27 Díaz Nosty, *La comuna asturiana*, p. 136.

28 Largo Caballero, *Escritos*, pp. 150–8, and *Mis recuerdos*, p. 136; Rosal, *1934*, pp. 257–61; Rosal, *Historia de la UGT*, vol. I, pp. 387, 401–2; Alvarez del Vayo, *The Last Optimist*, pp. 263–6.

29 Antonio Ramos Oliveira, *La revolución española de octubre* (Madrid, 1935), pp. 55–61; Martínez Barrio, *Memorias*, p. 251.

30 See Grossi, *L'insurrection*, pp. 57, 119; José Canel (pseud. José Díaz Fernández), *Octubre rojo en Asturias* (Madrid, 1935), pp. 31, 43; Vidarte, *El bienio negro*, pp. 267–85, 334.

31 Munis, *Jalones*, pp. 130–40; Maurín, *Segunda revolución*, pp. 144–67; testimony of Madrid CNT secretary, Miguel González Inestal, to the author; Enrique Castro Delgado, *Hombres made in Moscú* (Barcelona, 1965), pp. 176–83; Andrés Nin, *Los problemas de la revolución española* (Paris, 1971), pp. 156–7; Santos Juliá Díaz, 'Fracaso de una insurrección y derrota de una huelga: los hechos de octubre en Madrid', *Estudios de Historia Social*, no. 31, October– December 1984; Juliá, *Historia del socialismo*, pp. 126–9.

32 Benavides, *La revolución fue así*, p. 372.

33 Munis, *Jalones*, p. 154; 'Ignotus', *Anarquismo*, pp. 176–9.

34 Grossi, *L'insurrection*, pp. 108, 114ff.; Canel, *Octubre rojo*, p. 33.

35 Grossi, *L'insurrection*, pp. 155–6; Canel, *Octubre rojo*, pp. 151–7. The most detailed reconstructions of the events in Asturias are by Paco Ignacio Taibo II, *Historia general de Asturias*, vol. VII, *Octubre 1934: el ascenso*, and vol. VIII, *Octubre 1934: la caída* (Gijón, 1978), and David Ruiz, *Insurrección defensiva y revolución obrera: el octubre español de 1934* (Barcelona, 1988).

36 J. Costa i Deu and Modest Sabaté, *La veritat del 6 d'octubre* (Barcelona, 1936), recounts the revolutionary events in Lerida, Gerona and other parts of provincial Catalonia where the Alianza Obrera had influence.

37 Azana, *Obras*, vol. III, pp. 74–6; Munis, *Jalones*, pp. 140–7. On Dencàs and the policy of the Generalitat, see Enric Ucelay da Cal, *La Catalunya populista: imatge, cultura i política en l'etapa republicana (1931–1939)* (Barcelona, 1982), pp. 208–20.

38 Maurín, *Segunda revolución*, pp. 123–44; Josep Dencàs, *El 6 d'octubre des del Palau de Governació* (Barcelona, 1935, reprinted 1979), pp. 77–9. It has been claimed that Dencàs was a rightist provocateur; see Brenan, *Labyrinth*, p. 284,

and Consuelo Berges, *Explicación de octubre* (Madrid, 1935), p. 121. Cf. Andrés Nin, 'Los acontecimientos de octubre en Barcelona', *Leviatán*, no. 18, October–November 1935.

39 General López de Ochoa, *Campaña militar de Asturias en octubre de 1934 (narración táctico-episódica)* (Madrid, 1936), pp. 11–12, 26–9; Gil Robles, *No fue posible*, pp. 140–1; Jalón, *Memorias*, pp. 128–31; Vidarte, *El bienio negro*, pp. 358–9; Francisco Aguado Sánchez, *La revolución de octubre de 1934* (Madrid, 1972), pp. 188–93; Gabriel Cardona, *El poder militar en la España contemporánea hasta la guerra civil* (Madrid, 1983), pp. 203–5.

40 Gil Robles, *No fue posible*, p. 140; Joaquín Arrarás, *Franco* (Valladolid, 1939), p. 186; Brenan, *Labyrinth*, p. 288. The actual campaign is described, from the army's point of view, in López de Ochoa, *Campaña militar*, and, from the Civil Guard's point of view, in Aguado Sánchez, *La revolución*, pp. 253 ff.

41 Jalón, *Memorias*, pp. 139–40; Aguado Sánchez, *La revolución*, pp. 193–6, 257–8; Benavides, *La revolución fue así*, p. 330; Díaz Nosty, *La comuna asturiana*, pp. 164, 240–4, 314; Ballbé, *Orden público*, p. 372.

42 Arrarás, *República*, vol. II, pp. 614, 637–8, and *Historia de la cruzada española*, 8 vols (Madrid, 1939–43), vol. II, p. 259; Franco, '*Apuntes*', p. 12.

43 On the repression, see *ABC*, 13 October 1934; Ignacio Carral, *Porqué mataron a Luis de Sirval* (Madrid, 1935), pp. 37–60; Díaz Nosty, *La comuna asturiana*, pp. 355–72; José Martín Blázquez, *I Helped to Build an Army: Civil War Memoirs of a Spanish Staff Officer* (London, 1939), pp. 12–33.

44 Tusell and Calvo, *Giménez Fernández*, p. 57.

45 *DSC*, 9 October 1934; *La Mañana*, 7, 11 October 1934. *El Debate*, 11 October 1934, reported that in Madrid alone there were already 2000 prisoners. Total figures for the arrests are difficult to find. The lowest respectable figures are those of Malefakis (*Agrarian Reform*, p. 342), who gives 15,000–20,000. Jackson (*Republic*, p. 161) gives 30,000–40,000, and Buckley (*Life and Death*, p. 166) gives 60,000. The prisoners' fate is described in Leah Manning, *What I Saw in Spain* (London, 1935), pp. 54–135. See also Carral, *Luis de Sirval*, passim. On the *ayuntamientos*, see Salazar Alonso, *Bajo el signo*, p. 129; Vidarte, *El bienio negro*, p. 397.

46 Frederic Escofet, *Al servei de Catalunya i de la República*, 2 vols (Paris, 1973), vol. I, *La desfeta*, pp. 147–93; Sánchez y García Saúco, *La revolución de 1934*, pp. 146–8.

47 Robinson, *Origins*, p. 194; Madariaga, *Spain*, p. 435.

48 Ramos Oliveira, *La revolución española*, pp. 161–2; Berges, *Explicación de octubre*, pp. 89–90; Hidalgo, *¿Por qué fuí lanzado?*, pp. 83–9; Martín Blázquez, *I Helped*, p. 34.

6 THE LEGAL ROAD TO THE CORPORATE STATE

1 Robinson, *Origins*, p. 194; Madariaga, *Spain*, p. 435.

2 *JAP*, 27 October 1934; *El Debate*, 9, 17, 21, 24, 31 October, 4 November 1934; *DSC*, 5 November 1934; Antonio Elorza, 'El sindicalismo católico en la segunda República', in Antonio Elorza, *La utopía anarquista bajo la segunda República española* (Madrid, 1973), pp. 295–350. For the subsequent activities and fiercely rightist tone of the CESO, see Juan José Castillo, 'El Comité Nacional Circunstancial de la Confederación Española de Sindicatos Obreros 1936–1938', *Revista Española de la Opinión Pública*, no. 38, October 1974.

3 *DSC*, 14, 15 November 1934; *El Debate*, 24 October, 2, 3, 8, 14 November 1934; Alcalá Zamora, *Memorias*, p. 298.

4 *El Debate*, 24 October, 16, 17 November 1934; *Leviatán* no. 7 (November 1934); *DSC*, 15 November 1934; Gil Robles, *No fue posible*, pp. 141–5; Tusell and Calvo, *Giménez Fernández*, pp. 60–1.

5 Francisco Franco Salgado-Araujo, *Mi vida junto a Franco* (Barcelona, 1977), p. 123.

6 Arrarás, *Cruzada*, vol. II, p. 277; Gil Robles, *No fue posible*, pp. 141–9.

7 Ballbé, *Orden público*, p. 376.

8 *DSC*, 6, 7, 14, 15 November 1934.

9 Gil Robles, *No fue posible*, pp. 152–3, 157–8; *DSC*, 21 December 1934; *El Debate*, 28 December 1934; Antonio Rodríguez de las Heras, *Filiberto Villalobos: su obra social y política (1900–1936)* (Salamanca, 1985), pp. 218–20, 233–4, 257–65; De la Cierva, *La guerra civil*, p. 458; Jackson, *Republic*, p. 170.

10 *El Debate*, 24 November, 1, 5, 7, 20, 21 December 1934, 2, 6 February, 1, 19 March 1935; Gil Robles, *No fue posible*, pp. 172–88; Malefakis, *Agrarian Reform*, pp. 347–55; Robinson, *Origins*, pp. 200–2; Tusell and Calvo, *Giménez Fernández*, pp. 74–95, 110; Jackson, *Republic*, p. 169. See also Mercedes Cabrera Calvo-Sotelo, 'La estrategia patronal en la II República (II): el bienio negro', *Estudios de Historia Social*, nos 10–11, July–December 1979, pp. 150–4.

11 A graphic picture of a *pueblo* in Toledo is provided by Arturo Barea, *La forja de un rebelde* (Buenos Aires, 1951), pp. 483–90.

12 *JAP*, 10, 24 November, 8 December 1934, 2, 11 February, 16 March 1935; Gil Robles, *No fue posible*, p. 203.

13 *El Debate*, 3 September 1934.

14 *El Debate*, 22, 23 December 1934, 12 January 1935.

15 *El Debate*, 12 January 1935; Gil Robles, *No fue posible*, pp. 165–8; Pabón, *Cambó*, p. 299.

16 *El Debate*, 4, 20 January, 3 March 1935; *CEDA*, 1 May 1935.

17 *El Debate*, 10 February, 19, 27 March 1935; Lerroux, *La pequeña historia*, pp. 374–5; Gil Robles, *No fue posible*, pp. 212–17; Alcalá Zamora, *Memorias*, pp. 301–2; Jackson, *Republic*, pp. 161–7.

18 Viñas, *La Alemania nazi*, p. 172.

19 *El Debate*, 2, 3, 21, 23, 28, 30 April, 4, 7 May 1935; Gil Robles, *No fue posible*, pp. 218–31; Lerroux, *La pequeña historia*, pp. 387–91.

20 Diego Martínez Barrio, *Orígenes del Frente Popular espanōl* (Buenos Aires, 1943), pp. 66–7.

21 *DSC*, 15, 27 February 1935.

22 *El Debate*, 12 May 1935.

23 *El Debate*, 16, 18 May, 27 August 1935; Gil Robles, *No fue posible*, pp. 232–44; De la Cierva, *La guerra civil*, pp. 488–90; Arrarás, *Franco*, pp. 191–9; Manuel Goded, *Un 'faccioso' cien por cien* (Zaragoza, 1939), pp. 23–4; Payne, *Politics and the Military*, pp. 304–6.

24 Franco Salgado-Araujo, *Mi vida*, p. 122.

25 Gil Robles, *No fue posible*, pp. 234–43; Antonio López Fernández, *Defensa de Madrid* (Mexico City, 1945), pp. 40–3.

26 Iribarren, *Mola*, p. 44; Ricardo de la Cierva, *Francisco Franco: biografía histórica*, 6 vols (Barcelona, 1982), vol. II, p. 162.

27 Gil Robles, *No fue posible*, pp. 238–40; Azaña, letter to Prieto of 7 August 1935, *Obras*, vol. III, p. 604.

28 Brenan, *Labyrinth*, p. 293, says, 'It was at this time that those concrete trenches were dug in the Sierra de Guadarrama overlooking Madrid that proved so useful to General Mola's levies in the Civil War.' Identical accusations were made in *ABC*, 31 July 1936, and in *Solidaridad Obrera*; see S. Cánovas Cervantes, *Apuntes históricos de Solidaridad Obrera* (Barcelona, 1937),

p. 31. See also Alcalá Zamora, *Memorias*, pp. 334–5; Arrarás, *Franco*, pp. 193–4.

29 Seco Serrano, *Época contemporánea*, p. 133.

30 *Documents on German Foreign Policy 1918–1945*, ser. C, vol. IV (London, 1964), documents 303, 330, 445; Earl of Avon, *Facing the Dictators* (London, 1962), p. 256; Buckley, *Life and Death*, pp. 175–6; *El Debate*, 27 August, 15 September 1935.

31 *El Debate*, 7, 16 May 1935; *Arriba*, 13 June 1935; Robinson, *Origins*, pp. 204–5.

32 *El Debate*, 14 May, 14 June 1935; De la Cierva, *La guerra civil*, p. 487.

33 Tusell and Calvo, *Giménez Fernández*, pp.114–16, 127–32; Seco Serrano, *Epoca contemporánea*, p. 138; Primo de Rivera, *Obras*, pp. 631–42.

34 *El Debate*, 21 May, 2, 21 June, 6 July, 19 September 1935; *Boletín del Ministerio de Trabajo, Sanidad y Previsión*, August, September 1935.

35 'Emilio Ruiz' (Juan Andrade), 'La política pre-supuestaria Radical–Cedista', *Leviatán*, no. 15 (July 1935); *Boletín del Ministerio de Trabajo*, June, October, December 1935, January 1936.

36 *El Debate*, 2 July 1935; *CEDA*, 1 July 1935; *DSC*, 12 July 1935.

37 *El Debate*, 3 July 1935; Malefakis, *Agrarian Reform*, p. 358.

38 *El Debate*, 21, 28 May 1935; *Arriba*, 13 June 1935 (which graphically illustrated its report of the Uclés meeting with a photograph of pigs jostling for swill); *JAP*, 14 March, 27 April, 1 June 1935.

39 Manuel Portela Valladares, *Memorias: dentro del drama español* (Madrid, 1988), p. 147.

40 *El Debate*, 14, 20, 23 June, 2, 3 July 1935; *JAP*, 1 July 1935.

41 *El Debate*, 3 September 1935.

42 *JAP*, 22 June, 1, 14 July 1935; De la Cierva, *La guerra civil*, pp. 508–10.

43 *JAP*, 16 March, 8 June, 27 July, 31 August, 28 September 1935; Gil Robles, *No fue posible*, p. 194.

44 *CEDA*, 30 November 1935; *JAP*, 17 August, 7 September, 5 October 1935; *El Debate*, 10 November 1935. The fascist leader, Ramiro Ledesma Ramos, regarded the CEDA as a 'fascisticised' force; see Ramiro Ledesma Ramos, *¿Fascismo en España?*, 2nd edition (Barcelona, 1968), p. 72.

45 *El Debate*, 25 June 1935; Lerroux, *La pequeña historia*, pp. 392–4; Gil Robles, *No fue posible*, p. 285; Primo de Rivera, *Obras*, p. 609.

46 Joaquín Chapaprieta Torregrosa, *La paz fue posible* (Barcelona, 1971), pp. 207–33; Gil Robles, *No fue posible*, pp. 286–91; Pabón, *Cambó*, pp. 433–5; *El Debate*, 20, 24–26 September 1935.

47 Mendizábal, *Aux origines*, pp. 221–2; Chapaprieta, *La paz fue posible*, pp. 234–5; Portela Valladares, *Memorias*, pp. 146–7.

48 *DSC*, 2 October 1935. Their concern might have been greater had they known that on 11 September the German Embassy in Madrid had replied in the affirmative to the government feelers of March regarding a possible collaboration between the Spanish police and the Gestapo in the fight against 'communism'; see Viñas, *La Alemania nazi*, pp. 440–6.

49 *DSC*, 22 October 1935; Chapaprieta, *La paz fue posible*, pp. 257–62; Gil Robles, *No fue posible*, pp. 292–304; Pabón, *Cambó*, pp. 440–6.

50 Chapaprieta, *La paz fue posible*, pp. 262–80; Gil Robles, *No fue posible*, pp. 304–12; *DSC*, 28 October 1935; Primo de Rivera, *Obras*, pp. 665–8; Lerroux, *La pequeña historia*, pp. 446–55; Pabón, *Cambó*, pp. 446–50; *El Debate* 23, 27, 29, 30 October 1935.

51 Cortés Cavanillas, *Gil Robles*, p. 151.

52 Serrano Súñer, *Entre el silencio y la propaganda*, pp. 38, 78, and in numerous conversations with the author.

53 Chapaprieta, *La paz fue posible*, pp. 292–305; Gil Robles, *No fue posible*, pp. 341–58; Pabón, *Cambó*, pp. 452–8. Samper later alleged that the CEDA leader had turned a blind eye to the Radicals' financial immorality in return for being left to carry out his own plans in the Ministry of War; see Martínez Barrio, *Orígenes*, pp. 82–3.
54 *JAP*, 12 October 1935; *El Debate*, 10 November 1935.
55 Tusell and Calvo, *Giménez Fernández*, pp. 154–5; Chapaprieta, *La paz fue posible*, pp. 318–21; Alcalá Zamora, *Memorias*, p. 340.
56 Tusell and Calvo, *Giménez Fernández*, pp. 156–7.
57 During the Civil War, Gil Robles told a Portuguese journalist that the initiative for a coup was his; see Armando Boaventura, *Madrid-Moscovo: da Ditadura a República e a guerra civil de Espanha* (Lisbon, 1937), pp. 191–2. On the projected coup, see also Franco's letter to Gil Robles, April 1937, quoted in Jaime del Burgo, *Conspiración y guerra civil* (Madrid, 1970), pp. 228–9; Ansaldo, *¿Para qué...?* pp. 110–11.
58 *El Debate*, 10–15 December 1935; Gil Robles, *No fue posible*, pp. 358–76; Chapaprieta, *La paz fue posible*, pp. 324–32; Pabón, *Cambó*, pp. 459–64; Arrarás, *República*, vol. III, pp. 267–71.
59 *El Debate*, 17, 18, 28 December 1935; *La Nación*, 14 December 1935; *La Época*, 17, 27 December 1935; *ABC*, 17 December 1935; Gil Robles, *No fue posible*, pp. 380–403; Portela Valladares, *Memorias*, pp. 152–60; Chapaprieta, *La paz fue posible*, pp. 353–77.
60 Gil Robles, *No fue posible*, p. 404; Arrarás, *República*, vol. IV, p. 41.
61 El Clero Vasco, *El pueblo vasco frente a la cruzada franquista* (Toulouse, 1966), pp. 105–39.
62 Gil Robles, *No fue posible*, pp. 404–30; Javier Tusell, *Las elecciones del Frente Popular*, 2 vols (Madrid, 1971), vol. I, pp. 42–133; *El Socialista*, 11, 18 January 1936 (which noted this chicanery with grim amusement); Tusell and Calvo, *Giménez Fernández*, pp. 162–5; Blinkhorn, *Carlism*, p. 204.
63 *El Debate*, 9 February 1936; *ABC*, 8 February 1936.
64 Gil Robles, *No fue posible*, pp. 431–4.
65 Chapaprieta, *La paz fue posible*, pp. 390–6.
66 Buckley, *Life and Death*, p. 188; Bowers, *My Mission*, p. 187; *El Socialista*, 19 January, 13 February 1936; Gil Robles, *No fue posible*, p. 472.
67 Viñas, *La Alemania nazi*, p. 147.
68 Buckley, *Life and Death*, p. 189; Tusell, *Elecciones*, vol. I, p. 217; Juan-Simeón Vidarte, *Todos fuimos culpables* (Mexico City, 1973), p. 37.
69 *El Debate*, 2 February 1936; Tusell, *Elecciones*, vol. II, appendix 7.
70 *El Debate*, 10, 11, 15 January, 9, 11, 14, 16 February 1936; Gil Robles, *No fue posible*, pp. 464–73.
71 *JAP*, 28 December 1935. The *JAP* issue for 21 December printed 'JEFE' 195 times on p. 3.
72 *El Sol*, 24 January 1936; *El Socialista*, 21 January 1936; *El Debate*, 7 February 1936; *JAP*, 14 February 1936.
73 *El Debate*, 3, 10, 17 January 1936; *El Socialista*, 18 January 1936.
74 See *El Defensor*, 24 January 1935, which made an eloquent and reasoned plea for the Right to moderate its aggressiveness; Tusell, *Elecciones*, vol. I, pp. 211–19, 230–4, 273–85; Ian Gibson, *La represión nacionalista de Granada en 1936 y la muerte de Federico García Lorca* (Paris, 1971), pp. 1–24.
75 *JAP*, 11 January 1936; Gil Robles, *No fue posible*, pp. 484–5; *Leviatán*, no. 20, January 1936.
76 *JAP*, 4 January 1936; *El Debate*, 3 January 1936; *El Socialista*, 18 January 1936.

77 *El Debate*, 3 January 1936; *El Socialista*, 30 January 1936; Bowers, *My Mission*, p. 182; Buckley, *Life and Death*, pp. 190–1; De la Mora, *In Place of Splendour*, p. 207.
78 *Ideal*, 3, 14, 15, 28, 29 January, 11, 12, 14, 16 February 1936; *El Defensor*, 14, 19, 22, 23, 28 January, 1, 11, 6, 15–20 February, 5–7 March 1936; *El Socialista*, 7 March 1936.
79 *El Socialista*, 18 January, 9 February 1936; Fraser, *In Hiding*, p. 116; Barea, *La forja*, pp. 522–9; Tusell, *Elecciones*, vol. II, pp. 123–91; Bécarud, *La segunda República*, pp. 152–3; Robinson, *Origins*, pp. 255–6, 387–8.
80 There has been endless controversy about the actual results. The most exhaustive national study to date is by Tusell, who gives the following figures: Left, 4,654,116; Centre, 526,625; Right, 4,503,505 (*Elecciones*, vol. II, p. 13). The only other monographic study, José Venegas, *Las elecciones del Frente Popular* (Buenos Aires, 1942), p. 65, favours the Left rather more: Left, 4,838,449; Centre, 449,320; Right, 3,996,931. The two general accounts which deal with the elections in most detail – Bécarud, *La segunda República*, p. 156, and Jackson, *Republic*, p. 193 – produce figures similar to those of Venegas.
81 Ministerio de la Gobernación, *Dictamen de la Comisión sobre ilegitimidad de poderes actuantes en 18 de julio de 1936* (Barcelona, 1939), pp. 31–45. The final composition of the Cortes was as follows: PSOE, 102; Azaña's Izquierda Repúblicana, 90; Martínez Barrio's Unión Repúblicana, 36; Companys's Esquerra, 36; PCE, 15; Portela Valladares's Centre Party, 18; Lliga, 12; Basque Nationalists, 9; Radicals, 4; conservative Republicans, 17; CEDA, 87; Agrarians, 15; Renovación Española and other extreme monarchists, 19; Carlists, 9.

7 SOCIALISM UNDER STRESS

1 Grossi, *L'insurrection*, p. 224.
2 On the FJS, see below. On the Trotskyists, see Resolución del Comité Central del Bloque Obrero y Campesino, *Las lecciones de la insurrección de octubre* (Barcelona, 1935), and 'Mont-Fort' (pseud. Joaquín Maurín, *Alianza Obrera* (Barcelona, 1935), both reprinted in Marta Bizcarrondo, editor, *Octubre del 34: reflexiones sobre una revolución* (Madrid, 1977), pp. 232–3, 236–7, 258–60.
3 On the Communists, see José Díaz, *Tres años de lucha*, 2nd edition (Paris, 1970), pp. 12–13; Rafael Cruz, *El Partido Comunista de España en la II República* (Madrid, 1987), pp. 209–12; Dolores Ibárruri, *El unico camino* (Paris, 1965), pp. 181–3.
4 Rosal, *1934*, pp. 284–93; Sánchez y García Saúco, *La revolución de 1934*, pp. 149–52; Díaz Nosty, *La comuna asturiana*, pp. 361–72; Munis, *Jalones*, pp. 167–8; Hidalgo de Cisneros, *Cambio de rumbo*, vol. II, pp. 95–101. Lerroux told Alcalá Zamora that he knew about Prieto's hiding place and escape plan and had decided to turn a blind eye – Alcalá Zamora, *Memorias*, p. 299.
5 Vidarte, *El bienio negro*, pp. 342–55; Rosal, *1934*, pp. 295–6, and *UGT*, vol. I, pp. 409–22.
6 Largo Caballero, *Mis recuerdos*, pp. 138–9; Ibárruri et al., *Guerra*, vol. I, p. 62; Luis Araquistain, 'Largo Caballero ante los jueces', *Leviatán*, no. 20, January 1936. Largo Caballero's statements in court are partially reprinted in Juliá, *Historia del socialismo*, pp. 353–4.
7 Castro Delgado, *Hombres made in Moscú*, p. 193; Mario de Coca, *Anti-Caballero*, p. 155; Alvarez del Vayo, *Last Optimist*, pp. 264–6; Munis, *Jalones*, pp. 134–40, 153; Eduardo Comín Colomer, *Historia del Partido Comunista de España*, 3 vols (Madrid, 1967), vol. II, pp. 325–7, 341–3; Tagüeña Lacorte,

Testimonio, pp. 67–72. Amaro del Rosal's own account and refutation of accusations of cowardice in *1934*, pp.257–68, and in numerous conversations with the author in Madrid.

8 Saborit, *Besteiro*, p. 251; Lamo de Espinosa, *Besteiro*, p. 98.

9 Largo Caballero, *Mis recuerdos*, pp. 143, 145. See Araquistain to Largo Caballero, 14 April 1935, reprinted in Juliá, *Historia del socialismo*, pp. 356–7; Ramos Oliveira to Largo Caballero, undated, quoted in Vidarte to Prieto, 10 July 1935, FPI/AH–22–24, and reprinted in Largo Caballero, *Escritos*, pp. 171–2

10 According to José Bergamín, a prominent left-wing Catholic intellectual, Largo Caballero's copy of the works of Marx and Engels was in Russian, which ensured that he could not have read them (in a conversation with the author in Madrid in 1977).

11 Juliá, *Azaña*, pp. 388–90. The public letter in Manuel Azaña, *Mi rebelión en Barcelona* (Madrid, 1935), pp. 5–8.

12 Azaña to Prieto, 25 December 1934, *Obras*, vol. III, pp. 589–90.

13 A. C. Márquez Tornero, *Testimonio de mi tiempo (memorias de un español republicano)* (Madrid, 1979), p. 115; Rivas Cherif, *Retrato de un desconocido*, p. 225.

14 Azaña to Prieto, 16 January 1935, *Obras*, vol. III, pp. 591–3.

15 Prieto to Azaña, 21 January 1935, in Juliá, *Historia del socialismo*, p. 358.

16 Juliá, *Azaña*, pp. 395–6.

17 Vidarte to Prieto, 20 March 1935, in *Documentos socialistas* (Madrid, n.d. [1935]), pp. 17–18; Vidarte, *Todos fuimos culpables*, p. 25.

18 The original of Prieto's letter to the PSOE executive is in FPI/AH–17. The text is reprinted in Carlos de Baraibar, *Las falsas 'posiciones socialistas' de Indalecio Prieto* (Madrid, 1935), pp. 139–45.

19 Nin, *Problemas*, pp. 155–8; Munis, *Jalones*, p. 183; Pelai Pagés, *Andreu Nin: su evolución política, 1911–1937* (Bilbao, 1975), p. 188. Trotsky later denounced as treachery the POUM's participation in the Popular Front; see Trotsky, *Révolution espagnole*, pp. 285–91.

20 *La Libertad*, 30 March 1935; *Documentos socialistas*, pp. 249–55; Vidarte, *El bienio negro*, pp. 393–8; Juliá, *Historia del socialismo*, p. 147.

21 *La Libertad*, 13 April 1935; Martínez Barrio, *Orígenes*, pp. 24–31; Santos Juliá, Díaz *Orígenes del Frente Popular en España (1934–1936)* (Madrid, 1979), pp. 31–3.

22 The text of the letter is reprinted in Baraibar, *Prieto*, pp. 197–200, and in *Documentos socialistas*, accompanied by a long message from González Peña to the Madrid section of the FJS, pp. 143–55. Largo Caballero, *Mis recuerdos*, p. 144, claimed to have received a letter from Peña endorsing *his* position. If so, it is strange that, given the no-holds-barred polemic at the time, the text was not published.

23 *Documentos socialistas*, pp. 179–87; Largo Caballero, *Escritos*, pp. 167–71.

24 Indalecio Prieto, 'La coalición de izquierdas', *El Liberal*, 14 April 1935.

25 [Carlos Hernández Zancajo], *Octubre-segunda etapa* (n.p., n.d. [Madrid, 1935]). There were two editions, of which the cheaper had no cover and smaller print. References given here are to that popular edition. See evidence by Carrillo in María Eugenia Yagüe, *Santiago Carrillo* (Madrid, 1977), p. 26, by Amaro del Rosal in Bizcarrondo, *Octubre del 34*, p. 50, confirmed personally by Carrillo to the author on 5 October 1977.

26 *Octubre*, pp. 26–31, 39–46, 52–5, 94.

27 Comín, *PCE*, vol. II, pp. 459–74; Stanley G. Payne, *The Spanish Revolution*

(London, 1970), pp. 164–5; Ricardo de la Cierva, *La historia perdida del socialismo español* (Madrid, 1972), pp. 189–90.

28 Largo Caballero, *Mis recuerdos*, p. 141; Santiago Carrillo, *Demain l'Espagne* (Paris, 1974), p. 32. Prieto believed otherwise; cf. Vidarte, *Todos fuimos culpables*, p. 30. In an interview published in *Claridad*, 7 December 1935, Largo Caballero stated that he agreed with much of the pamphlet but not with its demand for expulsions and for entry into the Third International.

29 *La Libertad*, 24 April 1935. At first Cordero had been in favour of ignoring the pamphlet; see Vidarte, *Todos fuimos culpables*, p. 30.

30 Saborit, *Besteiro*, pp. 251–7.

31 Serrano Poncela, *El Partido Socialista*, p. 156.

32 Julián Besteiro, *Marxismo y anti-marxismo* (Madrid, 1935). References are to the 4th edition (Madrid, 1967), pp. 16–23, 93–102, 107–13, 130–1. For a shrewd commentary, see Heywood, *Marxism*, pp. 158–9

33 Luis Araquistain, 'El marxismo en la Academia', 'Un marxismo contra Marx', 'La esencia del marxismo', *Leviatán*, nos 13–15, May–July 1935.

34 Julián Besteiro, 'Leviatán: el socialismo mitológico', 'Mi crítico empieza a razonar', *Democracia*, 15 June, 6 July 1935.

35 This aspect of Araquistain's thought is discussed at length in Paul Preston, introductory essay to Paul Preston, editor, *Leviatán: antología* (Madrid, 1976).

36 Indalecio Prieto, 'Mi derecho a opinar', 'La amnistía, base de la coalición electoral', 'El valor de la acción parlamentaria', 'Los roedores de derrotas', 'La planta exótica del caudillismo', *El Liberal*, *La Libertad*, 22–26 May 1935.

37 Azaña reminded Prieto of this in a letter of 20 April 1935, *Obras*, vol. III, p. 601.

38 Indalecio Prieto, *Posiciones socialistas: del momento* (Madrid, n.d. [1935]).

39 Enrique de Francisco wrote to Prieto on 24 April and 9 May 1935. Prieto's replies of 30 April and 14 May are reprinted in *Documentos socialistas*, pp. 31–59. Baraibar presented a copy of his *Las falsas 'posiciones socialistas' de Indalecio Prieto* to Largo Caballero on 30 June 1935 with a dedication which stated: 'You know better than anyone – my dear Don Francisco – the moral motives behind this book. Receive with it the affection, the limitless devotion of Carlos de Baraibar' (copy in private collection).

40 Baraibar, *Prieto*, pp. 22–6, 46, 67–9, 113. That many of Baraibar's accusations were false was proved by documents published by Prieto in *El Liberal*, 11 September 1935. See also the refutation of Baraibar by Antonio Gascón and Victoria Priego, *Por hoy y por mañana (leves comentarios a un libro firmado por Carlos Baraibar* (Madrid, 1935).

41 Correspondence between De los Ríos and the imprisoned members of the PSOE executive, in Largo Caballero, *Escritos*, pp. 175–85; commentary by Prieto in a letter to the Comité Nacional del PSOE, n.d. December 1935, FPI/AH–22–24.

42 Azaña to Prieto, 7 August 1935, *Obras*, vol. III, pp. 603–4. On the financing of *Claridad*, see Rosal, *1934*, p. 297.

43 Azaña, *Obras*, vol. III, pp. 229–93; Márquez Tornero, *Testimonio*, pp. 118–21.

44 Buckley, *Life and Death*, pp. 182–3.

45 *El Liberal*, 27, 29 August 1935; *Democracia*, 27 September 1935.

46 *Democracia*, 25 August 1935; *Claridad*, 20 July 1935; Rosal *1934*, p. 301.

47 *Democracia*, 13, 20 September, 8 November, 6 December 1935; *Claridad*, 29 July, 26 October, 30 November 1935.

48 *Democracia*, 13 September, 11 October 1935.

49 José Díaz Ramos, *Tres años de lucha*, (Paris, 1970), pp. 7–30, 33, 57.

50 *Claridad*, 27 August, 12, 19 October 1935.

51 Luis Araquistain, 'La nueva táctica comunista', *Leviatán*, no. 16, August 1935. Cf. Juliá, *La izquierda del PSOE*, pp. 184–201.

52 *Claridad*, 7, 14 December 1935.

53 Claudio Sánchez Albornoz, *De mi anecdotario político* (Buenos Aires, 1972), pp. 105, 116.

54 Largo Caballero, *Escritos*, pp. 167–72.

55 *Claridad*, 26 October 1935.

56 Minutes of meeting on 16 November 1935 of the executive committees of the UGT, FJS and PSOE, reprinted in Largo Caballero, *Escritos*, pp. 255–9; Juliá, *Historia del socialismo*, pp. 157–8; Helen Graham, *Socialism and War: The Spanish Socialist Party in Power and Crisis* (Cambridge, 1991), pp. 18–21.

57 De Francisco to Azaña, 16, 22 November 1935, Azaña to de Francisco, 21, 30 November 1935, FPI/AH–24–9; Vidarte to Prieto, 20 November 1935, Prieto to Vidarte, n.d. November 1935, in Largo Caballero, *Escritos*, pp. 276–81.

58 In the first edition, I followed Jacques Duclos, *Mémoires*, vol. II (Paris, 1969), pp. 106–10. The present account has been corrected in the light of Juliá, *Orígenes*, pp. 107–8, and Cruz, *El Partido Comunista*, pp. 240–50.

59 Largo Caballero to Comité Nacional del PSOE, 1 October 1934, FPI/AH–22–23; Largo Caballero, *Mis recuerdos*, pp. 146–7; Coca, *Anti-Caballero*, pp. 152–4.

60 *El Socialista*, 19, 25 December 1935; *Claridad*, 23 December 1935; minutes of the meeting of the Comité Nacional del PSOE, 16 December 1935, FPI/AH–24–1; Cabello and Vidarte to the Agrupación Socialista Madrileña, 21 December 1935, FPI/AH–19–14; Vidarte, *Todos fuimos culpables*, p. 26; Largo Caballero, *Mis recuerdos*, p. 148; Coca, *Anti-Caballero*, pp. 193–8; Juliá, *La izquierda*, pp. 22–3, 82–5.

61 *El Socialista*, 18, 19 December 1935; *Claridad*, 15 January 1936.

62 *El Socialista*, 22 December 1935, 4, 8–16 January 1936.

63 Payne, *Revolution*, p. 174; De la Cierva, *Socialismo*, pp. 200–1.

64 This account is based on a comparison of candidates in the 1933 and 1936 elections as listed in *El Debate*, 21 November, 5 December 1933, 18 February 1936.

65 Lamo de Espinosa, *Besteiro*, pp. 101–2, 125–33.

66 Vidarte, *Todos fuimos culpables*, pp. 38–40; *Claridad*, 25 January 1936. Largo Caballero had condemned Narciso Vázquez for having criticised the use of violence in October 1934. On Vázquez and Trejo, see Vidarte, *Cortes Constituyentes*, pp. 85, 608. Trejo was to be one of many prisoners pardoned by Franco but shot before the pardon arrived.

67 Letter of Largo Caballero to the UGT executive, 5 January 1936, reprinted in Rosal, *UGT*, vol. I, pp. 445–8.

68 *El Socialista*, 16 January 1936; Ibárruri et al., *Guerra*, vol. I, pp. 69–78; Largo Caballero, *Mis recuerdos*, pp. 150–1; Munis, *Jalones*, pp. 191–201; Vidarte, *Todos fuimos culpables*, pp. 27–35.

69 *Claridad*, 25, 30 January, 6 February 1935; *El Socialista*, 12 February 1936.

70 *Claridad*, 18 January 1936.

8 THE ABANDONMENT OF LEGALISM

1 *Boletín del Ministerio de Trabajo*, April 1936.

2 Munis, *Jalones*, p. 201; Díaz, *Lucha*, p. 149; Peirats, *CNT*, vol. I, p. 120; testimony of Miguel González Inestal to the author.

3 Vidarte, *Todos fuimos culpables*, pp. 40–55; Azaña, diary entry for 19 February 1936, *Obras*, vol. IV, p. 563.

4 Portela Valladares, *Memorias*, pp. 175–8; Gil Robles, *No fue posible*, pp. 492–3; Alcalá Zamora, *Memorias*, p. 347.

5 Franco, *'Apuntes'*, pp. 25–8; Arrarás, *Cruzada*, pp. 439–40; Gil Robles, *No fue posible*, pp. 492–3.

6 Franco, *'Apuntes'*, p. 30; Arrarás, *Cruzada*, p. 440; Gil Robles, *No fue posible*, pp. 492–5; Portela Valladares, *Memorias*, p. 184; Vidarte, *Todos fuimos culpables*, p. 49.

7 Portela Valladares, *Memorias*, pp. 184–5, 190; Arrarás, *Cruzada*, p. 441; B. Félix Maíz, *Alzamiento en España*, 2nd edition (Pamplona, 1952), p. 37; Franco interview in Boaventura, *Madrid–Moscovo*, pp. 207–8.

8 *El Socialista*, 19 February 1936; Goded, *Un 'faccioso'*, pp. 26–7; Martínez Barrio, *Memorias*, pp. 303–4; Gil Robles, *No fue posible*, pp. 497–8; Vidarte, *Todos fuimos culpables*, pp. 440–2.

9 For an entirely different interpretation of these events, see Tusell and Calvo, *Giménez Fernández*, pp. 170–5.

10 Rivas Cherif, *Retrato*, pp. 320–2. Azaña's own account may be found in his diary entry for 19 February 1936, *Obras*, vol. IV, pp. 567–9, and in a letter of 16 March 1936 to Rivas Cherif, reprinted in *Retrato*, pp. 662–5.

11 Portela Valladares, *Memorias*, pp. 186–7; Gil Robles, *No fue posible*, pp. 500–7; Tusell and Calvo, *Giménez Fernández*, pp. 173–7.

12 Azaña, diary entry for 20 February 1936, *Obras*, vol. IV, p. 572.

13 Moreno Gómez, *Córdoba*, pp. 352–68; Pérez Yruela, *La conflictividad*, pp. 205–7; Cobo Romero, *Labradores*, pp. 445–53; Eduardo Sevilla Guzmán, *La evolución del campesinado en España* (Barcelona, 1979), pp. 119–21; Malefakis, *Agrarian Reform*, pp. 364–9; Azaña to Rivas Cherif, 17 March 1936, in Rivas Cherif, *Retrato*, pp. 665–6. On Féliz Moreno's revenge, see Moreno Gómez, *Córdoba*, pp. 637–44; Larry Collins and Dominique Lapierre, *Or I'll Dress You in Mourning* (London, 1968), pp. 90–99.

14 *El Debate*, 6 March 1936; Gil Robles, *No fue posible*, p. 533.

15 *El Socialista*, 7, 8, 15 March 1936; speech of Rodolfo Llopis, *DSC*, 15 April 1936.

16 Azaña to Rivas Cherif, 21 March 1936, in Rivas Cherif, *Retrato*, p. 669; *El Debate*, 18, 19 March 1936. On Amós Salvador, see Portela Valladares, *Memorias*, pp. 197–8; Stanley G. Payne, *Spain's First Democracy: The Second Republic, 1931–1936* (Madison, Wis., 1993), p. 282.

17 Gil Robles, *No fue posible*, pp. 575–6; Tusell and Calvo, *Giménez Fernández*, pp. 180–3; Vidarte, *Todos fuimos culpables*, p. 53.

18 *El Socialista*, 22 March 1936; *Claridad*, 6 April, 30 May 1936.

19 Ministerio de la Gobernación, *Comisión sobre ilegitimidad*, pp. 40–3 and appendix I, p. 129; Robinson, *Origins*, pp. 255–6; Payne, *Spain's First Democracy*, pp. 296–301; Tusell, *Elecciones*, vol. II, pp. 190–1; Alcalá Zamora, *Memorias*, pp. 350–1; Gil Robles, *No fue posible*, pp. 541–7, attributes to Madariaga the opinions of Alcalá Zamora.

20 *DSC*, 20, 24, 31 March, 1, 2 April 1936.

21 *DSC*, 31 March 1936; *ABC*, 1 April 1936; Tusell and Calvo, *Giménez Fernández*, pp. 184–7.

22 Vidarte, *Todos fuimos culpables*, p. 71; Venegas, *Elecciones*, pp. 47–8; Gil Robles, *No fue posible*, pp. 548–9. Prieto wanted to annul all the Galician results. Cf. his own version in his prologue to Romero Solano, *Vísperas*, pp. 6–7.

23 *DSC*, 1, 2 April 1936. Castaño played an important role in the preparation

of the military uprising of July 1936 – Ronald Fraser, *Blood of Spain: The Experience of Civil War 1936–1939* (London, 1979), pp. 85–6.

24 Vidarte, diary entry for 3 April 1936, *Todos fuimos culpables*, p. 71; *El Sol*, 4 April 1936.

25 *DSC*, 7 April 1936; *El Debate*, 8 April 1936; *ABC*, 8 April 1936. Azaña's decision to postpone the municipal elections also took into account the imminent crisis over the President's mandate as well as difficulties over agreeing the joint Republican–Socialist candidacies – Azaña to Rivas Cherif, 4 April 1936, in Rivas Cherif, *Retrato*, p. 674.

26 Alcalá Zamora, *Memorias*, pp. 359–1.

27 Rivas Cherif, *Retrato*, pp. 323–4. Azaña's own account of this process is to be found in a lengthy letter – twenty-eight manuscript pages – to Cipriano Rivas Cherif, who was in Cuba. Begun on 16 March and taken up again on several occasions before finally being completed on 10 April, it is reprinted in Rivas Cherif, *Retrato*, pp. 662–79.

28 Azaña to Rivas Cherif, 10 April 1936, Rivas Cherif, *Retrato*, pp. 675–7.

29 *DSC*, 7 April 1936; Azaña to Rivas Cherif, 10 April 1936, Rivas Cherif, *Retrato*, pp. 677–9; Vidarte, *Todos fuimos culpables*, pp. 75–5.

30 It has been claimed that it was the left wing of the Socialist Party that had wished to be rid of Acalá Zamora because he was 'the last remaining guarantee of moderation within the Republican system' – Payne, *Revolution*, p. 192; De la Cierva, *Socialismo*, pp. 202–3, 214. The only evidence which supports such an affirmation consists of remarks made by Luis Araquistain, shortly before his death, to Juan Marichal, the editor of Azaña's writings – Marichal, introduction to Azaña, *Obras*, vol. III, pp. xxxi-xxxii. A penitent – but rather forgetful – Araquistain told Marichal that the Socialist Left neutralised both Azaña and Prieto, by making one President and stopping the other replacing him as Prime Minister, in order to prevent there being a strong figure at the head of the government. This view is not substantiated by the facts.

31 Azaña to Rivas Cherif, 14 May 1936, Rivas Cherif, *Retrato*, pp. 680–2; Vidarte, *Todos fuimos culpables*, pp. 96–7.

32 Azaña to Rivas Cherif, 14 May 1936, Rivas Cherif, *Retrato*, pp. 682–4; *Claridad*, 9, 10, 11, 12, 22 April 1936; Vidarte, *Todos fuimos culpables*, pp. 97–9; Largo Caballero, *Escritos*, pp. 299–300, and *Mis recuerdos*, p. 155; Julián Zugazagoitia, *Guerra y vicisitudes de los Españoles*, 2 vols (Paris, 1968), vol. I, p. 20; Alcalá Zamora, *Memorias*, pp. 360–73.

33 *DSC*, 15 April 1936; Robinson, *Origins*, pp. 259–60.

34 *El Socialista*, 18, 19 April, 8 May 1936; *Claridad*, 15, 16, 18 April 1936.

35 *ABC*, 4, 5, 11 March, 2, 19, 29 April 1936; Ansaldo, *¿Para qué?*, pp. 77–8; De la Mora, *In Place of Splendour*, pp. 214–15; Buckley, *Life and Death*, p. 129; Stanley G. Payne, *Falange: A History of Spanish Fascism* (Stanford, Calif., 1961), pp. 98–105. On the fascist tendencies of Sales and the Sindicatos Libres, see Colin M. Winston, *Workers and the Right in Spain 1900–1936* (Princeton, NJ, 1985), pp. 312–22.

36 Gibson, *Lorca*, pp. 40–3; *La Mañana*, 14 March 1936; *Claridad*, 14 April 1936; *El Sol*, 4, 11, 15, 21, 26 March, 6 April 1936; Bowers, *My Mission*, pp. 200–8.

37 Gil Robles, *No fue posible*, pp. 573–5.

38 Payne, *Politics and the Military*, p. 318, and *Falange*, pp. 104–5; Blinkhorn, *Carlism*, p. 257; Valls, *DRV*, pp. 227–31; Ramón Serrano Súñer, *Entre Hendaya y Gibraltar* (Madrid, 1947), p. 25.

39 Gil Robles, *No fue posible*, pp. 558–70; Gibson, *Lorca*, pp. 45–6.

40 Gil Robles, *No fue posible*, pp. 561–2; García Venero, *El general Fanjul*, pp. 208–12.
41 *Ya*, 23 April 1936.
42 Gil Robles, *No fue posible*, pp. 563–7; García Venero, *El general Fanjul*, pp. 226–8; Serrano Suñer, *Entre el silencio y la propaganda*, pp. 56–8.
43 *El Obrero de la Tierra*, 29 February, 7, 21, 28 March 1936.
44 Malefakis, *Agrarian Reform*, pp. 364–74.
45 *El Obrero de la Tierra*, 18 April, 1, 16, 23, 30 May, 13, 20, 27 June 1936; *Claridad*, 6, 9, 18 June 1936; Manuel Requena Gallego, *Los sucesos de Yeste (mayo 1936)* (Albacete, 1983), pp. 83–100. The events at Yeste on 29 May were debated in the Cortes on 5 June.
46 Prieto, *Discursos fundamentales*, pp. 255–73.
47 Vidarte, *Todos fuimos culpables*, pp. 115–18.
48 *Claridad*, 19 March 1936; Vidarte, *Todos fuimos culpables*, p. 66; Juliá, *La izquierda*, pp. 89–92.
49 Azaña to Rivas Cherif, 21 March 1936, Rivas Cherif, *Retrato*, p. 669.
50 Martín i Ramos, *Els orígens*, pp. 205–26; Ramón Casterás, *Las Juventudes Socialistas Unificadas de Catalunya ante la guerra y la revolución (1936–1939)*, 2nd edition (Barcelona, 1982), pp.113–30.
51 Fernando Claudín, *Santiago Carrillo: crónica de un secretario general* (Barcelona, 1983), pp. 35–43; Helen Graham, 'The Socialist Youth in the JSU: The Experience of Organisational Unity, 1936–8', in Martin Blinkhorn, editor, *Spain in Conflict 1931–1939: Democracy and its Enemies* (London, 1986), pp. 88–9; Burnett Bolloten, *The Grand Camouflage*, 2nd edition (London, 1968), pp. 115–16; *Claridad*, 2, 6 April 1936; Ricard Viñas, *La formación de las Juventudes Socialistas Unificadas (1934–1936)* (Madrid, 1978), pp. 50–63; Carrillo, *Demain l'Espagne*, pp. 48–9; Vidarte, *Todos fuimos culpables*, pp. 56–7.
52 *El Socialista*, 9 March 1936; *Claridad*, 7, 8, 11 May 1936; Juliá, *La izquierda*, pp. 124–38; Graham, *Socialism and War*, pp. 28–9.
53 *Claridad*, 12 April, 6, 7, 12 May 1936; Rosal, *UGT*, vol. I, p. 479; Vidarte, *Todos fuimos culpables*, pp. 100, 115–27, 664; Prieto, *Convulsiones*, vol. I, p. 164, and vol. III, pp. 135–6; Largo Caballero, *Escritos*, pp. 300–1; Prieto, *Discursos en América*, pp. 29–31; Juliá, *La izquierda*, pp. 101–7.
54 Arrarás, *République*, vol. IV, pp. 273–81; Gil Robles, *No fue posible*, pp. 616–27; *El Debate*, 24 April 1936; Tusell and Calvo, *Giménez Fernández*, pp. 198–200, 220–3; Payne, *Politics and the Military*, p. 330; Vidarte, *Todos fuimos culpables*, p. 136.
55 Vidarte, *Todos fuimos culpables*, pp. 147, 190–2; Prieto, *Convulsiones*, vol. III, pp. 143–4; Largo Caballero, *Escritos*, pp. 304–6, and *Mis recuerdos*, pp. 161–3; Ibárruri, *El único camino*, pp. 252–3.
56 Azaña to Rivas Cherif, 14, 18 May, 5 June 1936, Rivas Cherif, *Retrato*, pp. 679–92.
57 H. Edward Knoblaugh, *Correspondent in Spain* (New York, 1937), pp. 20–2.
58 Gil Robles, *No fue posible*, pp. 719, 728–30, 798; De la Cierva, *La guerra civil*, p. 742. For the fate of the money, see the correspondence between Gil Robles and Mola, 29 December 1936 and 1 January 1937, reprinted in Franco Salgado-Araujo, *Mi vida con Franco*, pp. 202–3.
59 Valls, *DRV*, pp. 231–4; De la Cierva, *La guerra civil*, pp. 743–4.
60 Juan Ignacio Luca de Tena, *Mis amigos muertos* (Barceolona, 1971), p. 68; Payne, *Politics and the Military*, p. 335; Gil Robles, *No fue posible*, p. 733.
61 Gil Robles, *No fue posible*, p. 780; Ramón Garriga, *El general Yagüe* (Barcelona, 1985), pp. 61–8.

62 Gil Robles, *No fue posible*, pp. 730–1, 787–8; Payne, *Politics and the Military*, p. 339.
63 *DSC*, 19 May 1936.
64 *El Debate*, 31 May 1936.
65 E. H. Carr, *The Comintern and the Spanish Civil War* (London, 1984), pp. 7–8; David T. Cattell, *Communism and the Spanish Civil War* (Berkeley, Calif., 1955), pp.39–43.
66 Santos Juliá Díaz, 'Economic Crisis, Social Conflict and the Popular Front: Madrid 1931–6', in Preston, *Revolution and War in Spain*, pp. 137–58; Alarcón Caballero, *El movimiento obrero en Granada*, pp. 426–36; Macarro, *La utopía*, pp. 460–8; Montañés, *Anarcosindicalismo*, pp. 128–32. Vera Coronel was shot without trial by the Nationalists in Zaragoza in the Civil War.
67 *Claridad* 19, 30 May, 9, 15, 19, 24 June, 8, 9 July 1936; *El Sol*, 9, 11, 15 June, 15 July 1936; Bolloten, *Camouflage*, pp. 22–3; Jackson, *Republic*, pp. 220–2; Julio Alvarez del Vayo, *Freedom's Battle* (London, 1940), p. 23.
68 *Claridad*, 20, 21 April 1936; Araquistain, articles in *Leviatán*, nos 22, 24, March and May 1936; *Mundo Obrero*, 23–8 March 1936; Rosal, *UGT*, vol. I, pp. 423–4.
69 *Claridad*, 9, 11 May 1936; Confederación Nacional del Trabajo, *El Congreso Confederal de Zaragoza 1936* (Madrid, 1978), pp. 224–6; Peirats, *CNT*, vol. I, pp. 119–22; John Brademas, *Anarco-sindicalismo y revolución en España*, (Barcelona, 1974), pp. 168–71; Juliá, *La izquierda*, pp. 237–48.
70 Munis, *Jalones*, pp. 208–13; Payne, *Revolution*, p. 199.
71 Vidarte, *Todos fuimos culpables*, pp. 162–3, 170.
72 Romero Solano, *Vísperas*, pp. 176–7.
73 *El Socialista*, 26 May 1936; *Claridad*, 26 May 1936; Graham, *Socialism and War*, pp. 36–8; Juliá, *La izquierda*, pp. 115–18.
74 *Claridad*, 20 May, 1 June 1936; Prieto, *Convulsiones*, vol. III, pp. 159–60.
75 *Claridad*, 30 June, 1, 2, 13 July 1936; *El Socialista*, 1, 2 July 1936; Vidarte, *Todos fuimos culpables*, pp. 192–6, 205–8; Jackson, *Republic*, pp. 221–2; Graham, *Socialism and War*, pp. 40–50.
76 Sánchez, *Maurín*, p. 81.
77 *DSC*, 16 June 1936.
78 *DSC*, 1 July 1936.
79 Vidarte, *Todos fuimos culpables*, pp. 213–17, contains an account by one of the officers present. For a graphic reconstruction of the background to the assassination, see Ian Gibson, *La noche en que mataron a Calvo Sotelo* (Barcelona, 1982), *passim*.
80 Gil Robles, *Discursos*, pp. 613–72.

EPILOGUE

1 Helen Graham, 'The Spanish Popular Front and the Civil War', in Helen Graham and Paul Preston, editors, *The Popular Front in Europe* (London, 1987), pp. 116–18; Tom Buchanan, *The Spanish Civil War and the British Labour Movement* (Cambridge, 1991), pp. 40–72.
2 Rosal, *UGT*, vol. I, pp. 489–91; Graham, *Socialism and War*, pp. 53–4.
3 Graham, *Socialism and War*, pp. 56–62.
4 Graham, 'The Spanish Popular Front', p. 118.
5 Burnett Bolloten, *The Spanish Civil War: Revolution and Counterrevolution* (Chapel Hill, NC, 1991), pp. 462–73; Graham, *Socialism and War*, pp. 86–103.

6 Julio Aróstegui, *Francisco Largo Caballero en el exilio: la última etapa de un líder obrero* (Madrid, 1990), pp. 118–50; Saiz Valdivielso, *Prieto*, pp. 215 ff.

7 José María Gil Robles, *La monarquía por la que yo luché (1941–1954)* (Madrid, 1976), pp. 240 ff.; Javier Tusell, *La oposición democrática al franquismo* (Barcelona, 1977), pp. 188–97.

8 José Ignacio Escobar, *Así empezó* (Madrid, 1974), p. 62.

9 Eugenio Vegas Latapie, *Los caminos del desengaño: memorias políticas*, vol. II, 1936–1938 (Madrid, 1987), pp. 295, 325. Gil Robles used notepaper headed '*ESTADO ESPAÑOL Representación en Lisboa*, – see letter to Mola reproduced in Franco Salgado-Araujo, *Mi vida*, p. 202. See also Arthur Koestler, *Spanish Testament* (London, 1937), pp. 22–5; FO 371/2057, W9964/9549/41, quoted in Glyn A. Stone, 'The Official British Attitude to the Anglo-Portuguese Alliance 1910–1945', *Journal of Contemporary History*, vol. X, no. 4 (October 1975), p. 745; *Documents on German Foreign Policy*, ser. D, vol. III (London, 1951), pp. 54–6; Gutiérrez Ravé, *Gil Robles*, pp. 198–9.

10 José Manuel Martínez Bande, 'Del alzamiento a la guerra civil verano 1936: correspondencia Franco/Mola', *Historia y Vida*, no. 93, 1975, p. 22; Vegas Latapie, *Caminos*, pp. 326–31.

11 Koestler, *Spanish Testament*, p. 33.

12 *La Gaceta Regional*, 18 October 1936.

13 Del Burgo, *Conspiración*, pp. 207–8.

14 Report of Roberto Cantalupo, Salamanca, 6 March 1937, Archivio Storico del Ministero degli Affari Esteri, Rome, Spagna Fondo di Guerra, b. 38, N. 464/226; Cabanellas, *La guerra de los mil días*, vol. I, pp. 622–3; Luciano González Egido, *Agonizar en Salamanca: Unamuno julio–diciembre 1936* (Madrid, 1986), pp. 95–6, 105.

15 González Egido, *Unamuno*, pp. 228, 245.

16 Armando Chávez Camacho, *Misión de prensa en España* (Mexico City, 1948), pp. 437–8.

17 Testimony of Gil Robles to the author in Madrid in 1970; interview with Manuel Fraga in María Mérida, *Testigos de Franco* (Barcelona, 1976), p. 76.

18 Burgo, *Conspiración*, pp. 221–2.

19 *The Universe*, 22 January 1937; Burgo, *Conspiración*, pp. 222–7.

20 *Sur* (Málaga), 25, 28 April 1937; Burgo, *Conspiración*, pp. 233–4.

21 Angel Alcázar de Velasco, *Serrano Suñer en la Falange* (Madrid, 1941), p. 98; Escobar, *Así empezó*, p. 62.

BIBLIOGRAPHY

1 PRIMARY SOURCES

Unpublished sources

(i) Archivo Histórico de la Fundación Pablo Iglesias (FPI) (Madrid):

    a) Actas de la Comisión Ejecutiva del Partido Socialist Obrero Español, 1931–6

    b) Correspondence files

    c) Francisco Largo Caballero, 'Notas históricas de la guerra de España 1917–1940', MS

(ii) Archivo Histórico Nacional (Madrid): Papeles de D. Luis Araquistain Quevedo

(iii) Archivio Storico del Ministero degli Affari Esteri, Rome: Spagna Fondo di Guerra

Parliamentary debates

Diario de sesiones de las Cortes Constituyentes de la República española, comenzaron el 14 de julio de 1931 (DSCC), 25 vols

Diario de las sesiones de Cortes, Congreso de los Diputados, comenzaron el 8 de diciembre de 1933 (DSC), 17 vols

Diario de las sesiones de Cortes, Congreso de los Diputados, comenzaron el 16 de marzo de 1936 (DSC), 3 vols

Trade union and party bulletins and congress reports

Boletín de Información de Acción Popular (Madrid), fortnightly, March 1932 to May 1933

Boletín de la Unión General de Trabajadores de España (BUGT) (Madrid), monthly, August 1929 to June 1936

CEDA – Organo de la Confederación Española de Derechas Autonomas (Madrid), fortnightly, May 1933 to November 1933

Confederación Nacional del Trabajo, *El Congreso Confederal de Zaragoza 1936* (Madrid, 1978)

Federación Nacional de Trabajadores de la Tierra, *Memoria del Comité Nacional para el II Congreso ordinario que ha de celebrarse en Madrid durante los días 17 y siguientes del mes de septiembre de 1932* (Madrid, 1932)

JAP – Organo nacional de las Juventudes de Acción Popular de España (Madrid), fortnightly, October 1934 to February 1936

PSOE, *Convocatoria y orden del día para el XII congreso ordinario del Partido Socialista Obrero Español* (Madrid, 1927)

PSOE, *Convocatoria y orden del día para el XIII congreso ordinario del Partido Socialista Obrero Español (Madrid, 1932)*

Renovación – Organo de la Federación de Juventudes Socialistas de España (Madrid), weekly, February 1933 to September 1934

La Unión Ferroviaria – Boletín del Sindicato Nacional Ferroviario (Madrid), monthly, 1933

Unión General de Trabajores, *Memoria y orden del día del XVII congreso, que se celebrará en Madrid los días 14 y siguientes de octubre de 1932* (Madrid, 1932)

Ministerial bulletins and reports

Anuario estadístico de España, 1931 (Madrid, 1931)

Boletín del Instituto de Reforma Agraria (Madrid), monthly, January 1933 to July 1936

Boletín del Ministerio de Trabajo y Previsón Social (Madrid), monthly, January 1931 to April 1936

Ministerio de la Gobernación, *Dictamen de la Comisión sobre ilegitimidad de poderes actuantes en 18 de julio de 1936* (Barcelona, 1939)

Ministerio de Justicia, *Causa general. La dominación roja en España. Avance de la información instruida por el ministerio público* (Madrid, 1944)

Ministerio de Trabajo y Previsión Social, *La crisis andaluza de 1930–1931* (Madrid, 1931)

Newspapers and periodicals

ABC (Madrid), daily, August 1923 to August 1936

Acción Española (Madrid), monthly, December 1931 to April 1936

Arriba (Madrid), weekly, March 1935 to February 1936

Avance (Oviedo), daily, November 1931 to October 1934

Claridad (Madrid), weekly (then daily from April 1936), July 1935 to July 1936

Comunismo (Madrid), monthly, May 1931 to October 1934

El Debate (Madrid), daily, January 1930 to July 1936

El Defensor (Granada), daily, December 1935 to June 1936

Democracia (Madrid), weekly, June 1935 to December 1935

La Época (Madrid), daily, April 1931 to April 1936

FE (Madrid), weekly, December 1933 to July 1934

Leviatán (Madrid), monthly, May 1934 to July 1936

El Liberal (Bilbao), daily, March 1935 to March 1936

La Mañana (Jaén), daily, April 1932 to July 1935

El Obrero de la Tierra (Madrid), weekly, January 1932 to July 1936

El Pueblo Católico (Jaén), daily, January 1931 to May 1933

El Socialista (Madrid), daily, August 1923 to August 1936

El Sol (Madrid), daily, August 1923 to July 1936

Tierra y Trabajo (Salamanca), weekly, November 1932 to May 1933

In addition to the above continuous runs of newspapers and periodicals, many shorter runs and odd copies were also consulted. These included:

El Adelanto (Salamanca)
Campo Libre (Madrid)
El Carbayón (Oviedo)
La Correspondence Militar (Madrid)
La Gaceta Regional (Salamanca)
El Heraldo (Madrid)
Ideal (Granada)
La Libertad (Madrid)
Mundo Obrero (Madrid)
La Nación (Madrid)
Región (Cáceres)
El Siglo Futuro (Madrid)
Sur (Málaga)
La Tierra (Madrid)
The Universe (London)

Printed documents: diaries, letters, speeches, memoirs and theoretical works by protagonists, and contemporary and eyewitness accounts

Alcalá Zamora, Niceto, *Los defectos de la constitución de 1931 y tres años de experiencia constitucional*, 2nd edition (Madrid, 1981)
Alcalá Zamora, Niceto, *Discursos* (Madrid, 1979)
Alcalá Zamora, Niceto, *Memorias* (Barcelona, 1977)
Alcázar de Velasco, Angel, *Serrano Suñer en la Falange* (Madrid, 1941)
Alvarez del Vayo, Julio, *Freedom's Battle* (London, 1940)
Alvarez del Vayo, Julio, *The Last Optimist* (London, 1950)
Andrade, Juan, *La burocracia reformista en el movimiento obrero* (Madrid, 1935)
Andrade, Juan, *Recuerdos personales* (Barcelona, 1983)
Angulo, Enrique de, *Diez horas de Estat Catalá* (Valencia, 1934)
Ansaldo, Juan Antonio, *¿Para qué...? De Alfonso XIII a Juan III* (Buenos Aires, 1951)
Araquistain, Luis, *El derrumbamiento del socialismo alemán* (Madrid, n.d. [1933])
Arnau, Roger, *Marxisme catalá i qüestió nacional catalana 1930–1936*, 2 vols (Paris, 1974)
Arrabal, Juan, *José María Gil Robles, su vida, su actuación, sus ideas* (Madrid, 1933)
Arrese, Domingo de, *Bajo la ley de defensa de la República* (Madrid, 1933)
Asociación Católica Nacional de Propagandistas de Oviedo, *Asturias roja: sacerdotes y religiosos perseguidos y martirizados (octubre de 1934)* (Oviedo, n.d. [1935])
Aunós, Eduardo, *La política social de la Dictadura* (Madrid, 1944)
Avon, Earl of, *Facing the Dictators* (London, 1962)
Azaña, Manuel, *Apuntes de memoria inéditos y cartas 1938–1939–1940*, edited by Enrique de Rivas, 2 vols (Valencia, 1990)
Azaña, Manuel, *Memorias íntimas de Azaña* (Madrid, 1939)
Azaña, Manuel, *Mi rebelión en Barcelona* (Madrid, 1935)
Azaña, Manuel, *Obras completas*, 4 vols (Mexico City, 1966–8)
Azaña, Manuel, and Rivas Cherif, Cipriano de, *Cartas 1917–1935 (inéditas)* (Valencia, 1991)
Azpeitia, Mateo, *La reforma agraria en España* (Madrid, 1932)

Baraibar, Carlos de, *Las falsas 'posiciones socialistas' de Indalecio Prieto* (Madrid, 1935)

Barea, Arturo, *La forja de un rebelde* (Buenos Aires, 1951)

Basque Clergy, *El pueblo vasco frente a la cruzada franquista* (Toulouse, 1966)

Belausteguigoitia, Ramón de, *Reparto de tierras y producción nacional* (Madrid, 1932)

Benavides, Manuel, *La revolución fue así* (Barcelona, 1935)

Benavides, Manuel, *El último pirata del mediterráneo*, 2nd edition (Mexico City, 1976)

Berenguer, Dámaso, *De la Dictadura a la República* (Madrid, 1946)

Berges, Consuelo, *Explicación de octubre: historia comprimida de cuatro años de República en España* (Madrid, 1935)

Besteiro, Julián, *Cartas desde la prisión* (Madrid, 1988)

Besteiro, Julián, *Marxismo y anti-marxismo* (Madrid, 1935, 4th edition 1967)

Besteiro, Julián, *Obras completas*, 3 vols, edited by Emilio Lamo de Espinosa (Madrid, 1983)

Boaventura, Armando, *Madrid-Moscovo: da Ditadura a República e guerra civil de Espanha* (Lisbon, 1937)

Bowers, Claude G., *My Mission to Spain* (London, 1954)

Buckley, Henry, *Life and Death of the Spanish Republic* (London, 1940)

Buenacasa, Manuel, *La CNT, los 'treinta' y la FAI* (Barcelona, 1933)

Bueno, Javier, *El Estado socialista: nueva interpretación del comunismo* (Madrid, 1931)

Bullejos, José, *La Comintern en España: recuerdos de mi vida* (Mexico City, 1972)

Bullejos, José, *España en la segunda República* (Mexico City, 1967)

Campoamor, Clara, *El voto femenino y yo* (Madrid, 1936)

Canals, Salvador, *El bienio estéril: perspectivas electorales* (Madrid, 1936)

Canel, José [José Díaz Fernández], *Octubre rojo en Asturias* (Madrid, 1935)

Cánovas Cervantes, S., *Apuntes históricos de Solidaridad Obrera* (Barcelona, 1937)

Carabias, Josefina, *Azaña: los que le llamábamos Don Manuel* (Barcelona, 1980)

Carral, Ignacio, *Porqué mataron a Luis de Sirval* (Madrid, 1935)

Carrillo, Santiago, *Demain l'Espagne* (Paris, 1974)

Carrión, Pascual, *Los latifundios en España* (Madrid, 1932)

Carrión, Pascual, *La reforma agraria: problemas fundamentales* (Madrid, 1931)

Casares, Francisco, *La CEDA va a gobernar (notas y glosas de un año de vida pública nacional)* (Madrid, 1934)

Castro Delgado, Enrique, *Hombres made in Moscú* (Barcelona, 1965)

Chapaprieta Torregrosa, Joaquín, *La paz fue posible: memorias de un político* (Barcelona, 1971)

Chávez Camacho, Armando, *Misión de prensa en España* (Mexico City, 1948)

Cierva, Ricardo de la, *Los documentos de la primavera trágica* (Madrid, 1967)

Clero Vasco, El, *El pueblo vasco frente a la cruzada franquista* (Toulouse, 1966)

Coca, Gabriel Mario de, *Anti-Caballero: una crítica marxista de la bolchevización del Partido Socialista Obrero Español* (Madrid, 1936)

Conze, Edward, *Spain Today: Revolution and Counter-Revolution* (London, 1936)

Cordero, Manuel, *Los socialistas y la revolución* (Madrid, 1932)

Cordón, Antonio, *Trayectoria (recuerdos de un artillero)* (Paris, 1971)

Cortés Cavanillas, Julián, *Gil Robles ¿monárquico?* (Madrid, 1935)

Cortés Cavanillas, Julián, *Vida, confesiones y muerte de Alfonso XIII* (Madrid, 1956)

Costa i Deu, J., and Sabaté, Modest, *La veritat del 6 d'octubre* (Barcelona, 1936)

Cripps, Stafford, et al., *Problemas de gobierno socialista* (Madrid, 1934)

Dencàs, Josep, *El 6 d'octubre des del Palau de Governació* (Barcelona, 1935, reprinted 1979)

Díaz, Carmen, *Mi vida con Ramón Franco* (Barcelona, 1981)

Díaz, José, *Tres años de lucha*, 2nd edition Paris, 1970)

Díaz Doin, Guillermo, *Como llegó Falange al poder: análisis de un proceso contrarrev-olucionario* (Buenos Aires, 1940)

Díaz Doin, Guillermo, *El pensamiento político de Azaña* (Buenos Aires, 1943)

Díaz Guisasola, Carmen, *Mi vida con Ramón Franco* (Barcelona, 1981)

Díaz del Moral, Juan, *Historia de las agitaciones campesinas andaluzas*, 3rd edition (Madrid, 1973)

Díaz Ramos, José, *Tres años de lucha*, 2nd edition (Paris, 1970)

Documentos socialistas (Madrid, n.d. [1935])

Documents on German Foreign Policy 1918–1945, ser. C, vol. IV, and ser. D, vol. III (London, 1964 and 1951)

Domingo, Marcelino, *La experiencia del poder* (Madrid, 1934)

Domingo, Marcelino, *La revolución de octubre* (Barcelona, 1935)

Duclos, Jacques, *Mémoires*, vol. II, *Aux jours ensoleillés du Front Populaire* (Paris, 1969)

Ehrenburg, Ilya, *España, república de trabajadores* (Madrid, 1976)

Escobar, José Ignacio, *Así empezó* (Madrid, 1974)

Escofet, Frederic, *Al servei de Catalunya i de la República*, 2 vols (Paris, 1973)

Franco Bahamonde, Francisco, *'Apuntes' personales sobre la República y la guerra civil* (Madrid, 1987)

[Franco Bahamonde, Francisco], 'Discurso de despedida en el cierre de la Academia General Militar', *Revista de Historia Militar*, Año XX, no. 40, 1966

[Franco Bahamonde, Francisco], *Hoja de servicios del Caudillo de España, Excmo: Sr. Don Francisco Franco Bahamonde y su genealogia*, edited by Esteban Carvallo de Cora (Madrid, 1967)

Franco Salgado-Araujo, Francisco, *Mi vida junto a Franco* (Barcelona, 1977)

García Palacios, Luis, *El segundo bienio (España en escombros)* (Madrid, 1936)

Garcitoral, Alicio, *El crimen de Cuenca* (Madrid, 1932)

Gascón, Antonio, and Priego, Victoria, *Por hoy y por mañana (leves comentarios a un libro firmado por Carlos Baraibar* (Madrid, 1935)

Gil Robles, José María, *Discursos parlamentarios* (Madrid, 1971)

Gil Robles, José María, *La monarquía por la que yo luché (1941–1954)* (Madrid, 1976)

Gil Robles, José María, *No fue posible la paz* (Barcelona, 1968)

Goded, Manuel, *Un 'faccioso' cien por cien* (Zaragoza, 1939)

González López, Emilio, *Memorias de un diputado de las Cortes de la República (1931–1938)* (La Coruña, 1988)

Gorkín, Julián, *El revolucionario profesional: testimonio de un hombre de acción* (Barcelona, 1975)

Grossi, Manuel, *L'Insurrection des Asturies*, 2nd edition (Paris, 1972)

Guerra, Francisco, *Casas Viejas: apuntes de la tragedia* (Jerez, 1933)

[Hernández Zancajo, Carlos], *Octubre – segunda etapa* (n.p., n.d. [Madrid, 1935])

Hidalgo, Diego, *¿Por qué fui lanzado del Ministerio de la Guerra? Diez meses de actuación ministerial* (Madrid, 1934)

Hidalgo de Cisneros, Ignacio, *Cambio de rumbo*, 2 vols (Bucharest, 1964)

Ibárruri, Dolores, *El único camino* (Paris, 1965)

Iglesias, Pablo, *Escritos*, 2 vols (Madrid, 1975)

'Ignotus' (Villar, Manuel), *El anarquismo en la insurreción de Asturias* (Valencia, 1935)

Iribarren, José María, *Mola, datos para una biografía y para la historia del alzamiento nacional* (Zaragoza, 1938)

Jalón, César, *Memorias políticas: periodista, ministro, presidiario* (Madrid, 1973)

Jellinek, Frank, *The Civil War in Spain* (London, 1938)
Jiménez de Asúa, Luis, *Anécdotas de las Constituyentes* (Buenos Aires, 1942)
Jiménez Asúa (Luis), Vidarte (Juan-Simeón), Rodríguez Sastre (Antonio) and Trejo (Anselmo), *Castilblanco* (Madrid, 1933)
Jupin, René, *La Question agraire en Andalusie* (Paris, 1932)
Kautsky, Karl, *El programa de Erfurt* (Madrid, 1933)
Knoblaugh, H. Edward, *Correspondent in Spain* (New York, 1937)
Koestler, Arthur, *Spanish Testament* (London, 1937)
Largo Caballero, Francisco, *Discursos a los trabajadores* (Madrid, 1934)
Largo Caballero, Francisco, *Escritos de la República*, edited by Santos Juliá Díaz (Madrid, 1985)
Largo Caballero, Francisco, *Mis recuerdos: cartas a un amigo* (Mexico City, 1954)
Largo Caballero, Francisco, *Posibilismo socialista en la democracia* (Madrid, 1933)
Largo Caballero, Francisco, *Presente y futuro de la Unión General de Trabajadores de España* (Madrid, 1925)
Ledesma Ramos, Ramiro, *¿Fascismo en España?*, 2nd edition (Barcelona, 1968)
León, María Teresa de, *Memoria de la melancolía* (Buenos Aires, 1970)
Lerroux, Alejandro, *La pequeña historia: apuntes para la historia grande vividos y redactados por el autor* (Buenos Aires, 1945)
Llaneza, Manuel, *Escritos y discursos* (Oviedo, 1985)
López de Ochoa, General Eduardo, *Campaña militar de Asturias en octubre de 1934* (Madrid, 1936)
López Sevilla, Enrique, *El Partido Socialista Obrero Español en las Cortes Constituyentes de la segunda República* (Mexico City, 1969)
Luca de Tena, Juan Ignacio, *Mis amigos muertos* (Barcelona, 1971)
Luca de Tena, Torcuato, *Papeles para la pequeña y la gran historia: memorias de mi padre y mías* (Barcelona, 1991)
Maíz, B. Félix, *Alzamiento en España*, 2nd edition (Pamplona, 1952)
Manning, Leah, *What I Saw in Spain* (London, 1935)
Marco Miranda, Vicente, *Las conspiraciones contra la Dictadura: relato de un testigo* (Madrid, 1930)
Márquez Tornero, A.C., *Testimonio de mi tiempo (memorias de un español republicano)* (Madrid, 1979)
Martín Blázquez, José, *I Helped to Build an Army: Civil War Memoirs of a Spanish Staff Officer* (London, 1939)
Martín-Sánchez Juliá, Fernando, *La reforma agraria italiana y la futura reforma española* (n.p., n.d. [Madrid, 1931])
Martínez Aguilar, Manuel, *¿A dónde va el Estado español? Rebelión socialista y separatista de 1934* (Madrid, 1932)
Martínez Barrio, Diego, *Memorias* (Barcelona, 1983)
Martínez Barrio, Diego, *Orígenes del Frente Popular español* (Buenos Aires, 1943)
Mateo Sousa, Eligio de, *Pasos al exilio* (Madrid, 1991)
Maura, Miguel, *Así cayó Alfonso XIII*, 2nd edition (Barcelona, 1966)
Maurín, Joaquín, *Hacia la segunda revolución: el fracaso de la Repúblic y la insurrección de octubre* (Barcelona, 1935)
Maurín, Joaquín, *Los hombres de la Dictadura* (Madrid, 1930)
Maurín, Joaquín, *La revolución española* (Madrid, 1932)
Medina Togores, José, *Un año de Cortes Constituyentes: impresiones parlamentarias* (Madrid, 1932)
Mendizábal, Alfred, *Aux origines d'une tragédie: la politique espagnole de 1923 à 1936* (Paris, n.d. [1937?])
[Moch] Picard-Moch, Germaine, and Moch, Jules, *L'Oeuvre d'une révolution: l'Espagne républicaine* (Paris, 1933)

Mola Vidal, Emilio, *Obras completas* (Valladolid, 1940)
Molins i Fábrega, N., *UHP: la insurreción proletaria de Asturias*, 2nd edition (Gijón, 1977)
Monedero Martín, Antonio, *La Confederación Nacional Católica-Agraria en 1920: su espíritu, su organización, su porvenir* (Madrid, 1921)
Monge Bernal, José, *Acción Popular (estudios de biologfía política)* (Madrid, 1936)
Mora, Constancia de la, *In Place of Splendour* (London, 1940)
Moral, Joaquín del, *Oligarquía y 'enchufismo'* (Madrid, 1933)
Morón, Gabriel, *El Partido Socialista ante la realidad política española* (Madrid, 1929)
Morón, Gabriel, *Política de ayer y política de mañana* (Mexico City, 1942)
Morón, Gabriel, *La ruta del socialismo en España* (Madrid 1932)
Munis, Grandizo, *Jalones de derrota, promesa de victoria* (Mexico City, 1948)
Nelken, Margarita, *Porqué hicimos la revolución* (Barcelona, 1936)
Nicolas, L., *A travers les révolutions espagnoles* (Paris, 1972)
Nin, Andrés, *Los problemas de la revolución española* (Paris, 1971)
Nin, Andreu, *Por la unificación marxista: escritos políticos* (Madrid, 1978)
Ossorio y Gallardo, Angel, *Mis memorias* (Buenos Aires, 1946)
Pabón, Jesús, *Palabras en las oposición* (Seville, 1935)
Pi Sunyer, Carles, *La República y la guerra: memorias de un politico catalán* (Mexico City, 1975)
Portela Valladares, Manuel, *Memorias: dentro del drama español* (Madrid, 1988)
Prieto, Indalecio, *Convulsiones de España*, 3 vols (Mexico City, 1967–9)
Prieto, Indalecio, *De mi vida: recuerdos, estampas, siluetas, sombras . . .* (Mexico City, 1965)
Prieto, Indalecio, *Dentro y fuera del Gobierno* (Madrid, 1935)
Prieto, Indalecio, *Discursos en América con el pensamiento puesto en España* (Mexico City, n.d. [1944])
Prieto, Indalecio, *Discursos fundamentales*, edited by E. E. Malefakis (Madrid, 1975)
Prieto, Indalecio, *Palabras al viento* (Mexico City, 1942)
Prieto, Indalecio, *Posiciones socialistas: del momento* (Madrid, n.d. [1935])
Prieto, Indalecio, *Yo y Moscú* (Madrid, 1955)
Primo de Rivera, José Antonio, *Obras*, 4th edition (Madrid, 1966)
Ramos Oliveira, Antonio, *Alemania: ayer y hoy* (Madrid 1933)
Ramos Oliveira, Antonio, *Nosotros los marxistas: Lenin contra Marx* (Madrid, 1932)
Ramos Oliveira, Antonio, *Politics, Economics and Men of Modern Spain* (London, 1946)
Ramos Oliveira, Antonio, *La revolución española de octubre* (Madrid, 1935)
Rangil Alonso, Félix, *El ensayo socialista en la República española* (Buenos Aires, 1934)
Reporteros Reunidos, *Octubre rojo: ocho días que conmovieron a España* (Madrid, n.d. [1935])
Ríos, Fernando de los, *Escritos sobre democracia y socialismo* (Madrid, 1974)
Ríos, Fernando de los, *El sentido humanista del socialismo* (Madrid, 1926)
Rivas Cherif, Cipriano de, *Retrato de un desconocido: vida de Manuel Azaña (seguido por el epistolario de Manuel Azaña con Cipriano de Rivas Cherif de 1921 a 1937)* (Barcelona, 1980)
Rodríguez de la Peña, José, *Los aventureros de la política: Alejandro Lerroux* (Madrid, n.d. [1916])
Romero Solano, Luis, *Vísperas de la guerra de España* (Mexico City, n.d. [1947])
Rosado, Antonio, *Tierra y libertad: memorias de un campesino anarcosindicalista andaluz* (Barcelona, 1979)

Rosal, Amaro del, *Historia de la UGT de España 1901–1939*, 2 vols (Barcelona, 1977)
Rosal, Amaro del, *1934: el movimiento revolucionario de octubre* (Madrid, 1983)
Ruiz Alonso, Ramón, *Corporativismo* (Salamanca, 1937)
Ruiz-Castillo Basala, José, *Funcionario republicano de reforma agraria y otros testimonios* (Madrid, 1983)
Ruiz del Toro, José, *Octubre: etapas de un período revolucionario en España* (Buenos Aires, 1935)
Saborit, Andrés, *Julián Besteiro*, 2nd edition (Buenos Aires, 1967)
Saborit, Andrés, *El pensamiento político de Julián Besteiro* (Madrid, 1974)
Salazar Alonso, Rafael, *Bajo el signo de la revolución* (Madrid, 1935)
Sánchez Albornoz, Claudio, *De mi anecdotario político* (Buenos Aires, 1972)
Sánchez, Manuel, *Maurín: gran enigma de la guerra civil y otros recuerdos* (Madrid, 1976)
Sánchez Guerra, José, *Al servicio de España* (Madrid, 1930)
Sánchez Guerra, Rafael, *Dictadura, indiferencia, República* (Madrid, 1931)
Santiago, Enrique de, *La Unión General de Trabajadores ante la revolución* (Madrid, 1932)
Sanz, Ricardo, *El sindicalismo español antes de la guerra: los hijos del trabajo* (Barcelona, 1935)
Sanz, Ricardo, *El sindicalismo y la política: los 'solidarios' y 'nosotros'* (Toulouse, 1966)
Sender, Ramón J., *Viaje a la aldea del crimen (documental de Casas Viejas)* (Madrid, 1934)
Serrano Poncela, Segundo, *El Partido Socialista y la conquista del poder* (Barcelona, 1935)
Serrano Súñer, Ramón, *Entre Hendaya y Gibraltar* (Madrid, 1947)
Serrano Súñer, Ramón, *Entre el silencio y la propaganda, la historia como fue: memorias* (Barcelona, 1977)
Suero Sánchez, Luciano, *Memorias de un campesino andaluz* (Madrid, 1982)
Tagüeña Lacorte, Manuel, *Testimonio de dos guerras* (Mexico City, 1973)
Trotsky, Leon, *Escritos sobre España* (Paris, 1971)
Trotsky, Leon, *La Révolution espagnole 1930–40*, edited by Pierre Broué (Paris, 1975)
Trotsky, Leon, *The Spanish Revolution (1931–1939)* (New York, 1973)
Trotsky, Leon, *The Struggle against Fascism in Germany* (New York, 1971)
Tusquets, J., *Orígenes de la revolución española* (Barcelona, 1932)
Valdés, Alejandro, *¡Asturias! (relato vivido de la insurrección de octubre)* (Valencia, n.d. [1935?])
Valverde, José Tomás, *Memorias de un alcalde* (Madrid, 1961)
Varela Rendueles, José María, *Rebelión en Sevilla: memorias de un gobernador rebelde* (Seville, 1982)
Vegas Latapie, Eugenio, *Los caminos del desengaño: memorias políticas, vol. II, 1936–1938* (Madrid, 1987)
Vidal i Barraquer Archives, *Esglesia i Estat durant la segona República espanyola*, 4 vols in 8 parts (Monastir de Montserrat, 1971–90)
Vidarte, Juan-Simeón, *El bienio negro y la insurreción de Asturias* (Barcelona, 1978)
Vidarte, Juan-Simeón, *Las Cortes Constituyentes de 1931–1933* (Barcelona, 1976)
Vidarte, Juan-Simeón, *No queríamos al Rey: testimonio de un socialista español* (Barcelona, 1977)
Vidarte, Juan-Simeón, *Todos fuimos culpables* (Mexico City, 1973)
Zugazagoitia, Julián, *Guerra y vicisitudes de los Españoles*, 2 vols (Paris, 1968)

2 SECONDARY SOURCES

Monographs and general works

Abad de Santillán, Diego, *Contribución a la historia del movimiento obrero español*, 3 vols (Puebla, 1962–71)

Aguado Sánchez, Francisco, *La revolución de octubre de 1934* (Madrid, 1972)

Aguilar Olivencia, Mariano, *El ejército español durante la segunda República* (Madrid, 1986)

Alarcón Caballero, José Antonio, *El movimiento obrero en Granada en la II República (1931–1936)* (Granada, 1990)

Alaya, José Antonio, *Murcia en la II República* (Murcia, 1984)

Alba, Victor, *La Alianza Obrera: historia y análisis de una táctica de unidad en España* (Gijón, 1977)

Alba, Victor, *El marxismo en España*, 2 vols (Mexico City, 1973)

Alexander, Martin, and Graham, Helen, editors, *The French and Spanish Popular Fronts: Comparative Perspectives* (Cambridge, 1989)

Alpert, Michael, *La reforma militar de Azaña (1931–1933)* (Madrid, 1982)

Alvarez, Ramón, *Eleuterio Quintanilla (vida y obra del maestro): contribución a la historia del sindicalismo revolucionario en Asturias* (Mexico City, 1973)

Andrés Gallego, José, *El socialismo durante la dictadura 1923–1930* (Madrid, 1977)

Aróstegui, Julio, *Francisco Largo Caballero en el exilio: la última etapa de un líder obrero* (Madrid, 1990)

Arrarás, Joaquín, *Franco*, 7th edition (Valladolid, 1939)

Arrarás, Joaquín, *Historia de la cruzada española*, 8 vols (Madrid, 1939–43)

Arrarás, Joaquín, *Historia de la segunda República española*, 4 vols (Madrid, 1956–68)

Aunós, Eduardo, *Itinerario histórico de la España contemporánea* (Barcelona, 1940)

Avilés Farré, Juan, *La izquierda burguesa en la II República* (Madrid, 1985)

Azpíroz Pascual, José María, *Poder político y conflictividad social en Huesca durante la II República* (Huesca, 1993)

Balcells, Alberto, *Crisis económica y agitación social en Cataluña (1930–1936)* (Barcelona, 1971)

Balcells, Alberto, *El problema agrari a Catalunya 1890–1936: la qüestió rabassaire* (Barcelona, 1968)

Balcells, Alberto, *El sindicalismo en Barcelona 1916–1923* (Barcelona, 1965)

Ballbé, Manuel, *Orden público y militarismo en la España contemporánea (1812–1983)* (Madrid, 1983)

Bar, Antonio, *La CNT en los años rojos (del sindicalismo revolucionario al anarcosindicalismo 1910–1926)* (Madrid, 1981)

Barragán Moriana, Antonio, *Conflictividad social y desarticulación política en la provincia de Córdoba 1918–1920* (Córdoba, 1990)

Barrio Alonso, Angeles, *Anarquismo u anarcosindicalismo en Asturias (1890/1936)* (Madrid, 1988)

Bécarud, Jean, *Le segunda Repúlica española* (Madrid, 1967)

Ben Ami, Shlomo, *Fascism from Above: The Dictatorship of Primo de Rivera in Spain 1923–1930* (Oxford, 1983)

Ben Ami, Shlomo, *The Origins of the Second Republic in Spain* (Oxford, 1978)

Bermejo Martín, Francisco, *La IIª República en Logroño: elecciones y contexto político* (Logroño, 1984)

Bernal, Antonio Miguel, *La propiedad de la tierra y las luchas agrarias andaluzas* (Barcelona, 1974)

Biglino Campos, Paloma, *El socialismo español y la cuestión agraria 1890–1936* (Madrid, 1986)

Bizcarrondo, Marta, *Leviatán y el socialismo de Luis Araquistain* (Glashütten im Taunus, 1974)

Bizcarrondo, Marta, editor, *Octubre del 34: reflexiones sobre una revolución* (Madrid, 1977)

Blas Guerrero, Andrés de, *El socialismo radical en la II República* (Madrid, 1978)

Blinkhorn, Martin, *Carlism and Crisis in Spain 1931–1939* (Cambridge, 1975)

Blinkhorn, Martin, editor, *Spain in Conflict 1931–1939: Democracy and its Enemies* (London, 1986)

Bolín, Luis, *Spain: The Vital Years* (New York, 1967)

Bolloten, Burnett, *The Grand Camouflage: The Spanish Civil War and Revolution, 1936–1939*, 2nd edition (London, 1968)

Bolloten, Burnett, *The Spanish Civil War: Revolution and Counterrevolution* (Chapel Hill, NC, 1991)

Bonamusa, Francesc, *Andreu Nin y el movimiento comunista en España (1930–1937)* (Barcelona, 1977)

Bonamusa, Francesc, *El Bloc Obrer i Camperol: els primers anys (1930–1932)* (Barcelona, 1974)

Brademas, John, *Anarco-sindicalismo y revolución en España 1930–1937* (Barcelona, 1974)

Brenan, Gerald, *Personal Record 1920–1972* (London, 1974)

Brenan, Gerald, *The Spanish Labyrinth*, 2nd edition (Cambridge, 1950)

Brey, Gérald, and Maurice, Jacques, *Historia y leyenda de Casas Viejas* (Madrid, 1976)

Broué, Pierre, and Témine, Emile, *The Revolution and the Civil War in Spain* (London, 1972)

Bruguera, F.G., *Histoire contemporaine d'Espagne 1789–1950* (Paris, 1953)

Buchanan, Tom, *The Spanish Civil War and the British Labour Movement* (Cambridge, 1991)

Burgo, Jaime del, *Conspiración y guerra civil* (Madrid, 1970)

Cabanellas, Guillermo, *La guerra de los mil días: nacimiento, vida y muerte de la segunda República española*, 2 vols (Buenos Aires, 1973)

Cabrera, Mercedes, *La patronal ante la II República: organizaciones y estrategia (1931–1936)* (Madrid, 1983)

Calero, Antonio M., *Movimientos sociales en Andalucía 1820–1936* (Madrid, 1976)

Cardona, Gabriel, *El poder militar en la España contemporánea hasta la guerra civil* (Madrid, 1983)

Carr, E. H., *The Comintern and the Spanish Civil War* (London, 1984)

Carr, Raymond, editor, *The Republic and the Civil War in Spain* (London, 1971)

Carr, Raymond, *Spain 1808–1939* (Oxford, 1966)

Casterás, Ramón, *Las Juventudes Socialistas Unificadas de Catalunya ante la guerra y la revolución (1936–1939)*, 2nd edition (Barcelona, 1982)

Castillo, Juan José, *Propietarios muy pobres: sobre la subordinación política del pequeño campesino* (Madrid, 1979)

Castillo, Juan José, *El sindicalismo amarillo en España* (Madrid, 1977)

Cattell, David, T., *Communism and the Spanish Civil War* (Berkeley, Calif., 1955)

Chamorro, Jesús Vicente, *Año nuevo, año viejo en Castilblanco* (Madrid, 1985)

Checkland, S.G., *The Mines of Tharsis* (London, 1967)

Cierva, Ricardo de la, *Bibliografía general sobre la guerra de España (1936–1939) y sus antecedentes históricos* (Madrid/Barcelona, 1968)

Cierva, Ricardo de la, *Francisco Franco: biografía histórica*, 6 vols (Barcelona, 1982)

Cierva, Ricardo de la, *Historia de la guerra civil española*, vol. I (Madrid, 1969)

Cierva, Ricardo de la, *La historia perdida del socialismo español* (Madrid, 1972)

Claudín, Fernando, *Santiago Carrillo: crónica de un secretario general* (Barcelona, 1983)

Clavero, Bartolomé, Ruiz Torres, Pedro, and Hernández Montalbán, Francisco J., *Estudios sobre la revolución burguesa en España* (Madrid, 1979)

Cobo Romero, Francisco, *Labradores, campesinos y jornaleros: protesta social y diferenciación interna del campesinado jiennense en los orígenes de la guerra civil (1931–1936)* (Cordoba, 1992)

Collier, George A., *Socialists of Rural Andalusia: Unacknowledged Revolutionaries of the Second Republic* (Stanford, Calif., 1987)

Collins, Larry, and Lapierre, Dominique, *Or I'll Dress You in Mourning* (London, 1968)

Comín Colomer, Eduardo, *Historia del Partido Comunista de España*, 3 vols (Madrid, 1967)

Contreras, Manuel, *El PSOE en la II República: organización e ideología* (Madrid, 1981)

Cruells, Manuel, *El 6 d'octubre a Catalunya* (Barcelona, 1971)

Cruz, Rafael, *El Partido Comunista de España en la II República* (Madrid, 1987)

Díaz Nosty, Bernardo, *La comuna asturiana: revolución de octubre de 1934* (Bilbao, 1974)

Ellwood, Sheelagh, *Prietas las filas: historia de Falange Española 1933–1983* (Barcelona, 1984)

Elorza, Antonio, *La utopía anarquista bajo la segunda República española* (Madrid, 1973)

Espín, Eduardo, *Azaña en el poder: el partido de Acción Republicana* (Madrid, 1980)

Fernández, Eusebio, *Marxismo y positivismo en el socialismo español* (Madrid, 1981)

Fontana, Josep, *Cambio económico y actitudes políticas en la España del siglo XIX* (Barcelona, 1973)

Forcadell, Carlos, *Parlamentarismo y bolchevización: el movimiento obrero español 1914–1918* (Barcelona, 1978)

Forner Muñoz, Salvador, *Industrialización y movimiento obrero: Alicante 1923–1936* (Valencia, 1982)

Fraser, Ronald, *Blood of Spain: The Experience of Civil War 1936–1939* (London, 1979)

Fraser, Ronald, *In Hiding: The Life of Manuel Cortes* (London, 1972)

Fusi Aizpurua, Juan Pablo, *Política obrera en el país vasco 1880–1923* (Madrid, 1975)

Fusi Aizpurua, Juan Pablo, *El problema vasco en la IIª República* (Madrid, 1979)

García Delgado, José Luis, editor, *La cuestión agraria en la España contemporánea* (Madrid, 1976)

García Escudero, José María, *Conversaciones sobre Angel Herrera* (Madrid, 1986)

García Escudero, José María, *El pensamiento de 'El Debate': un diario católico en la crisis de España (1911–1936)* (Madrid, 1983)

García Pérez, Juan, *Estructura agraria y conflictos campesinos en la provincia de Cáceres durante la II República* (Cáceres, 1982)

García Pérez Bances, Jesús, *Indalecio Prieto Tuero, 1883–1962* (Oviedo, 1983)

García Venero, Maximiano, *El general Fanjul: Madrid en el alzamiento nacional* (Madrid, 1967)

Garriga, Ramón, *El general Yagüe* (Barcelona, 1985)

Garriga, Ramón, *Ramón Franco, el hermano maldito* (Barcelona, 1978)

Germán Zubero, Luis, *Aragón en la segunda República* (Zaragoza, 1984)

Gibson, Ian, *The Death of Lorca* (London, 1973)

Gibson, Ian, *La noche en que mataron a Calvo Sotelo* (Barcelona, 1982)

Gibson, Ian, *La represión nacionalista de Granada en 1936 y la muerte de Federico García Lorca* (Paris, 1971)

Gil Novales, Alberto, editor, *La revolución burguesa en España* (Madrid, 1985)

Gil Pecharramán, Julio, 'Renovación Española: una alternativa monárquica a la segunda República', unpublished Ph.D thesis, Universidad Complutense de Madrid, 2 vols, 1983

Gómez Nazabal, José R., *Consideraciones en torno al ideario y la praxis del socialismo español 1879–1921* (San Sebastián, 1981)

González Egido, Luciano, *Agonizar en Salamanca: Unamuno julio–diciembre 1936* (Madrid, 1986)

González Sobaco, Antonio, *Los partidos políticos durante la segunda República en Castellón* (Castellón, 1986)

Graham, Helen, *Socialism and War: The Spanish Socialist Party in Power and Crisis, 1936–1939* (Cambridge, 1991)

Graham, Helen, and Preston, Paul, editors, *The Popular Front in Europe* (London, 1987)

Gutiérrez Molina, José Luis, *La idea revolucionaria: el anarquismo organizado en Andalucía y Cádiz durante los años treinta* (Madrid, 1993)

Gutiérrez Ravé, José, *Gil Robles, caudillo frustrado* (Madrid, 1967)

Harrison, Joseph, *The Spanish Economy in the Twentieth Century* (London, 1985)

Hennessy, C. A. M., *The Federal Republic in Spain 1868–1874* (Oxford, 1962)

Hernández Andreu, Juan, *Depresión económica en España, 1925–1934* (Madrid, 1980)

Hernández Armenteros, Salvador, *Jaén ante la segunda República: bases económicas, sociales y políticas de una transición* (Granada, 1988)

Heywood, Paul, *Marxism and the Failure of Organised Socialism in Spain 1879–1936* (Cambridge, 1990)

Ibárruri, Dolores, et al., *Guerra y revolución en España 1936–1939*, 4 vols (Moscow, 1967–77)

Jackson, Gabriel, *Costa, Azaña, el Frente Popular y otros ensayos* (Madrid, 1976)

Jackson, Gabriel, *Historian's Quest* (New York, 1969)

Jackson, Gabriel, *The Spanish Republic and the Civil War* (Princeton, NJ, 1965)

Jiménez Campo, Javier, *El fascismo en la crisis de la II República* (Madrid, 1979)

Juliá Díaz, Santos, *Historia del socialismo español (1931–1939)* (Barcelona, 1989)

Juliá Díaz, Santos, *La izquierda del PSOE (1935–1936)* (Madrid, 1977)

Juliá Díaz, Santos, *Madrid, 1931–1934: de la fiesta popular a la lucha de clases* (Madrid, 1984)

Juliá Díaz, Santos, *Manuel Azaña: una biografía política, del Ateneo al Palacio Nacional* (Madrid, 1990)

Juliá Díaz, Santos, *Orígenes del Frente Popular en España (1934–1936)* (Madrid, 1979)

Juliá Díaz, Santos, editor, *El socialismo en España: desde la fundación del PSOE hasta 1975* (Madrid, 1986)

Lacomba, Juan Antonio, *La crisis española de 1917* (Madrid, 1970)

Lamberet, Renée, *Mouvements ouvriers et socialistes: l'Espagne* (Paris, 1953)

Lamo de Espinosa, Emilio, *Filosofía y política en Julián Besteiro* (Madrid, 1973)

Lamo de Espinosa, Emilio, and Contreras, Manuel, *Filosofía y política en Julián Besteiro*, 2nd edition (Madrid, 1990)

Lannon, Frances, *Privilege, Persecution, and Prophecy: The Catholic Church in Spain 1875–1975* (Oxford, 1987)

Lannon, Frances, and Preston, Paul, editors, *Élites and Power in Twentieth-Century Spain: Essays in Honour of Sir Raymond Carr* (Oxford, 1990)

Lipset, Seymour M., and Rokkan, Stein, editors, *Party Systems and Voter Alignments* (New York, 1976)

López (Elsa), Alvarez Junco (José), Espadas Burgos (Manuel), and Muñoz Tinoco (Concha), *Diego Hidalgo: memoria de un tiempo difícil* (Madrid, 1986)

López Fernández, Antonio, *Defensa de Madrid* (Mexico City, 1945)

López López, Alejandro, *El boicot de las derechas a las reformas de la segunda República: la minoría agraria, el rechazo constitucional y la cuestión de la tierra* (Madrid, 1984)

Lorenzo, César M., *Les Anarchistes espagnols et le pouvoir, 1868–1969* (Paris, 1969)

Lozano, Jesús, *La segunda República: imágenes, cronología y documentos* (Barcelona, 1973)

Macarro Vera, José Manuel, *Sevilla la roja* (Seville, 1989)

Macarro Vera, José Manuel, *La utopía revolucionaria: Sevilla en la segunda República* (Seville, 1985)

Madariaga, Salvador de, *Spain: A Modern History* (London, 1961)

Majuelo, Emilio, *Luchas de clases en Navarra (1931–1936)* (Pamplona, 1989)

Malefakis, Edward E., *Agrarian Reform and Peasant Revolution in Spain* (New Haven, Conn., 1970)

Martin, Benjamin, *The Agony of Modernization: Labor and Industrialization in Spain* (Ithaca, NY, 1990)

Martín i Ramos, Josep Lluís, *Els orígens del Partit Socialista Unificat de Catalunya (1930–1936)* (Barcelona, 1977)

Martínez Barrio, Diego, *Memorias* (Barcelona, 1983)

Maurice, Jacques, *La reforma agraria en España en el siglo XX (1900–1936)* (Madrid, 1975)

Meaker, Gerald H., *The Revolutionary Left in Spain, 1914–1923* (Stanford, Calif., 1974)

Mérida, María, *Testigos de Franco* (Barcelona, 1976)

Míguez, Alberto, *El pensamiento filosófico de Julián Besteiro* (Madrid, 1971)

Mintz, Jerome, *The Anarchists of Casas Viejas* (Chicago, 1982)

Miralles, Ricardo, *El socialismo vasco durante la segunda República* (Bilbao, 1988)

Monreal, Antoni, *El pensamiento político de Joaquín Maurín* (Barcelona, 1984)

Montañés, Enrique, *Anarcosindicalismo y cambio político: Zaragoza, 1930–1936* (Zaragoza, 1989)

Montero, José Ramón, *La CEDA: el catolicismo social y político en la II República*, 2 vols (Madrid, 1977)

Moore, Barrington, Jr, *Social Origins of Dictatorship and Democracy* (London, 1967)

Moradiellos, Enrique, *El Sindicato de los Obreros Mineros de Asturias 1910–1930* (Oviedo, 1986)

Moreno Fernández, Luis Miguel, *Acción Popular Murciana: la derecha confesional en Murcia durante la II República* (Murcia, 1987)

Moreno Gómez, Francisco, *La República y la guerra civil en Córdoba*, I (Córdoba, 1982)

Morodo, Raúl, *Los orígenes ideólogicos del franquismo: Acción Española* (Madrid, 1985)

Muñoz Tinoco, Concha, *Diego Hidalgo: un notario republicano* (Badajoz, 1986)

Ojeda, Germán, editor, *Octubre 1934: cincuenta años para la reflexión* (Madrid, 1985)

Pabón, Jesús, *Cambó*, 3 vols (Barcelona, 1952–69)

Pagés, Pelai, *Andreu Nin: su evolución política, 1911–1937* (Bilbao, 1975)

Pagés, Pelai, *El movimiento trotskista en España '1930–1935'* (Barcelona, 1977)

Pascual Cevallos, Fernando, *Luchas agrarias en Sevilla durante la segunda República* (Seville, 1983)

Pastor Ugena, Alfredo, 'La Agrupación Socialista Madrileña durante la segunda

República', unpublished Ph.D thesis, Universidad Complutense di Madrid, 2 vols, 1985

Payne, Stanley G., *Falange: A History of Spanish Fascism* (Stanford, Calif., 1961)

Payne, Stanley G., *Politics and the Military in Modern Spain* (Stanford, Calif., 1967)

Payne, Stanley G., *Spain's First Democracy: The Second Republic, 1931–1936* (Madison, Wis., 1993)

Payne, Stanley G., *The Spanish Revolution* (London, 1970)

Peirats, José, *Los anarquistas en la crisis política española* (Buenos Aires, 1964)

Peirats, José, *La CNT en la revolución española*, 2nd edition, 3 vols (Paris, 1971)

Pérez Galán, Mariano, *La enseñanza en la segunda República española* (Madrid, 1975)

Pérez Ledesma, Manuel, *El obrero consciente: dirigentes, partidos y sindicatos en la II Internacional* (Madrid, 1987)

Pérez Yruela, Manuel, *La conflictividad campesina en la provincia de Córdoba 1931–1936* (Madrid, 1979)

Pertiñez Díaz, Miguel, *Granada 1936, elecciones a Cortes* (Granada, 1987)

Pradas Martínez, Enrique, editor, *8 de diciembre de 1933: insurrección anarquista en La Rioja* (Logroño, 1983)

Pradas Martínez, Enrique, *La segunda República y La Rioja (1931–1936)* (Logroño, 1982)

Preston, Paul, *Las derechas españolas en el siglo XX: autoritarismo, fascismo, golpismo* (Madrid, 1986)

Preston, Paul, *Franco: A Biography* (London, 1993)

Preston, Paul, editor, *Leviatán: antología* (Madrid, 1976)

Preston, Paul, *The Politics of Revenge: Fascism and the Military in 20th Century Spain* (London, 1990)

Preston, Paul, editor, *Revolution and War in Spain 1931–1939* (London, 1984)

Preston, Paul, *The Spanish Civil War 1936–1939* (London, 1986)

Ramírez, Manuel, *Las reformas de la IIª República* (Madrid, 1977)

Ramírez, Jiménez, Manuel, editor, *Estudios sobre la segunda República española* (Madrid, 1975)

Ramírez Jiménez, Manuel, *Los grupos de presión en la segunda República española* (Madrid, 1969)

Ramos Espejo, Antonio, *Después de Casas Viejas* (Barcelona, 1984)

Requena Gallego, Manuel, *Los sucesos de Yeste (mayo 1936)* (Albacete, 1983)

Ribas Ribas, Pedro, *La introducción del marxismo en España (1869–1939)* (Madrid, 1981)

Robinson, Richard A. H., *The Origins of Franco's Spain: The Right, the Republic and Revolution, 1931–1936* (Newton Abbot, 1970)

Rodríguez de las Heras, Antonio, *Filiberto Villalobos: su obra social y política (1900–1936)* (Salamanca, 1985)

Ruiz, David, *Insurrección defensiva y revolución obrera: el octubre español de 1934* (Barcelona, 1988)

Ruiz, David, *El movimiento obrero en Asturias* (Oviedo, 1968)

Ruiz, David, et al., *Asturias contemporánea 1808–1975* (Madrid, 1981)

Ruiz Manjón, Octavio, *El Partido Republicano Radical 1908–1936* (Madrid, 1976)

Sáez Alba, A., *La Otra 'cosa nostra': la Asociación Católica Nacional de Propagandistas* (Paris, 1974)

Saiz Valdivielso, Alfonso Carlos, *Indalecio Prieto: crónica de un corazón* (Barcelona, 1984)

Salas Larrazábal, Ramón, *Historia del Ejército popular de la República*, 4 vols (Madrid, 1973)

Sánchez Albornoz, Nicolás, *España hace un siglo* (Barcelona, 1968)

Sánchez y García Saúco, Juan Antonio, *La revolución de 1934 en Asturias* (Madrid, 1974)

Schmoll Mahoney, Barbara, 'José María Gil Robles: The Catholic Politician in the Second Spanish Republic', unpublished Ph.D thesis, St Louis University, 1974

Seco Serrano, Carlos, *Época contemporánea* (Barcelona, 1971)

Serrano, Vicente Alberto, and San Luciano, José María, editors, *Azaña* (Madrid, 1980)

Sevilla Guzmán, Eduardo, *La evolución del campesinado en España* (Barcelona, 1979)

Shubert, Adrian, *The Road to Revolution in Spain: The Coal Miners of Asturias 1860–1934* (Urbana, Ill., and Chicago, 1987)

Southworth, Herbert R., *Antifalange* (Paris, 1967)

Southworth, Herbert R., *El mito de la cruzada de Franco* (Paris, 1963)

Taibo, Paco Ignacio, II, *Historia general de Asturias*, vol. VII, *Octubre 1934: el ascenso* (Gijón, 1978)

Taibo, Paco Ignacio, II, *Historia general de Asturias*, vol. VIII, *Octubre 1934: la caída* (Gijón, 1978)

Tamames, Ramón, *La República, la era de Franco* (Madrid, 1973)

Termes, Josep, and Alquézar, Ramón, *Historia del socialismo español (1909–1931)* (Barcelona, 1989)

Thomas, Hugh, *The Spanish Civil War*, 3rd edition (London, 1977)

Townson, Nigel, 'The Collapse of the Centre: The Radical Republican Party during the Spanish Second Republic', unpublished Ph.D thesis, University of London, 1991

Tuñón de Lara, Manuel, *La España del siglo XIX 1808–1914* (Paris, 1961)

Tuñón de Lara, Manuel, *La España del siglo XX*, 2nd edition (Paris, 1973)

Tuñón de Lara, Manuel, editor, *Historiografía española contemporánea* (Madrid, 1980)

Tuñón de Lara, Manuel, *Luchas obreras y campesinas en la Andalucía del siglo XX* (Madrid, 1978)

Tuñón de Lara, Manuel, *El movimiento obrero en la historia de España* (Madrid, 1972)

Tuñón de Lara, Manuel, editor, *Sociedad, política y cultura en la España de los siglos XIX-XX* (Madrid, 1973)

Tuñón de Lara, Manuel, *Tres claves de la segunda República* (Madrid, 1985)

Tuñón de Lara, Manuel, et al., *Crisis del antiguo régimen e industrialización en la España del siglo XX* (Madrid, 1977)

Tusell, Javier, *Las elecciones del Frente Popular*, 2 vols (Madrid, 1971)

Tusell, Javier, *Historia de la democracia cristiana en España*, 2 vols (Madrid, 1974)

Tusell, Javier, *La oposición democrática al franquismo* (Barcelona, 1977)

Tusell, Javier, and Calvo, José, *Giménez Fernández: precursor de la democracia española* (Seville, 1990)

Ucelay da Cal, Enric, *La Catalunya populista: imatge, cultura i política en l'etapa republicana (1931–1939)* (Barcelona, 1982)

Valls, Rafael, *La Derecha Regional Valenciana 1930–1936* (Valencia, 1992)

Vega, Eulalia, *Anarquistas y sindicalistas durante la segunda República: la CNT y los sindicatos de oposición en el País Valenciano* (Valencia, 1987)

Velarde Fuertes, Juan, *El Nacional-Sindicalismo cuarenta años después* (Madrid, 1972)

Venegas, José, *Las elecciones del Frente Popular* (Buenos Aires, 1942)

Viñas, Angel, *La Alemania nazi y el 18 de julio* (Madrid, 1974)

Viñas, Ricard, *La formación de las Juventudes Socialistas Unificadas (1934–1936)* (Madrid, 1978)

Winston, Colin M., *Workers and the Right in Spain 1900–1936* (Princeton, NJ, 1985)

Yagüe, María Eugenia, *Santiago Carrillo* (Madrid, 1977)

Zapatero, Virgilio, *Fernando de los Ríos: los problemas del socialismo democrático* (Madrid, 1974)

Articles

Anes, Gonzalo, 'La agricultura española desde comienzos del siglo XIX hasta 1868', in Banco de España, *Ensayos sobre la economía española a mediados del siglo XIX* (Barcelona, 1970)

Aróstegui, Julio, 'Conflicto social e ideología de la violencia', in José Luis García Delgado, editor, *España, 1898–1936: estructura y cambio* (Madrid, 1984)

Aviv, Aviva and Isaac, 'Ideology and Political Patronage: Workers and Working Class Movements in Republican Madrid 1931–4', *European Studies Review*, vol. 11, no. 4, October 1981

Aviv, Aviva and Isaac, 'The Madrid Working Class, the Spanish Socialist Party and the Collapse of the Second Republic (1934–1936)', *Journal of Contemporary History*, vol. 16, no. 2, April 1981

Baraibar, Carlos de, 'La tración del Stalinismo', *Timón* (Buenos Aires), no. 7, June 1940

Bécarud, Jean, 'La acción política de Gil Robles', *Cuadernos de Ruedo Ibérico* (Paris), nos 28–9, December 1970 to March 1971

Bizcarrondo, Marta, 'Análisis económico y socialismo en la segunda República', *Estudios de Historia Social*, no. 14, July–September 1980

Bizcarrondo, Marta, 'La crisis socialista en la segunda República', *Revista del Instituto de Ciencias Sociales* (Barcelona) no. 21, 1973

Bizcarrondo, Marta, 'De las Alianzas Obreras el Frente Popular', *Estudios de Historia Social*, nos 16–17, January–June 1981

Bizcarrondo, Marta, 'Democracia y revolución en la estrategia socialista de la II República', *Estudios de Historia Social*, nos 16–17, January–June 1981

Bizcarrondo, Marta, 'Julián Besteiro: socialismo y democracia', *Revista de Occident* (Madrid) no. 94, January 1971

Bizcarrondo, Marta, 'El marco histórico de la revolución', *Estudios de Historia Social*, no. 31, October–Decembre 1984

Blas Guerrero, Andrés de, 'La radicalización de Francisco Largo Caballero, 1933–1934', *Sistema* (Madrid) no. 8, January 1975

Blinkhorn, Martin, ' "The Basque Ulster": Navarra and the Basque Autonomy Question under the Spanish Second Republic', *The Historical Journal*, vol. 17, no. 3, 1974

Blinkhorn, Martin, 'Carlism and the Spanish Crisis of the 1930s', *Journal of Contemporary History*, vol. 7, nos 3–4, 1972

Boyd, Carolyn P., ' "Responsibilities" and the Second Republic, 1931–1936', in Martin Blinkhorn, editor, *Spain in Conflict 1931–1939: Democracy and its Enemies* (London, 1986)

Cabrera Calvo-Sotelo, Mercedes. 'La estrategia patronal en la segunda República', *Estudios de Historia Social*, no. 7, October–December 1978

Cabrera Calvo-Sotelo, Mercedes, 'La estrategia patronal en la segunda República (II): el bienio negro', *Estudios de Historia Social*, nos 10–11, July–December 1979

Casanova, Julián, 'España, 1931–1939: República, protesta social y revolución', in *Revueltas y revoluciones en la historia* (Salamanca, 1990)

Castillo, Juan José, 'El Comité Nacional Circunstancial de la Confederación Española de Sindicatos Obreros 1936–1938', *Revista Española de la Opinión Pública* (Madrid), no. 38, October 1974

Claudín, Fernando, 'Dos concepciones de la vía española al socialismo', in *Horizonte español 1966*, 2 vols (Paris, Cuadernos de Ruedo Ibérico, 1966)

Díaz Elías, 'Fernando de los Ríos: socialismo humanista y socialismo marxista', *Sistema* (Madrid) no. 10, July 1975

Durgan, Andy, 'The Rise and Fall of Largo Caballero', *International Socialism*, vol. 2, no. 18, Winter 1983

Fusi Aizpurua, Juan Pablo, 'El movimiento obrero en España, 1876–1914', *Revista de Occidente* (Madrid) no. 131, February 1974

Gómez Molleda, Dolores, 'La inteligencia de izquierda en las constituyentes republicanas y su intento de transacción ideológica', *Studia Historica* (Salamanca), vol. 1, no. 4, 1983

Graham, Helen, 'The Eclipse of the Socialist Left: 1934–1937', in Frances Lannon and Paul Preston, editors, *Élites and Power in Twentieth-Century Spain: Essays in Honour of Sir Raymond Carr* (Oxford, 1990)

Graham, Helen, 'The Socialist Youth in the JSU: The Experience of Organisational Unity, 1936–8', in Martin Blinkhorn, editor, *Spain in Conflict 1931–1939: Democracy and its Enemies* (London, 1986)

Graham, Helen, 'The Spanish Popular Front and the Civil War', in Helen Graham and Paul Preston, editors, *The Popular Front in Europe* (London, 1987)

Harrison, Joseph, 'The Inter-War Depression and the Spanish Economy', *The Journal of European Economic History*, vol. 12, no. 2, Fall 1983

Heywood, Paul, 'De las difficultades para ser marxista: el PSOE, 1879–1921', *Sistema*, no. 74, September 1986

Heywood, Paul, 'The Development of Marxist Theory in Spain and the Frente Popular', in Martin Alexander and Helen Graham, editors, *The French and Spanish Popular Fronts: Comparative Perspectives* (Cambridge, 1989)

Juliá Díaz, Santos, 'Continuidad y ruptura en el socialismo español del siglo XX', *Leviatán*, IIª época, no. 17, Autumn 1984

Juliá Díaz, Santos, 'Corporativistas obreros y reformadores políticos: crisis e escisión del PSOE en la II República', *Studia Historica*, vol. 1, no. 4, 1983

Juliá Díaz, Santos, 'Fracaso de una insurrección y derrota de una huelga: los hechos de octubre en Madrid', *Estudios de Historia Social*, no. 31, October–December 1984

Juliá Díaz, Santos, 'El fracaso de la República', *Revista de Occidente*, supplement I, November 1981

Juliá Díaz, Santos, 'Gobernar ¿para quién? Debilidad de partidos y representación de intereses en la II República', *Revista de Derecho Político*, no. 12, Winter 1981–2

Juliá Díaz, Santos, 'Largo Caballero y la lucha de tendencias en el socialismo español (1923–1936)', *Annali della Fondazione Giangiacomo Feltrinelli*, 1983–4

Juliá Díaz, Santos, 'Un líder político entre dirigentes sindicales', *Revista del Ministerio de Obras Públicas y Urbanismo*, no. 305, December 1983

Juliá Díaz, Santos, 'Luchas obreras y políticas de Frente Popular en Madrid, 1931–1936', *Estudios de Historia Social*, nos 16–17, January–June 1981

Juliá Díaz, Santos, 'Organizaciones y prácticas obreras', *Arbor*, vol. CIX, nos 426–7, June–July 1981

Juliá Díaz, Santos, 'Raíces religiosas y prácticas sindicales', *Revista de Occidente*, no. 23, April 1983

Juliá Díaz, Santos, 'República, revolución y luchas internas', in *Anales de Historia de la Fundación Pablo Iglesias*, vol. 1 (Madrid, 1986)

Juliá Díaz, Santos, 'Sobre la formación del Frente Popular en España', *Sistema* (Madrid) no. 73, July 1986

Juliá Díaz, Santos, 'Los socialistas en la crisis de los años treinta', *Zona Abierta*, no. 27, January–May 1983

Juliá Díaz, Santos, 'Los socialistas y el escenario de la futura revolución', in Germán Ojeda, editor, *Octubre 1934: cincuenta años para la reflexión* (Madrid, 1985)

Juliá Díaz, Santos, 'La vigencia de Prieto', *Leviatán*, IIª época, no. 15, Spring 1984

Linz, Juan J., 'The Party System of Spain: Past and Future', in Seymour M. Lipset and Stein Rokkan, editors, *Party Systems and Voter Alignments* (New York, 1976)

Macarro Vera, José Manuel, 'Causas de la radicalización socialista en la II República', *Revista de Historia Contemporánea* (Sevilla), no. 1, December 1982

Madden, Marie R., 'The Status of the Church and Catholic Action in Contemporary Spain', *Catholic Historical Review*, XVIII, 1933

Malefakis, Edward E., 'Peasants, Politics and Civil War in Spain, 1931–1939', in Robert J. Bezucha, editor, *Modern European Social History* (Boston, Mass., 1972)

Martínez Bande, José Manuel, 'Del alzamiento a la guerra civil verano 1936: correspondencia Franco/Mola', *Historia y Vida*, no. 93, 1975,

Montero Gibert, José Ramón, 'La CEDA y la Iglesia en la II República española', *Revista de Estudios Políticos*, nos 31–2, 1983

Montero Gibert, José Ramón, 'La fascistización de la derecha española en la segunda República: el caso de la CEDA', mimeo

Montero Gibert, José Ramón, and Contreras, Manuel, 'Una constitución fragil: revisionismo y reforma constitucional en la II República española', *Revista de Derecho Político*, no. 12, Winter 1981–2

Nadal, Jordi, 'Spain, 1830–1914', in Carlo M. Cipolla, editor, *The Emergence of Industrial Society*, 2 vols (London, 1973)

Pérez Garzón, Juan Sisimio, 'La revolución burguesa en España: los inicios de un debate científico 1966–1979', in Manuel Tuñón de Lara, editor, *Historiografía española contemporánea*, (Madrid, 1980)

Preston, Paul, 'El accidentalismo de la CEDA: ¿aceptación o sabotage de la República?', *Cuadernos de Ruedo Ibérico* (Paris) nos 41–2, February–May 1973

Preston, Paul, 'Alfonist Monarchism and the Coming of the Spanish Civil War', *Journal of Contemporary History*, vol. 7, nos 3–4, 1972

Preston, Paul, 'The Creation of the Popular Front in Spain', in Helen Graham and Paul Preston, editors, *The Popular Front in Europe* (London, 1987)

Preston, Paul, 'Democrata por encima de todo: Indalecio Prieto y la creación del Frente Popular', *Revista del Ministerio de Obras Públicas y Urbanismo*, no. 305, December 1983

Preston, Paul, 'The "Moderate" Right and the Undermining of the Second Spanish Republic, 1931–1933', *European Studies Review*, vol. 3, no. 4, 1973

Preston, Paul, 'Spain's October Revolution and the Rightist Grasp for Power', *Journal of Contemporary History*, vol. 10, no. 4, 1975

Preston, Paul, 'The Struggle Against Fascism in Spain: *Leviatán* and the Contradictions of the Spanish Left 1934–1936', *European Studies Review*, vol. 9, no. 1, 1979

Rees, Timothy, 'The Political Mobilization of Landowners in the Province of Badajoz, 1931–1933', in Frances Lannon and Paul Preston, editors, *Élites and Power in Twentieth-Century Spain: Essays in Honour of Sir Raymond Carr* (Oxford, 1990)

Reig Tapia, Alberto, 'La tragedia de Manuel Azaña', *Historia Contemporánea* (Bilbao) no. 1, 1988

Romero Maura, Joaquín, 'El debate historiográfico acerca de la segunda República', *Revista Internacional de Sociología* (Madrid), 2nd ser., nos 3–4, July–December 1972

Ruiz, David, 'Clase, sindicatos y partidos en Asturias (1931–1934)', *Estudios de Historia Social*, no. 31, October–December 1984

Shubert, Adrian, 'A Reinterpretation of the Spanish Popular Front: The Case of Asturias', in Martin Alexander and Helen Graham, editors, *The French and Spanish Popular Fronts: Comparative Perspectives* (Cambridge, 1989)

Shubert, Adrian, 'Una revolución de auto-defensa: la radicalización de los mineros de Asturias 1921–1934', *Sistema*, no. 46, January 1982

Stone, Glyn A., 'The Official British Attitude to the Anglo-Portuguese Alliance 1910–1945', *Journal of Contemporary History*, vol. X, no. 4, October 1975

Tuñón de Lara, Manuel, 'El proyecto político de Manuel Azaña en la coyuntura de la República y la guerra', *Historia Contemporánea* (Bilbao) no. 1, 1988

Varela Ortega, José, 'Reacción y revolución frente a la reforma', *Revista Internacional de Sociología* (Madrid), 2nd ser., nos 3–4, July–December 1972

Vincent, Mary, 'The Politicisation of Catholic Women in Salamanca, 1931–1936', in Frances Lannon and Paul Preston, editors, *Élites and Power in Twentieth-Century Spain: Essays in Honour of Sir Raymond Carr* (Oxford, 1990)

Vincent, Mary, 'The Spanish Church and the Popular Front: The Experience of Salamanca Province', in Martin Alexander and Helen Graham, editors, *The French and Spanish Popular Fronts: Comparative Perspectives* (Cambridge, 1989)

Viñas, Miguel, 'Franquismo y revolución burguesa', in *Horizonte español 1972*, 3 vols (Paris, Cuadernos de Ruedo Ibérico, 1972)

INDEX

ABC, 51, 249, 255, 266; March 1934 printers' strike, 143, 144
Abyssinia, 190
Academia de Ciencias Políticas y Morales, 221
'accidentalism', 39–42
Acción Agraria Manchega, 58
Acción Castellana, 46
Acción Ciudadana y Agraria de Cuenca, 58
Acción Española, 56, 60
Acción Nacional, 4, 46, 135; Assembly December 1931, 56; and campaign against the Republic, 56; changes name to Acción Popular, 58; creation and growth, 43, 44, 55, 91; and 1931 elections, 47, 48; see also Acción Popular; Juventud de Acción Nacional
Acción Popular, 43, 124; and agrarian question, 102; and Civil War, 280; Covadonga rally, 165; and creation of the CEDA, 65; 1933 elections, 70–3 passim; 1936 elections, 202–9 passim; founded, 58; militia, 128; and monarchists in, 60; October 1932 Assembly, 62; and religious legislation, 55; and Unificación, 280, 281; see also Acción Nacional; Juventud de Acción Popular
Acción Popular Agraria de Badajoz, 58
Acción Regional Independiente de Santander, 62
Acción Republicana, 123, 159
ACNP, see Asociación Católica Nacional de Propagandistas

Agrarian Party, 135, 145, 197, 200
Agrarian Reform Statute, 100, 101, 125
Agrupación de Propietarios de Fincas Rústicas, 81, 82, 164, 165, 184
Agrupación Socialista Madrileña (ASM), 146; and 1935–6 Socialist schism, 234, 235, 261, 262, 263, 273; new programme in 1936, 270; supports Besteiro, 35, 104, 112; taken over by Caballeristas, 138, 261; see also Madrid
Aguirre y Lecube, José Antonio, 203
Aguirre, José María, 173
Aizpún Santafé, Rafael, 171, 191
Alba Bonifaz, Santiago, 127
Albacete, 118, 151, 228, 248
Albornoz y Liminiana, Alvaro de, 32, 253
Alcalá Zamora, Niceto: and 1930 Republican movement, 28; April 1935 crisis, 188; and Azaña, 113, 116; CEDA plot against, 183; and CEDA pressure, 145, 147, 159, 165, 197, 198; December 1935 crisis, 200, 201, 202; elections 1936, 229, 249; and February 1936 coup attempt, 242, 243; and Gil Robles, 189, 199, 200, 201; impeachment, 251, 252; and Lerroux, 146; and October 1934 crisis, 169, 170, 171, 173, 174, 177, 178; opposes post-October death sentences, 182, 187; becomes President, 92; and repression of CNT, 88, 89; resigns as Prime Minister, 92; September 1935 crisis, 195, 196; Socialist pressure to call elections, 123, 124, 132, 133, 160, 163,

Escamots, 176
Escofet Alsina, Captain Federico, 178
Escorial, El, 145, 146
La Época, 51
Esquerra Republicana de Catalunya,
123, 158, 176
Estadella Arnó, José, 151
Estat Catalá, 176
Estraperlo affair, 195, 197
Extremadura, 8, 97, 135, 147, 204
Eza, Vizconde de, 148

Fabian Society, see Labour Party,
British
FAI, see Federación Anarquista Ibérica
Fal Conde, Manuel, 266
Falange Española, 192; and Civil War,
279, 280, 281; and Jiménez Asúa
assassination attempt, 247; joined by
JAP, 257; under Francoism, 282;
violence against Popular Front, 246,
255, 272, 274
Fanjul Goñi, General Joaquín, 168, 182,
183, 188, 258; and Gil Robles, 189,
199, 201; and the 1936 conspiracy
and rising, 247
Fascism, 10, 121, 130, 222; Italian, 63,
64, 112, 113, 266
Federación Anarquista Ibérica (FAI),
90, 109
Federación de Artes Blancas, 133
Federación de Artes Gráficas, 96, 273
Federación de Juventudes Socialistas
(FJS), 128, 129; and Besteiro, 214,
220, 221; and 1930 conspiracy, 34;
and creation of the JSU, 262; and
electoral campaign of 1933, 118;
Fifth Congress, 139, 143; and joint
PSOE–UGT–FJS revolutionary
committee, 138, 162; and making of
Popular Front, 219, 230, 236; and
October 1934, 220, 228; and Octubre
– segunda etapa, 220, 221, 222, 223;
and PCE, 228, 229, 262; and Prieto,
217; radicalisation, 113, 117, 118, 134,
160; and Torrelodones summer
school, 113
Federación Española de Trabajadores,
255
Federación Nacional de Trabajadores
de la Tierra (FNTT), 9; and
Agrarian Reform Statute, 101; and
Castilblanco, 94; and CNT, 87;

foundation and growth in early
1930s, 30, 31, 78; opposes
revolutionary policy, 138;
radicalization, 122; restraint by, 96,
97, 98, 106, 133; resurgence in 1936,
246, 259, 260; and Right, 102, 103,
134, 135; and Socialist schism of
1936, 260, 263; and strike of June
1934, 149, 150, 151, 152, 153, 154, 157
Federación de Trabajadores de Banca
y Bolsa, 132
Federación de Trabajadores de la
Enseñanza, 155
Federation of Building Workers, 93,
122
Federation of Printing Workers, see
Federación de Artes Gráficas
Felipe, León, 215
Fernández Montes, Amador, 107, 175,
228, 234
Fernández Grandizo, Manuel, 154,
157, 213
Fernández Ladreda, José María, 62,
165
Fernández Ruano, Angel, 62
Figueroa y Torres, Alvaro, Conde de
Romanones, 73, 86
First World War, 10, 11
FJS, see Federación de Juventudes
Socialistas
FNTT, see Federación Nacional de
Trabajadores de la Tierra
Fonelas (Granada), 209
Fraga Iribarne, Manuel, 279
Francisco, Jiménez, Enrique de, 129,
130, 136, 159; and joint
PSOE–UGT–FJS revolutionary
committee, 138; in prison, 212; and
the making of Popular Front, 218,
223, 225, 230, 232; resigns from
PSOE executive, 232, 272; and the
1935–6 Socialist schism, 233, 235,
261
Franco Bahamonde, General
Francisco, 1; and Asturian rising,
176, 177; and Azaña military
reforms, 49, 51; as candidate in
Cuenca re-run elections, 257, 258; as
Caudillo, 172, 279; and Civil War,
277, 278, 279, 280; consulted on
military coups, 183, 201; and Diego
Hidalgo, 167, 168; and February
1936 coup attempt, 241, 242, 243,

WITHDRAWN
from
STIRLING UNIVERSITY LIBRARY